The British Mandate in Pal

The British Mandate over Palestine began just 100 years ago, in July 1920, when Sir Herbert Samuel, the first British High Commissioner to Palestine, took his seat at Government House, Jerusalem. The chapters here analyse a wide cross-section of the conflicting issues – social, political and strategical – that attended British colonial rule over the country, from 1920 to 1948.

This anthology contains contributions by several of the most respected Israeli scholars in the field – Arab, Druze and Jewish. It is divided into three sections, covering the differing perspectives of the main 'actors' in the 'Palestine Triangle': the British, the Arabs and the Zionists. The concluding chapter identifies a pattern of seven counterproductive negotiating behaviours that explain the repeated failure of the parties to agree upon any of the proposals for an Arab-Zionist peace in Mandated Palestine.

The volume is a modern review of the British Mandate in Palestine from different perspectives, which makes it a valuable addition to the field. It is a key resource for students and scholars interested in international relations, history of the Middle East, Palestine and Israel.

Michael J Cohen is Emeritus Professor of History at Bar-Ilan University, Israel. Among his key publications are *Churchill and the Jews; Truman and Israel; Fighting World War Three from the Middle East: Allied Contingency Plans, 1945–1954; Strategy and Politics in the Middle East: Defending the Northern Tier;* and *Britain's Moment in Palestine: Retrospect and Perspectives, 1917–1948.*

Routledge Studies in Middle Eastern History

The region's history from the earliest times to the present is catered for by this series made up of the very latest research. Books include political, social, cultural, religious and economic history.

16. The Druze Community and the Lebanese State
Between Confrontation and Reconciliation
Yusri Hazran

17. The Secret Anglo-French War in the Middle East
Intelligence and Decolonization, 1940–1948
Meir Zamir

18. Histories of the Jews of Egypt
An Imagined Bourgeoisie
Dario Miccoli

19. The Empress Nurbanu and Ottoman Politics in the Sixteenth Century
Building the Atik Valide
Pinar Kayaalp

20. Britain and the Arab Gulf after Empire
Kuwait, Bahrain, Qatar and the United Arab Emirates, 1971–1981
Simon C. Smith

21. Hebrew Popular Journalism
Birth and Development in Ottoman Palestine
Ouzi Elyada

22. The British Mandate in Palestine
A Centenary Volume, 1920–2020
Edited by Michael J Cohen

For a full list of titles, please visit: www.routledge.com/middleeaststudies/series/SE0811

The British Mandate in Palestine

A Centenary Volume, 1920–2020

Edited by
Michael J Cohen

With a foreword by
Professor Sari Nusseibeh

Routledge
Taylor & Francis Group

LONDON AND NEW YORK

First published 2020 by Routledge

2 Park Square, Milton Park, Abingdon, Oxon OX14 4RN

605 Third Avenue, New York, NY 10017

Routledge is an imprint of the Taylor & Francis Group, an informa business

First issued in paperback 2021

British Library Cataloguing-in-Publication Data
A catalogue record for this book is available from the British Library

Library of Congress Cataloging-in-Publication Data
A catalog record has been requested for this book

ISBN: 978-0-367-13343-6 (hbk)
ISBN: 978-1-03-217486-0 (pbk)
DOI: 10.4324/9780429026034

Typeset in Times New Roman
by Taylor & Francis Books

For Natalie, my beloved daughter.

Nietzsche was so right!

Contents

List of tables   x
List of contributors   xi
List of abbreviations   xiv
Foreword by Professor Sari Nusseibeh   xv

Editor's introduction   1
MICHAEL J COHEN

PART I
British perspectives   11

1 Colonial intrigue in the Middle East: *The Faysal – [Lawrence] –
   Weizmann Agreement, January 1919*   13
   MICHAEL J COHEN

2 The anti-Zionist 'Jewish Khazar' syndrome in the official
   British mind   29
   RORY MILLER

3 Churchill and Bevin: Thesis and anti-thesis?   45
   MICHAEL J COHEN

PART II
Arab perspectives   63

4 Between local Palestinian and pan-Arab nationalism among
   Palestinians during the British mandate: Akram Zuʿayter as an
   example   65
   MUSTAFA KABHA

5 The Palestinian political parties and local self-governance during
   the British Mandate: Democracy and the clan   83
   RAMI ZEEDAN

6 The rise and fall of the Palestinian Arab middle class   102
   ITAMAR RADAI

7 Difference, not fragmentation: Christians and Druze in
   Mandatory Palestine   119
   YUSRI KHAIZRAN

8 A troubled bond: The Palestinian-Arab national movement
   and the Arab states   136
   AVRAHAM SELA

PART III
Zionist perspectives   155

9 Zionism as a blessing to the Arabs: History of an argument   157
   HILLEL COHEN

10 Jewish immigration: The base of the Palestine triangle   172
   AVIVA HALAMISH

11 Zionist land acquisition: A core element in establishing Israel   189
   KENNETH W. STEIN

12 The origins of militant Zionism during the
   British Mandate   205
   COLIN SHINDLER

13 Is Zionism colonialism?   221
   YOAV GELBER

14 Chaim Weizmann: From the Balfour Declaration to the
   establishment of the state of Israel.   235
   JEHUDA REINHARZ AND MOTTI GOLANI

15 David Ben-Gurion's 'road map' to independence,
   May 1948   252
   TUVIA FRILING

PART IV
Conclusion 267

16 Arab-Zionist negotiations during the Mandate: An unbridgeable
   divide 269
   LAURA ZITTRAIN EISENBERG AND NEIL CAPLAN

   Select bibliography of English sources 285
   Index 287

Tables

5.1 1927: Local elections in Arab and mixed cities   92
5.2 1934: Local elections in Arab and mixed cities   94
5.3 1946: Local elections in Arab and mixed cities   96

Contributors

Neil Caplan is an Affiliate faculty member of the History Department at Concordia University, Montreal. Among his publications: *Futile Diplomacy*, a four-volume history of Arab-Zionist negotiations; and *The Israel-Palestine Conflict: Contested Histories.*

Hillel Cohen is Professor of Islamic and Middle East Studies and Arab-Jewish relations at the Hebrew University of Jerusalem. Among his publications: *Army of Shadows: Palestinian Collaborators in the Service of Zionism, 1917–1948*; and *Year Zero of the Arab-Israeli Conflict: 1929.*

Michael J Cohen is Emeritus Professor of History at Bar-Ilan University, Israel. Among his publications: *Fighting World War Three from the Middle East: Allied Contingency Plans, 1945–1954; Strategy and Politics in the Middle East: Defending the Northern Tier*; and *Britain's Moment in Palestine: Retrospect and Perspectives, 1917–1948.*

Tuvia Friling is a Professor at Ben-Gurion University of the Negev. He was Israel's State Archivist from 2001–2004. Among his publications: *Arrow in the Dark: David Ben-Gurion, the Yishuv Leadership and Rescue Attempts during the Holocaust; Critique du post-sionisme, Reponse aux "nouveaux historiens" Israeliens*, (editor); and *Ben-Gurion 1947–1949: The Secrets of the Birth of the State of Israel*, (joint editor).

Yoav Gelber is Emeritus Professor at the University of Haifa. Among his publications: *Palestine 1948: War, Escape and the Emergence of the Palestinian Refugee Problem; Nation and History: Israeli Historiography; Memory and Identity between Zionism and Post-Zionism*; and *Palestinian Time: Israel, Jordan and the Palestinians, 1967–1970.*

Motti Golani is Professor of Jewish History at Tel Aviv University. Among his publications: *Israel in Search of War: The Sinai Campaign, 1955–1956; Palestine between Politics and Terror, 1945–1947*; and co-author of vol. 3 of the Weizmann biography.

Aviva Halamish is Emerita Professor of History at the Open University of Israel. Among her publications: *The Exodus Affair: Holocaust Survivors* *and the Struggle for Palestine*; and *Kibbutz: Utopia and Politics: The Life and Times of Meir Yaari.*

Mustafa Kabha, is Professor of History, Philosophy and Judaic Studies at the Open University, Israel. Among his publications: *Writing up a Storm – The Palestinian Press Shaping Public Opinion*; and *The Palestinian People seeking Sovereignty and State.*

Yusri Khaizran, is an Adjunct Lecturer at the Hebrew University, Jerusalem. He is the author of *The Druze Community and the Lebanese State: Between Resistance and Reconciliation.*

Rory Miller is Professor of Government at Georgetown University in Qatar. Among his publications: *Desert Kingdoms to Global Powers: The Rise of the Arab Gulf*; and The Cambridge University Press series on *Intelligence and National Security in Africa and the Middle East* (co-editor).

Sari Nusseibeh is a retired Palestinian Professor of Philosophy and former President of the *Al-Quds* University in Jerusalem. He is the author of *Once Upon a Country: A Palestinian Life.*

Itamar Radai is Director of the Adenauer Program for Jewish-Arab Cooperation and a Research Fellow at Tel Aviv University. Among his publications: *Palestinians in Jerusalem and Jaffa, 1948: A Tale of Two Cities.*

Jehuda Reinharz is emeritus president and Professor of Modern Jewish History at Brandeis University. Among his publications: a 3-volume biography of Chaim Weizmann (vol. 3 with Motti Golani); *The Road to September 1939: Polish Jews, Zionists and the Yishuv on the Eve of World War II* (with Yaacov Shavit); and *Inside the Anti-Semitic Mind, The Language of Jew-Hatred in Contemporary Germany* (with Monika Schwarz-Friesel).

Colin Shindler is Emeritus Professor of Israeli Studies at the School of Oriental and African Studies, London University. Among his publications: *A History of Modern Israel; Israel and the European Left: Between Solidarity and Delegitimisation*; and *The Rise of the Israeli Right.*

Avraham Sela is Emeritus Professor of International Relations at the Hebrew University, Jerusalem. Among his publications: *Popular Contention, Regime, and Transition: The Arab Revolts in Comparative Global Perspective* (edited with Eitan Alimi and Mario Sznajder); and *Representations of Israeli and Palestinian Memories and Narratives of the 1948 War* (with Alon Kadish).

Kenneth W. Stein is Emeritus Professor at Emory University, Atlanta. Among his publications: *The Land Question in Palestine; Heroic Diplomacy: Sadat, Kissinger, Carter, Begin and the Quest for Arab-Israeli Peace*; and two documentary collections: *History, Politics and Diplomacy of the Arab-Israel Conflict*; and *Peace Negotiations between Israel, Egypt and the United States, 1973–1979.*

Rami Zeedan, is Assistant Professor of Israel Studies in the Jewish Studies Program at the University of Kansas. Among his publications: *Battalion of Arabs – the History of the Minorities' Unit in the IDF, 1948 to 1956* (in Hebrew).

Laura Zittrain Eisenberg is Teaching Professor at Carnegie Mellon University, Pittsburgh, PA. Among her publications: *My Enemy's Enemy: Lebanon in the Early Zionist Imagination, 1900–1948*; and, with Neil Caplan, *Negotiating Arab-Israeli Peace: Patterns, Problems, Possibilities.*

List of abbreviations

ABD	Archives of the Board of Deputies of British Jews
BGA	Ben-Gurion Archives
BG	Research Ben-Gurion Research Institute
CZA	Central Zionist Archives
DP	Displaced Persons
H.C.Deb.	House of Commons Debates
H.L.	House of Lords Debates
HMSO	His Majesty's Stationery Office
ISA	Israel State Archives
IZL	*Irgun Zwai Leumi* – National Military Organization. (Jewish terrorist underground in Palestine)
JNF	Jewish National Fund
LEHI	Fighters for the Freedom of Israel – or Stern Gang. (Jewish terrorist underground in Palestine)
NA	British National Archives
UN	United Nations
USNA	US National Archives
WA	Weizmann Archives

Foreword

Sari Nusseibeh

It cannot escape the notice of the reader of this volume that there is an imbalance in the presentations in favour of Israeli scholars. As the editor notes, Palestinian scholars on the whole did not feel inclined to participate. Why? There is, of course, first, the looming spectre of 'normalisation' – not wishing to give credence by participating in a joint volume to the impression that Israeli-Palestinian academic relations are 'normal'. But there is, also perhaps, the more fundamental wariness of engaging with Israeli scholars in an enterprise that seeks to unravel 'the story' of Israel's conception – as if, again here, credence may be given through such participation to the impression that 'Palestinian facts' about the matter have another side, or are a mere narrative.

Scholars, of course, are supposed to be 'neutral' or 'objective', but what is at issue in this case is less a question of how things happened as it is of whether what happened was 'right' or 'wrong'. Let me call this 'an ethical issue'. It is not hard to imagine how an ethical perspective can underlie, and therefore inform a historian's approach to the 'selection' or 'reading' of 'facts' – in other words, of 'how things happened'. From the Palestinian perspective, their country was unjustly 'usurped' by Zionists. From the Israeli perspective, it was rightfully 'reclaimed'. These are two starting points for 'writing history'. Inevitably, their incompatibility with one another will find itself reflected in the 'how' at the level of particular events – for instance, whether Palestinian refugees 'fled' or were 'driven out', or whether Britain connived with or undermined the Zionist project, or whether acquired land was 'bought' or 'swindled'. And so on. Different historical points of departure in this case assume more poignancy in particular since the scholars engaged in the study of Israel's birth – the *nakba* ('disaster' in Arabic) – are Israelis and Palestinians themselves, it is a study about their respective and recent histories, or history, and it is still an unfinished story, with both sides still being at war with one another – even in words – and with Palestinians, in particular, feeling greatly wronged, finding themselves left at the short end of the stick.

All this perhaps explains the reticence of Palestinian historians to participate in this volume, but likewise it may explain the readiness of their Israeli counterparts to participate. Indeed, this may more generally lie behind the observation that 'peace movements' have been more forthcoming and visible in Israeli society than among Palestinians. Feeling their national project largely accomplished, 'liberal' Israelis may feel more comfortable about affording a conciliatory disposition towards their enemy. Contrariwise, feeling almost totally dispossessed, Palestinians tend to see conciliatory moves on their part as a sign of capitulation. From the Israeli point of view, the image of an Israeli walking hand in hand with a Palestinian is a confirmation of Israel's victory in this drawn-out war. From the Palestinian point of view, it is seen as a sign of Palestinian surrender to the Israeli!

It is unclear whether this 'war' between Israelis and Palestinians will end any time soon. Indeed, it is many ways gathering both religious and chauvinist steam. There was a time when it seemed that claims and views could be reconciled. However, this is a case where the 'reconciliation' needed is less one over 'facts' than one to do with human dispositions. Even objective 'interests' do not seem to play a large part in determining political positions – as might be expected they do in international relations. But if dispositions are ever to change this must come about through unyielding efforts on the part of Israelis and Palestinians who have evolved sufficiently to see each other as human beings first and foremost, and who on this basis continue to work together and to look forward to a future where human values set their political sights. True, such a future may not come about, but neither will that other future where only one side can claim to have achieved total victory over the other. Regardless how the past evolved, the two sides have to make their bed together, or make do with never being able to sleep at peace.

Professor Sari Nusseibeh
formerly President of al-Quds University, Jerusalem

Editor's introduction

Michael J Cohen

In 1934 Isaiah Berlin made a short personal visit to Palestine and became an instant convert to Zionism. He wrote the following description of the country, through the prism of "English eyes and ... the filter of some very English metaphors". He compared Mandated Palestine to an English public school:

> The High Commissioner was the headmaster; the Colonial Office was the Board of Governors; the school itself was divided into the Arab house and the Jewish house. Most of the masters liked the Arab house, because its pupils were "gay, affectionate, high spirited and tough, occasionally liable to break out and have a rag and break the skulls of a few Jews or an Englishman perhaps".

The Jewish house, Berlin said, was full of able and rich boys,

> who were allowed too much pocket money by their parents, rude, conceited, ugly, ostentatious, suspected of swapping stamps unfairly with the other boys, always saying they know better, liable to work too hard and not play games with the rest.[1]

This centenary volume analyses a wide cross-section of the conflicting issues that attended the British Mandate in Palestine, which lasted from 1920 to 1948. Few issues can have generated such a volume of printed comment and violent polemic: in personal diaries and memoirs and, once the archives were opened, in scholarly works based on the primary sources.[2]

This volume assembles some of the key scholars who have published on this topic over the past 40 years. Some readers will note two 'absentees'. Most notable is Haj Amin al-Husayni, leader of the Palestinian Arab nationalist movement during this period. This is because none of the Arab scholars that I approached was willing to take on the task.[3] (On the absence of Arab scholars from this volume, see Professor Nusseibeh's insightful Foreword.) The second 'absentee' is Ilan Pappé, the Israeli expat who has become something of a popular cult figure, arguably the chief advocate of the Palestinian Arab cause on European University campuses. His absence here is due to his having crossed the clear line between academic integrity and propaganda. Fifteen years ago, he wrote

> My bias is apparent despite the desire of my peers that I stick to facts and the 'truth' when reconstructing past realities. I view any such construction as vain and preposterous.[4]

The Zionist movement's greatest achievement was the Balfour Declaration, published by the British government on 2 November 1917. This promised to facilitate the establishment in Palestine of a Jewish National Home – without defining in which part of Palestine that Home should be built. On 1 July 1920, 100 years ago, Sir Herbert Samuel, a Jew, the first British High Commissioner to Palestine took his seat at Government House Jerusalem. The Mandate for Palestine was not awarded officially to Britain by the League of Nations until two years later, in July 1922. Britain was obliged to report annually to the League's Permanent Mandates Commission, which monitored and on occasion censored Britain's actions in Palestine.

It has been claimed that the British neglected to observe the final *caveat* in the Declaration: "provided that nothing shall be done which may prejudice the civil and religious rights of the existing non-Jewish communities in Palestine or the rights and political status enjoyed by Jews in any other country".[5] This is only half true. By the late-1930s, with the clouds of World War Two on the horizon, the British effectively abandoned the Declaration. The Jewish National Home had become an imperial burden, deprecated by British officials. One of them, Elizabeth Monroe, later wrote that the Declaration "measured by British interests alone [was] one of the greatest mistakes in our imperial history".[6]

But talk of imperial mistakes reflects the cheap 'wisdom' that comes to some with hindsight. As I have written in another place:

> the very concept of 'mistakes' is misplaced, ahistorical…. Hindsight is a powerful reality changer … given the unique circumstances in which Britain found herself in 1917 the Declaration was universally regarded at the time (even by the anti-Zionist Lord Curzon) as a necessary, even brilliant wartime coup for British interests.[7]

By the late 1930s, the *Yishuv*[*] had matured into an embryonic state-in-the making of some 400,000. The British White Paper of 1939 condemned them to remain a permanent minority of one-third of Palestine's total population. However, the Holocaust and the interventions of the U.S. president after the war in Europe made it impossible for Britain to adhere to the 1939 policy.

---

* Yishuv: Palestine's pre-state Jewish community.

Lastly, when evaluating Britain's policy in Palestine, one cannot ignore the widespread anti-Jewish prejudice that pervaded wide sectors of the British elite, both in London and in the Middle East. In July 1922, William Ormsby-Gore, a future Colonial Secretary (1936–8), referred to this in a speech before the House of Commons:

> Then there is what I call quite frankly the anti-Semitic party ... those who are convinced that the Jews are at the bottom of all the trouble all over the world. Whether they are attacking an anti-Zionist ... or Zionists, or rich Jews, or poor Jews – it is the rich Jews who are all blood-suckers and the poor Jews all Bolshevists – they have that particular Hebrew mania, and they have fastened on Palestine with a view to paying off these mediaeval scores.[8]

This volume is divided into three sections, covering the differing perspectives of the main 'actors' in what has been called the 'Palestine Triangle':[9] the British, the Arabs and the Zionists.

British perspectives

The fundamental conflict of interests between the Palestinian Arabs and Zionists became clearly manifest – for anyone who wanted to see – long before the League of Nations awarded the Mandate for Palestine to Britain in late 1922. This was spelled out clearly by the Palin Report into the so-called *Nebi Musa* riots that broke out in Jerusalem during the Jewish Passover, in April 1920. Fortunately for the Zionist cause, the Palin report was stifled at birth. The Military Occupation regime (1918–20), which had been de-legitimised by charges of anti-Semitism, was dismissed *ad hoc* by Prime Minister Lloyd George. His government was convinced that the Zionists, with World Jewry behind them, were a powerful influence, whereas the Palestinian Arabs (many of whom still regarded Palestine as a southern province of Ottoman Syria) were not. Lloyd George installed Sir Herbert Samuel as Britain's first High Commissioner of Palestine, more than two years before the League of Nations officially awarded her the Mandate.

The home truths of the Palin Report remained to exasperate those Colonial Office officials who were charged with the day-to-day administration of Palestine. In April 1923, Sir John Shuckburgh, the founding head of the Middle East department of the Colonial Office, ventilated his frustrations in a private conversation with Sydney Moody, a Palestine government official on loan to London. Shuckburgh confessed to:

> a sense of personal degradation. He had always had this feeling during the two years he had been at the Colonial Office.... He could not go on, they could not go on, feeling this sense of equivocation. It was personally degrading and unworthy of the British Government.

[...]

We might logically rule Palestine as a conquered country, but after all could we, ought we, to force on the Arab population of Palestine a mass of alien immigrants mostly Russian and Polish? However good it might be for Palestine the Arabs did not want it, were bitterly opposed to it and deeply resented the treatment.

Moody responded with a heavy dose of pragmatic cynicism:

The historical and sentimental arguments [about the Jews] left me cold ... the Jews are the only people who are capable of rebuilding it [Palestine] because they have the necessary money, enthusiasm and manpower.[10]

In the first chapter, Michael Cohen re-visits the ill-fated, abortive Faysal-Weizmann Agreement of January 1919 – hailed by many as an Arab agreement to Zionist settlement in Palestine. He shows that the agreement was no more than a nineteenth century-style colonial deal whereby the Emir Faysal, the Bedouin leader of the Arab Revolt during World War One, 'forfeited' Palestine to the Zionists, in return for which Weizmann agreed to avail him of the Jews' fabled *richesse* (Weizmann spoke of £10 million!) and to deploy their political influence against the French in Syria. Each party was bluffing. Faysal hid the agreement from the Palestinian Arabs and Weizmann had no chance of mobilising the resources and influence he promised. The British were also to blame. Whereas the Cairo officials, and mavericks like T.E. Lawrence 'of Arabia' and Sir Mark Sykes encouraged the deal, hoping to 'biff' the French out of Syria – the government in London had promised Syria to the French before the war. Lawrence employed 'creative' translations to persuade Faysal and Weizmann to reach agreement. But the Lloyd George government had neither the will nor the resources to add Syria to its over-extended empire.

In Chapter 2, Rory Miller reveals that several senior government officials and members of the British political elite opposed the Zionist project, on the grounds that the Jewish population in Palestine was in fact descended from the ancient Khazars – a pagan people of Turco-Tartar stock, that appeared in Eastern Europe at some point after the fifth century – and converted to Judaism. The Khazar issue became part of a debate among senior British officials and members of the political elite over the legitimacy of Zionist aspirations in Palestine – on the grounds that the Zionists had no historical claim to the country.

In Chapter 3, Michael Cohen challenges the widely accepted stereotypes of Churchill, as the consistent supporter of the Jews and Zionism, in contrast to that of Bevin, a crass anti-Semite. He argues that the difference between the two was more in their public rhetoric, than in their fundamental beliefs. By the close of World War Two in Europe, there had developed a general consensus among Britain's political elite, including both Bevin and

Churchill, that the Balfour Declaration had been a mistake. Both men were equally opposed to the settlement in Palestine of the Jewish survivors of the Holocaust.

Arab perspectives

In Chapter 4, Professor Mustafa Kabha explores the philosophy of Akram Zuʿayter, one of the most influential Palestinian intellectuals of his time. The Arab inhabitants of the new entity of Palestine (prior to 1918, a part of Ottoman or Greater Syria), had lived for the previous 400 years under an Ottoman Caliph and administration. After the British conquest, and the separation of Palestine from modern-day Syria, they had to search for a new identity – between pan-Arabism and local Palestinian nationalism.[11]

In Chapter 5, Rami Zaydan discusses the formation of several Palestinian political institutions, i.e. the Supreme Muslim Council, the Arab Higher Committee, Arab local councils, and political parties. In 1923, there took place the only, albeit unsuccessful Palestinian Arab election, to a Legislative Council; and three municipal elections – in 1927, 1934, and 1946/7. Zaydan examines these elections and the effect they had on the formation of the Palestinian political parties at the national, and on local self-governance at the local level. He, and Dr Radai in the following chapter, describe the gradual alienation during the course of the Mandate of the Christian Arab and Druze minorities from the overwhelming Muslim majority.

In Chapter 6, Itamar Radai presents a historical and sociological analysis of the Palestinian Arab middle class during the Mandate. This class was bourgeois and educated, similar to the middle classes that developed in the West. Radai's central thesis is that the particular social and cultural characteristics of the Palestinian bourgeoisie prevented their full incorporation into the Palestinian National Movement, and led to its estrangement from both the national leadership, and members of the lower strata, especially the peasantry.

In Chapter 7, Yusri Khaizran discusses the social and political history of minority groups in Palestine – specifically the Druze and Arab-Christians.[12] He argues that these minority groups were alienated from the Arab Moslem majority by processes of radicalisation and Islamisation. The result was either indifference to Palestinian Arab nationalism, or the marginalisation of these groups during the Arab Revolt of 1936–39 and the 1948 war.

In Chapter 8, Avraham Sela examines the consequences of Britain's dual commitment to the Arabs and the Zionists. Unlike other Mandates in post-Ottoman territories, Britain was committed not only to preserve the civil and religious rights of the indigenous population – but also to facilitate the creation of a National Home for the Jews. Jewish immigration, land acquisition and settlement led to escalating Arab resistance, culminating in the 1948 war, with its disastrous results for Palestine's Arabs. He proposes a structural analysis of the social and political roots of the failure of Arab-Palestinian society to cope more effectively with the challenges posed by the British and the Zionists.

Zionist perspectives

In Chapter 9, Hillel Cohen refutes one of the Zionists' main propaganda claims – that far from harming Arab interests in Palestine, the Jewish National Home would bring blessings (mainly economic) to Jews and Arabs alike, if not to the Orient as a whole. He explores the sources and the essence of this promise, through the writings of various Zionist thinkers. He also examines the opposition to it in Arab and Western circles, as well as from within the Zionist camp itself.

In Chapters 10 and 11, Professors Aviva Halamish and Kenneth Stein assert that the two key pillars upon which the State of Israel was built were a. Jewish immigration and b. the purchase of Arab lands by the Zionists. It would appear that both are essentially correct.

Halamish asserts that Jewish immigration, notwithstanding Arab opposition and British attempts to prevent it, altered the demographic balance in Palestine drastically. It also had a decisive effect upon Arab-British-Jewish relations, and ultimately determined the political fate of the country.

In Chapter 11, Stein – author of what remains a classic monograph on Arab land sales to Jews[13] – demonstrates that by 1939 the Zionists had already created the territorial nucleus for a Jewish State. Palestinian and non-Palestinian Arabs sold off their lands to the Zionists, notwithstanding repeated British legislative to thwart the sales.

In Chapter 12, Colin Shindler examines the origins of Right-Wing Zionism – which he terms 'Military Zionism'. It began with the schism that occurred in 1938 between Vladimir Jabotinsky, the founder of Revisionist Zionism, and Menahem Begin, the father of the *IZL* terrorist underground, of the *Herut* Party, who in 1977 became Israel's first right-wing Prime Minister. Shindler highlights the fundamental differences between Jabotinsky and Begin, his accredited disciple. Jabotinsky, founder of the schismatic Revisionists, was against the creation of a Jewish underground, and preferred diplomacy to the use of armed force against the British. But his early death in 1940 allowed Begin to cherry-pick his teachings and to distort his views on the use of force.

In Chapter 13, Yoav Gelber refutes one of the most controversial allegations against Zionism: that the establishment of the Jewish National Home in Palestine under Britain's aegis was equivalent to Western colonialism. One of the first bodies to make this allegation was the first Palestinian Arab Congress, held in Jerusalem in January 1919. Islam recognised Judaism as a religion, not as a nationality, and therefore denied the national character of Zionism. In 1973, the colonialist stigma was lent authority by Maxime Rodinson – the eminent Franco-Jewish, Marxist historian, sociologist and orientalist. Gelber refutes the allegations and points out the fundamental differences between Zionism and colonialism. Like classical colonial movements, Zionism was also a movement of immigration and settlement. But here the similarities end. In all of its other characteristics, Zionism differed from other colonial movements.

The final chapters of this volume deal with the two giants of the Zionist pantheon during the Mandatory period: Chaim Weizmann, the consummate diplomat, who in 1949 became Israel's first President; and David Ben-Gurion, who by the 1930s had become the *Yishuv*'s unchallenged leader and father-figure. In 1948, the latter was the obvious and only choice for Israel's first Prime Minister.

Weizmann (1874–1952) was 12 years older than Ben-Gurion (1886–1973). During World War One, Weizmann not only earned himself an immortal place in Zionist history, but the income from his chemical patents set him on the road to riches. During the same period, Ben-Gurion was still an up-and-coming labour Zionist leader, who spent the latter years of the war in the United States. The author of the most recent biography of Ben-Gurion has speculated that it bothered Ben-Gurion that he had not been involved in securing the Balfour Declaration, that his initial dubiousness about it had a "sour tang to it – Weizmann had made history while he was sitting on Fifth Avenue [in New York city library] reading books".[14]

The two men could not possibly have been further removed from each other – not only in their relative prestige, but also in their socio-economic status and lifestyles (see Chapter 1). They never became colleagues, much less personal friends. The overall picture that emerges is their complementary roles in the Zionists' long struggle for statehood. On the one hand Weizmann, skilled in the diplomatic arts of backroom deals and compromise, whose major contributions to the Zionist cause were the securing of the Balfour Declaration in 1917, and in 1931, in securing the effective cancellation of the potentially-lethal Passfield White Paper.[15] (In effect, this was his last major diplomatic achievement.) On the other hand, Ben-Gurion's path to the leadership of the Zionist Movement took decades. In 1921, he was elected to become the first chairman of the *Histadrut*, the *Yishuv*'s all-embracing labour union; in 1930 he formed and headed *Mapai*, the *Yishuv*'s majority labour party. In 1935, with his election as chairman of the Jewish Agency's executive committee, he moved into the international arena.

After World War Two, the ageing Weizmann played only a marginal diplomatic role in the establishment of Israel, while Ben-Gurion prepared the *Yishuv* for statehood, and its fight for survival against the anticipated invasion of five Arab states. Ben-Gurion, traumatised by the Allies' failure to come to the aid of the Jews during the Holocaust, jettisoned the diplomatic path, which predicated relying on outside help. He became consumed by what he regarded as the categorical imperative of the immediate establishment of a Jewish state, built upon the mass immigration to Palestine of the Jewish survivors of the Holocaust. To this end, overriding the advice of his own experts, he pushed through the economic and military preparations that would guarantee Israel's future. Chapter 15 in this volume focuses on that climactic period in his life.

Such is Ben-Gurion's dominance of Zionist historiography that Weizmann's biographers complain that their subject has been neglected or forgotten.[16] There is some irony in this plaint, given that Professor Reinharz, Weizmann's biographer, has taken 25 years to publish the third and final volume of the massive biography (so far, only in Hebrew). The attempt to re-instate Weizmann's reputation is reflected in the subtitle of this third volume: *Architect of the Jewish State.*[17]

In Chapter 14, Jehuda Reinharz and Motti Golani assess Weizmann's long career. He rose to prominence first in 1917, due to the central role he played in securing the Balfour Declaration. In the same year, he was elected president of the British Zionist Federation and became the *de facto* leader of World Zionism. Weizmann's achievement in 1931, in securing the effective cancellation of the Passfield White Paper, was second only to that of 1917.

But from the mid-1930s, with a new world war looming, Britain's strategic interests in the Arab world became paramount. Weizmann's prestige waned. In May 1939, the Chamberlain government issued a new White Paper on Palestine, which severely restricted further Jewish immigration and land purchases, and promised the Palestinian Arabs an independent state within ten years. During the final decade of the Mandate, Weizmann remained Zionism's elder statesman. But with his influence in London in decline, Ben-Gurion wrested the movement's leadership from him. For most of his adult life Weizmann resided in London. He never built up his own constituency inside the *Yishuv* and took up permanent residence in Palestine only in 1946. By that time, he was an aged, half-blind invalid. In 1949, he was appointed the first President of Israel.

In Chapter 15, Tuvia Friling examines Ben Gurion's decisive role in the complex and multifaceted Zionist effort to establish the infrastructures of a Jewish state. After World War Two he took personal responsibility for this. He combined a strategic concept for the defence of the new state against the Arab states' anticipated invasion, with a messianic vision of an immediate mass immigration and absorption of two million Jews in Israel.

In the Conclusion, Chapter 16, Neil Caplan and Laura Eisenberg assert that an unbridgeable chasm separated the mutually exclusive Arab and Zionist claims to Palestine. However, this did not preclude sporadic diplo-matic efforts to arrive at a peaceful *modus vivendi*. Arab and Zionist leaders negotiated informally, directly and indirectly, via third party mediation, in secret and in public. All of their efforts failed, since neither side had any intention of making the concessions required. Rather, Caplan and Eisenberg claim, the two sides negotiated in order to impress a powerful third party, or for tactical reasons *other* than actually reaching agreement. Compromise became a non-starter, due to the sides' increasingly nationalistic insistence on what became irreconcilable red lines. The decision on what entity would replace British rule after May 1948 was made on the battlefield.

To some extent, this volume reflects the current state of scholarship of the history of the Palestine Mandate. Inevitably, some scholars hold different, at times opposing views. For example, on the question which factor was more essential to the building of the infrastructure of the Jewish State – Jewish immigration, or Zionist land acquisitions? (Chapters 10–11). Or the debate over which Zionist leader contributed more to the foundation of Israel – Chaim Weizmann, or David Ben-Gurion? (Chapters 14–15) As editor, I have allowed each contributor free academic expression. Thus, all contributions appear on the individual author's responsibility.

Finally, on a personal note, it gives me particular pleasure to present to the reader this Centenary volume of essays in the year of my own eightieth birthday.

Notes

1 Cited in Michael Ignatieff, *Isaiah Berlin: A Life*, New York: Metropolitan Books, 1998, p. 79.
2 In 1970, the Archives' 50-year closure law was reduced to 30 years. Numerous bibliographic compilations can be found on the internet. Many are blatantly subjective, excluding those sources that don't suit their narrative; for example, that of the Trans-Arab Research Institute: www.tari.org/index.php?option=com_content& view=article&id=25&Itemid=29, or the Jewish side, www.eretzyisroel.org/~samuel/ bibliography.html
3 One Israeli Arab and two Israeli Druze have written chapters for this volume. Over 150 sources are cited in Wikipedia's entry on the Mufti:
   https://en.wikipedia.org/wiki/Amin_al-Husseini#References
4 Ilan Pappé, *A History of Modern Palestine: One Land*, Cambridge: Cambridge University Press, 2006, pp.11–12.
5 For example, Charles Glass, *London Review of Books*, 7/6. 2001 Vol. 23/11, June 2001;
   'Balfour, Weizmann and the Creation of Israel', a review of Tom Segev; *One Palestine, Complete: Jews and Arabs under the British Mandate,* New York: Little, Brown, 2001; and Naomi Shepherd, *Ploughing Sand: British Rule in Palestine 1917–48*, London/New Brunswick, N.J.: Rutgers University Press, 2000.
6 Elizabeth Monroe, *Britain's Moment in the Middle East, 1914–1956*, London: Chatto & Windus, 1963, rev. 2nd ed., 1981, p. 43. During the war, Ms Monroe worked in the government's ministry of information (propaganda); after it, she worked as a journalist for the *Economist*; in 1961, she joined St Anthony's College, Oxford University, as a fellow in Middle Eastern History, where she helped to found its Middle East Centre's Archive.
7 Michael J. Cohen, *Britain's Hegemony in Palestine and in the Middle East: Changing Strategic Imperatives*, London/Portland, OR: Valentine Mitchell, 2017, p. 12. On Britain's anticipation that the Declaration would win over the large, influential Jewish community in the US, cf. James Renton, *The Zionist Masquerade: The Birth of the Anglo-Zionist Alliance, 1914–1918*, Basingstoke/New York: Palgrave MacMillan, 2007.
8 I.e. Glass, *London Review*... supra
9 Nicholas Bethell, *The Palestine Triangle: The Struggle for the Holy Land, 1935–1948*, New York: Putnam, 1979.
10 Evyatar Friesel, British Officials on the Situation in Palestine, 1923, *Middle Eastern Studies*, Vol. 23/2, 1987.

11 The Institute of Palestine Studies' website states that the first Palestinian National Congress was held in Jerusalem from January-February 1919; http://btd.palestine-studies.org/content/chronology-1919-1936 At that Congress, the Palestinians still referred to their country as a southern province of Greater Syria, and looked forward to being a part of Faysal's kingdom. Their second National Congress was held in Damascus; the third, in December 1920, was held in Haifa.

12 In 1920, an official British census found that 77,000 of Palestine's Arabs were Arabic-speaking Christians.

13 Kenneth W. Stein, *The Land Question in Palestine, 1917–1939*, Chapel Hill: University of North Carolina Press, 1984.

14 Tom Segev, *A State at Any Cost: The Life of David Ben-Gurion*, New York: Farrar, Straus and Giroux, 2019, p. 136 (in Hebrew, 2017). Ben-Gurion was doing research for a book that he and Ben-Zvi were writing on the history of Palestine.

15 On the 1930 Passfield White Paper, see Cohen, *Britain's Hegemony*, chapter 4.

16 Many biographies of Ben-Gurion have been published. The first, official one, running up to 1946, written by Shabtai Teveth, was published in Hebrew in 4 volumes, between 1976 to 2004; a single-volume English version, covering the period 1886–1948, was published in 1987; Anita Shapira published a single-volume biography in 2014; Ben-Gurion himself published prolifically, including six volumes of memoirs, between 1971–87; for a comprehensive bibliography on Ben-Gurion, cf. Segev's highly-acclaimed biography, supra.

17 Jehuda Reinharz, Motti Golani, *Chaim Weizmann: Architect of the Jewish State* (in Hebrew), Tel Aviv: Am Oved, 2020.

Part I
British perspectives

1 Colonial intrigue in the Middle East

The Faysal – [Lawrence] – Weizmann Agreement, January 1919[*]

Michael J Cohen

The negotiations between Chaim Weizmann and the Hashemite Emir Faysal, which resulted in a signed Agreement in January 1919, have been called by Neil Caplan, the scholar of Arab-Zionist negotiations, "perhaps the most famous of all" Arab-Zionist negotiations, which "might have become the basis of a long-term accord". His view has been endorsed by Yosef Gorni, a scholar of Zionist ideology, who called their contacts

> [t]he first and most important round of negotiations after World War 1, still spoken of as a missed opportunity for a Jewish Arab settlement.[1]

The Arab scholar A.L. Tibawi referred to their Agreement as "The 1919 attempt to secure an Arab Balfour declaration". In some contrast, Awni Abd al-Hadi, Faysal's Sorbonne-educated Palestinian secretary, later denied that Faysal had ever put his name to the Agreement. No 'authorised' version of their contacts has in fact survived, largely because they all passed through the subjective filters of the parties involved.[2]

I refer to the episode as a colonial 'intrigue' – since the idea was conceived by British officials in Cairo, and T.E. Lawrence 'of Arabia', the Agreement's midwife, helped secure it by deliberately mis-translating Faysal's and Weizmann's dialogue into what he believed would be acceptable to each side. At no juncture was this more pivotal than at the meeting at which the Agreement was signed.

In October 1918, the British completed the conquest of what had been Ottoman Syria. The territory came under the overall command of Gen. Allenby, with his HQ in Cairo.

Palestine was designated Occupied Enemy Territory Administration (OETA) South. The Military administration lasted less than two years. It was dismissed peremptorily after the first wave of Arab riots against the Jews in April 1920.

---

[*] I have transliterated Faysal's name thus, but have retained other forms when quoting.

Muddled policy-making

Any attempt to analyse the Faysal-Weizmann Agreement must take into account the incoherence, confusion and conflicts of interest that affected British imperial policymaking in the Middle East.[3]

In London, the government's *realpolitik* of supporting the Zionist cause in Palestine clashed with the Middle East Command's goal to establish a viable Arab status quo under British hegemony. Cairo and Jerusalem tried repeatedly to persuade London to rescind the Balfour Declaration. The Cairo officials hoped that their inflation of the Arab Revolt's achievements, together with Zionist support for Faysal might induce the French to accommodate Sherifian rule over the Syrian interior. But London adhered to the Foreign Office promise to the French in 1912 that Britain had no designs on Syria. In the summer of 1918, the cabinet decided to withdraw British forces from Syria.[4]

Two eccentric figures exerted a significant influence on Britain's 'desert war' – T.E. Lawrence and Lt. Col. Sir Mark Sykes. Lawrence has been called a 'tin-pot exhibitionist', Britain's 'hero and poster boy in promoting the war in the desert. In contrast, Sykes was the *eminence grise*, working behind the scenes, not always in tandem with Lawrence. Sykes' extensive reports from the Middle East – at times stretching the facts in order to sway his audience – established him as the government's expert on the region, at least until 1918. The Cairo officials regarded Sykes as "intellectually shallow and hopelessly verbose … pretending to far more knowledge … than he actually possessed". Lawrence called him a "bundle of prejudices and intuitions, half-sciences".[5]

Cairo's constant stream of warnings about Arab hostility to Zionism began on the morrow of the Balfour Declaration and continued throughout the period under discussion. Brigadier-General Gilbert Clayton (head of British intelligence in Egypt) complained that it was not easy "to switch over to Zionism all at once in the face of a considerable degree of Arab distrust and suspicion".[6] In a private letter to Gertrude Bell he wrote:

> The Arabs of Syria and Palestine see the Jew with a free hand and the backing of H.M.G. and interprets it as meaning the eventual loss of its heritage…. The Arab is right and no amount of specious oratory will humbug him in a matter which affects him so vitally.[7]

It might be speculated that Clayton attempted to 'square' this particular 'circle' by promoting the Faysal-Weizmann Agreement. Clayton was apparently the first to recommend to Weizmann that he should meet with Faysal.[8]

The Military's opposition to Zionism was tainted by anti-Semitic stereotypes. Major General Money (Chief Administrator of Palestine from

1918–19) believed that his work was being sabotaged by Jewish influence in London. He stayed just one year in Palestine. He explained to a friend:

> I am the more inclined to go since I see every prospect of the edifice I have built with some labour being pulled down by Messrs. Balfour, Lloyd George and their long-nosed friends.[9]

The military were obsessed also with what has been called the 'Judeo-Bolshevik bogey' – the fear that Zionist immigrants from Russia and Eastern Europe would import revolution into Palestine.[10] In April 920, following the Nebi Musa riots, Major-General Sir Louis Bols, Money's successor, reported to Allenby on:

> the undoubted existence of a ruling ring of Zionist Bolsheviks ... [with] destructive, tyrannical, and anti-Christian aims ... [who were] anti-British in every sense of the word.... The Jew should not be given any powers of government over Palestine.[11]

But Foreign Secretary Balfour dismissed the rights of the Palestinian Arabs:

> Zionism ... was rooted in age-long traditions ... and of far profounder import than the desires and prejudices of the 700,000 Arabs who now inhabit that ancient land.[12]

Weizmann – the Zionist autocrat

On the Zionist side, Weizmann's leadership was virtually a one-man show. The author of his three-volume biography describes his life's work as being "in many ways a history of the Zionist Movement".[13]

Weizmann's discovery of acetone in 1915 was a major contribution to the British war effort. His work for the government brought him into personal contact with three ministers who would exercise a significant influence on the Zionist cause: Balfour (Admiralty, 1915–16), Winston Churchill (Munitions, 1917–19) and David Lloyd George, Minister for Munitions (1915–16, Prime Minister, 1916–22).[14]

During the war, Weizmann enjoyed a meteoric rise in fame and fortune, from his government salaries and the income from his chemical patents. His new wealth brought a dramatic change in life-style, to a "magnificent establishment" in London, "serviced by a butler, a chauffeur [for his Rolls-Royce], a nurse-governess, cook and maids". He mixed easily with the British elite, and conducted much of his personal diplomacy at London's Savoy Grill. His social rise eased the way to his achievement in helping to secure the Balfour Declaration.[15]

After the war, intoxicated with success, Weizmann believed that he was uniquely equipped to understand the British. His complex personality has been described as "a combination of intellectual maturity and emotional instability". He never stooped to "coalition building or power sharing". His colleagues accused him of dictatorial megalomania. One could hardly imagine a deeper divide than that which separated Weizmann from the *Yishuv* (the Jewish community in Palestine). They took umbrage with his condescending, autocratic attitude. He did not apparently consult with any *Yishuv* leader about his démarche with Faysal.[16]

Weizmann gave only a cursory consideration to securing the agreement of the Palestinian Arabs to the Zionists' return. He soon fell in with Cairo's plan to promote the Hashemites over the heads of the Arabs.[17]

The Palestinian Arabs

In 1918, 650,000 Arabs lived in Palestine. Between 1882 and 1914, Palestine's Jewish population increased from 23,000 to 85,000. Just 35,000 were Zionists, settled in 40 rural settlements. Opposition to Zionism served as the primary catalyst of the Palestinian Arabs' national awakening, both before and after World War One. They supported a Greater Syria under Faysal, with local autonomy for Palestine.

Frequent Zionist statements about Jewish ambitions in Palestine were reproduced in the Arab press. In 1908, Dr Arthur Ruppin opened the first Zionist office in Jaffa. It monitored and translated relevant articles in the Arabic press, in Palestine, Egypt and Syria. It regularly sent German translations to the Zionist Head Office in Berlin, to Dr Jacobson in the Istanbul office, and to other Zionist leaders.[18]

In 1908 and again in 1913–14, Zionist representatives held talks with non-Palestinian Arab groups. These failed to produce any agreement. The Arabs insisted that the Jewish immigrants assimilate and become full Ottoman citizens. They expressed reservations about unlimited Jewish immigration and feared that the Jews would expropriate Arab lands.[19]

The last pre-war Zionist Congress, held in Vienna in September 1913, discussed future relations between Jews and Arabs in Palestine. But Weizmann adopted the set position – that it was just a question of 'enlightening' the Arabs about the benefits the Zionists would bring with them.[20]

After the war, some 40 Palestinian Arab political clubs formed, led mostly by senior notables from the leading clans. The most important was the Muslim-Christian Association (MCA). Another, exclusively Muslim club, *al-Nadi Al-Arabi* (the Arab Club), dominated by the Husayni clan, served as the main conduit for the Palestinians' ties with Damascus. Whenever the Palestinians questioned Faysal about his contacts with Weizmann, he vigorously denied ever having agreed to Zionist immigration into Palestine.[21]

Weizmann's first meeting with the Palestinians was in April 1918, at a dinner party at the house of Col. Storrs, the military governor of Jerusalem. He was chaperoned by British officers to the second meeting, his statement there vetted in advance by Gen. Clayton. At each meeting, he reassured the Arabs that the Zionists had no intention of setting up a Jewish state in Palestine, of ousting them from their current positions, or of expropriating any Arab lands. He asserted that the Jews and the Arabs could work in harmony. But he remained sceptical. He did not trust the Palestinians' "polite assurances of cooperation", and believed that their acquiescence depended upon Britain's determination to enforce the Balfour Declaration.[22]

At two further meetings, without British officers present, Weizmann was less discreet. On 8 May 1918, he told leaders of Jaffa's Arab community that the Jews regarded Palestine as their "sole homeland" and would invest in it "with a view to raising its living standards for the benefit of all its inhabitants."[23] Later in the month he met in secret with key Palestinian leaders – including Musa Kazem al-Husayni, the mayor of Jerusalem and Amin al-Husayni. Musa Kazem produced a copy of the *Elders of Zion* and asked if the Zionists were working according to it? The Palestinians suspected a British-Hashemite-Zionist plot at their expense. Musa Kazem asked that a Palestinian be present at any future meetings with Faysal. Amin Husayni repeated his request. The meetings served only to confirm each side's mutual suspicions. At subsequent meetings with British Intelligence officers in Cairo in June, Weizmann referred to the Palestinians as "a demoralized race with whom it is impossible to treat".[24]

But Weizmann had already agreed, the previous February, to meet with Faysal.

The Hashemites

Husayn's link with the British originated with his fear that the Turks would depose him from his Arabian emirate, the Hijaz. His significance for the Allies lay in his being a descendant of the Prophet, and the traditional guardian of Islam's holiest cities, Mecca and Medina. On 31 October 1914, the day on which Turkey declared war on the Entente powers, Lord Kitchener telegraphed Husayn's son Abdulla:

> If the Arab nation assist England in this war that has been forced upon us by Turkey.... It may be that an Arab of the true race will assume the Khalifate at Mecca or Medina.[25]

Kitchener had in mind only the Caliph's religious functions, but his message transformed Husayn's limited goals in the Hijaz into dreams of a Hashemite empire across the Arab Middle East. In March 1915, Husayn's son Faysal visited Damascus and made first contact with the Arab nationalists. He adopted their territorial demands, in return for which they committed to support Husayn, provided he could guarantee "British guarantees of Arab independence". From August 1915 to January 1916 Husayn conducted an inconclusive correspondence with Sir Henry MacMahon, the British consul in Egypt.[26]

Lawrence glorified the Hashemites: "the oldest, most holy, and most powerful family of the Arabs". In contrast, he stigmatised the Palestinian Arabs as "degenerate Levantines of mixed race and questionable character". After the war he admitted to Liddell Hart that he had deliberately exaggerated Faysal's importance, mainly "to get the British to support the Arabs". Sykes contrasted the 'virtues' of the Hashemites and the more-educated Syrians: "The fire, the spiritual fire, lies in Arabia proper, the intellect and the organising power lie in Syria and Palestine." Sykes feared the danger of "Peninsula nomads moving before intellectual Syrians are prepared and scheme falling through [for] want of organization".[27]

The Arab Revolt against the Turks began in June 1916. The British would exaggerate its achievements, in order to boost the Hashemites' claims to Syria against those of the French. But from the outset, it was dependent upon British supplies of arms, guidance and funding. In June 1916, the War Cabinet agreed to a monthly 'dole' of £50,000 to Husayn. By 1917, this had risen to £200,000 per month.[28]

Faysal's forces remained an ancillary right flank to Allenby's army, which from 1917–18 conquered Palestine. At the Peace Conference, Faysal made the absurd claim that he had mobilised 100,000 Arab tribesmen against the Turks (the real figure was between 5–10,000.) When Lloyd George declare that Arab help had been 'essential', Allenby added that their Revolt had been 'invaluable'. Allenby failed to mention that at the end of September 1918 he had stopped his troops at the gates of Damascus, to allow Faysal's forces to 'conquer' the city. Thus, in the words of one scholar, "history was rewritten to allow this fiction of the Arab conquest of Syria to become fact".[29]

The Faysal-Weizmann deal was apparently hatched in Cairo. In February 1918, Gen. Clayton first suggested to Weizmann that he meet Faysal.[30] Allenby told Weizmann that in his opinion, as in that of "most informed people", Faysal was:

> the only representative Arab whose influence was of more than local importance. By virtue of his personal qualities, and of his position as Commander in Chief of the Arab Army, he carried great weight in Arabia.[31]

Sykes' discovery of the benefits of Zionism for British interests were based on his anti-Semitic stereotypes. In March 1918, he tutored Faysal on the Jews' legendary wealth and influence.

> [B]elieve me I speak the truth when I say that this race, despised and weak, is universal … all-powerful, and cannot be put down.… In the councils of every state, in every bank, in every business, in every enterprise there are members of this race.

But he reassured Faysal that the Zionists were different:

> [R]emember these people do not seek to conquer you ... all they ask for
> is to be able to ... return to the land of their forefathers, to cultivate it, to
> work with their hands, to become peasants once more..... They do not
> seek wealth or power, that is in London and New York, in Rome and
> Paris ... in Vienna and in Berlin.[32]

On the eve of his meeting with Faysal, Weizmann sent his 'grand strategy' for
the Middle East to Balfour. He asserted that the Palestinian Arabs were not
capable of developing any national consciousness, and Faysal was not interested in them. He maintained that the real problem was economic, not
political, and there was plenty of land for the Zionists to develop, "without
any need for encroachment on the real rights of the Arab inhabitants of
Palestine". With unabashed *hubris,* he proposed not only that the Zionists be
allowed to buy the Wailing Wall – for which they would compensate the
Moslems handsomely – but concluded

> if you want to build up a strong and prosperous Arab kingdom, it is we
> the Jews who will be able to help him, and we only. We can give him the
> necessary assistance in money and in organizing power.... [The Zionists]
> are the natural intermediaries between Great Britain and the Hejaz.

Finally, he gave his 'considered' opinion:

> the Arab centre of gravity is not Palestine but the Hejaz, really the tri-
> angle formed by Macca [sic], Damascus and Baghdad.[33]

Balfour did not treat Weizmann's letter seriously. He referred it to Clayton,
who warned him against acting on its proposals. Two months later, Balfour
replied to Weizmann that it was "premature" to begin the complicated
reforms that he had proposed.[34]

On 4 June 1918, Weizmann talked with Faysal at Ma'an for an hour, via a
British interpreter, Colonel Joyce. Weizmann's report to his wife was euphoric:

> [Faysal] is the first real Arab nationalist I have met. He is a leader! He's
> quite intelligent and a very honest man ... he wants Damascus and the
> whole of northern Syria. He talked with great animosity against the
> French.... He expects a great deal from collaboration with the Jews! He is
> contemptuous of the Palestinian Arabs whom he doesn't even regard as
> Arabs![35]

Col. Joyce reported back that Weizmann had told Faysal that the Zionists did
not intend setting up a Jewish State in Palestine, but wished, under British
guidance:

to colonize and develop the country without encroaching on other legitimate interests …. a Jewish Palestine would assist the development of an Arab Kingdom … [which] would receive Jewish support.

All this made a very positive impression upon Faysal, even if he cautioned that he could not discuss the future of Palestine, as he did not represent an Arab government and "was greatly afraid of enemy propaganda". Joyce believed that Faysal would probably accept a Jewish Palestine if it helped Arab expansion to the north.[36]

In his talks with British Intelligence officers in Cairo, Weizmann pledged £10 million in order to secure the Hashemites' support. No one questioned his ability to raise this prodigious sum.[37] In his report to the Zionist Commission, Weizmann didn't mention the £10 million, but sufficed with reporting that Faysal had been very pleased with his offer to help him against the French in Syria.[38]

Gen. Clayton's (now Chief Political Officer in Palestine) assessment was ambiguous. He thought that local Palestinian opposition would disappear within a short time, *if* the Zionists proceeded along the lines proposed by Weizmann. But he warned the Foreign Office:

> The great majority of the more or less educated Arabs, however, regard any prospect of Zionist extension with fear and dislike …. these classes will spare no effort to induce in the peasantry a hostile attitude towards the Jews…. It is not difficult for them to persuade an ignorant and gullible population that Zionism is only another word for robbing them of their lands and even of their means of livelihood.[39]

At the end of October 1918, Dr Eder, the acting chairman of the Zionist Commission, reported to Weizmann on Faysal's 'grave financial situation' and his interest in a Zionist 'loan and financial advice'. On 2 November, confident of Faysal's desperate plight, the Commission organised public celebrations in Palestine to mark the first anniversary of the Balfour Declaration. This provoked Arab protests. From Jerusalem, High Commissioner Money warned: "The majority of Arabs were now stating openly that they preferred either Arab or Ottoman rule".[40]

After consultations with the Cairo officials, including Lawrence, Weizmann turned down Eder's recommendation to make Faysal a loan, for fear they would be accused of exploiting Faysal's 'financial embarrassment' in order to buy him off. It was agreed that any loan must be part of a "proper political agreement … ratified by the British government".[41]

But Lloyd George's strategy remained to secure control of Palestine (by virtue of the Balfour Declaration), and to maintain good relations with the French. At the beginning of December 1918, he agreed in secret with Georges Clemenceau, the French premier, to French rule over Syria – in return for British control of Palestine and the oil-rich district of Mosul.[42]

Weizmann continued to negotiate with Faysal. On 11 December 1918, they met at London's Carlton Hotel, with Lawrence again acting as interpreter. Faysal was furious – claiming, disingenuously, that he had only just discovered the existence of the Sykes-Picot agreement.[43] Faysal feared that the French would push his regime "back into the desert". He told Weizmann:

> The Arabs had set up some form of government centred at Damascus, but it was extremely weak. It had no money and no men. The Army was naked and had no ammunition.[44]

Weizmann feigned that he had known about the Sykes-Picot agreement since 1915.[45] He reassured Faysal that he opposed it and had asked the American Zionists to work against it. Faysal opined that the trouble in Palestine "was fomented by Turkish and pro-Turkish propaganda". When Faysal asked Weizmann what the Zionist programme was, he replied that they would develop Palestine so that it would be able to absorb four to five million Jews, without encroaching on "the ownership rights of Arab peasantry". The Jews would give Faysal "every assistance in brain and money, so as to help revive his country". Ten days later, Faysal was wined and dined at a dinner hosted by Lord Rothschild. Reading from a letter written for him by Lawrence, Faysal expressed his acquiescence in Weizmann's 'moderate Zionism'.[46]

On 3 January 1919, Weizmann and Faysal signed their agreement. Article III provided that "the Constitution and Administration of Palestine "will afford the fullest guarantees for carrying into effect" the Balfour Declaration. Article IV stated:

> all necessary measures shall be taken to encourage and stimulate immigration of Jews into Palestine on a large scale, and ... to settle Jewish immigrants upon the land ... the Arab peasant and tenant farmers shall be protected in their rights.

Article VII stated that the Zionist Organization would "use its best efforts to assist the Arab State in providing the means for developing the natural resources and economic possibilities" of Palestine.[47]

Faysal added a last-minute condition in Arabic – he would honour the agreement, "Provided the Arabs obtain their independence." According to George Antonius, and Tibawi, Lawrence changed this to "If the Arabs are established as I have asked". Lawrence's translation remains the authorised version.[48]

On 6 February 1919 Faysal appeared before the Council of Ten at the Peace Conference. He claimed full Arab independence, but left Palestine to one side, "in deference to its universal character". Clemenceau countered with a Lebanese Christian delegation that rejected "any plan to impose a 'nomadic' Hashemite dynasty on the 'advanced' races of Syria". Concurrently, the first Arab Congress in Jerusalem resolved to replace the name Palestine with "Southern Syria" and to call for its immediate annexation into [Faysal's] "Arab Kingdom".[49]

Two weeks later, the Zionist delegation appeared before the Council of Ten. Sylvain Levi, the French member of the delegation and last to speak, referred to the East European Jewish immigrants as "people who would carry with them into Palestine highly explosive passions conducive to very serious trouble in the country." The rest of the Zionist delegation was stunned, feeling that Levi had betrayed them. Robert Lansing, the US Secretary of State asked Weizmann: "What do you mean by a Jewish National Home?" Weizmann replied that they hoped that

> by Jewish immigration, Palestine would ultimately become *as Jewish as England is English* (author's emphasis).[50]

Weizmann's extempore remark proved to be a strategic mistake. It became a catchphrase for his less diplomatic colleagues – thereby confirming Arab suspicions that the Zionists' wanted nothing less than a Jewish State in Palestine. In 1922, the government's first White Paper on Palestine specifically repudiated him.[51]

Faysal's reaction came just one week later, on 1 March, in an interview with the French newspaper *Le Matin*. He warned that if the Jews "want to constitute a state and claim sovereign rights in this region, I foresee very serious dangers". The Zionists immediately arranged a meeting between him and Felix Frankfurter of the American Zionist delegation, to obtain a *démenti*. Eager to secure American support, Faysal virtually reversed himself. His reply, again hand-written by Lawrence, stated:

> Our deputation here in Paris is fully acquainted with the proposals submitted … by the Zionist Organisation to the Peace Conference, and we regard them as moderate and proper.[52]

But the Zionists' publication of Faysal's letter merely ignited sharp Arab protests. The Syrian Arabs refused to contemplate any 'secession' of their 'southern province'. At the first Syrian National Congress, convened in Damascus in May 1919, the Palestinians rejected the Balfour Declaration and the Sykes-Picot agreement, and resolved that both the Lebanon and Palestine should be included in a United Syria.[53]

On 12 August, Major J.N. Camp, a British Intelligence officer, warned that if Faysal's agreement with Weizmann became known generally, he would be regarded by the Arabs as a traitor. His evaluation of Faysal was less sanguine than Weizmann's:

> [H]e is capable of making contradictory agreements with the French, the Zionists and ourselves, of receiving money from all three, and then endeavouring to act as he pleases. This is an additional reason why his agreement with Weizmann is of little or no value.[54]

During the course of September 1919 September, Lloyd George decided to withdraw all British forces from Cilicia and Syria.[55] Unaware of the new reality, Weizmann wrote to Balfour:

> By cooperating with Feyzal [sic] we would gain the good will of both Damascus and Mecca, we would have peace in Syria and Palestine and, incidentally, get out of the impasse into which the present Anglo-Franco-Arab negotiations have got.[56]

Kinahan Cornwallis, head of the Arab Bureau, reported to London:

> [M]atters are at present at a deadlock since the Emir asks the Zionists to throw in their lot definitely with the Arabs against the French while Dr Weizmann is in favour of allowing the French to occupy the coastal districts saying that they can be squeezed out later.[57]

But Faysal was now a prisoner of the Syrian nationalists. On 3 October 1919, in an interview with London's *Jewish Chronicle*, he stated:

> [He] regarded Palestine not as an autonomous Jewish domain, but rather as a province of his future Arab kingdom ... when some Zionists speak about Palestine becoming as Jewish as England is English ... they are really talking unreasonably.[58]

The paper's correspondent insisted "practically the whole of Jewry imagine that the Balfour Declaration meant that the Jews were to be aided by HMG to set up a Jewish National Home which would ultimately become a Jewish State". He asked if this clashed in any way with Arab ideals? Faysal replied emphatically:

> To be sure they do.... We Arabs cannot yield Palestine as part of our kingdom, adding that the numbers of Jews that could possibly settle in Palestine for years to come cannot be more than a thousand or fifteen hundred per annum.

Weizmann's impromptu remark at the Peace Conference had come home to roost. By this stage, there was a total cognitive dissonance between the Zionists and the Arabs. The leaders of the *Yishuv* were stunned by Faysal's apparent *volte face*. On 8 October 1919, Menachem Ussishkin, acting chairman of the Zionist Commission, met with Musa Kazim al-Husayni, Mayor of Jerusalem. When Ussishkin insisted that the separation of Palestine from Syria was already a *fait accompli*, al-Husayni retorted that the Palestinian Arabs had already "repudiated the concessions made by the Amir". They would never agree to Palestine's separation from Syria, nor to any special privileges for the Zionists – notwithstanding any agreement that "Faysal may have made with Weizmann". He next chastised Ussishkin:

[J]ust as the mind of the European Jew is sharp and thoughtful, the mind of the Oriental is not so dense that he cannot see ... what is in store for him in the near future ... from the mass immigration of the Jews.... [T]hey want to drive us out of the land and to take possession of our houses and estates.[59]

At the beginning of October, Faysal reported to Foreign Secretary Curzon that the Syrian nationalists had accused him of betrayal, of selling off their lands to the Zionists. Many Arab nationalists, both in Syria and in Jerusalem, were working to oust the European powers and restore Syria to the Turks. The Syrian Congress rejected Zionist demands "in that part of southern Syria which is known as Palestine", and resolved that there should be "no dismemberment of Syria and no separation of Palestine or the coastal region". Curzon rejected Arab claims to Palestine and reminded him that in the 1915 correspondence, MacMahon had set aside Syria as a matter of French interest! He reiterated Britain's commitment to the French.[60]

Faysal agreed to the Zionists' request to meet with three of their leaders – Drs Shmaryahu Levin and Samuel Landman, and Ben Cohen, an American Zionist.[61] Accompanied by Awni Abd al-Hadi, Faysal rejected their request to sign a new draft of his agreement with Weizmann. Dr Levin asked Faysal to issue a statement on 2 November (the anniversary of the Balfour Declaration) to show the Jewish people that they could still rely on him. Faysal agreed to send a message, but then left the meeting. When asked by al-Hadi what had been unsatisfactory in the *Jewish Chronicle* interview, Levin replied "asking for Palestine to be a province of an independent Arabia was contrary to the aspirations of the Zionists". He added that Arab objections to Weizmann's phrase "Palestine was to be as Jewish as England is English", could not fail "to evoke disapproval among the Zionists".

Continuing their dialogue of the deaf, Al-Hadi retorted that the Balfour Declaration had "aroused the opposition of the Palestinian Arabs against the Jews". Zionist talk of Palestine as the land of the Jews had been "very offensive to the Palestinian Arabs who regarded Palestine as their country". He asked the Zionists to persuade "America to insist that Mesopotamia, Palestine and Syria should become an independent confederation, with an Arab King, under the League of Nations". He advised them to "limit themselves to colonization and development of their own culture and institutions".

Dr Levin asserted that the restoration of the Near East would require: "Jewish experts and Jewish capital". If the hope of a Jewish Palestine, promised by the Great Powers, was removed: "the Near East would not be able to attract those Jewish elements which were indispensable". Al-Hadi promised to do what he could to get Faysal to undo the damage done by his *Jewish Chronicle* interview. But Faysal's vague message, which paid "homage to the sincerity of the Zionist leaders", failed to meet their expectations.[62]

Weizmann ventilated his frustration at the final dénouement of his agreement. In a letter to the Zionist Bureau, he excoriated the British

> [who] think of us as a set of capitalists and exploiters ready to come down on the poor innocent Arab peasant and tear him to pieces.... [They] jump rapidly to the conclusion that Tel Aviv is nothing but a Bolshevik colony, Jerusalem is no more than a community of old, lazy, derelict, creatures – rather repulsive, living on charity.[63]

But he also insisted that the *Yishuv* should have shown more tact towards the British, berating their complaints against the officials' anti-Semitism.[64] In a private letter to Dr Eder, he ventilated his personal alienation from the *Yishuv*:

> I think an end must be put to the hysterical state into which a part of the Palestinian population has apparently worked itself.... They seem to excel in a game of showing cheap heroism and fictitious martyrdom, and candidly I am beginning to sympathise with the British Administration more than I ever did before.

He warned that if the *Yishuv* continued along its current path, it would have to take full responsibility "towards the Jewish world [and] the British government" for raising the funds necessary for building up the country.[65]

Conclusion

The Faysal-[Lawrence]-Weizmann deal was an ill-conceived colonial chimera. The scholar of Arab-Zionist negotiations (four volumes) asserted that their Agreement might have become "the basis of a long-term accord". But this is somewhat at odds with his conclusion:

> The gap between the basic national-political demands and the perceived "vital" interests of Palestinian Arabs and Zionists was so wide as to be virtually unbridgeable.[66]

It might be conjectured that the only 'agreement' that the Palestinians would have accepted would have been the limitation of the Jews' status and numbers in Palestine to their pre-war dimensions.[67] Obviously this was a non-starter for the Zionists. Faysal's surreptitious contacts with Weizmann only heightened the Palestinians' animosity and suspicions of Zionist goals. As declared by Izzat Darwaza, a Palestinian delegate to the Syrian Congress in June 1920, his countrymen "would not agree to Palestine's being sacrificed on the altar of [Syrian] independence". Nor would the Syrian nationalists. Once they discovered Faysal's secret agreement with Weizmann, they, not Faysal, dictated the subsequent course of events. Only the British army could have prevented the French from taking over Syria – but this was never an option for the British government.

In 1917, Weizmann had wielded to great effect the myth of Jewish power and influence. But after the war, there was never any chance of his mobilizing these assets for Faysal in Syria. Given his experience with senior ministers during the war, Weizmann might have appreciated that Lawrence and Sykes were peripheral figures in the confused labyrinths of British policy-making. This was not 1917 all over again. Balfour was not a key arbiter of British policy – not in 1917, and certainly not after the war. Nor did he ever give Weizmann any hint that he agreed with his surrealistic ideas. Fifty years later, Britain's last ambassador to occupied Egypt commented ruefully:

> In the Middle East the British never saw the writing on the wall until they hit their heads against it.[68]

Notes

1 Neil Caplan, Faisal Ibn Husain and the Zionists: A Re-examination with Documents, *The International History Review*, vol. 5/4, 1983, p. 561; idem, *Futile Diplomacy, vol. I, Early Arab-Zionist Negotiation Attempts, 1913–1931*, London: Frank Cass, 1983, pp. 36–46; Yosef Gorni, *Zionism and The Arabs, 1882–1948: A Study of Ideology*, Oxford: Clarendon Press, 1987, p. 86.

2 A.L. Tibawi, T.E. Lawrence, Faisal and Weizmann, *Royal Asian Society Journal*, vol. 56, 1969, p. 160; Suleiman Mousa, *Lawrence: An Arab View*, London: Oxford University Press, 1966, p. 228.

3 Bruce Westrate, *The Arab Bureau: British Policy in the Middle East, 1916–1920*, University Park, Penn.: Pennsylvania State University Press, 1992, pp. 24–7; Michael D. Berdine, *Redrawing the Middle East: Sir Mark Sykes, Imperialism, and the Sykes-Picot Agreement*, London: I.B. Tauris, 2018, pp. 45, 66–8.

4 James Barr, *A Line in the Sand, Britain, France and the Struggle that Shaped the Middle East*, London: Simon and Schuster, 2011, pp. 13–14.

5 Robert H Lieshout, *Britain and the Arab Middle East: World War 1 and its Aftermath*, London/New York, 2016, pp. 1–2; Westrate, *The Arab*, pp. 145, 153; T. E. Lawrence, *Seven Pillars of Wisdom*, London: Jonathan Cape, 1946, p. 57.

6 Clayton to FO, 18 April 1918, in Bernard Wasserstein, *The British in Palestine: The Mandatory Government and the Arab-Jewish Conflict, 1917–1929*, London: Royal Historical Society, 1978, p. 24.

7 Clayton to Bell, 8 December 1917, in Lieshout, *Britain and*, p. 471, note 146.

8 On Cairo's (especially Wingate's) support for the Hashemite-led Arab revolt, ibid., pp. 127–9.

9 A. J. Sherman, *Mandate Days: British Lives in Palestine, 1918–1948*, New York: Thames & Hudson, 1998, p. 53.

10 cf. Wasserstein, *The British*, p. 11.

11 Bols to Allenby, 21 April 1920, ibid., p. 67.

12 Balfour memo of 19 August 1919, Syria, Palestine and Mesopotamia, in *Documents on British Foreign Policy 1919–39*, London: HMSO, 1961, p. 345.

13 Jehuda Reinharz, *Chaim Weizmann*: vol. 2, *The Making of a Statesman*, New York, Oxford University Press, 1993, p. vii.

14 Ibid., pp. 47–8, Ben Halpern, *A Clash of Heroes: Brandeis, Weizmann, and American Zionism*, New York: Oxford University Press, 1987, pp. 55–6.

15 Reinharz, ibid., pp. vii–viii, 50–1, 60–9; Norman A Rose, *Weizmann: A Biography*, New York: Viking, 1986, pp. 157, 246–7.
16 Reinharz, ibid., pp. 185–6, 242, 288–9, 292, 369, 392; Rose, ibid., pp. 67–8, 246.
17 cf. Chaim Weizmann, *Trial and Error*, New York: Schocken Books, 1949, p. 236.
18 Caplan, Faisal, pp. 16–17; Neville Mandel, Attempts at an Arab-Zionist Entente: 1913–1914, *Middle Eastern Studies*, vol. 1/3, 1965, pp. 238–267; Ya'acov Roi, 'The Zionist Attitude to the Arabs 1908–1914', *Middle Eastern Studies*, vol. 4/3, 1968, pp. 206–7. Roi's and Mandel's articles are based primarily on Zionist sources.
19 Roi, ibid., pp. 198–242; Caplan, *Futile*, vol. I, pp. 18–27.
20 Roi, ibid., pp. 204–5, 216–17, Mandel, Attempts, pp. 259–65.
21 Yehoshua Porat, *The Emergence of the Palestinian-Arab National Movement, 1918–1929*, London: Frank Cass, 1974, pp. 86–9, 104.
22 Reinharz, *Weizmann* 2, pp. 250–1.
23 Sahar Huneidi, *A Broken Trust, Herbert Samuel, Zionism and the Palestinians*, London/New York: I.B. Tauris & Co., Ltd, 2001, p. 31.
24 Reinharz, *Weizmann*, 2, pp. 252–3, Caplan, *Futile*, vol. I, p. 33.
25 Elie Kedourie, *England and the Middle East, The Destruction of the Ottoman Empire, 1914–1921*. London: Bowes & Bowes, 1956, pp. 17–18.
26 Michael J Cohen, *The Origins and Evolution of the Arab-Zionist Conflict*, Berkeley: University of California Press, 1987, pp. 11–28; Lieshout, *Britain*, pp. 42–3, 77–80.
27 Lawrence minute of 25 February 1921, FO 371/6375, E2354, and 'Syria: The Raw Material', in Report of 25 February 1918, in Wasserstein, *The British*, pp. 12–13; Lieshout, *The British* p. 105; Berdine, *Redrawing*, p. 56.
28 Liesehout, ibid., pp. 183–7; Berdine, ibid., pp. 155–9.
29 Elie Kedourie, The Capture of Damascus, 1 October 1918, *Middle Eastern Studies*, vol. 1/1, October 1964; Matthew Hughes, Elie Kedourie and the Capture of Damascus, 1 October 1918: A Reassessment, *War & Society*, 23/1, 2013.
30 Caplan, *Futile*, vol. I, p. 36, idem, Faisal, p. 564.
31 Weizmann, *Trial*, p. 232.
32 Sykes to Faysal, 3 March 1918, FO 882/3, NA
33 Weizmann to Balfour, 30 May 1918, F.O. 371/11053/125475. NA.
34 Clayton to Foreign Office, June 16, 1918, F.O. 371/11053/130342, Balfour to Weizmann, 26 July 1918, FO 371/3395, NA.
35 Weizmann to Vera, 17 June 1918, *The Letters and Papers of Chaim Weizmann* (*WL*), vol. VIII, Dvorah Barzilay and Barnet Litvinoff, editors, New Brunswick, N.J.: Transaction Books, 1977, p. 210.
36 Clayton to Foreign Office 12.6.18, based on Joyce's handwritten notes, Caplan, *Faisal*, p. 570.
37 Symes to Foreign Office, 13 June 1918, FO 800/221, NA, Clayton to Balfour, 1 July 1918, Weizmann Archives (WA)
38 Weizmann report to Zionist Commission, 16 June 1918, Caplan, *Faisal*, p. 572.
39 Clayton report, 16 June 1918, FO 371/3395, NA.
40 Money to Cairo, 20 November 1918, copied to Foreign Office, FO 371/3386, NA; Reinharz, *Weizmann*, vol. 2, p. 281.
41 Weizmann letters to Gen Clayton, and to Eder, 5 November 1918, *WL*, IX, pp. 9-20.
42 Howard Sachar, *The Emergence of the Middle East, 1914–1924*, New York: Alfred A. Knopf, p. 253.
43 Faysal and his father had discussed it with Sykes and Picot when the latter visited the Hijaz in May 1917, Kedourie, *Labyrinth*, pp. 165–6, 176–9.
44 Weizmann's report to Sir Eyre Crowe, 16 December 1918, FO 371/3420, NA.

45 At a meeting with the Zionists in February 1917, Sykes reassured them: "the British had given the French no pledge in Palestine". Weizmann learned of the agreement in April 1917, from C.P. Scott, editor of the *Guardian* newspaper. Weizmann, *Trial*, pp. 189, 191.

46 Faysal's dinner speech, written by Lawrence, in Caplan, *Faisal*, pp. 576–8.

47 For the full text, Cohen, *The Origins*, pp. 144–7.

48 Awni Abd al-Hadi later accused Lawrence of having "tricked Faysal disgracefully", Caplan, Faisal, p. 580, Tibawi, *Feisal*, p. 160.

49 Caplan, ibid., p. 564, Isaiah Friedman, *British Pan-Arab Policy, 1915–1922: A Critical Appraisal*, New Brunswick/London: Transaction, 2010, chapter 8.

50 Meeting of 23 February 1919, Weizmann, *Trial*, p. 245, Reinharz, *Weizmann*, 2, pp. 219, 299. Weizmann cited as a precedent the "outstanding success" of the French in Tunisia.

51 Reinharz, ibid., p. 299; in 1922, overriding Weizmann's protests, Samuel rebuffed his remark in the government's first White Paper on Palestine: "Phrases have been used such as that Palestine is to become 'as Jewish as England is English'. His Majesty's Government regard any such expectation as impracticable". Cmd. 1700, 3 June 1922.

52 Faysal – Frankfurter, in Lawrence's handwriting, 1 March, 1919, Caplan, *Futile,* vol. I, pp. 149–50.

53 Reinharz, *Weizmann* 2, p. 281.

54 Caplan, *Faisal*, pp. 590–1.

55 Kedourie, *England*, pp. 165–6.

56 Caplan, *Faisal*, p. 592.

57 Kinahan Cornwallis to FO, 25 September 1919, FO 371/4183, NA.

58 For this and following, cf. FO 371/4183, NA.

59 Caplan, *Futile,* vol. I, 1, pp. 157–9.

60 Curzon to Faysal, 9 October 1919, FO 371/4183, NA.

61 Meeting on 19 October 1919, Caplan, *Futile,* vol. I, 159–62.

62 Faysal to Levin, 31 October 1919, Caplan, Faisal, p. 599.

63 Weizmann to Zionist Bureau, London, 7 November 1919, Reinharz, *WL,* IX, p. 238.

64 Ibid.

65 Weizmann to Eder 8 June 1920, ibid., pp. 354–5.

66 Caplan, *Futile*, vol. I, p. 127.

67 Ibid., p. 122.

68 Humphrey Trevelyan, *The Middle East in Revolution*, London: MacMillan, 1970, p. 7.

2 The anti-Zionist 'Jewish Khazar' syndrome in the official British mind

Rory Miller

During the crucial period between 1939 and 1948, as a decision on the final status of Palestine loomed ever closer, a small but influential group of current and former British politicians and civil servants, diplomats and soldiers, and academics and theologians, became increasingly active in their attempts to oppose any move from mandatory rule to a Jewish state in all or any part in Palestine. Among this group some had first come into contact with the Palestine issue through missionary work or government service. Others had less experience of Palestine itself but had come to see any abandonment of the Arabs in Palestine as one more ignominious nail in the British imperial coffin. Others still had developed a sympathy for the Arab cause in general and the Arabs of Palestine in particular out of a romantic infatuation with one type of Arab, the Bedouin, which had nothing to do with the realities of modern Palestine.

Whatever their motives, by the late 1930s, this cross-section of the British establishment had taken up the challenge set down by Sir Ronald Storrs, Governor of Jerusalem and Judea between 1920 and 1926, and himself a central member of this constituency, that the 'extreme and logical' thing that pro-Arabs could do would be to 'devote time, brains and cash' to the Arab cause in Palestine.[1]

The most concrete manifestation of this new activism was the establishment during the final decade of the mandate of several organisations dedicated to Palestinian Arab cause. These included, most notably, the Palestine Information Centre, the Arab Centre, the Middle East Parliamentary Committee (MEPC), the Committee for Arab Affairs (CAA), the Anglo-Arab Association, the Anglo-Arab Friendship Society and the Arab Friendship Committee.

I have discussed these groups elsewhere in detail,[2] but their primary objective was to influence public opinion by promoting national campaigns, gaining access to the media to present their views and by attempting to influence the political debate on the fate of Palestine. According to its 1937 charter, for example, the Palestine Information Centre's goal was 'supplying information to the press and influential persons on the Palestine issue'.[3] This chapter focuses on one of the more intriguing arguments disseminated by members of the British pro-Arab elite involved in groups like the Palestine Information Centre as they attempted to influence policy circles managing the mandate in its final decade: the Khazar theory.

The Khazars were a pagan people of Turco-Tartar stock who appeared in Europe, most likely southern Russia and the Caucasus, at some point after the fifth century. In circa AD740, the King of the Khazars and his ruling elite converted to Judaism and Judaism became the state religion of the Khazar people. At the height of its power, the Khazar empire's territorial claims and political influence extended westward to Kiev in the Ukraine, to Khwarizm in the East, north into the Lower Volga basin and as far south as the Northern half of the Caucasus.

Proponents of the Khazar theory in the Palestine debate were not interested in the imperial exploits of the Khazars, or the more academic questions of whether their conversion to Judaism had covered the whole population or only the ruling elite or whether the rabbinic or Karaite form of Judaism was adopted.[4] What preoccupied them was the fate of the Khazar people post-conversion, once they scattered from their homes in the Caucasus into what is now Russia and Poland, following the destruction of their empire sometime between the middle of the tenth and the late twelfth centuries.

As Salo Wittmayer Baron eloquently explained in the third volume of his monumental *A Social and Religious History of the Jews*, which addressed the Khazars in some detail, this migration resulted in the resettlement of "many [Khazar] offshoots into the un-subdued Slavonic lands, helping ultimately to build up the great Jewish centres of eastern Europe".[5] By the time of the mandate, these 'great Jewish centres' were at the heart of Jewish cultural and intellectual life, as well as home to the largest concentrated Jewish population in the world – almost seven million Jews, living in Poland (almost 3 million), Russia (2.5 million), Romania, Lithuania, Latvia and Carpatho-Russia (1.5 million). From the Zionist perspective, these vibrant and Zionist-conscious communities were an important consideration in the politics of mandatory Palestine, for two reasons: 1) Palestine's ultimate fate rested on being able to turn the existing Jewish minority in Palestine into a majority of the country's population; 2) the immigrants needed to change the demographic reality on the ground would inevitably come from Eastern and Central Europe.

Writing at this time, the famed historian and active Zionist Lewis Namier described these communities as the "glacier of Jewry", compared to the Jews of Western and Central Europe, whom he characterised as "the fringes of the glacier from which no river can spring and by which one must not judge the nature and future of the glacier itself".[6] For this reason, Zionist leaders, publicists and supporters like Namier spared no effort in presenting the migration of these Jews to Palestine as a return to their ancestral homeland. During 1941, discussions between senior Zionists and Colonial Secretary Lord Moyne, Namier rejected any territorial alternative to Palestine as a way of solving the Jewish problem on exactly these grounds. The commitment to

Palestine, he explained, was not only an expression of "national and religious feeling, deep longing and love for the land", but also because "our claim to the land of our fathers, fully acknowledged under the mandate, and to a Return which for more than two thousand years has formed the essence of our national existence".[7]

The historian Walter Laqueur has argued that before 1948 there was only a limited number of Zionist and anti-Zionist arguments in the battle over Palestine.[8] The possibility that the vitally important Jewish communities of Eastern Europe could be directly descended from the Khazars, a pagan tribe converted to Judaism in the middle ages, posed an ethnological challenge to some of the key Zionist arguments that did exist – those that emphasised the direct connection of Europe's Jews to historical events in Palestine and stressed the biblical underpinnings of the Zionist endeavour.

For the duration of the mandate, British Arabists had been preoccupied with the success that Zionists had in framing their case in the above terms. Sir Ronald Storrs labelled the Zionist claims to Palestine on biblical grounds as the 'Abrahamic Declaration', implying that just as the Balfour Declaration had given political credibility to Zionist aspirations in Palestine at the expense of the Arabs who lived there, the Bible had given historical and religious credibility to those same claims.[9] Similarly, Dr Maud Royden-Shaw, the noted missionary, who became a champion of Arab rights in Palestine during the second part of the mandate, expressed concern that support for Zionism was due to the fact that "the average Englishman gets all his knowledge of Palestine out of the Bible".[10]

It is interesting how devout Christians of this era, such as Royden-Shaw and Frances Newton, another leading British female opponent of Zionism, overcame their natural inclination to accept the literal meaning of the Bible when it clashed with their opposition to Zionist claims. Royden-Shaw would ruminate on this apparent contradiction. Her opposition to Zionism, she explained, did not contradict her belief in God as set out in the Bible because some of the most ardent Zionists were communists who did not believe in God.[11]

Sir Edward Spears, the former soldier, parliamentarian and British ambassador to the Levant during the World War Two, was the most active proponent of Palestinian Arab rights during the final mandatory era.[12] He shared Royden-Shaw's concerns over the effectiveness of Zionist historical and Biblical claims to Palestine, arguing that the "average well-meaning citizen ... his biblical memories, generally as vague as his knowledge of geography, induce him to feel that somehow Palestine is or should be a Jewish land".[13] Countering such feelings was challenging. The Rt. Rev. W.H. Stewart, Bishop of the Church of England in Jerusalem, responded to a letter from Spears requesting a "refutation on biblical grounds of the Jewish claim to Palestine",[14] by noting the difficulty of using a theological argument against Zionism. He also warned of the futility of trying to argue against Zionism on biblical terms because every argument against the biblical right of Jews to Palestine could be countered by an equally convincing argument in favour.[15]

The Khazar theory had been introduced into the policy debate over Palestine and the wider Jewish question in 1920, the same year that Britain was assigned the mandate. In 1919, an Anglo-American Mission to Poland had been established and led on the British side by Sir Stuart Samuel, president of the Board of Deputies of British Jews. The mission was tasked with investigating allegations of mistreatment of Jews by the recently established government of the Second Polish Republic. The commission reported its findings in 1920. A majority report concluded that mistreatment had occurred and was a result of "a widespread anti-Semitic prejudice aggravated by the belief that the Jewish inhabitants were politically hostile to the Polish State".[16]

Captain Peter Wright, a member of the British delegation, refused to sign off on these findings and instead issued a minority report. Among many other points of historical and contemporary interest, his dissenting opinion noted how during the eighth and ninth centuries "there was a great kingdom of Tartars to the north of the Black Sea – called the Chazars [sic] – of which a large, and the upper portion, were converted to Judaism". He then noted, somewhat randomly, that "Tartars are still the only people who show any inclination for conversion to Orthodox Judaism". Speaking the following year on the findings of the Mission's report, he repeated these claims, stating that one thousand years previously a "large portion of the inhabitants of the Tartar Kingdom of the Chazars [sic] to the north of the Black sea converted to Judaism". He then argued that this "Jewish stream from the East" had been long-time residents in Poland and that "except for the purpose of proving a point, they [the Jews of Poland] cannot be called strangers there, nor can the Slavs be considered very much more native than they".[17]

Wright's focus on the Khazar theory in both his minority report and in his subsequent contribution to the public debate on the Samuels Mission is significant for three reasons: He explicitly linked the Khazar heritage of Poland's Jews to their long-time status as Poles; he was hostile to Zionism, and a vocal opponent of the Balfour Declaration when it was announced two years earlier; and he framed the Polish-ness of the country's Jews in terms of their growing identification with Zionism and the Jewish future in Palestine. In his minority report, he summed up concisely what he considered the Polish-Jewish attitude to be: "We Jews are a nation. All we need is a country. Our country is Palestine and until we can have it as a national home we want to be organized as a nation in Poland".

By the late 1930s, *Kristallnacht*, the German annexation of Austria and the occupation of Czechoslovakia, provided a forewarning of the fate awaiting the Jewish communities of the East, whom Wright had argued were not even Jews at all, at the hands of the Nazis. At the same time, the primary concern of Britain, the mandatory power in Palestine, was to win the Arab world to its side in its Middle Eastern rivalry with Nazi Germany and fascist Italy. In January 1939, the Colonial Secretary, Malcolm MacDonald, concluded that "active measures must be taken" to improve Anglo-Arab relations.[18]

This resulted in the promulgation of the Palestine White Paper on 17 May 1939. During the early years of the mandate, the level of Jewish immigration into the country was based on economic rather than political criteria and dependent on the number of extra immigrants that it was believed the economy could adequately support. This principle was first laid down in the (Churchill) White Paper of 1922, which stated officially that "immigration cannot be so great in volume as to exceed whatever may be the economic capacity of the country at the time to absorb new arrivals".[19] This was most publicly reiterated in a letter from Prime Minister Ramsay MacDonald to Zionist leader Chaim Weizmann in February 1931.[20] Even though the principle of economic absorptivity was problematic, and adherence to it depended on the existing political circumstances (for example, during the Arab Revolt of the late 1930s, the Palestine administration took political, as well as economic, considerations into account when deciding levels of Jewish immigration), it was still primarily perceived by the Zionists, if not their Arab interlocutors in Palestine, as a non-political approach to a controversial issue.

The 1939 White Paper officially changed Jewish immigration from an economic to a political issue. It provided for the "admission, from the beginning of April [1939] of some 75,000 immigrants over the next five years.... After the period of five years no further Jewish immigration will be permitted unless the Arabs of Palestine are prepared to acquiesce in it". The White Paper also imposed severe restrictions on the Jewish purchase of land, and envisaged an independent state in which the Jews would comprise no more than one-third of the total population. The following July, MacDonald announced that all Jewish immigration into Palestine would be suspended from October 1939 until March 1940.[21] In practice, the immigration clauses of the White Paper set down the principle that the Arabs of Palestine had the final say on levels of Jewish immigration into that country. This angered the Zionist movement because it undermined the possibility of a manufactured Jewish majority in Palestine and because it demonstrated total indifference to the humanitarian needs of Jews under Nazi occupation.[22]

Speaking in the debate on the White Paper in the House of Commons on 22 May 1939, Anthony Crossley, the Unionist MP for Stretford, acknowledged that his "task to-day [is] to deploy the Arab case in this Debate". In doing so, he argued that Askhenzi Jews, whom he described as "the ordinary modern European Jew" were "descended from Tartar and Hittite tribes in Asia Minor and was converted to the Jewish faith in the eighth or ninth century". On these grounds, he argued, "not only are these people [Jewish immigrants into Palestine from this group] not going back to the same land, but they are not the same people".

Crossley's statement earned an immediate response from James de Rothschild, MP for the Isle of Ely. Taking issue with Crossley's attempt to use "ethnological reasons" to argue that the "people who are returning to Palestine now are not the same Jews as used to be there 1,500 years ago", de

Rothschild countered with the standard Zionist trope that over the previous 1,500 years "these people, their parents, their grandparents, their ancestors, have prayed from day to day for the return of themselves and their children to the land which they revered. Surely, that is a sufficient claim".

Intrigued by this parliamentary exchange, Foreign Office grandee H. Lacy Baggallay, initiated an internal Foreign Office investigation into the matter under the heading 'Origins of Polish and Russian Jews'. Baggallay was one of the most senior Foreign Office officials dealing with Palestine during the final years of the mandate and his objective in launching an enquiry, he explained, was to take the opportunity provided by Crossley's Commons' statement to consider whether the 'modern European Jew is descended from Tartar and Hittite tribes converted to the Jewish faith in the eighth or ninth century'.[23]

In his internal Foreign Office memorandum on the matter, Baggallay noted that he had heard "similar arguments brought forward before", in particular the claims made by Captain Peter Wright in 1920 at the very beginning of the mandatory period. Baggallay then raised two key questions that in his opinion merited further comment: whether the Khazar theory was supported by any leading historians and, if so, whether it was regarded by them to be "(a) 'quite impossible' (b) 'reasonable, though not proved' or (c) 'a strong probability or certainty'".[24]

Soon after, Baggallay also considered the claims made in a letter by Charles A. Kincaid, H.M. Consul at Berne, published in the London *Times* at the end of May 1939. In his letter, Kincaid argued that the "Palestine immigrant Jews are not descended from the ancient Hebrews, but are the descendants of Poles and Germans converted from Paganism in the early middle ages by Jewish missionaries". Baggallay"s first reflection on Kincaid's interjection was that his suggestion that "most of the European Jews are descendants of converted Poles and Germans ought to please Herr Hitler".[25] Baggallay then noted that Kincaid had introduced a "third variant of the theory",[26] that "the ... so-called Palestine Arabs are not pure Arabs but are largely descended from ancient Jews", and he concluded with the view that if Crossley and Kincaid were correct then "there is more of the ancient Israeli blood among the so-called Arabs than any other section of humanity".[27]

Interestingly, this view – that Jews had less of a claim to Palestine than members of other religions – became a common refrain of opponents of Israel after its establishment in 1948. A 1952 pamphlet published by the United Nations Educational, Scientific and Cultural Organization (UNESCO) put it:

> The home to which ... so many other Ashkenazim Zionists have yearned to return has most likely never been theirs.... [i]n anthropological fact, many Christians may have much more Hebrew-Israelite blood in their veins that most of their Jewish neighbours.

Or as the academic Professor Ray L. Cleveland, observed three decades later, the Palestinian claim to descent from the ancient Hebrews and Judeans is as strong or stronger than that of most Jewish communities. It is well established, for instance, that the Khazars, who converted to Judaism over a millennium ago, are a major ancestral group to Jews of Eastern Europe.[28]

In 1939, Sir Stephen Gaselee, a highly-regarded polymath, who served as Foreign Office historian and librarian, was charged by Baggallay to shed light on these questions. In taking up the challenge, Gaselee drew on two main sources. The first was the available literature on the Khazars. This included volumes of annotated fragmentary primary source documents on the Khazars published in 1912 and 1923, as well as Yarmolinsky's bibliographical essay on the Khazars that had been published earlier that same year in *The Bulletin on the New York Public Library*.[29] The second group of sources came from the much larger, and far more controversial literature on race that was published from the mid-nineteenth century onwards, a period when racial characteristics were widely viewed as major determinants of culture, behaviour, character and even societal progress.

Gaselee's report drew specifically from the work of William X. Ripley from the late 1890s and from the more recent work of Julius Huxley and A.C. Haddon, whom he considered "very high authorities" on the matter.[30] The final internal Foreign Office report, completed by Gaselee within a week of being commissioned, supported two points made by Ripley and Huxley and Haddon in their works: that the Jews "[are] not a nation nor even an ethnic unit but rather a socio-religious group" (Huxley and Haddon) and that they are "not a race but only a people" (Ripley).

On the issue of the Khazar conversion, Gasellee concluded that there was "no reason to doubt about a large-scale conversion to Judaism of the Chazars", a view endorsed soon after by two major works on the Khazars by Abraham Poliak in Hebrew in 1944 and by D.M. Dunlop in English, exactly one decade later.[31] Gasellee was much more cautions than Crossley, Kincaid or Baggallay in coming to a conclusion on the issue of whether the Jews of contemporary Eastern Europe were the direct descendants of the Khazars and therefore had no claim to Palestine. Rather than take a position on such a politically-charged matter in the midst of the debate over the White Paper, in the shadow of the rising racially-driven Nazi programme in Europe, he chose instead to note only that there was "room for argument as to the extent to which it [the Khazar conversion] affected Ashkenazim generally".[32]

Critics of Britain's role in Palestine, and the wider Middle East, during the mandatory era commonly viewed Baggallay as a cunning, shadowy mastermind of anti-Zionist obstructionism in Whitehall. Most notably, Elie Kedourie accused him of being "so intent on refuting Zionist arguments" that he lost no opportunity and spared no effort in trying to find aspects of the Palestine debate that were unfavourable to Zionist claims.[33] Certainly, the speed at which he moved to have Crossley's parliamentary claims investigated by the Foreign Office appears to suggest that he was looking to find an effective argument with which to counter calls for Jewish immigration into Palestine at this highly uncertain time. On the other hand, after R.A. Butler, under-secretary of state for foreign affairs at the Foreign Office, believed that Gasellee's report had "to a great extent" backed up what Crossely had said and asked whether it was possible to send it back to Crossley "for his own interest", Baggallay approved, as long as it was made clear that the information was "of a scholarly and not a political complexion".[34]

The historian Bernard Wasserstein has noted that by the early years of the Second World War "Quasi-Scientific notions" on the origins of East Europe's Jews were "making the rounds of London clubs".[35] In these terms it is worth nothing that on receipt of the Foreign Office report, Crossley told Butler that "the ethnic claim is *so often advanced* that I had just thought it worthwhile in the debate to throw that home-made bomb".[36] Crossley himself contributed to the spread of this idea by forwarding the Gasellee report to Sir Dennison Ross in order to get his "written comments and opinion".[37] Ross was a renowned orientalist and linguist, reputed to speak over thirty languages, who served at the time as the first director of the School of Oriental and African Studies (SOAS) at the University of London.[38] Similarly, as Wasserstein notes, in 1941, Oliver Hardy, Anthony Eden"s private secretary, was informed by the distinguished archaeologist Sir Leonard Woolley over dinner that "the Jews of Central Europe were not real Jews, but a Mongoloid race converted to Judaism in early times; hence their distinctive mongoloid appearance".[39]

The Crossley-Ross and Woolley-Hardy interactions are typical of how issues like the Khazar theory that were relevant to key political discussions of the day were circulated between a relatively small and closely-knit elite linked professionally, through common social circles and the same clubs. Take Woolley for example. Though he was not as public in his opposition to Zionism as contemporaries like Sir Ronald Storrs and Sir Edward Spears, he was still viewed by Zionists in the early war years as the leader of an informal movement in elite circles that was attempting to "jettison Zionism as a cheap sop to the Arabs".[40]

In 1941, Wooley submitted a memorandum to Professor Rushbrook Williams at the Ministry of Information which stressed the importance of the Moslem world to the British Empire and argued the necessity of educating American opinion on this issue, adding "Americans are prone to think of Palestine as a Jewish country threatened by 'Arabs': their views are largely based on the Bible and on Zionist propaganda which has been very skilfully done".[41] Rushbrook Williams forwarded this memorandum to Colonial Secretary Lord Moyne who then reached out to Woolley and asked whether he himself would be prepared to go to the United States to present the British position over the Middle East.[42]

Woolley enthusiastically accepted Moyne's invitation, and the Colonial Secretary in turn reached out to two other key stakeholders – Anthony Eden at the Foreign Office and Leo Amery at the India Office. Moyne reassured both that Woolley's duties would be limited to providing "general background of Arab and Moslem affairs rather than to express opinions on controversial problems".[43] But he failed to convince either of the merits of the proposed trip. Amery wondered whether Woolley, whom he personally held in "great regard", was the "right person" and was "perhaps a little identified with the Arabs".[44] For his part, Eden vetoed the proposal because the dispatch of an "unofficial or semi-official lecturer" would "stir up controversy regarding the Palestine problem", something that was not desirable at that moment in time.[45]

Moyne served as Colonial Secretary between 1941 and early 1942 and then Deputy Minister of State and Minister of State in Cairo until his assassination by Zionist extremists in November 1944. Michael J Cohen has argued that while Moyne must hold ministerial responsibility for a number of decisions that undermined Zionist aspirations during the early war years, most notably his refusal to establish a Jewish division inside the British army, he was by no means the main instigator of Britain's anti-Zionist policy.[46] Even up until his assassination many within the mainstream Zionist movement held quite a positive view of Moyne.[47]

However, he differed profoundly with his Zionist interlocutors in his view on the historical right of Jews to emigrate to Palestine, perhaps explaining why, unlike Amery or Eden, he was supportive of Woolley's possible tour of the United States. Moyne is on record repeatedly expressing his preference for the Jews to find an alternative homeland to Palestine. In August 1941, in a meeting with David Ben-Gurion in London, Moyne asked why the Jews insisted on gaining control of Palestine, and questioned whether it would not be better if the Jewish state was set up in East Prussia, once its German inhabitants had been expelled by the allies after the war had been won. In response Ben-Gurion answered "You may be able to expel the Germans, but the Jews will not go there; it will take machine guns to force them to go". A response Moyne dismissed as naïvete.[48]

Moyne's belief that the Jewish problem should be settled outside of Palestine was undoubtedly a function of many considerations including British imperial and wartime interests and Palestinian Arab rights. But like Woolley and many of his peer-group he was also on the record casting doubt on the historical or racial connection of Europe's Jews to biblical Palestine. As he explained in a speech in the House of Lords a few months after leaving his role as Colonial Secretary, "[though it is] very often loosely said that the Jews are Semites [these features] ... have been bred out of the Ashkenazim by an admixture of Slav blood".[49]

Moyne put forward this argument in a House of Lords Debate on Palestine in June 1942, just one month after a meeting of the Zionist leadership at the Biltmore Hotel, New York, officially called for the creation of a Jewish Commonwealth in all of western Palestine. The Biltmore Declaration, as it became known, set down an explicit and practical challenge to opponents of

Zionist national aspirations once the war ended and the future of Palestine returned to the top of the political agenda: How to make the case against the relocation to Palestine of Europe's Jewish survivors of the recently liberated Nazi extermination camps.

This was a central consideration of those inside and outside government concerned with the fate of Palestine in the years between the end of the Second World War and the establishment of Israel in 1948. Many arguments were put forward by a wide-range of individuals and groups committed to preventing the establishment of a Jewish state. The three most common were that 1) the White Paper had put a final limit on Jewish immigration; 2) the Zionists were cynically using the humanitarian argument to open the way for immigration that would result in their political domination of the country; and 3) in order to achieve this demographic goal Zionists had brainwashed through propaganda Jews and non-Jews alike into believing that Palestine was the only answer to the tragedy that had befallen European Jewry.

Spears, for example, repeatedly argued in the post-war years that the White Paper had finally settled the political question of Palestine, but that Zionists were treating Jewish refugees as political pawns rather than tragic victims of the war, and that this manipulation of Holocaust survivors was the "cruelest deception".[50] Likewise, Sir John Hope-Simpson, the career civil servant who had authored the 1930–31 report commissioned by the British government on Immigration, Land Settlement and Development in Palestine. In this report, and during the 1930s, his argument against Jewish immigration into Palestine had been based on economic and social considerations inside Palestine. After 1945, he argued instead that Zionist propaganda not legitimate Jewish rights was the only reason large-scale immigration into Palestine was being given serious consideration.[51]

For men like Spears and Hope-Simpson these arguments coalesced and were rooted in the Khazar theory. During his evidence at the hearing of the Anglo-American Committee of Inquiry into Palestine and the Jewish Question held in 1946,[52] Spears estimated that only 4,000 of the 400,000 Jews returning to Palestine could claim that they were returning to the home of their ancestors in Israel, because the great majority of immigrants had "no racial connection to Palestine even in the distant past [are]not descendants of the Israelites who migrated to Palestine from Egypt".[53] Similarly, Hope-Simpson argued in 1946 that Jewish immigrants to Palestine were "in ... no sense returning to their homeland.... [T]hey have in them not one drop of Hebrew blood.... [D]escended from pagans who converted to Judaism many centuries ago".[54]

Jewish and Arab opponents of Zionism also increasingly adopted the Khazar theory in the post-1945 era for the same reasons: as a way to delink the victims of the humanitarian catastrophe in Europe from any ancestral links to Palestine as a way of preventing further Jewish immigration. In the British case, the theory was widely adopted by the Jewish Fellowship, the most influential Anglo-Jewish anti-Zionist body. An article in its newspaper, *The Jewish Outlook*, in 1947, entitled 'The Jewish Race: Anthropological, Geographical and Historical Facts to Defeat Political Zionist Theory', made the case against Zionism on the grounds that Palestine was "a country with which the Khazars in all their history had neither geographical nor ethnic association".[55] In the United States, Alfred Lilienthal, one of the most well-known members of the anti-Zionist American Council for Judaism, also promoted the Khazar argument widely. Like his Anglo-Jewish counterparts, Lilienthal argued that the "Khazars are the lineal ancestors of Easter European Jewry is a historical fact ... these 'Ashkenazim Jews' .... have little or no trace of Semitic blood".[56]

Another Jewish group, the League for Peace with Justice in Palestine, adopted the Khazar theory as its main argument against Zionist-national aspirations. Founded by the successful businessman Benjamin Freedman, the League spent large sums of money in promoting the Khazar theory in the media. In early May 1946, for example, Freedman's League ran a full-page advertisement in the *New York Herald Tribune*, under the heading 'Political Zionists Exploit Untruths About Palestine'. It argued that the existence of the Khazars contradicted the Zionist claim that there "exists a Jewish race or nation".[57] Freedman would subsequently develop this argument in his pamphlet *Facts are Facts* which, under the sub-heading 'Chazars' retold the historic conversion of the Khazars, "people of Turkish origin whose life and history are interwoven with the very beginnings of the history of the Jews of Russia".[58]

In the period before World War Two, the main focus of Arab arguments against Zionist claims were their rights under the McMahon-Husayn agreement and the illegitimacy of the Balfour Declaration.[59] However, in the post-1945 era, the Khazar theory increasingly became a staple of Arab arguments against Zionism in London, Washington and at the United Nations.

During his evidence before the United Nations Special Committee on Palestine (UNSCOP), in 1947, Jamal Husseini of the Arab Higher Committee opposed Zionist claims to Palestine on the grounds that "Western Jews known as Ashkenazim are descendants of the Khazars who converted to Judaism".[60] This view was subsequently adopted by India's representative on the Special Committee, Sir Abdur Rahman, who during deliberations asked rhetorically if "[the] Khazars of Eastern Europe .... were converted to Judaism; can their descendants possibly claim any rights simply because the ancestors of their co-religionists had once settled in Palestine?"[61] Similarly, following the UNSCOP deliberations, Faris al-Khouri,[62] the Syrian representative at the United Nations, argued against the Committee's majority report findings on the grounds that they failed to take into account the fact that the Khazar issue proved there was no historical link between Jewish immigrants and Palestine.

Conclusion

The Khazar theory was by no means the only argument used by opponents of Jewish national aspirations in Palestine during the mandate era. Nor was it the only one put forward, despite the lack of factual evidence to back it up. In October 1945, for example, five MPs (three of whom were members of the Middle East Parliamentary Committee (MEPC) and the Committee for Arab Affairs (CAA), circulated a memorandum in parliament claiming that by December 1944, 35,000 European Jews living in Palestine had applied for permission to return to Europe after the war.[63] In considering these claims, J. M. Martin of the Colonial Office acknowledged that 'we have heard a good deal recently [of this as an] argument used against immigration into Palestine'.[64] However, it had very little basis in fact. C.V. Shaw, the chief secretary of Palestine, was of the view that "there is as yet no sign of any 'backflow' on a large scale", adding that speculation of even 15,000 Jews wanting to leave "was a considerable exaggeration".[65]

What makes the Khazar theory so intriguing is that during the final years of the mandate, it became an issue on which Arab and Jewish opposition to Zionism became intertwined with the arguments of British Arabists. Cecil Hourani who worked for the Arab League in Washington in the years between 1945 and 1948 claimed in his autobiography that Benjamin Freedman had convinced Arab leaders in the West, especially Jamal Husseini of the value of using the Khazar theory in the battle against Zionism.[66] Hourani's claim is backed up by an internal Foreign Office assessment of Arab interactions with Jewish anti-Zionist activists that also noted Freedman's role in promoting the Khazar theory in Arab policy-making circles.[67]

All three groups championed the Khazar theory precisely because it was, in the words of Arthur Koestler, "maliciously interpreted as a denial of Israel's right to exist". Koestler, whom Sir Ronald Storrs once referred to as that "half Jew Magyar writer", himself wrote a book on the Khazars in the mid-1970s. In it he agreed with the anti-Zionists of the pre-1948 era that the Khazars were the real ancestors of European Jewry. But he differed with them completely on what this meant for the Zionist endeavour. Rather than de-legitimizing it, he argued, it had no relevance at all. What mattered, in his view at least, was that the Jews were a national group that had undertaken "a century of peaceful Jewish immigration and pioneering effort which provided ethical justification for the state's legal existence".[68]

Koestler's excursus on the Khazars was widely dismissed as the ramblings of an aging intellectual contrarian,[69] but his take does illuminate why the "wild and woolly Khazars",[70] as one commentator labelled them, have continued to capture the imagination in the decades since 1948. They have been the inspiration for poetry, like 'The Khazar Poet' by Leo Haber, with its haunting refrain, "We are a nation of Jews; of Jews, I repeat, converted by the harmful views of a demented King".[71] They have also, not surprisingly, continued to play such a central part in anti-Israeli arguments and polemics.

As American academic, Glenn A. Perry summed up in a scholarly article of the mid-1980s:

> It is quite likely that the European Jews are in large part descendants of the Khazar tribes of the early Middle Ages who converted to Judaism ... people have a right to whatever national identities they choose, even mythical ones, but to use this as a justification for uprooting the population of another country is another matter.[72]

Notes

1 Sir Ronald Storrs, *Orientations*, London: G. Putnam's Sons, 1937, p. 379.
2 Rory Miller, *Divided Against Zion: Opposition in Britain to a Jewish State in Palestine, 1945–1948*, London/New York: Routledge, 2000.
3 Frances Newton, *Fifty Years in Palestine*, Wrotham: Cold Harbour Press, 1948, p. 282.
4 On the debate over the Khazar conversion to Judaism, Leon Nimoy's review of Dunlop's *The History of the Jewish Khazars* in *The Jewish Quarterly Review*, XLVI, no. 3, January 1956, pp. 78–81.
5 Salo Wittmayer Baron, *A Social and Religious History of the Jews*, Vol. III, New York: Columbia University Press, 1957, second edition, revised and enlarged, p. 206. On the Khazar conversion see Chapter XIX, pp. 196–221, also the very detailed and informative endnotes on the Khazar chapter which give a detailed bibliographical account of sources for the study of the Khazar conversion in several languages, pp. 323–5.
6 Lewis Namier, The Jews, *The Nineteenth Century*, CXXX, no. 777, November 1941, p. 270.k
7 Lewis Namier to Lord Moyne, 10 June 1941, British National Archives (NA) FO371/27044.
8 Walter Laqueur, Zionism and its Liberal Critics, 1896–1948, *Journal of Contemporary History*, 6, 1971, p. 171.
9 Manuscript Diary of Sir Ronald Storrs, 27 January 1947, Box 6/6, Storrs Papers, Pembroke College, Cambridge.
10 Transcript of Radio discussion The Future of Palestine, *The Listener*, XXXIV, no. 877, 1 November 1945, p. 480.
11 Royden-Shaw's evidence before the Anglo-American Committee, London 29 January 1945, Archives of the Board of Deputies of British Jews, (ABD), ACC3121/C14/30/4, p. 63. For Newton's argument on this issue see her memoirs *Fifty Years in Palestine*, p. 306
12 On Spears' pivotal role in the anti-Zionist movement in Britain in the final years of British rule in Palestine see Rory Miller, Sir Edward Spears' Jewish Problem: A Leading anti-Zionist and His Relationship with Anglo-Jewry, 1945–1948, *The Journal of Israeli History*, 19/1, Spring 1998, pp. 41–60.
13 Spears's preface to M.F. Abcarius, *Palestine Through the Fog of Propaganda*, London: Hutchinson & Co., 1946, p. 9.
14 Sir Edward Spears to Rt. Rev. W.H. Stewart, 26 March 1945, Box 4/6, Spears papers, Middle East Centre, St. Anthony's College, University of Oxford.
15 Correspondence of Rt. Rev. W.H. Stewart to Sir Edward Spears, 7 April 1945, Box 4/6, Spears papers.

16 Full text of The Jews in Poland: official reports of the American and British Investigating Missions, https://archive.org/stream/cu31924028644783/cu31924028644783_djvu.txt

17 Ibid., full text of the Captain Wright Report, pp. 33–49.

18 See Colonial Office memorandum, Suggestions for increased propaganda for Palestine to deal with German and Italian Propaganda, sent to Rushbrook Williams of the Ministry of Information, 20 January 1939, CO 733/387/20; also Owen Tweedy's memorandum, Publicity: Propaganda in the Middle East, 29 November 1938, CO 733/387/2, NA.

19 Correspondence with the Palestine Arab Delegation and the Zionist Organisation, and Statement of British Policy on Palestine, Cmd. 1700, London: His Majesty's Stationery Office (HMSO), 1922.

20 MacDonald to Weizmann, 13 February 1931. A copy of this letter can be found in Appendix 3 in Norman Rose, *Lewis Namier and Zionism*, Oxford: Oxford University Press, 1980, pp. 171–6.

21 Cmd. 6019, *Palestine, A Statement of Policy, May 1939*, part 2: Immigration, pp. 1–11, London: HMSO, 1939.

22 Chief Rabbi Isaac Herzog, *The Times*, 16 May 1939; *The Jewish Case against the White Paper*, London: The Zionist Organization, 1945; The MacDonald White Paper of 1939, London: Zionist Organization, 1945.

23 Baggallay, 'The Origins of Polish and Russian Jews', 26 May 1939, FO371/23250, NA.

24 Ibid.

25 Baggallay's comments on Kincaid's letter, 2 June 1939, ibid.

26 Ibid.

27 Charles A. Kincaid, Letter in *The Times*, 31 May 1939.

28 *What is Race?* Paris: UNESCO, 1952, p. 223; Ray L. Cleveland, The Zionist Obfuscation of Palestinian History, *International Journal of Islamic and Arabic Studies*, 2/1, 1985, p. 29.

29 S. Schechter An Unknown Khazar Document, *The Jewish Quarterly Review*, 3/2 (1912), pp. 181–219; A. Yarmolinsky et al., The Khazars, *Bulletin on the New York Public Library*, 42, 1939, pp. 697–710.

30 William Z. Ripley, *The Races of Europe: A Sociological Study*, New York: D. Appleton and Company, 1899; Julius Huxley and A.C. Haddon, *We Europeans: A Survey of Racial Problems*, London: Jonathan Cape, 1935.

31 Abraham Poliak, *Kazaria: History of a Jewish Kingdom in Europe*, Tel Aviv: Bialik-Masada Foundation, 1944; D.M. Dunlop, *The History of the Jewish Khazars*, Princeton: Princeton University Press, 1954.

32 S. Gasellee, The Origins of Polish and Russian Jews, 1 June 1939, FO 371/23250, NA.

33 Elie Kedourie, *In the Anglo-Arab Labyrinth: The McMahon-Husayn Correspondence and its Interpretations, 1914–1939*, Cambridge, London/New York: Cambridge University Press, 1976, pp. 270–83.

34 Butler to Crossley, 26 June 1939, FO 371/23250, NA; also 'Internal Minute on permission to send FO findings to Crossley', in idem.

35 Bernard Wasserstein, *Britain and the Jews of Europe, 1939–1945*, London/Oxford: Institute of Jewish Affairs/ Clarendon Press, 1979, p. 117. As one expert on Polish Jewish history would subsequently point out, apart from the Khazar theory other speculations over the origins of East European Jewry at this time included their descent from the Jews from Ancient Greece and Byzantium, Babylon or Persia; and that they came from tribes exiled from Jerusalem after the destruction of the temple in Jerusalem 8–6 century BCE, See Bernard Weinryb, Origins of East European Jewry, *Commentary*, December 1957, p. 511.

36 A. Crossley to R.A. Butler, 29 June 1939, and R.A. Butler to A. Crossley, 10 July 1939, both in FO 371/23250, NA. (My italics).

37 Crossley to Butler, 29 June 1939, ibid.
38 J.E. Mackenzie to Butler, 1 July 1939, ibid.
39 Hardy's diary entry of 7 August 1941 is quoted in full in Bernard Wasserstein, *Britain and the Jews of Europe, 1939–1945*, London/Oxford: Institute of Jewish Affairs, Clarendon Press, 1979, p. 117.
40 Richard Meinertzhagen, *Middle East Diary, 1917–1950*, London: The Cresset Press, 1959, p. 183 [diary entry, 5 July 1940].
41 Sir Leonard Woolley, 'Memorandum on the Educating American Opinion on the Importance of the Moslem World to Great Britain', July 1941, FO371/27044, NA.
42 See 'Extract from note of conversation between Lord Moyne and Sir Leonard Woolley', 31 July 1941, ibid.
43 Lord Moyne to Anthony Eden, 7 August 1941, ibid.
44 M.J. Clauson (India Office) to C.G. Eastwood, (Colonial Office), 11 August 1941, ibid.
45 Anthony Eden to Lord Moyne, 25 August 1941, ibid.
46 Michael J Cohen, The Moyne Assassination, November 1944: A Political Analysis, *Middle Eastern Studies*, 15/3, October 1979, pp. 360–361, also Bernard Wasserstein, The Assassination of Lord Moyne, *Jewish Historical Society of England, Transactions*, XXVII, 1978–1980, pp. 72–83.
47 See, for example, Blanche Dugdale's diary entry of March 12 1941, which noted how Chaim Weizmann had 'quite an encouraging talk with Lord Moyne', in Norman Rose, (ed.), *Baffy: The Diaries of Blanche Dugdale, 1936–1947*, London: Vallentine Mitchell, 1973, p. 182.
48 Minutes of Jewish Agency Executive Meeting, 4 October 1942 and 7 November 1943, Central Zionist Archives (CZA), Jerusalem
49 *H.L.* vol. 123, col. 198, 9 June 1942; also Bernard Wasserstein, *Britain and the Jews*, p. 117.
50 Edward Spears, A Reply to Dr Parkes, in *Palestine Controversy: A Symposium*, London: Fabian Colonial Bureau, 1945, p. 23.
51 John Hope-Simpson, The Palestine Statement, *Fortnightly*, January 1946, pp. 23–4.
52 The Anglo-American Committee comprised six members from Britain and the United States. The committee's terms of reference were to examine conditions in Palestine as they related to the issues of Jewish immigration and settlement and to examine the position of Europe's Jewish population that had survived the Holocaust. Viewed as the crucial forum for deciding the fate of Palestine in this era its hearings were held in several locations (most notably Washington, London and Jerusalem) from late 1945 until March 1946.
53 Evidence of Spears before the Anglo-American Committee, 3121/C14/30/4, pp. 34–7, ABD/ACC.
54 Hope-Simpson to Spears, 18 January 1946, Box 4/3, Spears papers.
55 The Jewish Race: Anthropological, Geographical and Historical Facts Defeat Political Zionist Theory, *The Jewish Outlook*, 2/1, June 1947, p. 12.
56 Alfred M. Lilienthal, *What Price Israel*, Chicago: Henry Regnery, 1953, p. 222.
57 Political Zionists Exploit Untruths About Palestine, *New York Herald Tribune*, 2 May 1946.
58 Benjamin Freedman, *Facts are Facts*, New York: League for Justice and Peace in Palestine, 1947.
59 Kedourie, *In the Anglo-Arab Labyrinth*, p.270.
60 For a full transcript of Husseini's speech before UNSCOP see the *Zionist Review*, 3 October 1947, p.4.
61 Quoted in Bernard Weinryb's Origins of East European Jewry, *Commentary* (December 1957), p. 509.
62 Al-Khouri served as Syrian prime minister between 1944–45 and 1954–55.

63 'Memorandum on Palestine', MSS Brit.Emp.s, 365 Box 176/3, Fabian Colonial Bureau Archive, Rhodes House Library, Oxford.
64 Martin to Shaw, 25 September 1945, FO371/52600, NA.
65 Shaw to Martin, 7 October 1945, ibid.
66 Cecil Hourani, *An Unfinished Odyssey: Lebanon and Beyond*, London: Weidenfeld & Nicolson, 1984, p. 61.
67 T.E. Bromley, British Embassy, Washington D.C., to Sinclair of the British Consulate, New York, 7 September 1946, FO371/522557, NA.
68 Arthur Koestler, *The Thirteenth Tribe: The Khazar Empire and its Heritage*, London: Hutchinson & Co., 1976, p. 224.
69 On Koestler's Khazar exposition see also Simon Szyszman, La Question Des Khazars Essai De Mise Au Point, *The Jewish Quarterly Review*, LXXIII, no. 2, October 1982, pp. 189–202.
70 Leon Nimoy, Dunlop's History of the Jewish Khazars, *The Jewish Quarterly Review*, XLVI, no. 3, January 1956, p. 78.
71 Leo Haber, 'The Khazar Poet', *Commentary*, April 1956, p. 358.
72 Glenn E. Perry, The Program for Dispossession and its Continuing Implementation, *International Journal of Islamic Studies*, 2/1, 1985, p. 3.

3   Churchill and Bevin

Thesis and anti-thesis?

Michael J Cohen

Winston Churchill

The late Martin Gilbert, the prolific author of Churchill's official biography, has asserted that he "never deviated" from his support of the Jews, and the Zionists:

> [he] felt an affinity with the Jewish struggle: both to survive and to attain statehood … [and was] a persistent opponent of anti-Semitism.[1]

From 1949, after Israel had vanquished five Arab states on the battlefield, Churchill declared repeatedly, in private and in public, that he had been a Zionist "since the days of the Balfour Declaration", that he had favoured "a free and independent Israel all through the dark years when many of my most distinguished countrymen took a different view".[2] Neither statement was true. Churchill did not earn his exalted position in the pantheon of Zionist heroes until 1939. Prior to that he gave them plenty to be unhappy about.

An intriguing comparison might be drawn between Churchill's extended influence on how historians viewed World War Two, and Gilbert's creation of the myth of Churchill's lifelong dedication to the Jews and to Zionism. Churchill created his own historical legacy. After he lost the General Election in July 1945, he began writing his multi-volume history of World War Two, helped by a backroom, well-paid research team – the 'Syndicate'. He was granted the unique privilege of access to secret government documents. Professor Reynolds has shown how Churchill rejected evidence that did not suit his purpose and manipulated facts in order to create the heroic image which he hoped would promote his return to number 10 Downing Street.[3] In his turn, Gilbert was given exclusive access to Churchill's private papers until 1995.[4]

Ernest Bevin

Bevin was a self-made man, who went out to work at the age of 11, first as a labourer and then as a lorry driver.[5] He had the temperament of a born fighter and was one of the leading founders of the powerful Transport and General Workers' Union, the largest trade union in Britain. In 1940, he was a natural choice for Churchill's wartime coalition, in which he served as Minister of Labour and National Service. He emerged from the war an admired national leader.

When Labour won the 1945 general election, Bevin was Foreign Secretary Eden's choice to succeed him. At the Foreign Office, Bevin soon became master in his own house. Even if Bevin had no formal secondary education, his Oxbridge officials admired the quality and originality of his mind. Above all, they knew that they could rely on him to get their policies through the cabinet – the acid test of any minister.[6]

Bevin's main legacy as Foreign Secretary was the formation of NATO, of which he was one of the principal architects. Palestine was a painful irritant, but never a cardinal issue in British foreign policy. Bevin once confided to a close adviser that he had two preoccupations when dealing with Palestine. The first was his fear that it would "poison Anglo-American relations". The second was "the danger of alienating the Arabs".[7]

Whereas Churchill earned his place in the Zionist pantheon only in 1939, when he spoke up against the Palestine White Paper of that year, conversely, Bevin earned his notoriety as an anti-Semite in 1945, when Foreign Secretary. His important influence in favour of the Zionist cause in 1930 is frequently air-brushed out of the Zionist narrative.[8]

Most Gentiles did not share the Jews' emotional trauma following the Holocaust, certainly not the Zionists' conviction that the Jewish survivors should be allowed to migrate to Palestine – especially not if against the will of the Arab majority there.

Both Bevin and Churchill shared the general post-war consensus that the Great Powers had just expended enormous human and financial resources in order to defeat Nazism and to make Europe a safe place for the Jews to continue to live in.

On 1 August 1946 (one week after the King David hotel atrocity in Jerusalem),[9] Churchill gave crude testimony in the Commons to this consensus:

> The idea that the Jewish Problem can be solved or even helped by a vast dumping of the Jews of Europe into Palestine is really too silly to consume our time in the House of Commons this afternoon. I am not absolutely sure that we should not be in too great a hurry to give up the idea that European Jewry may live in the countries where they belong.[10]

This was the antithesis of the most fundamental Zionist doctrine – the Ingathering of the Jewish Exiles into Palestine – which they believed had just been vindicated by the Holocaust.

Bevin himself must bear the major responsibility for the anti-Semitic stereotype that stuck to him. (Although his colleagues rejected the idea that he had ever been an anti-Semite.) His impromptu asides may be explained, if not justified, by a combination of his mounting frustration with the intractability of the Palestine problem; his growing conviction that the

Zionists were mounting an insurrection to coerce the government to adopt a pro-Zionist solution in Palestine; his resentment of President Truman's interventions on the Zionists' behalf, which he had good grounds for believing stemmed from his domestic political agenda;[11] his fury at the murders of British soldiers in Palestine by Jewish terrorists; and by his deteriorating health.[12] All these combined to produce a series of irascible, insensitive outbursts.

Bevin earned his anti-Semitic stereotype in November 1945. On the 13th, he announced the appointment of an Anglo-American Committee of Inquiry (AAC) to "examine the status of the Jews in former Axis-occupied countries and to determine how many could be reintegrated into their lands of origin". The Americans had forced him to add to its terms of reference: "how many would be impelled to migrate to Palestine or to other countries outside Europe". In an editorial the next day, the London *Times* lauded his statesmanship.[13] But at his press conference on the 14th, Bevin went off script, and in a characteristically impromptu, blunt aside, stated

> if the Jews, with all their sufferings, want to get too much to the head of the queue, you have the danger of another anti-Semitic reaction.[14]

As noted by one retrospective, Bevin's comment, with its "height of insensitivity"

> helped fashion Bevin's image in most Jewish eyes – particularly in the United States – as a dyed-in-the-wool anti-Semite, even as Hitler's heir.[15]

Zionist leaders reacted with outrage and hysteria. Some warned that his speech spelled "the end of Zionism", that the government intended to "wipe out the Jewish race", that it was "the biggest defeat for Zionism since the Balfour Declaration".[16]

Bevin had dared to voice in public the fears of many other, more discreet members of the British elite. The risk of anti-Semitic reactions in England remained one of the key themes in subsequent debates in the House of Commons. Continuing outrages against British forces in Palestine did eventually provoke widespread anti-Semitic riots in London and in many northern cities in the summer of 1947.[17]

****

I have chosen to monitor and to correct both the Churchill and the Bevin stereotypes through the prism of a key debate on Palestine held in the Commons on 26 January 1949.[18] British forces had been evacuated from the country the previous May; Israel had emerged triumphant from the first Arab-Israeli war; peace talks between Egypt and Israel were under way on the Island of Rhodes.

Of all those MPs present in the debate, Churchill had the most experience of executive power and influence over Palestine: as Colonial Secretary from

1921–22, as Chancellor of the Exchequer from 1924–1929, and as Prime Minister from 1940–45.

In January 1949, Churchill was an ageing, ailing man, aged 74.

The anti-Semitic card

The anti-Semitic stigma that had stuck to Bevin was exploited to the full, not only by Zionist propaganda, but also by Churchill. In Bevin's opening statement on 26 January 1949, he confronted the accusation head-on. After referring to the perils of anti-Semitism raising its head in Britain, he asserted

> There has never been in this country the anti-Semitism which we have unfortunately seen elsewhere, and I hope there never will be.

Next, acknowledging his own shortcomings, Bevin made a jest at his own expense:

> it has been said that His Majesty's Government muddied the waters and that they have not handled the Palestine problem with dignity and consistency. I am often told that I have not sufficient dignity. I always console myself that what I lack in that field I make up in weight.[19]

Responding as Leader of the Opposition, Churchill first commended Bevin's firm stand against Communism. But he next lashed out at his "astounding mishandling" of the Palestine problem:

> No one ever made such sweeping declarations of confidence in himself … and no one has been proved by events to be more consistently wrong on every turning-point and at every moment…. Every opportunity for obtaining a satisfactory settlement was thrown away…. All this is due not only to mental inertia or lack of grip on the part of the Ministers concerned, but also, I am afraid, to the very strong and direct streak of bias and prejudice on the part of the Foreign Secretary.

This last comment provoked cries of protest in the House, but they did not deter Churchill from continuing his diatribe against Bevin:

> I do not feel any great confidence that he has not got a prejudice against the Jews in Palestine…. I am sure that he thought the Arab League was stronger and that it would win if fighting broke out.[20]

However, given Churchill's own record regarding the Jews, his speech can only be regarded as another example of his notorious political opportunism. This was not his 'finest hour'. Churchill was hardly the one to preach to Bevin. He had a few 'anti-Semitic skeletons' in his own locker. In June 1914, he had been accused in the Commons by a fellow-MP of "Jew-baiting"[21] One sympathetic biographer has argued that a convincing case could be made against Churchill for 'Jew-baiting' in 1920, when he adopted the populist line that the Jews were responsible for Bolshevism. He told Lloyd George that the Jews had played "a leading part in Bolshevik atrocities" and were "the main instigators of the ruin of the Empire".[22] He developed these themes at length in an article he published in February 1920, in the popular *Illustrated Sunday Herald*.[23]

Churchill's article brought down upon him the wrath of the Anglo-Jewish community. *The Jewish Chronicle*, its weekly organ, accused him of waging:

> the gravest, as it is the most reckless and scandalous campaign in which even the most discredited politicians have ever engaged.[24]

The *Illustrated* article has been dismissed as a one-off slip-up. One sympathetic biographer asserted, "At no time in his career had he employed such brutal language against Jews; nor would he do so again in the future".[25] But neither this biographer, nor the MPs attending the 1949 debate knew about Churchill's further, jaw-dropping indiscretion. This was revealed only in 2007, when Richard Toye, a Cambridge historian, published a study of the rivalry between Churchill and Lloyd George. His book included extracts of an article written for, and approved and paid for by Churchill in 1937. The ghost-writer was Marshall Diston, formerly a member of Moseley's New Party. It contained the crudest of anti-Semitic stereotypes:

> The Jew in England is a representative of his race. Every Jewish money-lender recalls *Shylock and the idea of the Jews as usurers*. And you cannot reasonably expect a struggling clerk or shopkeeper, paying forty or fifty per cent interest on borrowed money to a *"Hebrew bloodsucker"* to reflect that, throughout long centuries, almost every other way of life was closed to the Jewish people; or that there are native English moneylenders who insist, just as implacably, upon their *"pound of flesh"*[26] (author's emphases).

There is no little irony in the article's references to Shylock and to Jewish 'bloodsuckers', considering that Churchill himself was, and for many years would remain dependent on Jewish largesse – in the currency of gifts and free holidays on the lavish estates and on the yachts of Jewish magnates.[27] It was Churchill good fortune that his repeated attempts to publish the article were in vain.

The Balfour Declaration

Churchill's boast that he had been a Zionist all of his life, or at least since the Balfour Declaration, also bears closer examination. Churchill was not a member of the inner war cabinet that approved the issue of the Declaration in 1917. When he was appointed Colonial Secretary, in February 1921, he inherited, reluctantly, the obligation of executing the policy it had promised.

Churchill's first priority after the war was to appease the Turks. He feared that the occupation of the former Ottoman territories, would alienate the Muslims in the Empire, and provoke Kemal Attatürk – the founder of modern Turkey – to join forces with the Red Army and re-conquer the Middle East.[28]

In May 1921, following the second wave of Arab riots against the British in Palestine, he urged the government to make peace with Atatürk, to "get out of Mesopotamia & Palestine", complaining that the two mandates would "cost [£] 9 million a year for several years".[29] He also sent private, written appeals to Lloyd George. On the last occasion, on 2 June 1921, he warned the Prime Minister that it was becoming impossible to maintain the British position either in Palestine or in Mesopotamia, and

> the only wise and safe course would be to take advantage of the postponement of the Mandates and resign them both and quit the two countries at the earliest possible moment, as the expense to which we will be put will be wholly unwarrantable.[30]

One of the most intimate profiles of the Lloyd George coalition's Palestine policy is to be found in the diary of Col. Richard Meinertzhagen, Churchill's military adviser at the Colonial Office:

> Our main trouble is the apathy of our big men towards Zionism. Winston Churchill really does not care or know much about it. Balfour knows, and talks a lot of platitudes but his academic brain is unable to act in a practical way. Lloyd George has sporadic outburst of keenness but fails to appreciate the value to us of Zionism or its moral advantages.[31]

At a meeting of the cabinet in August 1921, Churchill made it clear that he was pursuing the government's Zionist policy under duress. He protested against the extra expenses involved in Palestine – "almost wholly needed due to our Zionist policy":

> The whole country is in ferment. The Zionist policy is profoundly unpopular with all except the Zionists. Both Arabs and Jews are armed and arming, ready to spring at each other's throats.... It seems to me that the whole situation should be reviewed by the Cabinet. I have done and am doing my best to give effect to the pledge given to the Zionists by Mr Balfour on behalf of the War Cabinet.... I am prepared to continue in this course, *if it is the settled resolve of the Cabinet*[32] (author's emphasis).

Lloyd George insisted that the honour of the government was tied up with the Balfour pledge, and any retreat would cause serious damage to Britain's prestige "in the eyes of the Jews of the world".[33]

In July 1922, Churchill was called upon to defend the government's Palestine policy, which had just been defeated by a motion in the House of Lords. He upbraided no less than 12 sitting MPs who had supported the Declaration in 1917, but now opposed it:

> We really must know where we are. Who led us along this path.... I remained quite silent. *I am not in the Black Book*. I accepted service on the lines laid down for me[34] (author's emphasis).

Churchill's rhetorical talent secured an overwhelming majority for the government's policy. During the 1920s, when Churchill served as Chancellor of the Exchequer (1924–29), his *diktat* of dipping into Palestine's budget surplus in order to subsidise Transjordan caused Field-Marshal Plumer, Palestine's High Commissioner, to resign in protest.[35]

The 1939 White Paper

With war against Hitler on the horizon, the 1939 White Paper on Palestine (which secured a majority in the Commons) was a clear act of appeasement of the Arab States by the Chamberlain government. It promised the Palestinian Arabs an independent state within ten years; Jewish immigration into Palestine would be restricted to a further 75,000 over the next five years, after which any further immigration would depend upon Arab consent. This would guarantee the Palestinian Arabs a two-thirds majority[36]

The Zionists were delighted by Churchill's opposition and printed his speech as a publicity (propaganda) pamphlet. They were prepared to overlook the fact that just seven months previously, he had aired his own plan for the restriction of Jewish immigration into Palestine. His opposition to the 1939 policy was due both to his frustration at being kept in the political wilderness for over ten years, and to his belief that no nation would ally itself with Britain unless convinced that her word could be trusted.

In the autumn of 1938, Britain faced a series of international crises: in Europe, the Munich crisis over Hitler's demands on Czechoslovakia, and in the Middle East, Italian advances in Libya, and the Arab Rebellion in Palestine. From 9–10 November 1938, the *Krystallnacht* pogrom raged in Germany, leaving 91 Jews killed, and hundreds more beaten up and raped. The pogrom shocked all of Europe. The European press was full of graphic descriptions of Nazi acts of barbarism. Yet despite wide public revulsion at the barbarity of *Krystallnacht*, powerful elements in British politics and business continued to admire Hitler and his regime.[37]

On 21 November 1938, the House of Commons held a special debate on the problem of Jewish refugees fleeing Nazi-dominated Europe.[38] Sir Samuel Hoare, the Home Secretary, referred to the risks of anti-Semitic protests in England if too many Jews were allowed into the country:

> [T]here is the making of a definite anti-Jewish movement. I do my best as Home Secretary to stamp upon an evil of that kind. That is the reason why I have prohibited demonstrations in certain parts of London where inevitably they would stimulate this evil movement.[39]

Two weeks later, Churchill presented to the Commons his own plan for restricting Jewish immigration into Palestine.[40] He began by crowing over his own role the previous year in preventing the House from committing itself to the partition of Palestine – "this most absurd and most inflammatory scheme".[41] He continued:

> the problem in Palestine was excessive Jewish immigration ... which the Arabs believed, with some justification, was jeopardizing their majority.

In what was a partial preview of the 1939 White Paper, he proposed to

> fix the immigration of the Jews into Palestine for 10 years at a certain figure which at the end of the 10-year period will not have decisively altered the balance of the population as between Arab and Jew.[42]

On the next day, the *Jewish Chronicle* lambasted Churchill. His proposal "might well be regarded as a welcome success by many even of those who find themselves in the Mufti's camp".[43]

But all this was forgotten and forgiven by the Zionists when Churchill voted against the Palestine White Paper. A close reading of his speech reveals that in fact he agreed with the main points of the new policy: the immigration restrictions, the harsh restrictions on further Zionist purchases of land, and the provision setting up an independent Palestinian state within 10 years. Churchill believed that Zionist dreams must wait until the impending war was over, and Britain's own strategic interests had been secured.

Churchill opposed just one, albeit key provision of the new policy – the grant to the Arabs of a veto on all further Jewish immigration after five years:

> After the period of five years no further Jewish immigration will be permitted unless the Arabs of Palestine are prepared to acquiesce in it. Now, *there is the breach; there is the violation of the pledge*; there is the abandonment of the Balfour Declaration .... Jewish immigration during the next five years will be at a rate which, if the economic absorptive capacity allows, will bring the population up to approximately one-third of the total population of the country. After that the Arab majority, twice

as numerous as the Jews, will have control, and all further Jewish immigration will be subject to their acquiescence.[44]

Churchill's attack on the new policy was part of his general onslaught on the Chamberlain government's appeasement of Nazi Germany:

Shall we relieve ourselves by this repudiation?.... What will our potential enemies think?... Will they not be tempted to say: They're on the run again. This is another Munich, and be the more stimulated in their aggression.... Never was the need for fidelity and firmness more urgent than now. You are not going to found and forge the fabric of a grand alliance to resist aggression, except by showing continued examples of your firmness in carrying out ... the obligations into which you have entered.[45]

Churchill's agreement to the five-year restriction on Jewish immigration was confirmed in a private letter written by Colonial Secretary MacDonald to Prime Minister Chamberlain on 16 January 1940:

I doubt whether, in his heart of hearts, he [Churchill] disagrees with our land policy; he certainly regards it as consistent with the Mandate, for he told me in the lobby that he might have supported us [in May 1939] if it hadn't been for the Arab "veto" on immigration after five years.[46]

The years immediately preceding World War Two were undoubtedly years of crisis, in which every British patriot felt the need to put Britain's own interests first. Churchill put his Zionism on hold. As he had told his friend Lord Melchett in July 1937, it might take "5, 10 or even 20 years" to overcome the current crisis.[47]

Churchill's support for a Jewish state in Palestine

In the January 1949 Commons debate, Churchill's most specious claim was arguably that had he remained Prime Minister after World War Two, he would have set up a Jewish State in Palestine.

As wartime Prime Minister, Churchill told his coalition cabinet that he would cancel the 1939 White Paper – but only *after* the war had ended. But his wartime coalition was deliberately stingy in its allocation of immigration certificates and managed to extend the five-year immigration quota of 75,000 until the end of 1946 (more than two years beyond the White Paper's May 1944 deadline).

But effectively, Churchill gave up the Zionist cause in November 1944, after Jewish terrorists assassinated Lord Moyne, his personal friend and his appointee as Minister of State for the Middle East resident in Cairo.[48] He ordered the secretary of the cabinet to shelve the partition plan for Palestine that had been on the cabinet's agenda. He never met again with Weizmann and turned down all requests to meet with any Zionist leader. In the spring of 1945, he turned down a Colonial Office request to bring the partition plan before the cabinet. Six months after the assassination, John Martin, Churchill's personal secretary, admitted to a disgruntled Ben-Gurion "it had been impossible to broach the Palestine question with him since the murder".[49]

In November 1944, just a few days before the assassination, he had promised Weizmann to make a generous (to the Jews) partition of Palestine after the war. In May 1945, when the Zionists asked him to make good on his promise, they regarded his procrastination as a blow to their intelligence (see below).

Nonetheless, in January 1949, Churchill berated the Labour administration:

> Every opportunity for obtaining a satisfactory settlement was thrown away. Immediately after the end of the Japanese war [in August], we had the troops in the Middle East and we had the world prestige to impose a settlement on both sides. That chance was missed.[50]

Churchill's polemic was disputed by Prime Minister Attlee:

> May I ask the right hon. Gentleman, if he thought that could have been done, why did he not do it after the war? [Germany surrendered on 7 May 1945] He was in power.... He said that we could settle the question immediately after the war, when there were plenty of troops there ... there were several months at the end of the war when the right hon. Gentleman was in the position to do that.... [Churchill] knows – every hon. Member opposite knows – that the right hon. Gentleman shirked the question.[51]

Clement Davies, leader of the Liberal party, expressed his surprise at Churchill's claim that "the Tory Party had a wonderful and perfectly clean record in regard to establishing a home for Jews in Palestine". He referred to Churchill's own opposition to the Conservatives' policy in the late 1930s, "when he accused the then Government of vacillation, infirmity of purpose, lack of policy and lack of decision".[52]

However, had the MPs listening to Churchill in January 1949 been privy to the confidential, still-closed government documents of 1945, they would have been astounded to learn that his policy towards the Middle East during his final months in office was almost diametrically opposed to the hypothetical actions that he now vaunted. At the end of January 1945, when the Chiefs of Staff informed him that security in the Middle East could be guaranteed only by the transfer of troops from operations against the German and the Italians. Churchill's response, irritable and disparaging, reflects his enduring nineteenth century imperialist, patronizing mindset:

As long as we keep our troops well concentrated, a certain amount of local faction fighting can be tolerated and we can march in strength against the evil-doers. I am therefore not admitting the need of great reinforcements.

Suppose a lot of Arabs kill a lot Jews or a lot of Jews kill a lot of Arabs, or a lot of Syrians kill a lot of French or vice versa, this is probably because they have a great desire to vent their spite upon each other.... We really cannot undertake to stop all these bloodthirsty people slaying each other if that is their idea of democracy and the New World.... We are getting uncommonly little out of our Middle East encumbrances and paying an undue price for that little.[53]

On 1 July 1945, with the General Elections just four days off (after he had told the Zionists that their demand for a Jewish state would have to await the peace conference), Churchill, in a confidential note to his Colonial Secretary and to his Chiefs of Staff, expressed his exasperation with American interference in Palestine and expressed his desire to relieve Britain of the Mandate:

I do not think that we should take the responsibility upon ourselves of managing this very difficult place while the Americans sit back and criticize.... I am not aware of the slightest advantage which has ever accrued to Great Britain from this painful and thankless task. Somebody else should have their turn now.[54]

This became his idée fixe. As head of the Conservative Opposition, Churchill urged the Labour administration repeatedly to return the Palestine Mandate to the United Nations. On 24 October 1946, he stated in the Commons:

The burden may yet be too heavy for one single country to bear. It is not right that the United States, who are so keen on Jewish immigration into Palestine, should take no share in the task, and should reproach us for our obvious incapacity to cope with the difficulties of the problem.[55]

Zionist disillusion with Churchill

At the end of the war, the Zionists were totally disillusioned with Churchill. He had retreated from the cabinet's 1940 decision to set up a Jewish Division and had not taken any action to stop the mass murder of the Jews at Auschwitz.[56] His single wartime 'contribution' to the Zionist cause was the belated creation of a Jewish Brigade (one-third of the size of a Division) in September 1944 – a force that his cabinet banned from fighting in the Middle East.[57]

In November 1944, just three days before Moyne's assassination, Churchill had promised Weizmann a 'generous partition' (i.e. Jewish state) in Palestine. On 22 May 1945, Weizmann signed a Jewish Agency memorandum sent to

Churchill, demanding "a clear statement by the Allies that they intended to establish a Jewish state in Palestine, as an 'independent member of the British Commonwealth'". Churchill replied that he must defer any consideration of a solution to the Palestine problem until the Peace Conference.[58]

At a meeting of the Zionist Political Committee in London, Ben-Gurion protested that Churchill's reply was:

> The greatest blow they had received.... The Jewish people had been let down completely.... For him [Churchill] the delay was an escape, a way out.... The Jewish people had been let down completely.... They were absolutely powerless and helpless, but it was most evil to deceive their people.[59]

The Zionists were especially bitter about the Allies' failure to carry out the Zionists' 1944 request to bomb the Auschwitz death camp. In August 1946, Churchill would claim in the Commons that until the war had ended, he had no idea

> of the horrible massacres which had occurred, the millions and millions that have been slaughtered. That dawned on us gradually after the war was over.[60]

It is impossible to determine now to what extent his memory was actually failing him. But it should be remembered that during this same period, his memory was good enough to manipulate the facts in his memoirs of World War Two. Churchill's personal involvement in the Auschwitz bombing episode does not appear in his war memoirs. Prof Reynolds, the historian of his memoirs, has suggested that the omission was due to pangs of guilty conscience:

> To print his exhortations of July 1944 [to bomb Auschwitz] would ... draw embarrassing attention to how little was actually done.[61]

Weizmann, a lifelong Anglophile, whose affinity with Churchill had been one of the Zionists' greatest assets, thought that his postponement of their request to fulfil his 1944 promise was an insult to their intelligence. On June 27 1945, he told a further meeting of the Political Committee:

> The P.M., General Smuts, the late President Roosevelt, had all let them down, maybe not intentionally, but inadvertently. *They made promises which they did not carry out or mean to carry out* .... He felt very bitter .... Nobody cared what happened to the Jews. *Nobody had raised a finger to stop them being slaughtered*. They did not even bother about the remnant which had survived[62] (author's emphases).

In a Commons debate at the end of January 1947, Churchill supported the Labour government's policy of returning the Palestine mandate to the United Nations. He declared that since Britain had no strategic interest in Palestine and never had:

> then the responsibility for stopping a civil war in Palestine between Jew and Arab ought to be borne by the United Nations, and not by this poor overburdened and heavily injured country. I think it is too much to allow this heavy burden to be put on our shoulders costing £30 million a year and keeping 100,000 men from their homes. I see absolutely no reason why we should undergo all this pain, toil, injury and suffering.[63]

Conclusion

The Zionists never spoke out in public against Churchill, throughout his long career. In June 1945, notwithstanding their disillusion, they still expected him to win the impending 'khaki' election. Ben-Gurion ordered his colleagues not to publicise their disillusion with him. It would not have been politic to make an enemy of him. When Churchill lost the election, their Political Committee discussed whether to pay a tribute to him. Weizmann stated that although his last letter had been a "stab in the back", they were still indebted to him for his "famous speech against the [1939] White Paper", and for the mobilisation of the Jewish Brigade.[64]

Weizmann remained determined to keep on the right side of Churchill. He continued to write flattering letters to the great man, even though Churchill refused to receive him. In November 1947, the Jewish Telegraph Agency published a special issue of its Bulletin to mark the 30th anniversary of the Balfour Declaration. In October 1947, in a private letter to the editor, Weizmann pleaded with him to include Churchill's name in the list of Western statesmen who had helped bring about the Declaration. His letter encapsulates the Zionists' true feelings about Churchill:

> [J]ust at this moment he has more or less withdrawn from Zionist work because he is disgusted by the terrorists and terrorism.... I have never attempted to see him in the last few months.... I have on purpose included his name among the founders of the Jewish National Home together with Balfour and Lloyd George, although his role was comparatively small. It would be useful if you would give it prominence in your bulletin and send it on to him. He is rather sensitive.[65]

The great disparity between Churchill's statements and actions was noticed long ago by the late A.J.P. Taylor, not a specialist on Zionism:

> Only Churchill continued to show sympathy with the Jews until the murder of Lord Moyne, and there is nothing more striking in the story

than the total failure of the supposedly all-powerful prime minister to enforce his will on numerous occasions.[66]

Bevin was 'guilty' of something that the well-educated politician rarely did – of indiscreet, straight talking in public. Although Bevin was prone to go off script, J. P. Morgan, the Labour intellectual and historian, has summarised Bevin's views as:

> far more than the emotional product of one prejudiced, insensitive personality. It summarized the measured response of the Attlee government as a whole to a political and communal problem virtually incapable of solution.[67]

In fact, Bevin's Palestine policy enjoyed a large degree of all-party even nation-wide support. Churchill's main criticism of him was that he had not withdrawn from Palestine sooner. If we set aside Churchill's polemical fireworks in the House of Commons, his fundamental position on Palestine was very similar to Bevin's. However, as leader of the Opposition after the war, he was, as usual, on the make politically.[68] But so far as we know, Bevin had none of Churchill's numerous skeletons in his locker.

Notes

1 Martin Gilbert, *Churchill and the Jews*, London: Simon and Schuster, 2007, inside cover blurb and pp. 9, 42–3, 282–3, 295, 303, 307; see my review, 'The Churchill-Gilbert Symbiosis: Myth and Reality', *Modern Judaism* 2008 vol. 28/2, pp. 204–28, and Michael J Cohen, *Churchill and the Jews*, London: Frank Cass, 2003.
2 For example, his speeches to Zionist leaders in New York, 29 March, 1952, and in the House of Commons, 10 November 1952, in Gilbert, *Churchill and*, pp. 280, 282, 285.
3 At the time, government documents were closed for 50-years. In 1969, this was reduced to 30-years. cf David Reynolds, *In Command of History: Churchill Fighting and Writing the Second World War*, London: Penguin, 2004. Churchill's memoirs were published in six volumes, from 1948–1954
4 Gilbert produced eight volumes of the official biography, and 17 'companion' volumes of original documents.
5 The following is based on Sir Alan Bullock, *The Life and Times of Ernest Bevin*, Vol. 3: *Foreign Secretary, 1945–1951*, London: Heinemann, 1983; Kenneth O. Morgan, *Labour in Power, 1945–1951*, Oxford: Clarendon Press, 1984, Dixon, *Double*, p. 179.
6 Interviews in 1978 with Sir Harold Beeley, Bevin's principal adviser on Palestine, and Sir John Beith, in charge of illegal immigration to Palestine, cf Michael J Cohen, *Palestine and the Great Powers, 1945–1948*, Princeton: Princeton University Press, 1982, p. 18.
7 Cf. Benjamin Grob-Fitzgibbon, *Imperial Endgame: Britain's Dirty Wars and the End of Empire*, Basingstoke: Palgrave MacMillan, 2011, p. 385, note 73.
8 Without going into any detail, Weizmann brushes off Bevin's role in 1930 with the comment "but then Mr Bevin had wanted my services". As Foreign Secretary, Weizmann found him "overbearing, quarrelsome". Cf. Chaim Weizmann, *Trial*

and Error, New York: Schocken Books, 1949, p. 440; for Bevin's role in 1930, cf. Michael J Cohen, The British Mandate in Palestine: The Strange Case of the 1930 White Paper, *European Journal of Jewish Studies*, vol. 10, 2016, pp. 79–107.

9 On 22 July, Jewish terrorists, Menahem Begin's *Irgun*, blew up the entire south wing of the hotel, killing 91 men women and children.

10 House of Commons Debates (H.C.Deb.) 5th series, vol. 426, col. 1258, 1 August 1946.

11 On the American Jewish Zionist lobby, see Michael J Cohen, *Truman and Israel*, Berkeley/Los Angeles: University of California Press, 1990, Chapter 5.

12 Bevin arrived at the Foreign Office a sick man. The stress of international crises reduced him to complete exhaustion and recurrent heart-attacks, Piers Dixon, *Double Diploma*, London: Hutchinson, 1968, pp. 210 ff.

13 Bevin's speech on 13 November 1945, H.C.Deb., vol. 415, cols. 1927–34, *The Times*, 14 November 1945.

14 Ibid.

15 Norman Rose, '*A Senseless, Squalid War*': *Voices from Palestine, 1945–1948*, London: The Bodley Head, 2009, p. 83, also Weizmann, *Trial*, p. 440.

16 Protocols of the Jewish Agency Executive, 14 November 1945, vol. 42, Central Zionist Archives (CZA), cited in Cohen, *Palestine and*, p. 67.

17 The riots in July 1947 were ignited by the kidnapping and hanging in Palestine of two British sergeants by Jewish terrorists; cf. Cohen, *Palestine and the Great*, pp. 242–50.

18 All citations from the 26 January 1945 debate are in H.C.Deb., vol. 460, cols. 925–1059.

19 Ibid., col. 929.

20 Ibid., cols. 952–53.

21 H.C.Deb., 5th series, vol. 64, col. 1151; on the prevalence of anti-Semitism among the British upper classes, cf. Michael J Cohen, *Britain's Moment in Palestine: Retrospect and Perspectives, 1917–48*, London/New York: Routledge, 2014, pp. 5–25.

22 Norman Rose, Churchill and Zionism, in *Churchill: A Major New Assessment of His Life in Peace and War*, Robert Blake, Roger Louis, eds. Oxford/New York: Oxford University Press, 1993, pp. 150–1, Gilbert, *Churchill and*, pp. 37–44.

23 Cohen, *Churchill and*, pp. 55–6.

24 Ibid., p. 56.

25 Rose, Churchill and Zionism, p. 151.

26 Richard Toye, *Lloyd George & Churchill: Rivals for Greatness*, London: MacMillan, 2007, pp. 318–22.

27 For details, cf. Cohen, 'The Churchill-Gilbert Symbiosis', notes 25–26.

28 Cf. Richard Toye, *Churchill's Empire: The World that Made Him and the World He Made*, New York: Henry Holt and Co. 2010, pp. 148–9. In 1920, the Muslim population of the Empire was 87 million, including 70 million in India and 13 million in Egypt; also Cohen, *Churchill and*, pp. 62–5.

29 Martin Gilbert, *Winston S. Churchill*: vol. IV, *The Stricken World, 1916–1922*, Boston: Houghton Mifflin Company, 1975, p. 590, also Toye, *Churchill's Empire*, p. 147.

30 Churchill to Lloyd George, June 21, 1921, Gilbert, *Churchill*, vol. IV, companion vol. 2, London: William Heinemann Ltd., 1977, pp. 1489–91.

31 Richard Meinertzhagen, *Middle East Diary, 1917–1956*, London: The Cresset Press, 1959, entry for 5 July 1921, pp. 101–2.

32 Churchill memo for cabinet, CP 3213, 11 August 1921, in Cab 24/127, NA; Cohen, *Churchill*, pp. 117–22.

33 Cabinet discussion on 18 August 1921, Cab 23/26, NA

34 H.C.Deb., vol. 156, 4 July 1922, cols. 327–42. "Black Book" refers presumably to that place where the schoolmaster notes the names of children who misbehave.

35 Cf. Cohen, *Britain's Moment*, pp. 175–9.

36 On the 1939 White Paper, cf., ibid., Chapter 6.

37 Over 30,000 middle class Jews were rounded up and incarcerated in concentration camps; Over 1000 synagogues and prayer houses were burned and destroyed, and some 7,500 Jewish-owned businesses were smashed and looted. On 13 November, German Jewry was ordered to stop all business and trading activity by the end of the year. cf. *The Guardian*, 12 November 1938, and its 75th anniversary edition, 8 November 2013.

38 Cf. H.C.Deb., 21 November 1938, vol. 341 cols. 1428–83.

39 Ibid., col. 468.

40 On 20 October, he had publicised his plan in a Daily *Telegraph* article; on this, and Jewish opprobrium of it cf. Gilbert, *Churchill and*, pp. 142–43.

41 Debate on 24 November 1938, H.C.Deb., vol. 341, col. 2033.

42 Ibid., cols. 2036–38.

43 Gilbert, *Churchill and*, pp. 153.

44 H.C.Deb., vol. 347 cols. 2173–6.

45 Ibid., cols. 2177–8.

46 Prem 1/420, NA.

47 Cohen, *Churchill*, p. 177.

48 Michael J Cohen, The Moyne Assassination, November 1944: A Political Analysis, *Middle Eastern Studies*, 15/3, October 1979; Bernard Wasserstein, 'The Assassination of Lord Moyne', *Transactions of the Jewish Historical Society of England*, 27, 1982. Only Gilbert continued to insist that even though Churchill was shocked by the murder of Moyne, he "refused to allow it to deflect him from his Zionist sympathies". Gilbert, *Churchill and*, p. 229.

49 Prem 4/5/11, notes of April-May 1945, in FO 371/45377, NA, Z4/302/29, CZA.

50 H.C.Deb., vol. 460, col. 947.

51 ibid., cols. 947, 954, 1052. Churchill's wartime coalition was disbanded at the end of May 1945. He presided over a caretaker government until late July 1945.

52 H.C.Deb., vol. 460, col. 962.

53 Churchill note of 29 January 1945, Prem 3/296/9, NA

54 Churchill to Colonial Secretary and Chiefs of Staff, 1 July 1945, FO 371/45377, NA.

55 debate on 23 October 1946, also on 24 May, in H.C.Deb., vols. 427, 423.

56 cf. Cohen, *Churchill* (2003), pp. 203–27, 348–56.

57 Cohen, ibid., pp. 225–7.

58 Weizmann to Churchill, 22 May, Churchill to Weizmann, 9 June 1945, The Weizmann Archives (WA).

59 Meeting of Zionist Political Committee, 13 June 1945; Z4/302/29, CZA.

60 Churchill speech in the Commons, 1 August 1946, 1946, H.C.Deb., vol. 426, col. 1258; detailed information about the mass murders of Jews at Auschwitz was being leaked to the British since April 1944; one report given to Churchill by Eden described the camp's four crematoria, with a daily burning capacity of 10–12,000 bodies. The report stated that in this single camp, some 1.5 million Jews had been done to death over the previous 1.5 years, cf. Prem 4/5/10, and FO 371/42809, NA.

61 Reynolds, *In Command*, p. 455. On Churchill's veto of the bombing project, cf. Cohen, *Churchill and*, (2003), pp. 348–56.

62 Protocol of meeting, Z4/302/30, CZA.

63 Speech on 31 January 1947, H.C.Deb., vol. 432, cols. 1348–9.

64 Meeting of Zionist Political Committee, 27 July 1945, Z4/302/29, CZA.

65 Weizmann to Jacob Landau (founding editor of Jewish Telegraphic Agency) 19 October 1947, WA.

66 A.J.P. Taylor review of Bernard Wasserstein, *Britain and the Jews of Europe, 1939–1945*, Oxford: The Clarendon Press, 1979, *English Historical Review*, vol. XCV/375, April, 1980, pp. 388–92. Churchill's private archives were not open until 1995, so Wasserstein was not aware that Churchill had in fact vetoed the bombing of Auschwitz.

67 Morgan, *Labour in Power*, p. 209.

68 Richard Crossman referred to this during the January 1949 Commons Debate: "I did not want any party point scored from either side of the House. I regret, however, that the Right Hon. Member for Woodford [Churchill] had deliberately scored such party points on an issue which is far too important for party policies." H.C.Deb., col. 984.

Part II
Arab perspectives

4 Between local Palestinian and pan-Arab nationalism among Palestinians during the British mandate

Akram Zuʿayter as an example

Mustafa Kabha

This chapter deals with the role of Akram Zuʿayter (1909–96) in the development and shaping of Palestinian nationalism throughout the British Mandate. In addition, he is considered a major pivot of Palestinian nationalist education. Zuʿayter served as an educator, journalist, politician and historian. His creative journey began in the early twentieth century and continued until his death in 1996. I will concentrate here on Zuʿayter's role during the British Mandate until 1948, when he left Palestine for Jordan. There, he filled different political positions, in foreign affairs, and as head of committees, etc.

The history of the Palestinian people in the twentieth century was shaped by three triangles. One was external, and consisted of Britain (and the other superpowers), pre-state Zionism and the State of Israel, and the Arab world, encompassing Arab countries and their vested interests. The second triangle relates to aspects of national identity: the pan-regional Arab dimension, the national Palestinian dimension, and the political Islamic dimension. The third triangle was social and intrinsic: the veteran, traditional, family-based elite, the intellectual middle class that entered politics mainly from the 1930s, and working-class groups whose young, armed representatives burst into the political sphere at crucial junctions, taking advantage of both traditional and modern leadership. These triangles remained in force throughout the modern history of the Palestinian people, albeit with different players, in the contexts of the changing political and historical circumstances.[1]

Most historians investigating the history of the Palestinian people begin their analyses with one of two major events in the annals of the Zionist-Arab conflict: the commencement of Jewish-Zionist immigration from Europe in 1882, or the promise given by the British to the Zionists in the Balfour Declaration in 1917, in which they promised to assist Jewish efforts to construct a Jewish national homeland in Palestine. Recognition of these events as focal points has at its roots in the assumption that the unique Palestinian national consciousness developed in response to the budding Zionist enterprise. Other historians choose starting points indicative of more authentic origins. One such option is the local revolt initiated in 1834, aimed against the tyrannical regime established in Palestine by Ibrahim Pasha, son of the Egyptian ruler Muhammad 'Ali.[2] In a more far-reaching attempt, others identify Dahir al-'Umar, the eighteenth-century ruler of the Galilee, as the founder of the first 'Palestinian national state'.[3]

These scholars tie the development of the modern Palestinian identity to that of the wider regional and modern Arab identity – a disputable viewpoint. We have no evidence that a nationalist Palestinian doctrine existed, whether declared or implied, in those earlier times. Nor is there evidence of intrinsic manifestations of local-nationalist identity, as distinguished from the affiliation with other parts of Greater Syria, Bilad al-Sham. On the contrary, contemporary sources show that feelings of alliance with the regional Ottoman system remained intact until the demise of the empire following the First World War. This traditional Islamic sense of identification was retained during the pre-war years, increasingly manifested by conspicuous displays of Arab consciousness, which evolved despite the policy of 'Turkifization' introduced by the Young Turks. Many contemporary pioneers of Arabism and Palestinian consciousness were in fact Arabic-speaking Christians, whose ties to the Muslim Ottoman Empire had been shaky to begin with.

It is possible to recognise the initial development of both an Arab and a Palestinian modern identity as occurring in the transition between the nineteenth and twentieth centuries. The Arab dimension of this identity evolved as an inseparable part of shifts occurring in the entire region. The local Palestinian dimension was a result of unique problems involving Palestine and the growing conflict with the Zionist movement. The first signs of this local dimension included, among other things, the emergence of exceptional modern newspapers, *Al-Karmil*, established in Haifa in 1908 by Najib Nassar, and *Filastin*, established by the cousins 'Issa Dawoud, and Yusuf Hanna al-'Issa, in Jaffa in 1911. The newspapers' names reflect familiarity with the scenery of the homeland. Articles published in these and similar newspapers reveal the gradual formation of a Palestinian consciousness, in acknowledgement of the threat posed by Jewish immigration to Palestine and its Arab residents.[4] Jewish immigrants, arriving in the Second Aliyah that began in 1904, declared goals of 'conquering the land' and 'conquering labor'. Undoubtedly, these declarations contributed to the consolidation of an Arab movement based on nationalist, local-patriotic, *watani* foundations.[5] At this point, a Palestinian Arab national consciousness began to develop. It has continued to motivate its adherents to this very day. From the beginning, these sentiments were anchored in pan-regional Arab identity, and so they remain. The Arab dimension of the Palestinian entity derived both from its purely historical-cultural affiliation and from its need for support from the Arab world in its battle for Palestine. The history of the Palestinians in the twentieth century manifests a gradually changing emphasis from pan-Arab to uniquely Palestinian, a shift facilitated by the permutations of the fight for Palestine and deeply affected by intrinsic transformations, both social and political in nature.

It is possible to contend that, in the years prior to the First World War, only a limited number of intellectuals possessed this complex, modern national identity. The working classes were the first to come into contact with Zionist immigrants, but they probably interpreted the threat inherent in the presence of the newcomers in traditional terms of protecting the pan-Islamic and pan-Arab region. After the war an Arab government was established in Damascus, headed by Faisal Ibn al-Husayn and leaders of the Arab revolt, resulting in the enhancement of modern Arab aspects among the intelligentsia and the elite. Faisal's supporters, who included Palestinians, recognised Palestine as the southern part of Greater Syria. Many local Palestinians deferred to the government in Damascus. This is evident from the newspaper *Surya al-Janubiyya* (southern Syria), published at the time in Jerusalem, not the least from its name. Newspaper names regularly reflected the spirit of the times and the different emphases of the new modern identity. Aside from *Surya al-Janubiyya*, edited by 'Arif al-'Arif and Hasan al-Budayri, another newspaper published in Jerusalem during these years was *Mir'at al-Sharq* [*Mirror of the East*] edited by Boulos Shihada. The newspaper reflected a general Eastern sense of identity, seeking to blur ethnic-national and religious differences between all residents of the East. The local-patriotic, Palestinian dimension was consistently manifested by the newspaper *Filastin*, edited by 'Issa al-'Issa, which renewed its publication after the First World War. The names of new organisations, for example, the Muslim-Christian Associations and the Palestinian Arab General Congress, were another mark of the emerging, modern Palestinian Arab identity. In addition to its association with pan-Arabism, and its contemporary Damascus focus, the Palestinian entity derived some of its motivation from objection to the Balfour Declaration, the assurances it gave, and its threat to the future of Palestine. As early as in 1918, members of the Muslim-Christian Association in Jaffa voiced a 'protest against the aspirations of the Jews and the subordination of the Arabs' demands. The 'protest' included statements specifically emphasising the uniqueness of the Arab population of Palestine and the fundamental connection of this population to the land as a disparate territory: "Palestine, the homeland of our fathers".[6]

The emphasis on any one dimension of the Arab-Palestinian (or Palestinian-Arab) identity has always been related to social, political, and strategic processes within Palestinian society. With the beginning of the British Mandate in 1920 and the internationally distinct political definition of Palestine, the Arabs of Palestine abandoned the idea of Greater Syria and a pan-Eastern identity. From this point on they gradually became focused on the Arab-Palestinian identity, increasingly stressing the national dimension. A glance at books published in this period, primarily educational textbooks, shows that most of the writers used the name 'Palestine' and defined its Arab residents as 'Palestinians'. For example, 1923 saw the publication of Husayn Rawhi's book *Concise Geography of Palestine*.[7] Educator Khalil al-Sakakini published a *History of Palestine following the Great War* in 1925.[8] Two other educators,

'Umar al-Salih al-Barghuti and Khalil Tawtah, composed a *History of Palestine.*[9] They wrote in the introduction, "In attempting to document the history of Palestine we fulfil the duty of each and every person to learn the history of his country and his nation before studying that of others."[10]

In the political sphere as well, institutions and organisations emphasizing national identity and its Arab and Palestinian dimensions were established in the 1920s. While the British attempted to address the Arab population of Palestine as a conglomerate of variegated religious groups, this approach was countered by the nonspecific Muslim-Christian Associations, precursors of the Arab Palestinian General Congress [al-Mu'tamar al-'Arabi al-Filastini al-'Am].[11] Members of the Executive Arab Committee, an organisation demanding recognition of the nationalist ideology and its rights, headed by Mousa Kathim al-Husayni, were chosen from among this congress. Although the British never acknowledged the Executive Arab Committee (as they did its rival, the Jewish Agency), they did occasionally hold dialogues with its president and members, and some say that it was indeed recognised de facto.

Under the new circumstances formed by the British Mandate, in light of the conflict with Zionism and with no autonomous, official governmental Arab systems (which existed in other Arab countries), the Palestinian-Arab national movement found it difficult to become stabilised. The family-based factions of the traditional elite became further entrenched, hampering attempts at founding a modern system. These conflicting factions had existed for many years but were dormant during the late Ottoman period and re-emerged in force during the first decade of the British Mandate. The British encouraged traditional factionalism and rivalries between the families of the elite. In 1921, the British authorities initiated the Muslim Higher Council, an organisation created to provide religious leadership, which they then proceeded to recognise as representing the Arabs of Palestine, as opposed to the Executive Arab Committee, which was a nationalist organisation. The Muslim Higher Council succeeded in aggravating the factionalism. British authorities directed the Nashashibi-led group to municipal positions and awarded the rival Husayni-led group precedence on the religious council. In 1912, Haj Amin al-Husayni was appointed mufti of Jerusalem, and a year later he became head of the Muslim Higher Council. This set in motion the development of strong rivalries and factionalism at the expense of modern national forms of organisation.

The elements of national politics introduced by families of the Palestinian elite, together with the relative stability enjoyed in the region and in the world in general in the 1920s, helped calm matters during this decade. However, with the transition to the 1930s a new era began. Facing the crises emerging both globally and regionally, the existential need to form modern organs of a national movement – political parties, popular committees, journals, and armed units – arose once again. This coincided with a process of social change that strengthened Arab sentiments at the expense of local Palestinian identity. Establishment of the al-Istiqlal (Independence) Party (officially in 1932, but unofficially as early as 1930) marked the advent of a new generation of intellectuals becoming active in national politics, most originating from the middle class. This generation began developing a modern political system as an alternative to the old elite with its family-based rivalries. In contrast to the hegemony of the 1920s elite, the 1930s generation espoused a new national agenda in which a more patent attempt was made to use concepts incorporating pan-Arab modern unity. Efforts to achieve liberation from British rule replaced the apportioning of positions under British patronage.

In addition, the Zionist-Palestinian conflict in the 1930s deteriorated and became more violent. Fortification of the Jewish settlement by waves of immigrants escaping declining circumstances in Europe, in addition to impoverished conditions in Arab villages due to the economic crisis, led the extensive lower classes of Palestinian society to begin taking part in political activities from the onset of this decade. The new members were mostly organised in armed bands that operated clandestinely and attacked British and Jewish targets. The one leader most identified with the attempts of villagers and members of the urban proletariat to take to arms and terrorise their opponents was Shaikh 'Izz al-Din al-Qassam. Born in Syria in 1881, al-Qassam was a teacher at the Islamic School in Haifa and a preacher and imam at a local mosque. He was killed on 19 November 1935, in a battle with British forces near Jenin. He has remained a symbol, not only of armed participation of popular groups in Palestinian politics but also of the development of political Islam as an additional dimension and component of the Palestinian movement.

Important stages in Zu'ayter's life

Akram Zu'ayter was born in Nablus in 1909. His father, Umar Zu'ayter, was the Mayor of Nablus. Nablus was a major city with a central part in the rebirth or reawakening of Palestinian education. The city's reputation as one that resisted the occupation during the nineteenth century caused the governors of the Ottoman Empire to pay it special attention.[12]

In addition, it had a commercial relationship with the nearby and coastal cities of Jordan, Syria and Egypt. This relationship exposed the people of Nablus to technological developments. Commercial and business interests encouraged villagers to relocate to Nablus, increasing the territory of the city westward in the direction of 'Anabta, thus earning it the name of Magareb Nablus, while in the east it expanded towards the Jordan valley, earning it the name of al-Mashareq.

Zu'ayter was exposed to an educated group of people since early childhood. He listened to their conversations, constantly attentive to the people who used to visit his father throughout the tribulations affecting the city of Nablus and the Palestinians.

During this period the Palestinians continued to wage their nationalist struggle. The population of Palestine after World War One stood at 700,000, of whom 642,000 were Arabs. Seventy per cent of the Arabs were farmers, 22% city dwellers and 8% Bedouin.[13]

The *al-Najah* Nationalist School – first step to forming a unique nationalist voice

In joining the *al-Najah* school, Zu'ayter had the opportunity to be exposed and introduced to the Arab public. Muhammad 'Izzat Darwza (director of the school from 1921–26), a citizen of Nablus, had a great impact on Zu'ayter's national voice. In 1932 Zu'ayter and Muhammad formed the al-Esteqlal political party.

> Muhammad 'Izzat Darwaza described his teaching style, which focused on nationalist developments: From the beginning I would gather all the high school students every Tuesday afternoon and deliver a lecture on matters of behavior, literature, nationalism, Islam, history and sociology. Students were allowed to question me on these issues and I answered them. This tradition continued for six years.[14]

Zaki al-Nqqash, a science teacher from Beirut, and Ahmad Abdullah Harlo, an American convert and English teacher, are both mentioned in Zu'ayter's diary. Abdullah taught English at the *al-Najah* School for many years. He managed to influence his students mainly in matters of human heritage, art, literature and other educational issues.[15]

The influence of his father's death on Zu'ayter

> My father was the governor of Nablus and a prominent Palestinian leader, particularly in the district of Nablus, which was painfully affected by his death. Never before had so many residents of Nablus participated in the funeral of one man. I was only fifteen years old and I admired my father for his shrewdness, the sympathy he demonstrated towards both national and religious issues, for his strong personality, his attractiveness, determination, courage, and his patience in the field. My grief was not only for the loss of a father. I was sad to lose his gratification. I cried the entire funeral. Maybe I cried to see the burial of such intellect.[16]

These are the words of Zu'ayter describing the painful death of his father in his diary and explaining how proud he was of him. He understood his father's significance for the district and for the Palestinians in general. However, the strongest statement that Zu'ayter heard and stored in his memory, which influenced him for the rest of his life, were the words of his former teacher, Zaki al-Naqash, during the funeral: "Your father left you the ultimate goal – to be your father".

Losing his father was not just an emotional disaster, it also meant losing the family breadwinner and provider. His eldest son, Adel, was a law student at the Sorbonne University in Paris. But the death of Akram's father occurred at the beginning of his first term at the American University of Beirut. He found himself beset by both the loss of his father and the need to secure and finance his studies. Zu'ayter describes this era:

I had paid my tuition and I began my studies a little late since my father died in November 1924. I worked all hours of the day and night to catch up with my studies; this enormous effort was physically harrowing.[17]

The American University of Beirut

Zu'ayter settled down quickly and soon endeared himself to students and staff members on the campus. After overcoming his initial financial battles, Zu'ayter became more and more confident and eventually did well in his studies. Qustanten Zreq speaks of his relationship with Zu'ayter:

We met during the 1924–1925 school year, my first year of studies at the American University of Beirut in the Faculty of Science and Literature. The university listed staff and students by the English alphabet and the surnames Zu'ayter and Zurayq were at the end of the list. We subsequently spent the entire academic year together and developed a great relationship which lasted the rest of our lives.[18]

Their faith in Arab nationalism and in the ideology of Arab unity ignited a long-lasting relationship between the two. The Beirut campus afforded a warm environment for the students to express their thoughts and a great number of students from Arab countries such as Egypt, Jordan, Saudi Arabia and Iraq, welcomed this ideology and gathered around it.

The primary core of the Arab nationalist party began its activities on campus and called for the unity and independence of Arab countries. Zu'ayter, Zurayq and other members of the party contributed to the development of this ideology and of the party, to the benefit of the Arab community and in accordance with political sectionalism.

Regarding his educational activities on campus Zu'ayter states:

I was active in organisations such as al-'Urwa al-Wuthqa [the strong connection], Zahrat al-Aadab [flower of literature] and others. In addition, I spoke at most of the competitions and debates. I won first prize, and second prize for Zahrat al-Aadab.[19]

All these activities were in addition to his formal studies at the university. He was under great pressure and his health suffered. The doctors advised him to return to Nablus to rest. However, the health problems were aggravated by the family's financial difficulties, which regretfully caused him to leave the university and return to Nablus.

Returning to Nablus – the conflict with Bowman of the Department of Education

At the beginning of the 1925–1926 school year, Zuʿayter was appointed to teach at the al-Hashemiyya School. His family and friends congratulated him on receiving this position, but he had higher ambitions. Zuʿayter described his feelings: "I returned home, informed my brother and my family and they congratulated me. But I went to my room and closed the door behind me and cried, asking myself whether I was destined to remain a primary school teacher".[20]

However his brother's encouragement and the supportive atmosphere at the school motivated Zuʿayter to change his views. He described his first day at the school:

> I was warmly welcomed by the school principal, ʿAlaa al-Den, and the teachers as well. In addition, by Sheik Husni al-Gabwa and Ragib Malhas. The principal introduced me to the students. Although I was not happy with this job I promised myself to increase and maximize my productivity at the school. I understood the value of delivering my ideology and broadcasting the seeds of nationalism to my students from an early age. The Moroccan revolution, led by Muhammad ʿAbd al-Karem, and the Syrian revolution, led by Sultan al-Atrash, served as major resources for our discussions of nationalism. As a result, my students grew eager and awaited my classes.[21]

The next year Zuʿayter was transferred to the al-Salahiyya high school and worked with Nur al-Den al-ʿAbbasi, the school principal (father of the poet ʿEsam al-ʿAbbasi, later of Haifa). At this school Zuʿayter focused increasingly on nationalist issues. He created a literature institute for the school's students and wrote national songs for different occasions. He also began writing for the *al-Shura* newspaper, published by Muhammad ʿAli al-Taher from Nablus in Cairo.

The British Department of Education, most of all Humphrey Bowman, its Director, focused on the political activists. He was very disturbed by their ideology and its dissemination throughout the educational system. Bowman wrote to the district inspector of Nablus, asking that Zuʿayter be transferred to ʿAkka high school, located at the time in the al-Jazzar Mosque.

In 1927, an earthquake caused massive damage to the district while Zuʿayter was present at the school. He gave a detailed description of the earthquake:

We had not yet left the school when we saw the doors collapse. The late Ahmad Al-Bustami, the Arabic teacher, left without his robe and his socks. The school guard ran inside the school but found only the robe and not the socks and he was forced to leave without them.[22]

Relocation to 'Akka

The relocation did not fulfil his ambitions. Zu'ayter wished to join the Law School of the Jerusalem University. At first, he refused to relocate and wrote to Bowman asking to remain. But Bowman refused: "We are transferring you to a peaceful atmosphere".

Bowman assumed that by relocating Zu'ayter to 'Akka he would isolate him from all the national activists of the districts of Nablus and Jerusalem. Shortly after the relocation, Bowman was disappointed to discover that Zu'ayter had formed a new network of activists in 'Akka and Haifa in addition to broadcasting his ideology amongst his new students. Zu'ayter quickly endeared himself to the local residents of the city. He stated his feelings joyfully:

I loved 'Akka and its gentle people, I enhanced their loyalty. I explained to the tourists visiting the city the principles of the national party. They all supported and trusted me. In addition to my formal teaching classes, I insisted on teaching Arabic literature and history, and I used these classes to spread my ideology. My students were so excited and motivated that new speakers were born out of this group.[23]

Khalil al-Sakakeni, the Arabic language inspector at the time, visited the school and attended one of Zu'ayter's classes. He wrote in his report:

The students are highly motivated. They understand their studies. The students behave properly in class, as manifested by their body language, tone of voice and pronunciation. I have never seen or experienced this at any other school in Palestine. Surprisingly, I saw that the students related to the topic as if they had written the articles rather than just studying them. However that was exactly how Zu'ayter himself behaved, as if they incorporated his own spirit.[24]

Zu'ayter began travelling very often to Haifa and started writing for the *al-Yarmouk* newspaper, owned by Rashid al-Haj Ibrahem, and published by Hani Abu Muslih; also for the *al-Zuhor* newspaper, owned and published by Jamil al-Bahri. However, in order to avoid a conflict with the Department of Education, Zu'ayter started using pseudonyms, such as Ibn al-Sahari or Ibn al-Badiya [son of the desert].[25]

At that time a warm relationship developed between him and Ahmad al-Shuqayri, As'ad al-Shuqayri's son. Akram described this relationship:

al-Shuqeri would often visit me at my office, complaining about his father – but I did not express my opinion on that matter since he was still living at his father's house. We spent many nights discussing public issues. I noticed his enthusiasm and his intellect by the way he avoided confrontation, notwithstanding his strong criticism of those whom he did not like.[26]

The height of his demonstrative writings: 1929–1939

In the summer of 1929, Acre was beset by al-Buraq protesters. At the time, Zu'ayter was spending his summer vacation in Nablus, far from his students. He followed the news closely, wishing to see the outcome of the spirit of his ideology. On his return to 'Akka after the summer vacation, Zu'ayter joined protests against British conduct towards the Palestinians throughout the al-Buraq protests. He was the most influential architect of Palestinian public opinion. He wrote an article in the *al-Yarmok* newspaper in Haifa and in *al-Iqdam* in Jaffa. It was the most important article he wrote and it was written under a pseudonym, 'Arabi Abi'. It protested the physical punishing of a group of students from Nablus and Safed. The title of his article was 'Oh executioner – palsy in your hands – transfer but do not beat them'. He wrote that students were the motivated group and the future of the nation, destroyed by the coloniser. He urged the people to protest and fight – explaining about the dark clouds of the future:

> We ask every one of the followers of Muhammad, the sons of Khalid and 'Umar, the youngsters of today, the men of tomorrow and the flowers of this nation, to stop the English people – Oh executioner – palsy in your hands – transfer but do not beat them.[27]

However, Bowman and his group discovered the identity of the writer and Zu'ayter was never forgiven, particularly when his students distributed the newspaper and the article widely. He would have been forced to collaborate with the British authorities in order to retain his job – but he refused, and lost his job. For Zu'ayter this was preferable to collaboration.

From teaching to journalism

After resigning from the Department of Education, Zu'ayter was accepted to study law at the University of Jerusalem. At the same time, he became closer to the Palestinian political establishment. He was incidentally introduced to Bulus Shehada, owner of the *Mir'at al-Sharq* newspaper. Shehada was a well-known politician and educator.[28]

It was not easy for Zu'ayter to accept Shehada's offer to join the newspaper, since they did not share the same ideology. Zu'ayter rejected any contact with the British until their complete withdrawal from Palestine.

Nevertheless, Zu'ayter accepted Shehada's offer, on one condition – that he be allowed to express himself freely. But Shehada asked that he refrain from criticizing colleagues employed by the political establishment, such as Ragheb al-Nashashebi, As'ad al-Shuqayri, Suleman Tuqan, Umar Salih al-Bargouthi, and Ahmad Samih al-Khalidi. Zu'ayter told Shehada that he would not tolerate any renunciation of the national cause. Shehada demanded that Zu'ayter consult him before publishing any item related to those colleagues.[29]

There was no time to test this agreement. Palestinian society was torn between the government and the opposition, which adhered to Zu'ayter's ideology. Zu'ayter facilitated the increasing growth of *Mi'rat al-Sharq* throughout Palestine, also al-Jami'a al-'Arabiyya and *al-Karmel*.

His first article published in *Mir'at al-Sharq* was entitled 'Istiqlaliyon', the Independent. In it he wrote about unity and about the significance of achieving Palestinian independence at any price: "If we cannot achieve it right now, we shall live it in our hearts – and keep advancing towards it".[30] His articles in *Mir'at al-Sharq* focused on several issues:

- Do not trust the United Nations since it is a British device. He called upon the people to follow the steps of the Indians, the statements of Gandhi, Nehru, Muhammad Ali and others.
- Treat the prisoners with respect, encourage them and visit them whenever possible.
- Attack those who sell land to the enemy and accord them no respect.
- Encourage youth organisations to be more involved in nationalism.

This attitude made him one of the most influential people in Palestinian public opinion, in two different domains. The first was the effort to inculcate in the new generation a new ideology associated with their nationality; the second was criticism of Palestinian political leaders who did not behave accordingly.

In the first domain Zu'ayter published several articles aimed at recharging the spirit of the young, under a pseudonym, 'Tha'ier' – Rebel. In one of his articles he encouraged the young: "The struggle for freedom – *jihad* – can only survive with your help – that of the youth; we shall be prepared and well organized and return to the field".[31]

He strongly criticised the traditional political leaders and their methods. In one of his articles: 'Confused determination and detestable fear', he criticised Musa Kathem al-Husseini, the highest representative of the Palestinian governing body:

It seems that the enforcement committee never understood the significance of sacrifice, which is the smallest and most basic rule for freeing the nation. Prison is the last concern of those who serve their country. It is about time for our leaders to understand that our nation will never receive what they desire with this detestable fear.

Zuʿayter increased his demands that the leaders be a model for the nation and follow in the steps of Gandhi and Nehru in India, Mustafa Kamal and Saʾad Zaglul in Egypt – leaders who served their nation and were models for their people. He also insisted that the national faction be allowed to join the battlefield.[32]

In another article, 'The land is in danger and the leaders are fighting among themselves', he wrote:

> Every sheik should devote his days and nights to thinking about how to rescue the land, every youngster should give his heart and soul to protect the land, every woman should cry loudly to beat the enemy, every teacher should make his students soldiers of the land, every rich man should spend his money for the land, educated people should design and orga-nize the political parties, writers should uplift the spirit of the nation, preachers should instill the spirit of resistance in people's hearts.[33]

The controversy with Commissioner Roach over monitoring the press

Zuʿayter's articles and his ability to influence the Palestinian public could not be hidden from the British officers. They started applying pressure when Zuʿayter's tone changed to threats and when he used the newspaper to create a national army and a headquarters to recruit youngsters willing to join it. In May 1930, Zuʿayter presented his idea in an op-ed in *Mir'at al-Sharq*:

> A loyal group of youngsters capable of joining the workforce has decided to build our defence army – the basic idea is obvious from the title. An idea has started circling around the villages and cities of Palestine to awaken the national spirit, to teach people how to protect the land and the local industry and products. Any one of you who is willing to con-tribute one or two weeks of his time, any loyal youth who is capable of working, we call upon you to join the defence army. The land is in danger, anyone who can work without talking can join without fear. Palestine is calling you.[34]

This article aroused the youth and they began calling the newspaper's office to join up. The British authorities lost their patience with Zuʿayter – at first, he was called to the office of General Quigley, head of the investigation depart-ment in Jerusalem. He was asked to reduce the level of aggressiveness in his articles, to support the British authorities and to calm the people.[35] Soon after that he was called to the office of Keith Roach, District Commissioner of Jerusalem, who repeated the same demand. But Zuʿayter ignored both. Before long he was arrested for one week and then banished from Jerusalem for one year. At that time Zuʿayter became the first Palestinian journalist to be incarcerated for his political activities. This prevented him from writing for *Mir'at al-Sharq*. Zuʿayter had completed an important stage of his journal-istic career. It did not take long before *Mir'at al-Sharq* ceased to exist.[36]

The second stage of Zu'ayter's journalistic career began in June 1931, when he joined the *al-Haya al-Maqdisiya* newspaper. He signed an agreement with Khayr al-Den al-Zirakli and 'Adel Jaber to write his own daily column in the newspaper, 'Our national life'.[37] In this section Zu'ayter repeatedly raised the spirit of the youth, shaped their nationalist ideology and criticised the national leadership. In one of his articles, 'Youth', he wrote:

> There are two different types of youth – The first are those blinded by their desires. They do not care what is happening in their land. They feel it yet they do nothing because they have ears but do not hear, they have eyes but do not see, hearts with no feelings, they are the living dead, children in the image of men. The second type are those whose *Jihad* takes the form of debates, articles and protests, claiming that they have no organisation to lead them from words to deeds.[38]

We can assume that Zu'ayter's criticism of the youth was directed at those who did not respond to his calls to participate in the national struggle and to protect the land. He expressed such criticism repeatedly. In one of his other articles, 'Ink on Paper', he wrote:

> Our disaster with our fighters has come to a fitting conclusion in our satisfaction with written reports. We do not think of implementing them and if we do it is only for a short period of time. The enemy understands this and they no longer fear us. We have become careless about what we say or decide, confident that our anger is just a passing cloud. Our national parties lack continuity and persistence. If we wish to decide something without implementing it we should not decide it in the first place. Organisations earn respect as do individuals. Organisations that reach decisions which are mere ink on paper do not garner any respect. Political parties that reach decisions but do not implement them have no self-respect and should be ignored.[39]

Soon after, in August 1931, Kher al-Den al-Zirakly left Palestine for Egypt. Zu'ayter became the main publisher of the newspaper. In addition to his section 'Our national life' he began writing the newspaper's editorial. He strongly criticised the Palestinian leaders who attended the tea party given by the British commissioner for Jaffa and Jerusalem, who resigned in 1931. In an article, 'Tea and Blood', he wrote:

> The authorities are ignorant of their national dignity, while thousands of our youth are taken to prisons and they do nothing about it. British weapons are shooting our elderly, youth, children, and women, our women yell at the British soldiers. At this time all Palestinians should unite. Instead, our leaders went to thank the British commissioner for Jaffa and Jerusalem. This man is responsible for the Palestinian struggle.

His soldiers open the prison doors, he is in charge of the bloodshed in Nablus, and this is the man with whom our leaders feel an urgent need to party. Don't they feel the pain of their thousands of incarcerated brothers while they sit drinking tea with the commissioner?[40]

Soon after writing this article, on 31 August 1931, Zu'ayter was called again to the office of Inspector-General Spicer. Munif al-Husini, publisher of *al-Jami'a Alarabiyya* – the Arabic University – was present as well, and Spicer issued a warning to them both for their provocative articles.[41]

Under pressure of the new commissioner, whilst the owner of the newspaper was still in Cairo, Zu'ayter announced the closing of the newspaper, especially having discovered that one of his colleagues had been spying on them for British commissioner Roach.[42]

Zu'ayter's return to the educational system: teaching at *al-Najah* National School

Zu'ayter was forced to leave Jerusalem and return to Nablus. He received an offer to teach Arabic and history at the *al-Najah* School – which was both a relief and good for his spirit. He began teaching on 21 September 1931. He described his return in his diary:

I was very happy to resume teaching. Educating children from an early age is for me the holiest job. Teaching is the best platform for spreading the spirit of nationalism, classes are an opportunity to produce men. I have never felt a difference between being a journalist and being an educator. As a journalist I would appeal to the public and here I am educating a new generation in order to form a good nation.

Joining the National School will not mark the end of my national political activities and I will never stop writing newspaper articles on public affairs.[43]

Upon leaving the field of journalism and returning to teaching, Zu'ayter thought that he would now be free of the government's Department of Education. He was a member of the Arab Independence Party and he described the party:

We discussed the possibility of building an Independence Party, to rescue the country from the internal arguments between the opposition and the governors, and to be fair with both, to maintain the correct focus and to stay away from tribal conflicts.[44]

That was his dream. But his plan did not succeed since the party could not avoid conflicts between the major families and tribes. Nevertheless, Zu'ayter continued writing in the Palestinian newspapers and attacking land speculators. Even while heading the Independence Party he continued to teach at the school until the end of the 1932–33 academic year.[45]

Teaching in Iraq

In 1933, Zuʿayter participated in the memorial service for the late King Hussein. The Iraqi Department of Education asked him to teach the subject 'The nationalist direction' at the teachers' seminar. At that time, he wrote an article in *al-Istiqlal*, the Independence, an Iraqi newspaper, in which he spoke of Arab nationalism under a pseudonym, al-Qaʾaqaʾa.[46] He also joined the national workers' union. Before long he became principal of the high school, which was a branch of the Science College. He advanced rapidly and drew widespread attention.

However, things did not go according to plan. Some of the Iraqi intelligentsia opposed his appointment as school principal. He also faced opposition from the communists and some locals, particularly minorities, who insisted on the idea of 'Iraq for the Iraqis'. Zuʿayter described this opposition: "Once again I am attacked. At first I did not mind, and I have heard that Junes al-Bahri has had similar experiences. Then I understood that our national work would not be easy".[47]

When Zuʿayter realised the inherent complications he resigned from his position, at the end of the 1933–34 academic year. While he was on summer vacation in Palestine, Sadeq al-Bassam, the Iraqui Minister of Education, tried to persuade him to stay. A group of Iraqi, Syrian and Palestinian activists eventually succeeded in convincing him and he returned for one more year, 1934–35.

Leader of the revolution and organiser of the 1936 protest

In July 1935 Zuʿayter returned from Iraq.[48] He continued with his nationalist activities, convincing the people to rebel. He also sent a letter to the Iraqi education department: "Palestine will be destroyed if the Palestinians do not start the *Jihad* and the Arab world does not support them in their struggle".[49]

After returning from Iraq, Zuʿayter was in Nablus when Sheik ʿIzz al-Din al-Qassam called the people to rebel against the British. In November 1935, in an armed clash with British forces, the sheik was killed. Zuʿayter began writing once again for Palestinian newspapers and organizing new Palestinian associations. He was the main organiser of protests against the seventeenth memorial service for Lord Balfour together with many others from Palestinian cities, trade unions, and journalists.

Zuʿayter was not happy with the existing situation. He demanded in his articles that the traditional leaders encourage and allow the youth to join in the struggle. Al-Qassam's revolt served his interests and many youngsters turned against the traditional leaders.

On the eve of the sheik's funeral, Zuʿayter wrote an article for the newspaper of the Islamic university:

> Tomorrow we will attend the funeral of the Sheik, leader of the Muslim youth association, the Imam of the big Mosque, and all those who died with him on the battlefield in defense of the land. I invite the Palestinian leaders to join the funeral; the Egyptian leader al-Nahhas always came to the funerals of the freedom fighters. Is there any Palestinian leader who will join the funeral of the Muslim scholar and leader?[50]

But few of them came to the funeral. Zuʿayter attacked the leaders in his articles and became even tougher on them in November 1936. He organised the funeral at Zahrat al-Sharq in Haifa and thousands of Palestinians and others showed up. He also wrote another article for the Islamic university newspaper: *Alzaʾama Alhqqa* [*The True Leaders*]: "It is incorrect to call someone a leader in a country that is soon to be destroyed. The leadership consists of *jihad* – freedom fighters – and death. Thus from today our Mujahiden are the leaders".[51]

It was a very stressful time for Palestinian society, engaged in fighting the British and attempting to halt Jewish immigration to Palestine. Yet most of the journalists began criticizing the leaders and telling them what to do.[52] Zuʿayter was the architect of this organisation and the architect of the 1936 protest. The organisation gave a good example in Palestine and many other Arab countries. However, all this activity aroused the British authorities, and Zuʿayter was once again arrested, this time for six months. He was the first educated Palestinian to be incarcerated and remained in prison from June to November 1936. Soon after his release from prison he emigrated to Beirut and Damascus, where he operated as a member of the *jihad* committee.

Shortly after the end of the revolt in Palestine, he moved to Baghdad, where he joined the revolution of ʿAali al-Kilani. He became responsible for documenting and writing. When this revolution failed, he emigrated to Turkey to begin a new life, confirming his loyalty to the Arab world.

Conclusion

Zuʿayter understood the nature and complexity of identity formulation and affiliation in his earliest childhood years. He prepared himself to assist people in identifying their affiliation. In his writings in the press, his books and speeches, he found a successful way of conveying his ideology. He also continued to serve this ideology and not surprisingly, in the 1920s, within a short period of time, Zuʿayter became a well-known public figure, with an ability to influence others. He became known as a 'Leader of the Youth'.

As a result, he began receiving formal invitations from different parties to deliver speeches. He also became known as a major journalist with the ability to influence Palestinian public opinion. He wrote for *al-Yarmouk* in Haifa from 1929 until 1948, including the period of the 1936–39 strike and revolt, when he wrote for five different newspapers.

Within a very short time Zu'ayter was recognised as an intellectual and educated Palestinian. His subjectivity, nationalism and phraseology forged his place as the creator of Arab nationalism, not only at the Palestinian level, but also at the Pan-Arab level as well. He conveyed his ideology mostly to the student community and the politicians.

Zu'ayter was obliged to sacrifice everything to ensure the delivery of his ideology. He was forced to leave the educational system in 1929, eventually becoming a refugee. Despite all the challenges and difficulties he encountered, Zu'ayter was never a fundamentalist or a fanatic. Zu'ayter was always able to communicate effectively and to support his ideology pragmatically, rather than emotionally.

His efforts in the field enabled him to become a journalist, educator and politician in Palestine, Jordan and Iraq throughout the twentieth century. In his last two decades he became a documentary producer and publisher.

Notes

1 Mustafa Kabha, *The Palestinian People seeking Sovereignty and State*, Boulder, CO/London: Lynne Rienner Publishers, 2013, pp. 3–14.
2 See Baruch Kimberling and Joel Migdal, *Palestinim, 'Am Behivazruto* [Palestinians: The Making of a People], Jerusalem: Keter, 1998.
3 That is, the Palestinian national movement developed in resistance to Ottoman rule, and was headed for eighty years by Dahir al-'Umar and his sons. The Palestinian National Information Center, www.pnic.gov.ps
4 On the role of the press in the formation of a national consciousness in this period, see Mustafa Kabha, *Writing up a Storm – The Palestinian Press Shaping Public Opinion*, London: Vallentine Mitchell, 2007, pp. 9–12.
5 Rashid Khalidi, *Palestinian Identity: The Construction of Modern National Consciousness*, New York: Columbia University Press, 1997.
6 Akram Zu'aytir, *Watha'iq al-Haraka al-Wataniyya al-Filastiniyya, Min Awraq Akram Zu'aytir* [Documents of the Palestinian National Movement: From the Papers of Akram Zu'aytir], Beirut: Mu'assat al-Dirasat al-Filustiniyya,1979.
7 Husayn Rawhi, *Al-Mukhtasar fi Gughrafiyyat Filastin* [Concise Geography of Palestine], Jerusalem: L.J.S Printing Press, 1923.
8 Khalil Al-Sakakini, *Filastin Ba'd al-Harb al-'Uthma* [Palestine After the Great War], Jerusalem: Matba'at Dar al-Aytam, 1920.
9 Umar al- Salih Al-Barghouti and Khalil Tawtah, *Tarih Filastin* [A History of Palestine], Jerusalem: Makatbat al-Thaqafa, 1925.
10 Ibid., pp. 5–9.
11 The congress was part of the General Syrian Congress; it acquired its new name as the concept of 'Greater Syria' was replaced gradually by 'Palestine for the Palestinians'.
12 Bashara Domani, Rediscovering Palestine: The People of the Mountain of Nablus – 1700–1900, in *Episodes of the Palestinian Cities* (3), Beirut: Palestinian Studies Institution, 1998.

13 Muhammad 'Urabi Nakhla, *The Mechanism of Palestinian Society*, Kuwait: Linkwork Publications, 1882, pp. 187–95.
14 Muhammad 'Izzat Darwaza, *Muzakkarat, 1884–1987* [Diary] vol. 1, Beirut: The Western Islamic House, 1993, p. 522.
15 Akram Zu'ayter, *Bawaker Al-nedal* [Zu'ayter's Diary], 1909–35, Beirut: The Arabic Institution for Research and Publication, 1994, p. 7.
16 Ibid., p. 8.
17 Ibid., p. 9.
18 Sariy Zu'ayter, (ed.), *The Memory of Akram Zua'yter, the Loyal Memorial of the Nation*, Amman: 1997, p. 3.
19 Zu'ayter, *Bawaker Al-nedal*, pp. 12–13.
20 Ibid., pp. 15–16.
21 Ibid., p. 16.
22 Ibid., p. 21.
23 Ibid.
24 Report in CO 733/315, British National Archives, (NA)
25 Mustafa Kabaha, *Tahta 'Ayn al-Raqeeb*, al-Sihafa al-Filastiniyya wa dawroha fi al-Kifah al-Watani bayna al-Harbayn al-'Alamiyatayn [under the eyes of the Censor, the Palestinian press in the National Movement between the Two World Wars] Beit Berl College, Israel: The Center of Arabic Literature, 2004.
26 Zu'ayter, *Bawaker Al-nedal*, p. 35.
27 *Al-yarmouk* newspaper, 22 October, 1929.
28 Ami Ayalon, *The Press in the Arab Middle East, A History*, Oxford/New York: Oxford University Press, 1995, pp. 95–100.
29 Kabha, *Tahtai Ein Alraqeb*, p, 72.
30 *Mir'at al-Sharq*, 7 January 1930.
31 Ibid., 5 February 1930.
32 Ibid., 19 February 1930.
33 Ibid., 30 March 1930.
34 Ibid., 5 April 1930.
35 Zu'ayter, *Bawaker Al-nedal*, p. 139.
36 Ibid.
37 Ibid., p. 268.
38 *al-Hayat*, 15 June 1931.
39 Ibid., 30 June 1931.
40 Ibid., 28 August 1931.
41 Zu'ayter, *Bawaker Al-nedal*, p. 335.
42 Ibid., p. 336.
43 Ibid., p. 361.
44 Ibid., pp. 385–6.
45 *al-Jami'a al-'Arabiyya*, 9 September 1932.
46 Zu'ayter, *Bawaker Al-nedal*, p. 590.
47 Ibid., p. 591.
48 Zu'ayter's diary, p. 3.
49 Zu'ayter, *al-Haraka al-wataniyya*, p. 5.
50 Ibid., pp. 7–8.
51 *al-Jami'a al-'Arabiyya*, 20 November 1935.
52 Zu'ayter, *al-Haraka al-wataniyya*, 10 January 1936.

5 The Palestinian political parties and local self-governance during the British Mandate

Democracy and the clan

Rami Zeedan

This chapter discusses the various election cycles that the Palestinian Arabs went through during the period, and their effect on the formation of the Palestinian political parties, both at the national, and the local government levels. During this period, many Palestinian political institutions were formed: the Supreme Muslim Council, the Arab Higher Committee, Arab local councils and political parties.

The relatively short period of 30 years of the British Mandate over Palestine was fraught with massive changes.[1] The mandate determined the Palestinian territory as we know it in modern history.[2] This contributed, along with the national awakening in the region, among other societal changes, to the establishment of Palestinian Arab society.[3] At the same time, the *Yishuv* was absorbing massive Jewish immigration, establishing new settlements, and establishing the political structure for the future state.[4] The Ottoman Millet System was modestly changed by the British, in the form of the Religious Communities Ordinance of 1926.[5] As a result, each resident of the mandate was associated with a specific millet.[6] Thus, religious authority became the only kind of political leadership formally recognised by the government of the mandate. As such, the social structure remained segregate along religious and kinship lines, while setting the stage for sectarian politics.[7]

The Palestine mandate is considered a critical period for the emergence of Palestinian nationalism. The period highlights the formation of many Palestinian institutions, such as the Supreme Muslim Council, the Arab Higher Committee, Arab municipal councils, and political parties. During this period there was only one, unsuccessful election attempt, for a Legislative Council in 1923, and three municipal election cycles – in 1927, 1934, and 1946/47. This chapter focuses on local Arab self-governance during the period, political rivalry at the national level, and the competition between clans.

Arab-Palestinian leadership at the national level

Palestinian political parties and organisations were developing as early as 1918, such as the Arab Literary Club and the Executive Committee for Opposition.[8] The most important were the Muslim Christian Associations

(MCA).[9] Within a few years, branches were established in many Palestinian cities. The MCA formed the Palestinian Arab Congress as a national body; but its leadership was based mainly on members of wealthy families, land-owners, notables, and religious leaders. Musa Kazim Husseini was the head of the Executive Committee of the Palestinian Arab Congress from 1922 until 1934.[10] In the seventh and last Congress, held in Jerusalem in 1928, the Congress elected 48 members to its Executive Committee. These represented all the towns, districts and religions.[11]

The most important decision taken by the Palestinian Arab Congress was to boycott the 1923 elections to the Legislative Council.[12] The reason for the boycott was the under-representation of Arabs in the council proposed by the 1922 White Paper.[13] This was the result of the decision to include British appointed officials in addition to the 12 elected representatives.[14] As a result, only 107 Muslim secondary electors were elected out of 670 seats, only 19 Christians out of 59, and only eight Druze out of 15, while among the Jews – 79 out of 79 were elected.[15]

The almost-complete Arab boycott of the elections prompted a protest in the House of Lords against the government's support for Zionism. Lord Islington, a veteran opponent of Zionism, protested that the whole Arab electorate had refrained from voting, "in protest against the new Constitu-tion", as laid down in the recent White Paper. This, he protested, was "a definite violation of the pledge made by Great Britain to the Arab commu-nity", which had had an unfortunate affect "upon the whole Arab and Moslem world". The Colonial Secretary conceded that the result was dis-appointing, but did not agree that "the whole electorate" had refrained from voting.[16] However, the Lords' protest was political, against the government's policy in Palestine. It was never followed by any British campaign for the civic rights of the Palestinian Arabs. The Legislative Council election results were declared void, and an advisory council appointed in its stead.[17] In 1935, Sir Arthur Wauchope, the British High Commissioner, renewed the proposal to set up a Legislative Council – but in March 1936, the project was defeated in parliament, largely due to the efforts of a Zionist lobby.[18] The elections of 1923 were the only ones held in mandatory Palestine.

During the 1920s, Haj Amin al-Husseini established his leadership. He was appointed by the British to the role of the Grand Mufti of Jerusalem in 1921, and in 1922, as the president of the Supreme Muslim Council.[19] Four others were also elected: Sheikh Muhamad Murad-the Mufti of Haifa, Abdel-Latif Salah from Tulkarem, Said al-Shawa from Gaza, and Abdullah al-Dajani from Jaffa.[20] The 1929 riots marked the beginning of the reign of Haj Amin al-Husseini as the dominant leader among the Palestinians.[21] His main rival was Raghib Nashashibi, the mayor of Jerusalem from 1920 to 1934. This rivalry between them was at the top of the Palestinian political divide between the "Supporters" of Husseini [*Majlisiyeen*], and his "Opponents" [*al-Mu'arada*], most of whom were supporters of the Nashashibis.[22] This represented the state of affairs of the Arab leadership at the time – traditional rivalries among the leading families that helped to form an aristocracy that comprised mainly Muslim landowners, the wealthy, and the well-educated.[23] These leaders assumed pre-eminence during Ottoman times and they or their descendants continued their control over the organised religious, political, and social life of the Arab community during the mandatory period.[24]

During the 1920s, several Arab parties were established with support from the British, mainly to help counter the leadership of the Husseinis. The Arab National party was established in Jaffa in 1923. Among its founders was Fakhri Nashashibi. The Palestinian People 's Party was established in 1925 in Nablus, led by Adel Zuaiter and Abdul Latif Salah. The Agricultural Party was founded in al-Dawayima in 1923. These three parties failed to mobilise any significant popular support, and they ceased their activities within a relatively short period. Following the political division among the opposition, the Palestinian Free Party was established in Jaffa in 1927.

During the first years of the mandate, the Palestinian Arabs supported King Faisal, and a Pan Arabism that envisioned Palestine as part of a Greater Syria.[25] However, they abandoned the idea after Faisal's defeat by the French in July 1920. The 1929 riots are considered to be a turning point in the conflict over Palestine.[26] It was seen as the culmination of the shift towards local, Palestinian Arab nationalism – that began with Faisal's defeat in 1920.[27] In any case, there were still parties that called for pan-Arabism or pan-Islamism – such as the Arab Nationalist Bloc, which was established in 1929, and the Muslim Youth Organization, which was established in Nablus in 1930.

The death of Musa Kazim Husseini in 1934 and the failure to agree on a permanent chairperson, resulted in the cessation of the operations of the executive committee of the Palestinian Arab Congress.[28] It opened the opportunity for Haj Amin to take over the leadership of the Palestinians officially, after he had established his leadership internally among Muslim Palestinians, and internationally among Arabs and Muslims.[29] Raghib Nashashibi was defeated in the Jerusalem mayoralty elections of 1934 by a candidate supported by Haj Amin. This further widened the Nashashibi–Husseini divide and was the background for the establishment of new political parties in the 1930s, which again represented the interests of particular families and individuals.[30]

The two main parties were the "Husseini party" and the "Nashashibi party". The Palestinian Arab Party was established in 1935 by Jamal Husseini, influenced by Haj Amin. This consolidated the power of the Husseini clan and their supporters.[31] The National Defense Party was established in Jaffa in 1934 by Raghib Nashashibi, which did likewise for the Nashashibi clan and their supporters. It was founded after Raghib Nashashibi lost his re-election campaign for the Jerusalem mayoralty. The National Defense Party was considered as a continuation of early efforts by the British to help Arab parties that opposed the Husseinis.[32]

Two other parties were formed that were not attached directly either to the Nashashibis or the Husseinis. The Independence Party of Palestine was established in Jerusalem in 1932 by Muhammad Izzat Darwaza and other supporters of pan-Arabism, who had worked previously with King Faisal.[33] The party did not gain much popular support and was not based on any prominent Palestinian clan. However, it did gather support among the middle-class. In 1935, a small group was formed in Haifa, the Palestine Youth Congress, which was generally regarded as Husseini supporters.[34] Among its founders was Yaqub al-Ghussein. Two additional, smaller parties operated for short periods only. The Arab Reform Party was established in Jerusalem in 1935 by Hussein Khalidi, the mayor of Jerusalem from 1934 to 1937.[35] The party's supporters were mainly from Jerusalem and Ramallah. It was associated with the Husseinis. The National Bloc Party that was established in Nablus in 1935, was associated with Nashashibis.

These developments in the Palestinian leadership in the 1930s continued the political rivalry between the Nashashibis and the Husseinis. However, they also added a new political rivalry between the traditional leadership and the growing, well-educated, urban-based leadership. Thus, it is not surprising that these new groups emerged mainly in big cities, such as Jerusalem, Jaffa, Nablus, and Haifa.

The 1936–1939 Arab revolt was the ideological and political implementation of Palestinian national demands when all the Palestinian political leaders joined forces.[36] It is believed that Arab anger, following the manhunt and killing of Sheikh Izzedin al-Qassam, a member of the Supreme Muslim Council, triggered the series of events that led to the beginning of the revolt.[37] In the beginning, Palestinian unity was established, by forming the Arab Higher Committee (HAC), in April 1936.[38] The Committee brought together all Palestinian political organisations and parties.[39] Haj Amin was its chairman. The HAC replaced the Executive Committee, following a gap of two years without any Palestinian organisation leading at the national level.[40]

In contrast to the Executive Committee, the HAC did not comprise an elected leadership. Its 12 members were from the Palestinian elite, representing the six parties that existed at the time – the Youth Congress, the Arab Independence Party, the National Defense Party, the Palestinian Arab Party, the National Bloc Party, and the Reform Party.[41] It included Muslim Arabs as well as Christian Arabs, such as Ya'qub Farraj, an Arab Orthodox, who was a representative of the National Defense Party.[42] The massive Arab support in the demonstrations, as part of the Arab revolt, showed that the Arab Higher Committee enjoyed considerable popular support.[43]

During the second phase of the revolt, from summer 1937, Palestinian unity was lost, when the rivalry between the Nashashibis and the Husseinis turned violent. Haj Amin wanted to continue the fight against the British, while Raghib Nashashibi claimed that through negotiations with the British they could achieve more for the Palestinian cause. Despite being declared illegal by the British, the HAC managed to continue until 1939 when it ceased operations.[44] By the end of the revolt, supporters and opponents were fighting each other.[45]

During the stagnation period from 1939 to 1945, due to the Second World War, there was no clearly recognised Palestinian national leadership.[46] In the meantime, there arose another wave of Palestinian political parties. In 1944, the Palestinian Communist party – previously Jewish dominated, in the 1920s-1930s – split up and an Arab-led communist party was established.[47] Their efforts resulted in the formation of the National Liberation League.[48] Among its founders was Emile Habibi, Emile Touma, and Moussa al-Dajani. In 1946, the Muslim Brotherhood of Palestine was established. Among its founders were Shaykh As'ad al-Imam, Muhammad al-Amad, and Shaykh 'Abd al-Bari Barakat. In addition, semi-military groups were established, such as al-Najjada, which was established in Jaffa by Muhammad Nimr al-Hawari.[49]

However, these new organisations proved unable to lead the Palestinian cause. The involvement of the Arab league in 1946 sponsored the establishment of the Second HAC, support by the Palestinian parties.[50] Once again Haj Amin took control, while his supporters and the Palestinian Arab Party dominated its leadership.

Local governance in British Mandatory Palestine

Until the mid-nineteenth century, the Ottoman Empire was based mainly on a centralised government.[51] It also included sub-divisions that were controlled by Ottoman officials.[52] In the 19th Century, the Ottomans reorganised their administration. The Ottoman Vilayet Law (1864), laid the foundation for local government in rural areas by appointing *Mukhtars* as village chiefs.[53] The Municipalities Ordinance (1877) provided the legal framework for local municipalities in urban communities as differentiated from rural ones.[54] Based on this legislation, by the end of the Ottoman rule over Palestine there were 22 recognised municipalities.[55] These Ottoman administrative structures in Palestine helped maintain the segregated social structures that were based on social groups organised by religious sectarianism and kinship while leaving no place for political change and new leadership that was not based on the notables.[56] The elite of notable families dominated society, economically, by continued ownership of lands, and politically, by dominating Muslim religious bureaucracy, and local administration in the form of *Mukhtars* and council members.[57]

From 1918 to 1920, the British military administration in Palestine mainly maintained the status quo without changing the Ottoman laws that were in effect until the end of the First World War.[58] The administrative structure of districts and sub-districts was changed; however, the local government structure remained the same.[59] Except for a few, those Mayors holding appointments from the Ottoman period were allowed to continue in their positions.[60]

In the first years of the mandate, 65% of the total population of 757,000 was agrarian, living in villages or tribal areas.[61] Those living in municipalities were spread in the 22 municipalities recognised by the Ottomans (out of a total of 1,026 localities). This included 20 Arab or Arab-majority municipalities, as well as Jerusalem and Tiberias, the only mixed cities with a Jewish majority.

With the transition to a British civilian administration in 1920, the British government announced its intention to advance local self-government in the country.[62] The Local Councils Ordinance of 1921, which was intended for rural areas (amended in 1941) and the Municipal Corporations Ordinance of 1934, were designed to lay the ground for a structured local self-governance in Palestine.[63] This legislation allowed the British to recognise some cities, regional councils, local councils, and *Mukhtars.*

The Municipalities Ordinance of 1877 remained in effect until the Municipal Corporations Ordinance of 1934 was enacted. The High Commissioner appointed mayors and council members who represented the leading families. For example, in Safed, the British appointed four mayors during the period 1918 to 1926.[64]

1927: The first local elections

The Local Councils Ordinance of 1921 set the regulations for local elections, including the requirement of residency and payment of taxes for eligibility to vote.[65] As a result, in most municipalities, only men who were heads of a household and owned property were eligible. The Municipal Franchise Ordinance of 1926 detailed further the requirements of local elections.[66] Eligible voters were men, older than 25 years, Palestinian citizens, not disabled, without a criminal record, the owner of a property within the municipal area who had paid the minimum property or municipal taxes.[67] The right to be elected was given to male citizens above the age of 30, who had paid taxes at a higher rate than the minimum required for the right to vote.[68]

The first municipal elections in mandatory Palestine were held in 1927 in all the recognised municipalities (Table 5.1). Only in Gaza were the election results not approved, due to complaints of improper management.[69] In these elections, the number of eligible voters was not reported for all municipalities. However, for those municipalities where information is available, it is clear that only a minority of the residents were eligible to vote, ranging between 3.3% to 6.5%, out of the total. Nonetheless, the government claimed enthusiastically that the "newly-elected Municipal Councils are fully representative of the constituencies".[70]

In many of these elections, such as in Jerusalem, Haifa, Jaffa, Hebron, Gaza, and other municipalities in the north, the competition was between Husseinis and their supporters and the opposition led by the Nashashibis.[71] This helped establish centres of opposition in these municipalities.[72] The 1927 elections ended with victories for the opposition. In Jerusalem, Haifa, Jaffa, and Safed the opposition's victory was facilitated by the help of the Jewish voters.[73] In Arab cities without any Jewish residents, supporters of the Husseini camp won the elections, i.e. in Jenin, Tulkarem, Lydda, Hebron, Bethlehem, Ramallah, Majdal, Gaza, Beersheba, and Beisan.[74]

Elections in other villages were not systematically reported by the British, as was the case in the 22 municipalities. One report of such elections in Qalqilya, states that none were held. Instead, "each *hamouleh* nominated two members, the last nomination and appointment being in July of 1927".[75] In the case of

Qalqilya, no elections were held during the entire course of the mandate.[76] Although more evidence is required, this might shed light on the situation in other villages. The leadership of the notables was maintained, and clans and extended families still controlled the political structure.

1934: The second local elections

As of 1931, 62% of the Palestine population of more than one million was agrarian, living in villages or tribal areas[77] – a small decrease from 65% in 1922. Besides formal definitions of rural and urban, most of these muni-cipalities were not yet in fact of urban character, except four cities: Jer-usalem, Jaffa, Tel-Aviv, and Haifa.[78] The other municipalities were described by the British as "...convenient centres for the marketing of rural products, or as large villages".[79] Palestinian society was seen by the British as quasi-feudal.[80] In any case, the local government structure included only 23 recognised municipalities. Thirty-eight villages were recognised to have local councils, out of which 11 were Arab villages. This was a minority compared to the 1,072 localities that did not have a municipality or a local council.

The next election cycle after 1927 was scheduled for 1930; however, due to the 1929 riots, elections were postponed until 1934.[81] The British feared that Hus-seini's supporters might gain more power following the impact of the 1929 riots and the withdrawal of the 1930 White Paper.[82] Most council members and mayors were permitted to continue in their positions. The Municipal Corpora-tions Ordinance of 1934 replaced the Ottoman Municipalities Ordinance of 1877. Elections were held in all the municipalities following the new legislation. The new legislation gave the right to vote to male residents of Palestine, aged 25 or over, who had paid municipal taxes of at least 1 Mil per year.[83] The right to be elected was given to those male residents, aged 30 or above, who had paid municipal taxes of at least 3 Mil per year.[84] The High Commissioner appointed from the newly elected council members a mayor and a deputy mayor. However, in contrast to previous legislation, this time the High Commissioner could appoint a council member as mayor, regardless of the actual results, or which council member received more votes.

As shown in Table 5.2, formal elections were held in 14 municipalities, while in the remaining seven municipalities no elections were held, because the number of candidates equalled the number of vacancies. Therefore, the candidates were appointed by the High Commissioner. In any case, a UN report states that as of 1935 there were 22 elected municipal councils in mandatory Palestine, without mentioning the different methods of "election".[85]

This time, in contrast to 1927, the Husseinis were victorious. The Nasha-shibis and their supporters lost Jerusalem, while the Husseinis and their sup-porters won a majority of council seats in Jenin, Nablus, Ramallah, Bethlehem, Hebron, and Gaza.[86] However, the High Commissioner still appointed mayors who were council members that supported the Nashashibis.

Opposition mayors were also elected in Gaza, Jenin, Nazareth, Lydda, Ramleh, Safed, and Hebron[87] In other municipalities, the opposition did not win any seats. Having no other legal choice, the High Commissioner appointed mayors who were from the Husseini camp.[88] For example, in Acre, Majdal, Tulkarem, Beisan, Jericho, and Beersheba.

In the 1934 elections, like the 1927 elections, the number of eligible voters was not reported for all municipalities. However, as shown in Table 5.2, for those municipalities where information is available, it is clear that, once again, only a minority of residents – between 2.7% to 9.1% – were eligible to vote, except for Beersheba with 26.2%.

1946: The third local elections

According to the Municipal Corporations Ordinance of 1934, local elections were scheduled for every five years.[89] Thus the next election cycle after 1934 was scheduled for 1939. However, elections were postponed until after the Second World War, due to security concerns.[90] Some council members and mayors were dismissed by the British, in a move that was seen as punishment following the 1936–39 Arab revolt. As a result, in 1939 eight Arab municipalities were managed by appointed commissions, not by an elected leadership. By 1945, some Arab and mixed municipalities were also managed by appointed commissions, including Jerusalem, Haifa, Tiberias, and Gaza.

As shown in Table 5.3, local elections were held in 1946 in 16 out of 22 municipalities.[91] In seven municipalities, the same mayor that had been elected in 1934 was re-elected. One was reappointed with no elections. In total, 14 new mayors were appointed following the results of the 1946 elections. The Husseini-Nashashibi rivalry ended this time with more gains for the opposition camp, as in 1927, and in contrast to 1934. Again, as in 1934, the High Commissioner appointed mayors who were council members that support the opposition, as in Jenin, Nablus, Bethlehem, Hebron, and Gaza.

In this election cycle, there is more information on the number of eligible voters. In some municipalities, there was a modest improvement in the number of eligible voters. The average percentage of residents that were eligible to vote was for the first time 10%, while Haifa (20.2%) and Jaffa (21.2%) enjoyed the highest percentages.

Conclusions

There was a minimal degree of Arab local governance during the mandate. A municipality or a local council existed only in less than 5% of about 1,000 Arab localities. Therefore, the vast majority of Arab localities were operated by the traditional local leadership. The Peel Royal Commission (1936–37) noted that the mandate had helped the *Yishuv* establish local self-government; however, it had failed to encourage the same pattern among the Arabs.[92]

Local politics were controlled mainly by clan-politics, which was also the case in many municipalities and local councils. They were aligned to the nation-level rivalry between the Nashashibis and Husseinis. Some accuse the British of staging the political divide among the Palestinians.[93] Further, British legislation did not encourage the Arabs to support the establishment of elected local councils in their villages. The number of eligible voters remained very low, due to the restrictions of gender, age and high taxation. This resulted in the perpetuation of a leadership based on notables, clan leaders, extended families and religious leaders. In that sense, local Arab self-government continued the same pattern of the Ottoman Mukhtar – a tool that served mainly the central government.[94]

Arab local self-government was too dependent on the High Commissioner's rule. Most of the critical positions in the municipalities were appointed by him: mayors and deputy mayors, treasurers, sanitary inspectors, doctors and veterinarians. The High Commissioner also supervised the municipalities' budgets. The Municipal Corporations Ordinance of 1934 gave the district governor the authority to supervise the budgets of the municipalities, its activities, and also to dismiss council members and replace them with appointed officials. In addition, the legislation provided the district governor with more flexibility in appointing a mayor. For that reason, some mayors were merely representatives of the mandate government more than representatives of their people.

Elections were not held regularly. Local elections were held only in three elections cycles – in 1927, 1934 and 1946. In addition, they were held in only a small portion of the municipalities. In most of these elections, candidate represented clans, or clan-alliances, not political parties. In many of the municipalities, only a list of pre-agreed lists of candidates was submitted. This forced the cancellation of many elections and the acceptance of the candidates as the elected representatives. Thus, most Palestinians were not involved in voting and did not experience the process of electing local representatives.

Members of the local councils and mayors came from wealthy families. Despite the limited extent of their independence, the municipalities were the arena of competition between the families of the urban elite, mainly because of the prestige of the public office and the possibility of influencing the appointment of officials. For example, the Jerusalem municipality was established in 1864; until 1920, there were 17 different appointed mayors, of which seven were members of the Husseini clan.[95]

Previous research states that the Palestinian leadership at the national level was selected in different patterns. In the first stage, the leadership was elected; in the second, it was the result of a party coalition, and in the third, it was appointed.[96] In this study, we conclude that this was different at the local level during the mandate. During the entire period, most of the local Arab leadership was appointed in the form of village *Mukhtar*s and local councils. Only in less than 20 Arab and mixed municipalities, and not during all of this period, were Arab leaders at the local level elected. British conceptions of democracy were for home consumption only, never exported to the colonies.

Table 5.1 1927: Local elections in Arab and mixed cities

District	Sub-district	Munici-palities	Election day	Population (as of 1922[97])	Eligible voters[98]	Percentage of eligible voters	Elected Mayor[99]
Southern	Gaza	Gaza	8–9 April 1927	17,480	N/A	N/A	Elections results cancelLed
		Khan Yunes	6 April 1927	3,890	N/A	N/A	Haj Salim Effendi Hussain Jaser al-Agha
		Majdal	7 April 1927	5,064	N/A	N/A	Taj-Eddin Sha'th
	Beersheba	Beersheba	12 April 1927	2,356	N/A	N/A	Taju effendi Sha't
	Jaffa	Jaffa	27–29 May 1927	47,709	2,713	5.6%	Assem Bey al-Said
	Ramleh	Ramleh	2 May 1927	7,312	N/A	N/A	Sheikh Mustafa al-Khairi
		Lydda	26 April 1927	8,103	N/A	N/A	Ahmed Effendi Husseini
Jerusalem	Jerusalem	Jerusalem	5–7 April 1927	62,578	2,055	3.3%	Raghib Nashashibi
	Hebron	Hebron	13–14 April 1927	16,577	N/A	N/A	Sheikh Mukhlis Hammuri
	Ramallah	Ramallah	24 March 1927	3,104	N/A	N/A	Musa Effendi Khalil Musa
	Bethlehem	Bethlehem	27 March 1927	6,658	N/A	N/A	Nicolas Attalah Effendi Shahin
		Beit Jala	27 March 1927	3,101	N/A	N/A	Jiries Effendi Juma Abu Awad
Northern	Nablus	Nablus	7 April 1927	15,947	N/A	N/A	Suleiman Bey Abdel Razak Tukan
	Jenin	Jenin	31 March 1927	2,637	N/A	N/A	Aref Effendi Abdulrahman

Tulkarem	Tulkarem	13 April 1927	3,350	N/A	N/A	Abdulrahman Effendi al-Haj Ibrahim
Baisan	Baisan	30 March 1927	1,941	N/A	N/A	Haj Mahmud Effendi Abdullah el-Safadi
Haifa	Haifa	16–18 May 1927	24,684	N/A	N/A	Hassan Bey Shukri
	Shafa 'Amr	*	2,288	N/A	N/A	Da'ud Sulaiman Talhami
Acre	Acre	11 April 1927	6,420	N/A	N/A	Abdul Fatah el-Sa'adi
Nazareth	Nazareth	9 April 1927	7,424	N/A	N/A	Selim Effendi Bishara
Tiberias	Tiberias	26 April 1927	6,950	452	6.5%	Zaki Haddef
Safad	Safad	12 April 1927	8,761	329	3.8%	Mohamed Effendi Hasan Abd al-Rahman

* No official information was found regarding the elections in Shafa 'Amr and Jericho.

Table 5.2 1934: Local elections in Arab and mixed cities

District	Sub-district	Municipalities	Election day	Population (as of 1931)[100]	Eligible voters[101]	Percentage of eligible voters	Elected Mayor[102]
Southern	Gaza	Gaza	26 June 1934	17,046	840	4.9%	Fahmi Effendi Husseini
		Khan Yunes	23 November 1935	N/A	N/A	N/A	Al-Saidi Abdul Rahman Mohammed el-Farra
		Majdal	9 June 1934	6,226	170	2.7%	Yusef Nijim
	Beersheba	Beersheba	7 June 1934	2,959	775	26.2%	Taj-Eddin Sha'th
	Jaffa	Jaffa	7 July 1934	N/A	N/A	N/A	Assem Bey al-Said
	Ramleh	Ramleh	9 July 1934	N/A	N/A	N/A	Sheikh Mustafa al-Khairi
		Lydda	-*	-	-	-	Ahmed Effendi Husseini
Jerusalem	Jerusalem	Jerusalem	26 September 1934**	90,503	3,650	4.0%	Dr. Hussein Fakhri Effendi al-Khalidi
	Hebron	Hebron	5–6 July 1934	N/A	N/A	N/A	Sheikh Mukhlis Effendi Hammuri
	Ramallah	Ramallah	-*	N/A	N/A	N/A	Dr. Saadallah Qassis
	Bethlehem	Bethlehem	-*	6,815	331	4.9%	Issa Effendi al-Bandak
		Beit Jala	5 April 1934	N/A	N/A	N/A	Andria Mansour
Northern	Nablus	Nablus	-*	17,189	747	4.3%	Suleiman Bey Abdel Razak Tukan
	Jenin	Jenin	8 August 1934	2,706	163	6.0%	Fahmi Effendi 'Aabushi
	Tulkarem	Tulkarem	12 August 1934	N/A	N/A	N/A	Abdulrahman Effendi al-Haj Ibrahim

Baisan	Baisan	13 August 1934	N/A	N/A	N/A	Muhammad Sa'id Effendi Halbuni
Haifa	Haifa	-**	-	-	-	Hassan Bey Shukri
	Shafa 'Amr	-				Jabbour Yousef Jabbour
Acre	Acre	9 October 1934	7,897	718	9.1%	Husni Effindi Muhammad Khalifa
Nazareth	Nazareth	28 July 1934	8,756	458	5.2%	Selim Effendi Bishara
Tiberias	Tiberias	-*	-	-	-	Zaki Haddef
Safad	Safad	26 July 1934	9,441	510	5.4%	Salah Effendi 'Ezz al-Din Qaddura

* No elections were held in these municipalities – Bethlehem, Ramallah, Lydda, Nablus, and Tiberias.[103] The reason is that the number of candidates submitted equalled the number of vacancies.

** No elections were held in most of the divisions in Jerusalem and Haifa for the same reason.[104] No official information was found regarding Jericho.

Table 5.3 1946: Local elections in Arab and mixed cities

District	Sub-district	Munici-palities	Election day[105]	Population (as of 1945)[106]	Eligible voters[107]	Percentage of eligible voters	Elected Mayor[108]
Gaza	Gaza	Gaza	4 February 1946	34,170	1,622	4.7%	Rushdi Effendi al-Shawa
		Khan Yunes	8 September 1946	11,220	450	4.0%	Al-Saidi Abdul Rahman Mohammed el-Farra
		Majdal	6 May 1946	9,910	329	3.3%	Al-Sayyid Abu-Sharkh
Lydde	Jaffa	Jaffa	28 April 1947	94,310	20,000	21.2%	Dr. Yousef Heikal
	Ramleh	Ramleh	10 November 1946	15,160	N/A	N/A	Sheikh Mustafa al-Khairi
		Lydda	29 November 1946	16,780	N/A	N/A	Muhammad Effendi al-Kayyaly
Jerusalem	Jerusalem	Jerusalem	*	157,080	26,700	17.0%	-
		Bethlehem	1 April 1946	8,820	590	6.7%	Issa Effendi al-Bandak
		Beit Jala	15 May 1946	3,710	N/A	N/A	Wadi'a Effendi Musa al-Da'amas
	Hebron	Hebron	22 December 1946	24,560	980	4.0%	Sheikh Muhammad 'Ali al-Ja'abari
	Ramallah	Ramallah	15 April 1946	5,080	800	16.0%	Khalil Salah
Samaria	Nablus	Nablus	6 May 1946	23,259	1,619	7.0%	Suleiman Bey Abdel Razak Tukan
	Jenin	Jenin	23 March 1946	3,990	327	8.2%	Hilmi Effendi 'Aabushi
	Tulkarem	Tulkarem	-				Hashim Al Jayousi

Haifa	Haifa	*	138,300	28,000	20.2%	Shabtai Levi
	Shafa 'Amr	-	3,640	N/A	N/A	Jabbour Yousef Jabbour
Galilee	Acre	28 July 1946	12,360	1,341	10.8%	Husni Effindi Muhammad Khalifa
	Baisan	4 March 1946	5,180	N/A	N/A	Ahmad Effendi Abu 'Ali
	Nazareth	19 May 1946	14,200	1,150	8.1%	Selim Effendi Bishara
	Tiberias	*	11,310	1,900	16.8%	Shimon Dahan
	Safad	*	11,930	510	4.3%	Zaki Qaddura
(not affiliated)	Beersheba	27 February 1946	5,570	N/A	N/A	Shafiq Effendi 'Arafat Mushtaha

* Elections in Jerusalem, Haifa, Tiberias, and Safad were last held in 1934. Instead, a commission was appointed.[109]

Notes

1   Roger Owen, *State, Power and Politics in the Making of the Modern Middle East*, London: Routledge, 2013, pp. 5–22.
2   Bernard Lewis, Palestine: On the history and geography of a name, *The International History Review* 2/1, 1980, pp. 1–12.
3   Baruch Kimmerling, *The Palestinian People: A History*, Cambridge: Harvard University Press, 2009, pp. 3–37.
4   Anita Shapira, *Israel: A History*, Lebanon, MA: University Press of New England, 2012, pp. 65–137.
5   Great Britain, Report by His Majesty's Government to the council of the League of Nations on the administration of Palestine and Trans-Jordan for the year 1929, London: His Majesty's Stationery Office (HMSO), 1929.
6   Great Britain, Palestine Order in Council, 1922, London: HMSO, 1922.
7   Ibid.
8   Bayan Nuweihid Al-Hout, The Palestinian political elite during the mandate period, *Journal of Palestine Studies* 9/1, 1979, pp. 85–111.
9   Kimmerling, *The Palestinian People*, pp. 67–101.
10   Hasan Ahmed Naser Mu'tasem, Jerusalem municipality and political conflict: 1918–1942, *International Journal of History and Philosophical Research* 4/1, 2016, pp. 1–15.
11   Al-Hout, The Palestinian political elite, pp. 85–111.
12   Neil Caplan, The Yishuv, Sir Herbert Samuel, and the Arab Question in Palestine, 1921–25, in *Zionism and Arabism in Palestine and Israel*, edited by Sylvia G. Haim and Elie Kedourie, London: Routledge, 2005.
13   Neil Caplan, *Palestine Jewry and the Arab Question, 1917–1925*, London: Routledge, 2012, pp. 107–82.
14   Great Britain, Palestine Order in Council, 1922.
15   Reply by the Duke of Devonshire, the Colonial Secretary, to Lord Islington, House of Lords Debates (H.L.Deb.), 53, 27 March 1923, cols. 658–9.
16   Ibid., cols. 639, 644–6, 658–9.
17   Elie Kedourie, Sir Herbert Samuel and the government of Palestine, *Middle Eastern Studies* 5/1, 1969, pp. 44–68.
18   Michael J Cohen, *Palestine: Retreat from the Mandate, The Making of British policy, 1936–45*, London/New York: Paul Elek, 1978, p. 12.
19   Philip Mattar, *The Mufti of Jerusalem: Al-Hajj Amin al-Husayni and the Palestinian National Movement*, New York: Columbia University Press, 1992, pp. 19–32.
20   Taysir Jabara, Dirasat fi Tarikh Filastin alhadith [Studies in the History of Modern Palestine], Palestine: Hebron University Press, 1980.
21   Ilan Pappe, Haj Amin and the Buraq Revolt, *Jerusalem Quarterly* 18, 2003, pp. 6–16.
22   Jamal Ibrahim, Sirae Alflstynyn Bayn Majlasiiyn waMuearidin bein 1920–1934, waDawr Sulutat Alaintidab fi 'Iitharatiha waTaeziziha (Alaintikhabat Albaladiat Anmwdhjaan) [The Palestinians' conflict between the Supporters (Majlisiyeen) and their Opponents during 1920–1934 and the role of the mandate authorities in stirring and strengthening it (municipal elections as a model)], *Journal of Al-Quds Open University* 36/1, 2014, pp. 181–224.
23   Don Peretz, Palestinian social stratification: the political implications, *Journal of Palestine Studies* 7/1, 1977, pp. 48–74.
24   Ibid.
25   Abbas Kelidar, States without foundations: The political evolution of state and society in the Arab East, *Journal of Contemporary History* 28/2, 1993, pp. 315–39.
26   Hillel Cohen, *Year Zero of the Arab-Israeli Conflict 1929*, Lebanon, MA: Brandeis University Press, 2015, pp. 207–54.
27   Rashid Khalidi, *Palestinian Identity: The Construction of Modern National Consciousness*, New York: Columbia University Press, 2010, pp. 145–76.

28 Zvi Elpeleg, Shmuel Himmelstein, *The Grand Mufti: Haj Amin al-Husseini, Foun-der of the Palestinian National Movement*, London: Routledge, 2012, pp. 29–35.
29 Freas Erik, Hajj Amin al-Husayni and the Haram al-Sharif: A Pan-Islamic or Palestinian Nationalist Cause? *British Journal of Middle Eastern Studies* 39/1, 2012, pp. 19–51.
30 Naser, Jerusalem municipality, pp. 1–15
31 Abboushi Wasef, The road to rebellion: Arab Palestine in the 1930s, *Journal of Palestine Studies* 6/3, 1977, pp. 23–46.
32 Muhammad Muslih, Arab politics and the rise of Palestinian nationalism, *Journal of Palestine Studies* 16/4, 1987, pp. 77–94.
33 Muhammad Muslih, The rise of local nationalism in the Arab East, in *The Origins of Arab Nationalism*, edited by Rashid Khalidi, Lisa Anderson, Muhammad Muslih, and Reeva S. Simon, New York: Columbia University Press, 1991, pp. 167–88.
34 Shmuel Dothan, Attempts at an Arab-Jewish agreement in Palestine during the thirties, *Studies in Zionism* 1/2, 1980, pp. 213–238.
35 Naser, Jerusalem municipality, pp. 1–15.
36 Ted Swedenburg, *Memories of Revolt: The 1936–1939 Rebellion and the Palestinian National Past*, Fayetteville: University of Arkansas Press, 2003, pp. 76–106.
37 Mahmoud Yazbak, From poverty to revolt: economic factors in the outbreak of the 1936 rebellion in Palestine, *Middle Eastern Studies* 36/3, 2000, pp. 93–113.
38 Al-Hout, The Palestinian political elite, pp. 85–111.
39 Martin S. Widzer, Becoming a state: Zionist and Palestinian movements for national liberation, University of Denver, Electronic Theses and Dissertations, 2015, pp. 118–45.
40 Elpeleg and Himelstein, The grand mufti, pp. 29–35.
41 Al-Hout, The Palestinian political elite, pp. 85–111.
42 Laura Robson, Communalism and nationalism in the Mandate: the Greek Orthodox controversy and the national movement, *Journal of Palestine Studies* 41/1, 2011, pp. 6–23.
43 Jacob Norris, Repression and rebellion: Britain's response to the Arab Revolt in Palestine of 1936–39, *The Journal of Imperial and Commonwealth History* 36/1, 2008, pp. 25–45.
44 Thomas Mayer, Arab unity of action and the Palestine question, 1945–48, *Middle Eastern Studies* 22/3, 1986, pp. 331–349.
45 Kanafani Ghassan, *The 1936–39 Revolt in Palestine*, New York: Committee for Democratic Palestine, 1972, pp. 35–60.
46 Al-Hout, The Palestinian political elite, pp. 85–111.
47 Joel Beinen, The Palestine Communist Party 1919–1948, *MERIP Reports* 55, 1977, pp. 3–17.
48 Johan Franzéen, Communism versus Zionism: The Comintern, Yishuvism, and the Palestine Communist Party, *Journal of Palestine Studies* 36/2, 2007, pp. 6–24.
49 Haim Levenberg, *Military Preparations of the Arab Community in Palestine, 1945–1948*, London: Frank Cass, 1993, pp. 126–45.
50 Mayer, Arab unity, pp. 331–49.
51 Farid Al-Salim, *Palestine and the Decline of the Ottoman Empire: Modernization and the Path to Palestinian Statehood*, London: I.B. Tauris, 2015, pp. 1–17.
52 Donald Quataert, *The Ottoman Empire, 1700–1922*, Cambridge: Cambridge University Press, 2005, pp. 90–110.
53 Al-Haj, Henri Rosenfeld, *Arab Local Government in Israel*, Westview, Boulder: Westview Press, 1990, pp. 1–22.
54 Ibid.
55 Rashid Sabri Nidal, Rania Yaser Jaber, Managerial performance of Palestinian local authorities, *Transforming Government: People, Process and Policy* 1/4, 2007, pp. 350–63.

56 Al-Haj, Rosenfeld, Arab local government, pp. 1–22.
57 Beinen, The Palestine Communist Party, pp. 3–17.
58 Gideon Biger, *The Boundaries of Modern Palestine, 1840–1947*, London: Routledge, 2004, pp. 41–79.
59 John J. McTague, The British Military Administration in Palestine 1917–1920, *Journal of Palestine Studies* 7/3, 1978, pp. 55–76.
60 Ylana Miller, *Government and Society in Rural Palestine, 1920–1948*, Austin: University of Texas Press, 1985.
61 J. B. Barron, *Report and General Abstracts of the Census of 1922, 23 October 1922*, Jerusalem: Greek Convent Press, 1923, p. 5.
62 Ibid., pp. 1–4.
63 Government of Palestine, Local Councils Ordinance 1921, Jerusalem: The Palestine Gazette, No. 42, 1 May 1921; Government of Palestine, Municipal Corporations Ordinance 1934 Notices, No. 1, Jerusalem: The Palestine Gazette, No. 414, 12 January 1934, Supp. 1, p. 1.
64 Mustafa Abbasi, Safad fi 'Eahd Alaintidab Albritanii 1917–1948: Dirasah Aijtimaeiah Wasiasiatah [Safed in the British Mandate period 1917–1948: a social and political study], Beirut: Institute for Palestinian Studies, 2005, pp. 45–54. The four were Nayef Sobh, Mohammed Salim Shama, Saeed Mahmoud Murad, and Mohamed Hassan Abd al-Rahman.
65 Great Britain, The Local Councils Ordinance 1921.
66 Government of Palestine, The Municipal Franchise Ordinance 1926, Jerusalem: The Palestine Gazette, 11 October 1926, pp. 528–533.
67 Ibid.
68 Ibid.
69 Government of Palestine, Orders Under the Franchise Ordinance, 1926, Jerusalem: Palestine Gazette, No. 196, 1 October 1927, p. 690.
70 Great Britain, Report by His Majesty's Government to the Council of the League of Nations on the administration of Palestine and Trans-Jordan for the year 1927, London: HMSO, 1927.
71 Elyakim Rubinstein, Yehudim Ve-aravim Be'retz Yisrail (1926–1933) Yerushalaim V'Arim Acherot [Jews and Arabs in the Municipalities of Eretz Israel (1926–1933) Jerusalem and other cities], *Katedra* 51, 1989, pp. 122–47.
72 Peretz, Palestinian social stratification, pp. 48–74.
73 Ibrahim, The Palestinians' conflict, pp. 181–224.
74 Ibid.
75 Government of Palestine, Letter from the District Commissioner of Samaria to the Chief Secretary of the Government of Palestine on "Municipal and Local Council Elections", Jerusalem, 3 December 1947, File:" Elections to Municipal and local Councils", Israel State Archive (ISA)- G-41-47.
76 Ibid.
77 Eric Mills, *Census of Palestine: Population of Villages, Towns and Administrative Areas*, Jerusalem: Greek Convent & Goldberg Presses, 1932.
78 Eric Mills, Census of Palestine 1931, Alexandria: Government of Palestine, Volume I, Palestine Part I, Report, 1933, p. 12.
79 Ibid.
80 Peretz, Palestinian social stratification, pp. 48–74.
81 Ibrahim, The Palestinians' conflict, pp. 181–224.
82 Ibid.
83 Government of Palestine, Municipal Corporations Ordinance No. 1 1934.
84 Ibid.
85 United Nations Special Committee on Palestine, Report to the General Assembly: Official records of the second session of the general assembly, Lake Success: United Nations Special Committee on Palestine, Supplement no. 11, Vol. 1, 1947.

86   Ibrahim, The Palestinians' conflict, pp. 181–224.
87   Abbasi Mustafa, The Arab Community of Safed 1840–1918 A Critical Period, *Jerusalem Quarterly* 17, 2003, pp. 49–58.
88   Ibrahim, The Palestinians' conflict, pp. 181–224.
89   Great Britain, Municipal Corporations Ordinance No. 1 of 1934.
90   Tamir Goren, The Position of the Leadership of the Jewish Yishuv on the Mayoralty of Haifa and Preparations for Elections, 1940–1947, *Israel Affairs* 14/1, 2008, pp. 29–48.
91   Government of Palestine, Sir Henry Gurney, Chief Secretary to the Government of Palestine, Internal report on the status of overdue elections, Jerusalem: Government of Palestine, 13 January 1948, File: Elections to Municipal and local Councils, ISA- G-41–47.
92   Great Britain, Palestine Royal Commission Report, Cmd 5479, 1937. London: HMSO
93   Ibrahim, The Palestinians' conflict, pp. 181–224.
94   Miller, *Government and Society.*
95   Ibid.
96   Al-Hout, The Palestinian political elite, pp. 85–111.
97   Barron, Report and General Abstracts.
98   Al-Haj, Rosenfeld, Arab local government in Israel, pp. 1–22; Tamir Goren, The Second World War as a turning point in Arab–Jewish relations: The case of Jaffa and Tel Aviv, *Middle Eastern Studies*, 54/2, 2018, pp. 216–237, Naser, Jerusalem municipality, pp. 1–15, Abbasi, Safed in the British Mandate, pp. 45–54, Rubinstein, Jews and Arabs, pp. 122–47; Tamir Goren, Tel Aviv and the question of separation from Jaffa 1921–1936, *Middle Eastern Studies*, 52/3, 2016, pp. 473–87.
99   Government of Palestine, Orders Under the Franchise Ordinance, 1926, Jerusalem: The Palestine Gazette, March to October, 1927.
100 Mills, Census of Palestine 1931.
101 Abbasi, Safed in the British Mandate, pp. 45–54; Al-Haj and Rosenfeld, Arab local government, pp. 1–22; Naser, Jerusalem municipality, pp. 1–15.
102 Government of Palestine, Municipal Corporations Ordinance 1933 notices, Jerusalem: The Palestine Gazette, No. 350, 23 March 1933, 23 March 1934 to 28 December 1934, 17 January 1935 to 3 December 1935.
103 Government of Palestine, '*Municipal Corporations Ordinance 1934 notices*', 15 May 1934 to 29 September 1934.
104 Ibid., 10, 21 September 1934.
105 Government of Palestine, Sir Henry Gurney, Municipal Corporations Ordinance, 1946 notices, Jerusalem: The Palestine Gazette, supplement 2, from 24 January to 14 December 1946.
106 Government of Palestine, Village statistics, 1943, Jerusalem, 1 April 1945.
107 Al-Haj, Rosenfeld, Arab local government, pp. 1–22; Abbasi, Safed in the British Mandate, pp. 45–54.
108 Government of Palestine, Municipal Corporations Ordinance 1946 notices: Jerusalem: The Palestine Gazette, supplement 2, 20 February to 26 December 1946; Letter from the District Commissioner of Haifa to Chief Secretary to the Government of Palestine on Municipal and Local Council Elections, Jerusalem, 2 December 1947, File: Elections to Municipal and local Councils, ISA- G-41–47.
109 Government of Palestine, Letter from the District Commissioner of Jerusalem to Chief Secretary to the Government of Palestine on "Municipal and Local Council Elections", Jerusalem, 11 November 1947, File: Elections to Municipal and local Councils, Government of Palestine, Letter from the District Commissioner of Haifa, ibid.

6 The rise and fall of the Palestinian Arab middle class

Itamar Radai

Research on the Palestinian-Arab middle class under the British Mandate, begun only recently, has focused on economic patterns.[1]

This chapter focuses on the rise of the Palestinian Arab middle class during the Mandate. The main hypothesis is that particular bourgeois social and cultural characteristics prevented the full incorporation of the middle class into the Palestinian-Arab National Movement, and even led to an estrangement between the middle class and the national leadership, as well as members of lower strata, especially the villagers. Members of the middle class, mostly Christians but Muslims also, espoused in their daily life modern habits, ideas and customs, as a means to distinguish between themselves and other classes, similarly to their parallels in the West, and like their contemporaries elsewhere in the Eastern Mediterranean. Those gaps reached their climax during the years of revolt (1936–39), which was a kind of prelude to the cataclysmic events of 1948 that marked the end of the Mandate era.

The rise of the middle class

The Palestinian Arab upper middle class first appeared during the late Ottoman period. Beginning in the mid-nineteenth century, Ottoman administrative reforms and the influence of the European powers set in motion economic and social changes and rapid development in the coastal cities of Palestine, which experienced an increase in economic activity and saw the growth of educational institutions. The same happened in Jerusalem. An educated middle class began to emerge. Many of its members were migrants from villages into the cities who owed their wealth to trade and to government and municipal jobs. The middle class was composed disproportionately of Christians. They played a central role in commerce, some of them Arabs and others members of Eastern communities, such as Armenians and Greeks. The growth of the cities widened the longstanding fissure that separated the urban and rural populations, which began to take the form of a divide between the more modern and secular coastal region and the conservative and traditional mountain country.[2]

The rise of the middle class accelerated during the British Mandate. The Christians were largely an urban community, and many of them gained knowledge and skills via the European education they received in church missionary schools. They thus provided a qualified pool of candidates for government service and played central roles in the newly formed Mandate civil administration. In 1921 about two-thirds of government positions were filled by Christians, who made up about a tenth of the Arab population of Palestine. By 1938 the proportion had declined, but half of government officials were still Christians. They also dominated the white-collar professions – doctors, lawyers, engineers, architects, journalists, and educators, who provided services to the civil service, to merchants, to landowners, and to the wealthy. In 1931, more than half the Arabs in the professions and nearly half in the financial professions were Christians.[3] At that time, the settled population of Palestine numbered, according to the 1931 British census, 966,761 people, out of whom 693,147 (72%) were Muslims, 174,600 (18%) were Jews, while only 88,907 (9%) were Christians.[4]

The upper middle class built new neighbourhoods and even entire quarters in the three large cities, places such as the 'Abbas neighbourhood in Haifa; the 'Ajami, Nuzha, and North Jabaliyya neighbourhoods in Jaffa; and Jerusalem's southern neighbourhoods of Talbiyya, Baq'a, and Qatamon. The concentration of government offices in Jerusalem, the city's large Christian population, and its proximity to other Christian centres in Bethlehem and Ramallah made the city a magnet for educated Christians and Muslims and home to the largest upper middle-class population during the Mandate period. At the same time the Arab middle-class neighbourhoods became the favourite lodging place for British Army officers and Government officials, often renting apartments or houses with their families. Some well-to-do Jewish families, mainly of Middle European origin, also moved into the same neighbourhoods.[5] The predominance of government officials in the ranks of the new bourgeoisie was evident mainly in Jerusalem, while in the coastal towns such as Haifa and Jaffa the backbone of the middle class tended to rely more on entrepreneurship.[6]

The educator Khalil al-Sakakini, author of one of the best Palestinian personal diaries of the period, was one of the landlords in these neighbourhoods. Having initially resigned from government service following the appointment of a Jewish (and Zionist) High Commissioner Herbert Samuel, Sakakini finally re-joined the government in the late 1920s as chief inspector of Arabic Language studies in the department of education. He soon became well-to-do, not only thanks to his appointment, but also due to revenues from his innovative elementary school reading textbooks, not only in Palestine but throughout the Arab world. Following his retirement from the public service in 1938 he opened a private high school (that fostered both liberal and national values), which became an important centre for the dissemination of Arab culture and nationalism. Sakakini introduced numerous innovations in his school, such as eliminating examinations and grading, forgoing religious studies, and creating an atmosphere of camaraderie and equality between students and teachers. He also endeavoured to implement the same principles of equality and openness in his family. His economic success reached its zenith, perhaps, already in 1937, when he finished building a private home in the affluent, bourgeois Qatamon neighbourhood of Jerusalem.[7]

In a letter to his son, Sari (a student in the USA), Sakakini described the building process, his pedantic observation over each detail and his sources of inspiration, as well as the influence on his socio-economic status:

> I do not wonder why the people are marveling how I built a house, me, the poorest beggar. Until today, each time I wore a new *tarbush* everybody noticed and used to greet and congratulate me, so how come I built now a house? And moreover, I spent without any calculation: the builders, the carpenter, the locksmith, the floorer, the whitewasher, and the painter are the best.[8]

Four days after moving into their new house, Sakakini described how the new home, built in western bourgeois style room division, influenced the life of his family and their surroundings:

> It is amazing how within four days we became totally new people ... we guide all the visitors from room to room, this is a bedroom, this is a library, this is a leaving room, so I decided to hang at home a map, in which I will design each room [and its function].[9]

In her memoirs, Sakakini's daughter Hala describes the high quality of the construction in the middle-class areas as simple, modern style, with meticulous detail. Personal taste was demonstrated everywhere, in the mason craft, roof-tiles that many houses had, bars and parapets. The residents were highly conscious of both their external appearance and the exterior of their houses, and used to assiduously cultivate them along with the courtyards and gardens.[10] The affluent and fashionable Arab neighbourhoods in Southern Jerusalem, from Abu Thor in the east to Qatamon in the west, and from Talbiyya to Upper Baq'a, consisting largely of private family homes, constituted a "garden suburb" of Jerusalem. Bourgeois neighbourhoods such as 'Ajami and Northern Jabaliyya in Jaffa, 'Abbas in Haifa, the resort mountainous towns of Ramallah and Bayt Jala, and even the al-Rimal neighbourhood in Gaza, or the more affluent parts of coastal towns such as Lydda and Ramla, did their best not to remain behind. In Jerusalem, the low population density in the Southern neighbourhoods gave rise to a pastoral feeling of living close to nature and to the agricultural cycle of the surrounding villages, such as al-Maliha and Bayt Safafa, whose farmlands adjoined the new neighbourhoods. The proximity to the villages permitted the purchase of fresh farm produce, which the villagers supplied daily, door to door.[11]

In such a pastoral atmosphere, and against the backdrop of the events of the 1948 War, recollections by former residents of the area often tend towards idealisation. Hala al-Sakakini described the daily ride to school as an idyllic social experience, with passengers vying to pay the fare, while "the conductor in the meantime would wait patiently for the outcome of that argument". According to Sakakini, each passenger used to greet the driver and his fellow passengers, regardless if he knew them, and was answered accordingly. Passengers about to get off used to invite their fellow passengers for a coffee, and were turned down curtly.[12] However, it is clear that social harmony prevailed in these bourgeois neighbourhoods, owing to the overall uniformity of the residents' cultural and socio-economic background. It was a cohesive, mutually supportive community for which, as is characteristic in bourgeois middle classes, the education of the young generations was a first priority.[13]

Typically with a bourgeois society, the middle class families [had] attributed great importance to the education of both males and females, who were usually educated separately. They were usually not sent to government schools, but attended private prestigious (and expensive) schools, mostly run by western Christian missions. Multi-lingual education contributed to a cosmopolitan atmosphere, while many houses spoke several languages. But Arabic was the common tongue.[14] The sisters Hala and Dumya al-Sakakini, for example, spoke fluent German from their childhood in the German colony neighbourhood, near Baq'a in Southern Jerusalem. Until the Second World War, when the Germans were evicted by the British, they frequented a German school. They received their lessons in English conversation and pronunciation from a British resident of the area, Clarissa Graves (the sister of Robert Graves, the author). The Christian sisters were also given private lessons in the Quran, meant for their general knowledge of classic and contemporary Arabic. Upon graduating from school in Jerusalem they were sent to college in Beirut – quite a rare phenomenon among young Palestinian Arab women. Hala graduated as a teacher of English, and Dumya as a teacher of science. Both could have expected to continue their career until marriage – which might be one of the reasons why they never got married. However, young men going to academic studies abroad were more common, in their hundreds, throughout the period. The closest universities abroad were the American universities in Beirut and Cairo. Those who could afford it travelled to universities in Europe, and some even in the USA. Their knowledge and cultural influence added to the cosmopolitan atmosphere in the bourgeois areas.[15]

Sports, another characteristic of the bourgeois lifestyle, were present as well. Like many friends and neighbours, the Sakakini sisters had gymnastics and swimming classes taken at the YMCA club, which functioned as a cultural, social, and leisure hub for the bourgeoisie. They used to watch their brother Sari in the same place, playing tennis against Robert Mushabbek, another member of their social circle. The YMCA was the encounter place for Arabs, Greeks, Armenians and Jews. The tennis and squash playgrounds, the swimming pool, youth clubs, library, concert hall, and the cafeteria served them all in a typical British colonial atmosphere. Another sports and social hub was the Arab sports club in Baq'a. Hiking and Biking were also popular, as recorded Hala, who used to bike together with her neighbor Jean Zaphyriades, a Palestinian Greek.[16]

Leisure habits included hanging out in European style garden cafes in the resort town Bayt Jala, south of Jerusalem, near Bethlehem, as well as Ramallah to the north of the city. Some vacationed in Lebanon, Syria, and Egypt, while the most affluent travelled to Europe.[17] The Christian Arab amateur musician, Wasif Jawhariyya, who first got a job as a clerk under the British military regime (1918–1920), and then moved to the civil Jerusalem district commissioner's office, travelled for the first time in his life to Syria and Lebanon in the summer of 1922. He wrote: 'When I reached economic stability, thank God – and could implement this plan'. Jawhariyya and his brother Khalil travelled by car through Haifa, in northern Palestine, to Beirut, where they stayed in a state-of-the-art hotel, and from there travelled from village to village resorts in the Lebanon Mountains – 'Aley, Bahamdun, and Sofar. There he felt "like a Bedouin in New York". Jawhariyya admired not only the Lebanese vistas, but also the sophisticated reception and service they encountered at the resorts, the hotels, restaurants, and cafes, which they obviously were not accustomed to in Ottoman Jerusalem, where they grew up.[18]

The thrust towards modernity was apparent also in their possession of consumer products. As early as in the 1930s and 1940s, some of the bourgeois residents had electric appliances such as refrigerators, cooking ovens, radios, and gas stoves. Some of the most affluent even had their own automobiles – a rare luxury in the 'Old World' prior to the 1950s.[19] The symbol of the new modernity was the telephone. In 1937 there were in Jerusalem, for example, about 350 telephone lines owned by Arabs, including private homes, institutes, companies, or businesses (out of 2,300 private telephone lines, mostly owned by Jews or Britons). About 160 lines were owned by Christians (Arabs, Armenians, and Greeks), among them many white-collar professionals, and importers of foreign goods, such as automobiles. 120 telephone lines were owned by Muslim members of the middle class, while only 50 were owned by members of the veteran notable families, the old elite of Jerusalem.[20]

Khalil al-Sakakini, who acquired a telephone in his new residence for the first time in his life on June 1937, described enthusiastically in a letter to his son in America the revolutionary influence of the new device on his and his family's lives:

> Perhaps I forgot to let you know that we had acquired a telephone. The meaning of the telephone, sir, is that we are now connected to the world, first, and to each other, then. […] I go in the morning to my work, and as

soon as I arrive I pick up the phone and ask the operator for my home number. "Hello, My darling [sic], I just arrived and start working". Later, when I am feeling tired or bored, or troubled, I immediately rush to the phone. The telephone, the telephone! I don't know how people could live without a telephone![21]

However, the telephone was not the only symbol of socio-cultural gaps between the bourgeoisie and other, lesser affluent segments of society, as manifested by their consumption patterns. Food products such as European patisseries or American food brands such as Heinz Ketchup or Kellogg's Cornflakes that were deemed prestigious, were also among the bourgeois trademarks.[22]

Many middle-class members purchased commodities, such as imported garments and furniture, at the Spinney's chain of department stores. They donned European attire, the women's dresses and shoes according to the latest fashion in Europe, also the men's suits and ties. The *Tarbush* (Fez) was the only Middle-Eastern traditional garb that some of the men used to don. Spinney's shops also offered food departments and even meat butcheries in western style. The more conservative preferred the traditional butcher shops in the Old City markets. Intercultural hybridity was well manifested in food consumption: alongside the department stores and grocery shops, there was also daily distribution of vegetables, fruits, and live chickens were brought to the doors by rural women from the neighbouring villages, adjusting their merchandise on baskets carefully balanced on their heads. Fresh bread was delivered on a cart, and fresh milk on a mule. Peddlers sold a variety of goods, from linen to ice cream. Wood for heating was delivered on camels, and kerosene on horse-drawn carts. Craftsmen such as shoemakers and knife grinders, offered their services on the streets, as well as in the Old City markets.[23]

Despite the thrust towards modernity, traditional Arab and Middle Eastern cultural characteristics were preserved, mainly among the older generation. Young women discussed in social saloons topics, apart from politics, fashion, and 'the ideal home'; i.e. 'the meaning of being civilized', 'our society and the old maid', and 'outdated attitudes among our elders'.[24] The elders, such as 'Isa al-Toubbeh (1882–1973), the *Mukhtar* (traditional community leader) of the Christian Orthodox community in Jerusalem, who also lived in Qatamon, donned a *Tarbush,* a Middle Eastern urban symbol, roughly equivalent to the hat in the West. They preferred to smoke a *Narghileh* (Hookah, a Middle Eastern smoking pipe). Like many of his older community members, who belonged also to the middle class, Toubbeh was fluent in Greek and in Ottoman Turkish, but did not speak western languages. As many younger and older members of the middle class he used to read the Arabic dailies, both Palestinian and Egyptian. His younger son, Jamil Toubbeh, performed in his mission school, Terra Sancta, *Mawawil* (traditional Arab vocal music) of the

Egyptian singer Muhammad 'Abd al-Wahhab. He later accredited 'Abd al-Wahhab as the "Frank Sinatra of the Arab World".[25] This declaration seems to encapsulate the intercultural hybridity of the Palestinian-Arab middle class under the British Mandate.

The middle class and the national movement: Muslims and Christians

Just prior to the outbreak of the Arab Revolt in 1936, about 50,000 Arabs lived in the bourgeois neighbourhoods of the three large cities. Of these, 35,000–40,000 were Christians. (In fact, a few thousand of the Christians were not Arabs but Greeks, Armenians, Germans, and members of other ethnic groups. However, the Greeks and Armenians for the most part assimilated gradually into the Christian Arab population, and were extensively involved in the social life of the larger Palestinian Arab middle class.) The Muslims who lived in these neighbourhoods were influenced by the values of their neighbours and maintained social ties with them. However, they tended to be more traditional, especially with regard to the status of women. But by and large their lifestyle was very much like those of the Christian members of the middle class.[26] However, the very same Muslims tended to complain about the overrepresentation of Christians in government institutions. Such grievances were voiced throughout the Mandate period. The British made some efforts to recruit more Muslims into their service, but Christians continued to dominate. The identification of the Christians specifically, and of the upper middle class as a whole, with the Mandate administration opened them up to charges of dual loyalty.[27]

From its inception, the Palestinian Arab national movement sought to bridge the old Christian-Muslim divide. However, despite the establishment of Muslim-Christian Associations and Christian participation in the Palestinian congresses of the 1920s, the Christian bourgeoisie remained a marginal player in the national movement, especially following the establishment of the Supreme Muslim Council in January 1922. The Christians active in the movement generally served as spokesmen or aides to Muslim leaders affiliated with the notable families. Both Muslims and Christians opposed the Balfour Declaration and the Zionist movement and viewed them as threats to their communities. Christian anti-Zionism was also influenced by a religious anti-Jewish tradition and their traditional economic rivalry with Jews under the Ottomans, which continued during the Mandate period in the framework of government service. Their involvement in anti-Zionist activity, if only in declarative form, was also intended to counter the pro-British label that was frequently attached to them. In fact, the Christians had trouble identifying enthusiastically with one of the two flags that the national movement raised in opposition to the British. The other flag, anti-Zionism, was as much theirs as the Muslims, but they maintained social ties with the British and only a few of them could wholeheartedly support the Muslim opposition to the West. They found themselves in a dilemma in the face of Muslim resistance to the Christian Mandatory regime. Many of them seem to have feared the prospect of an independent Palestinian Arab state dominated by Muslims; their preference was probably for a British Mandate unencumbered by the Balfour Declaration.[28]

The Palestinian Arab leadership's declared policy of cooperating with the Christians in the national movement did not preclude calls for the Christians to convert to Islam – some of which came from Christians themselves. The Christians recognised, or were compelled to acknowledge, the Muslim component in Arab history and culture. They often found themselves taking an apologetic stance to justify their separate existence as Christians.[29]

Khalil al-Sakakini was one of the most prominent Christians active in the national movement in the 1920s. Later, he seems to have had second thoughts. By 1935, when he was offered the appointment to be the first director of the Arab Department of the Mandate administration's broadcasting authority, he turned down the position, explaining that it would be better to appoint a Muslim to the post. This offer was delivered to Sakakini by the historian and government official George Antonius, himself a Christian. Antonius answered "My opinion is similar to [yours that a Muslim should be appointed], but where would we find a Muslim qualified for this job?" Sakakini did not record his response to this remark, which reflects arrogance and patronizing, not only towards Muslims but probably also, as a member of the middle class, towards the less educated strata in society. Finally, a talented Muslim candidate was appointed: Ibrahim Touqan, who became known later as the Palestinian national poet.[30]

In a letter that Sakakini sent in 1932 to his son Sari, which the latter translated and read to his college friends in the United States, he voiced his frustration, anger, and fear of the Muslim majority:

> No matter how high my standing may be in science and literature, no matter how sincere my patriotism is, no matter how much I do to revive this nation, even if I burn my fingers before its sight, as long as I am not a Moslem [sic] I am naught.
>
> If I enjoy any position in this land, if the people love me and respect me, it is because they think I am nearer to Islam than to Christianity, because I am wealthy in the Arabic language, because they fancy that I am a conservative and will not depart from Oriental customs under any circumstances. But if I were to struggle with a Moslem who is less founded in knowledge and heritage than I, I would not doubt that they would prefer him to survive.[31]

In the same letter to his son he addressed the gap in values between the Christian middle class and the rest of Palestinian Arab society:

> What would you say would happen if I donned a hat, if I said that Beethoven is the summit of music, preferring him to Abd al-Wahab [sic] or Um Kulthum, if I said that Khalil Mutran [a Christian Arab poet] is

more poetical than [Muslim Ahmad] Shawqi, or if I said that the Greek
or Latin or German or English languages are superior to the Arabic,
richer and more beautiful than it? [...] Still what would you think would
happen if I advocated that women should not be veiled, that we should
acquire western modes of living; if I said a pipe is better than a *narghile*
[water pipe] and that the association of young men and women [sic]
causes the elevation of both? Might you not think that if I said such
things they would shout, "He blasphemed; then stone him"?[32]

It should be recalled that Sakakini, a great proponent of Arabic culture, was
actually a devout smoker of the *narghile*.[33] But his major concern was his
profound apprehension about what the future held in store for his children,
for the education and way of life he had sought to grant them. He seems to
have understood that the Mandate government would not last forever. It is
also interesting that Sakakini, a political supporter of Hajj Amin al-Husayni,
Grand Mufti of Palestine and President of the Supreme Muslim Council,
whom he knew well personally, did not refrain from indirectly criticizing in
private the Husayni faction (and their socio-religious politics):

I tell you that whenever I think of you and your sisters' future, I am
alarmed for you. Do you suppose they consent to our sending you to
America? How they would have preferred that I had sent you at the
beginning of your school days to "The Garden of Knowledge" [Rawdat
al-Ma'arif, a national school in Jerusalem affiliated with the Husayni
circle], rather than to a church mission school, or to have entrusted your
training to Sheik [Muhammad al-] Saleh [the school's founder] or that I
had sent you to al-Azhar [the Islamic University in Cairo] or had persuaded you to study pre-Islamic poetry.[34]

In these terms, Sakakini was an authentic representative of the anxiety felt
by the Christians and by the middle class generally as its members watched
the conservatives and the Supreme Muslim Council grow in power. Yet,
paradoxically, in the national and social discourse, the middle class took a
hard nationalist line and called (largely through the press, a large part of
which was Christian) for solidarity among Palestinian Arabs of all
religions.[35]

This dualism, between national interests on the one hand and personal,
regional or sectarian ones on the other, was a constant in Palestinian Arab
society during the Mandate period (the *Yishuv* sometimes confronted
similar dilemmas). The historian Yosef Vashitz defined it as "civil versus
political society". He maintained that one could not doubt the integrity of
so many people. The contradictions arose from the fact that the Palestinian
Arab lived simultaneously in both societies, and each made different
demands on him.[36]

But it looks as if this was simply the natural tendency of both Christian and Muslim members of the middle class to accept the British Mandate regime in order to protect its own economic interests. This coexisted with their emotional and political identification with the national movement's opposition to Zionism. The government provided the middle class with vital services – water, electricity, mail, telephone, education, health, and sanitation. Its police and army forces guaranteed the security and social order that underpinned the middle class's economic position, and ensured its safety and economic status. As a result, very few middle-class Christians and Muslims took part in anti-government demonstrations throughout the period of British rule. Nearly all of them sat out the disturbances of the 1920s, whether because of their class and social interests, or because they – the Christians in parti-cular – feared that the violence might turn against them, and were carful not to endanger their recently acquired economic privileges. Sometimes their resentment was actively expressed. For example, when villagers, members of the 'Green Hand' band were brought to trial in Haifa in September 1929 for looting Jewish property in Safed and Acre, the local Arab lawyers refused to defend them.[37]

The Palestinian-Arab Revolt (1936–1939): village versus town

When the Arab Revolt broke out broke out in Palestine in 1936, the middle class remained mostly passive. Some Christian journalists who were in contact with Zionist institutions during the strike, offered to assist in restoring the peace. But cooperation between Christians and the Zionist movement was nevertheless uncommon.[38] Most simply kept quiet and carried on their middle-class lives, raising the hackles of the nationalists. In one instance, *al-Liwa'*, the Husayni newspaper, taunted the inhabitants of Qatamon and Upper Baq'a, "especially the [government] officials among them", i.e. the members of the upper middle class. These residents, the newspaper scoffed, continued to ride on Jewish buses "because their atrophied bodies cannot stand up to walking". Thus it both criticised their lack of national loyalty, and ridiculed their bourgeois lifestyle, by drawing a line between the two, as if they had grown from each other.[39]

Active participation in the strike did not mesh with the bourgeois way of life, which was dependent on the colonial regime. The middle class, in parti-cular the Christian middle class – which included both supporters of the Husaynis and of the opposition – took part in the Revolt in only a marginal way. The historian Yehoshua Porath was able to identify only four Christians among 282 people, about whom he collected information, who played an active role as commanders and organisers in the Rebellion.[40] At most they voiced sympathy for the Revolt, its cause, its leaders and activists, and even this was largely limited to the uprising's first stage. Khalil al-Sakakini, for example, wrote to his son of his admiration for Sami al-Ansari, a young Muslim teacher wounded in an assassination attempt on a British police officer who later died of his injuries. He wrote: "Another hero has fallen on the field of honor. Indeed, he is the greatest hero Palestine has known". While al-Ansari himself might have been seen as an urban member of the middle class, his participation in the revolt was in fact an exception, since the vast majority of active rebels were villagers.[41]

As early as December 1936 the rebels issued a virulently anti-Christian leaflet, accusing the members of that community of a series of crimes against the national cause. The Higher Arab Committee, alarmed at this development and fearing a break in its ranks, condemned the leaflet. But during the Revolt's second stage (fall 1937–summer 1939) rural Arabs and urban laborers again routinely voiced their resentment of the bourgeoisie by dictating anti-bourgeois and anti-Christian norms. They compelled women to wear veils and prevented men from wearing short pants, which were forbidden by Islam. Men were prohibited from wearing the *tarbush* and were forced to don the *kufiyya* and *'iqal*, the traditional headdress of the rural and Bedouin Arabs. The rebels also banned working on Fridays and resting on Sundays. Furthermore, they banned the use of electricity from the 'Jewish' electric company (most of the Arab clients were from the middle class – villages, even those close to the cities were not connected to the grid).[42] In the summer of 1938, Khalil Totah, headmaster of the prestigious 'Friends' Quaker School in Ramallah, described the ban on the *tarbush* and the enforcement of the *Kufiyya*:

> In about one week the whole Arab population changed its headwear from tarbush and *hal* into *iqals* [sic]. That was the rebels' order. It was to protect rebels from suspicion of the government. The transformation was like magic. All professional classes including supreme court judges are now wearing the [peasantry's] *iqal*.[43]

The Christian poet Iskander al-Khouri al-Baytjali, who served as a judge at the Haifa magistrate court, recorded in his memoirs a journey in his car during the revolt from Haifa to his residence in Jerusalem, in the Qatamon quarter. On the road from Haifa to Nablus he encountered an improvised roadblock, built of stones across the road. Khouri, who wore a rural *kufiyya* and *'iqal*, as ordered by the rebels, got out of his car and started to wave the *kufiyya*, hoping that the rebels who probably lay in ambush would come to his help, and also perhaps out of fear to be mistaken for a Briton. Finally, he had to remove the stones on his own, but after passing the roadblock, he "stopped and returned the stones to their place, out of fear of the rebels who built the roadblock, had I driven away without returning the stones as they were".[44]

Khalil Totah described in his diary a growing alienation between the middle class, mainly the Christians, and the rebels. Many of the anti-government measures taken by the latter, such as sabotaging the transportation, the postal services, the telephone and the electricity lines, had harmed the middle class and prevented them from pursuing their bourgeois lifestyle.[45] In many cases the rebels demanded money from the middle class, who showed a reluctance to finance the rebels. As the revolt was drawing to an end, British Military pressure on the rebels intensified. In March 1939 the British army even supplied 16 rifles to the residents of Ramallah to defend themselves from harassment and even worse threats from the rebellious villagers. Totah deemed the Army's measures "insufficient".[46] The social proximity to British officials sometimes led to awkward conversations, such as one that Totah recorded with Price-Gordon, the Assistant District Commissioner in charge of Ramallah, following a general strike proclaimed as mourning for 'Abd al-Rahim al-Hajj Muhammad, the general commander of the rebellion whom the British killed [in Battle]: "His idea was that the Christians should not have struck [...] I explained that the Christians could not do otherwise".[47]

The middle class's attitude to the villagers was somewhat ambivalent. On the one hand, they idealised the village and its inhabitants, whom they used to see as the epitome of nationalism and patriotism, similar to other national movements, typical of the Palestinian national movement in decades to come.[48] On the other hand they often treated them arrogantly, sometimes with scorn. Urban bourgeois people used to have themselves photographed dressed in mock-village attire, supposedly as a token of authenticity and attraction to the idyllic country style of life. At the same time, they mocked the very same villagers. Ghada Karmi mentioned her father Hasan, an inspector of Arabic at the department of education, a Muslim born in the rural town of Tulkarm, who later became a well-known linguist and Arabic-English dictionary author, ridiculing an educated member of their social circle for his rural origin:

> "So-and-so may call himself a university lecturer, but mark my words, the man is a peasant", he would say. "How do you know?" "Just look at his trousers", he would answer. "They're round". As peasants traditionally wore a type of loose trousers, they were unaccustomed to wearing city [European] clothes and hence, according to my father, when they adopted city wear they did not know how to iron their trousers properly [i.e. with a crease in their midst, a-la-bourgeois].[49]

The Karmi family was politically alienated from Hajj Amin al-Husayni and his faction. As such, when the latter began to violently dispose of his rivals, during the second phase of the revolt, Hasan Karmi was threatened by a gunman, working on orders from Hajj Amin. In December 1939, his older brother Mahmud Karmi, a teacher and journalist, was shot dead in Beirut. His assassin confessed to having been sent by Hajj Amin.[50] Like other Palestinian-Arab middle class and members of the elite, Mahmud Karmi had tried to find refuge in a neighbouring capital city, where he was finally reached by his enemies. Alongside Cairo, Beirut and well-known resorts such as 'Aley and Suq al-Gharb in the Lebanon Mountains were favorite shelters for the

Palestinian-Arab middle class during the revolt. Among those who escaped to the Lebanon were, besides Karmi, the Jaffa journalist 'Isa al-'Isa, founding editor of *Falastin,* the leading Arabic daily of the period in Palestine, as well as other prominent members of the middle class.[51]

Epilogue: disintegration and fall, 1948

The Qatamon neighbourhood and its fate might serve as a quintessential example for the Palestinian Arab middle class in 1948. On 30 April, the neighbourhood was taken by the Palmach, the Haganah elite force, after a fierce battle with Palestinian Arab rural fighters, led by Ibrahim Abu-Dayya, a commander from the village of Surif, north-west of Hebron. Palestinian Arab society in Jerusalem, which had been relatively cohesive, displayed resilience in the area of the Old City but weakness in the middle class neighbourhoods outside of its walls.

The case of Qatamon demonstrates clearly the extent to which the Palestinian Arabs (like other national groups) should not be viewed as monolithic. The process that led to the conquest of Qatamon, the collapse of civil society there, and the displacement of its inhabitants was a complex one, and the people who lived there held a wide variety of opinions about the war. Qatamon may be viewed as a microcosm of the Palestinian Arab middle class as a whole. It proves just how disparate were the declared national identifications of some members of the Palestinian Arab bourgeois upper middle class and their willingness to actually fight and make sacrifices for the national goals that their identities implied. In the end, this population's bourgeois values and way of life, alongside its practice of relying on the British authorities to defend them, led to a lack of will and ability to take part in the war effort. Other groups and individuals displayed no national identification at all, even for public consumption, and self-consciously pursued personal, family, and regional interests. For some, long opposition to the Husayni party prevented them from identifying fully with the political and military struggle led by the mufti. It appeared as if these city dwellers were largely socially alienated from most of the fighters (in areas such as Qatamon), who were primarily of rural origin. There can be no doubt that the Christian affiliation of the majority of the bourgeoisie, along with the presence of a significant Greek and Armenian non-Arab population, had an important impact on the level of national identification, participation in the national struggle, and the willingness of the middle-class civilian population to make sacrifices.[52]

Conclusion

The actions taken by villagers against the middle class, Christians in particular, during the Mandate, especially during the Revolt, were motivated by social, cultural, economic, and class factors. The middle class's reluctance to take part in violent resistance, especially during the Revolt, had the same origin. Another way the bourgeoisie coped with the attacks on them was to move to neighbouring countries until the situation improved.[53] This practice, which appeared again in late 1947 and early 1948, along with the passivity of the Christian and Muslim middle class, would later typify the beginning of the Palestinian-Arab *Nakba* (catastrophe: the common Palestinian term for the events of 1948).[54]

The events of 1948 were cataclysmic in their nature for the Palestinian Arab urban society, especially the middle class. Prior to the war, the urban population constituted about 35% of the entire Palestine Arab population. The middle class lost its mansions and properties in the urban centres, mostly in the three larger cities, and the majority went into exile. The Palestinian urban bourgeoisie, both as a social and as a cultural concept, had practically ceased to exist. As a result, claims cultural historian Manar Hasan in her recent book, the Palestinian national ethos, that experienced a revival in the 1960s, has chosen to concentrate on the village and the peasantry as national symbols.[55] While a full discussion of this phenomenon is outside the scope of this chapter, our findings show that the estrangement between the Palestinian national movement and the middle class dates well before 1948, and that middle class bourgeois characteristics had aggravated this rift and, in turn, contributed to the Palestinian debacle in their struggle. Middle classes have historically played central roles in national movements, often constituting their central support. The failure of the Palestinian-Arab national leadership to incorporate the bourgeoisie into their movement and to induce them to participate in the armed struggle seems to have been one of the principal reasons for the defeat of the Palestinian-Arab national movement during the Mandate, during the Arab Revolt and later, during the 1948 Arab-Israeli War.

Notes

1 See Sherene Seikaly, *Men of Capital: Scarcity and Economy in Mandate Palestine,* Stanford: Stanford University Press, 2016; Deborah Bernstein, Badi Hasisi, "Buy and Promote the National Cause": Consumption, class formation, and nationalism in Mandate Palestinian society, *Nations and Nationalism* 14/1, 2008, pp. 127–150.

2 Avaraham Sela, 'Hevra u-mosadot be-kerev 'arviyey Falastin bi-tekufat ha-mandat: tmura, hei'ader ni'ut u-krisa' [Palestinian Society and Institutions during the Mandate: Change, Lack of Mobility, and Downfall, in Avi Bareli and Nahum Karlinsky (eds), *Kalkala ve-hevra bi-yemey ha-mandat* [*Economy and Society in Mandatory Palestine*], Sde Boqer: Ben-Gurion Research Center, Ben-Gurion University of the Negev, 2003, p. 294; Ann Mosely Lesch, *Arab Politics in Palestine, 1917–1939,* Ithaca: Cornell University Press, 1979, p. 60. See also Mahmud Yazbak, *Haifa in the Late Ottoman Period, 1864–1914: A Muslim Town in Transition,* Leiden: Brill, 1998.

3 Sela, 'Hevra u-mosadot, p. 295; Yosef Vashitz, *ha -'Aravim be-Eretz-Israel,* [The Arabs in the Land of Israel] Merhavya: Hashomer Hatzair, 1947, p. 142; Don Peretz, 'Palestinian social stratification: The political implications', *Journal of Palestine Studies* 7/1, Autumn 1977, pp. 51–2.

4   *A Survey of Palestine*, prepared in December 1945 and January 1946, Jerusalem: Government Printer, vol. 1, p. 141, Table 1. Population of Palestine by Religions.

5   John Melkon Rose, *Armenians of Jerusalem: Memories of Life in Palestine*, London: Radcliffe, 1993, pp. 1–47, 106–114; David Kroyanker, *Shekhunot Yerushalayim: Talbiyyeh, Qatamon ve-ha-moshava ha-yevanit [Jerusalem Neighborhoods: Talbiyya, Qatamon, and the Greek Colony]*, Jerusalem: Keter, 2002, pp. 182–3, 279–82.

6   May Seikaly, *Haifa: Transformation of a Palestinian Arab Society, 1918–1939*, London: I.B. Tauris, 1995, pp. 220–221.

7   Khalil al-Sakakini, *Yawmiyyat Khalil al-Sakakini [Diaries of Khalil al-Sakakini]* ed. Akram Mussalam, Ramallah and Jerusalem: Institute for Jerusalem Studies, 2010, vol. 4, p. 140, 30 April 1919, pp. 163–4, 1 June 1919, vol. 6, p. 235, 20 December 1936, p. 362, 8 April 1937, pp. 369–70, 29 April 1937; See also "al-Sakakini, Khalil", in Ya'qub al-'Awdat, *Min a'lam al-fikr wal-adab fi filastin, [Persons of Thought and Literature in Palestine]* Amman: Wikalat al-tawzi' al-urduniyya, 1976, pp. 273–4, 276.

8   Sakakini, *Yawmiyyat*, vol. 6, p. 369, 29 April, 1937, Sakakini often referred to himself humorously, and in his less fortunate days called his favourite café "The beggars café" [Maqha al-sa'alik]. See also Salim Tamari, The Vagabond Café and Jerusalem's Prince of Idleness; Salim Tamari, *Mountain against the Sea: Essays on Palestinian Society and Culture*, Berkeley: University of California Press, 2009, pp. 176–189.

9   Sakakini, *Yawmiyyat*, vol. 6, p. 376, 25 May 1937.

10   Hala Sakakini, *Jerusalem and I*, Jerusalem: Commercial Press, 1987, p. 105.

11   Jamil Issa Toubbeh, *Day of the Long Night: a Palestinian Refugee Remembers the Nakba* Jefferson, North Carolina: McFarland, 1998, p. 27; Rose, *Armenians of Jerusalem*, pp. 108–9.

12   Sakakini, *Jerusalem*, pp. 103–4.

13   Toubbeh, *Day of*, p. 68.

14   Kroyanker, *Talbiyyeh*, pp. 182–3.

15   Sakakini, *Jerusalem*, pp. 16–17, 72–3.

16   Ibid., pp. 70–2, 93–4; Kroyanker, *Talbiyyeh*, pp. 182–3.

17   Sakakini, *Jerusalem and I*, pp. 91–2.; Rose, *Armenians of Jerusalem*, pp. 122–3; Wassif Jawhariyya, *al-Quds al-intidabiyya fi al-mudhakkirat al-Jawhariyya,* [Mandatory Jerusalem in the Jawhariyya memoirs] Jerusalem: Institute of Jerusalem Studies, 2005, pp. 425, 448–51, 487–88, also Salim Tamari, 'A Musician's Lot: The Jawhariyyeh Memoirs as a Key to Jerusalem's Early Modernity', in *Mountain*, pp. 71–92.

18   Jawhariyya, *al-Quds,* pp. 356–7.

19   Kroyanker, *Talbiyyeh, Qatamon ve-ha-moshava ha-yevanit*, p. 184; Andrea L. Stanton, *This is Jerusalem Calling: State Radio in Mandate Palestine*, Austin: University of Texas Press, 2013, pp. 168–194.

20   The Palestine Department of Post, Telegraph, and Telephone, *The Telephone Guide* (1937, Hebrew).

21   Sakakini, *Yawmiyyat*, vol. 6, p. 383 (20.6.1937).

22   Sakakini, *Jerusalem*, p. 63.

23   Sakakini, ibid., pp. 106–7; Rose, *Armenians of Jerusalem*, 106–7; Kroyanker, *Talbiyyeh, Qatamon*, p. 184.

24   Sakakini, ibid., p. 70.

25   Toubbeh, *Day of the Long Night*, pp. 15–19, 68–7; on the *tarbush* and its social significance see also Jawhariyya, *al-Quds,* pp. 568–70.

26   Ghada Karmi, *In Search of Fatima: A Palestinian Story,* London: Verso, 2002, pp. 87–127.

27 Bernard Wasserstein, "Clipping the Claws of the Colonizers": Arab Officials in the Government of Palestine, 1917–1948, *Middle Eastern Studies* 13/2, May 1977, p. 171.

28 Daphne Tsimhoni, The Arab Christians and the Palestinian Arab National Movement During the Formative Stage, in G. Ben-Dor (ed.), *The Palestinians and the Middle East Conflict,* Turtledove Press, 1978, Ramat-Gan, 1978, pp. 73–4, Mosely Lesch, *Arab Politics,* 60–1; Vashitz, *ha -'Aravim,* p. 143.

29 Tsimhoni, "The Arab Christians", pp. 74–5.

30 Sakakini, *Yawmiyyat,* vol. 6, pp. 176–7, 26 November 1935, also Stanton, *This is Jerusalem,* pp. 29–75.

31 Khalil al-Sakakini Jerusalem, to Sari al-Sakakini, Heidelberg College, Tiffin, Ohio, 12 December 1932, Israel State Archive (ISA), Jerusalem, RG 65, box 378, file 2646; For the Arabic original see Sakakini, *Yawmiyyat,* vol. 4, pp. 387–8, 22 December 1932.

32 Ibid.

33 Sakakini, *Kadha ana, ya dunya* [*Such am I, O world*], Jerusalem: Al-Matbaa Al-Tijariyya, 1955, p. 238, Cairo, 1 January 1949.

34 Khalil al-Sakakini to Sari al-Sakakini, 12 December 1932, ISA RG 65, box 378, file 2646.

35 See Sela, ' Hevra u-mosadot, pp. 303–304.

36 Yosef Vashitz, 'Tmurot hevratiyot ba-yishuv ha-'aravi shel Heifa bi-tqufat ha-mandat ha-briti' [Social Transformations in Haifa's Arab Society], in Bareli and Karlinsky, *Kalkala ve-hevra,* pp. 392–3.

37 Seikaly, *Haifa: Transformation,* pp. 223, 235 n. 23; Peretz, Palestinian Social Stratification, p. 56; Tsimhoni, The Christian Arabs, p. 74.

38 Quoted in Hillel Cohen, *'Shituf pe'ula' shel 'aravim falastinim 'im mosdot tziyo-niyyim bi-tequfat ha-shilton ha-briti u-ve-milhemt 1948, ve-ma'avaq ha-tenu'a ha-leumit ke-negdo* [Collaboration of Palestinian Arabs with Zionist Institutions during the British rule and in the 1948 War, and the National Movement's Struggle Against it], Unpublished PhD thesis, The Hebrew University of Jerusalem, 2002, pp. 104, 153.

39 N.A., Fresh reports on some splinters [khawarij], *al-Liwa',* Jerusalem, 12 May 1936.

40 Yehoshua Porath, *The Palestinian Arab National Movement: From Riots to Rebellion, 1929–1939,* London: Frank Cass, 1977, pp. 269–70.

41 Sakakini, *Yawmiyyat,* pp. 262–3, 13 June 1936; Bahjat Abu Gharbiya, *Fi Khi-damm al-nidal al-'arabi al-filastini: mudhakkirat al-munadil Bahjat Abu Ghar-biyyah, 1916–1949* [*In the Midst of the Palestinian-Arab Struggle: The Memoirs of Freedom-Fighter Bahjat Abu Gharbiyya, 1916–1949*] Beirut: Institute for Palestine Studies, 1993, pp. 68–77; also Matthew Hughes, A history of violence: The shooting in Jerusalem of British Assistant Police Superintendent Alan Sigrist, 12 June 1936, *Journal of Contemporary History* 45/4, 2010, pp. 725–43.

42 Porath, *From Riots,* pp. 267–9; Gudrun Krämer, *A History of Palestine: From the Ottoman Conquest to the Founding of the State of Israel.* Princeton: Princeton University Press, 2008, pp. 287–8; Ted Swedenburg, *Memories of Revolt: The 1936–1939 Rebellion and the Palestinian National Past,* Fayetteville: University of Arkansas Press, 2003, pp. 32–3, 151.

43 Thomas M. Ricks (ed.), *Turbulent Times in Palestine: The Diaries of Khalil Totah, 1886–1955,* Jerusalem and Ramallah: Institute for Palestine Studies, 2009, p. 231, 31 August 1938.

44 I. al-Khuri al-Baytjali, *Dhikrayati* [*My Memoirs*], Jerusalem 1973, Jerusalem: Matba'at al-ma'arif, 1973, pp. 110–111.

45 Ricks, *The Diaries of Khalil Totah,* pp. 233–4, 17–30 September 1938.

46 Ibid., pp. 253, 2 June 1939, 257, 13–14 March 1939

47 Ibid., pp. 259, 29 March 1939.
48 e.g. Ted Swedenburg, "The Palestinian Peasant as National Signifier", *Anthropological Quarterly* 63/1, 1990, pp. 18–30.
49 Karmi, *In Search*, pp. 17–20.
50 Ibid., pp. 9–11; 'Karmi, Mahmud', in al-'Awdat, *Min a'lam al-fikr*, pp. 542–3.
51 N. Tadros Khalaf (ed.), *Les Mémoires de 'Issa al-'Issa; Journaliste et intellectuel palestinien, 1878–1950,* Paris: Karthala, 2009, pp. 227–33.
52 Itamar Radai, *Palestinians in Jerusalem and Jaffa, 1948: A Tale of Two Cities,* London/New York: Routledge, 2016, pp. 65–82, 107–08.
53 Peretz, Palestinian Social Stratification, p. 55.
54 Radai, *Palestinians,* pp. 65–82.
55 Manar Hasan, *Smuyot me-ha-'ayin: nashim ve-he-'arim ha-falastiniyot* [*The Invisible: Women and the Palestinian Cities*], Tel Aviv: Van Leer Institute/ *Hakibbutz Hameuchad* Press, 2017, pp. 17–22, also Swedenburg, *The Palestinian Peasant*, pp. 18–30.

7 Difference, not fragmentation

Christians and Druze in Mandatory Palestine

Yusri Khaizran

Palestinian society during the Mandate period, like other societies in this region, was pluralistic from a religious point of view. This pluralism was not an obstacle to the formation of a national movement and a national discourse that emphasised the concept of unity vis-à-vis the Zionist enterprise. The integration of Christians into political and journalistic activity illustrates this even more, as Yehoshua Porat's works show. At the same time, Christian and certainly Druze participation in the Palestinian national struggle diminished, especially since the early 1930s. This trend coincided with the intensification of the Islamisation process of the national struggle. This process increased during the years of the revolt, deepening trends of alienation among these groups. Despite this, the poor participation of Christians and Druze in the active struggle was not the result of their religious differences, but mainly because of the failure of the Palestinian national movement to bridge the social, political and religious gaps within Palestinian society and to turn the rebellion into a formative event. In this sense, the ramifications of the revolt as an event that alienated the Christians and the Druze were not different in relation to other social groups in Palestinian society.[1]

Introduction

The 1931 census showed that the Christian population had reached nearly 92,000, which was about 11% of the total Palestinian population. The Greek Orthodox community was the largest Christian community, at around 43% of all Christians in Palestine. Roman Catholics constituted 20%, 14% for Melkite, 5% for Anglicans, with the Maronites at about 4%. As for the dichotomy between the city and countryside, the majority of Palestinian Christians lived in urban Jerusalem, Haifa, Jaffa, Nazareth, Ramallah, and Ramla.[2]

The Middle Class in mandatory Palestine was composed disproportionately of Christians, who played a major role in internal commerce. By the same token, Christians were disproportionately represented inside the Mandate's civil administration. They also dominated the professional sector – a great part of the doctors, lawyers, engineers, architects, journalists, and educators – who provided services to the civil service, merchants, landowners, and the wealthy. By the early 1930s, more than half the Arabs in the professions and nearly half in the financial were Christians.[3]

It is not a coincidence that the great majority of newspapers that appeared in Palestine during the late Ottoman period were founded or owned by Palestinian Christians. Out of a total of 39 newspapers from the late Ottoman period, 25 were owned and published by Christian journalists or communal institutions.[4] The development of journalism in late Ottoman Palestine gives only a single indication about Christian social and educational mobility in Mandatory Palestine. The names of two of these newspapers, established respectively by Najib Nassar and the El-Issa cousins, reflected an early identification with Palestine as a territorial and national sphere; these were *al-Karmel* established by Nassar and *Falastin* established by Isa El-Issa and Yussif El-Issa.[5]

Although the British Mandate showed no preference to Christians in Palestine, the Christian communities benefited from the continuation of the millet system and the civil and religious rights guaranteed by the unique character and terms of the Mandate itself.[6] They also formed a vital element of the middle class during this period, many gaining a modern education in mission schools, entering the free professions, and serving in the colonial administration. In 1921, while only constituting around a tenth of the Palestinian population, they formed two-thirds of all Arab administrative clerks. Although this number fell by half in 1938, they continued to be disproportionately represented in the administrative system.[7] The overwhelming majority of the residents of middle-class neighbourhoods in the large cities of Mandatory Palestine were also Christian – Arab and non-Arab. Thus, for example, around 13,000 of the 22,000 residents of south Jerusalem, a middle-class neighbourhood, were Christian, those in Jaffa numbering 17,000 of the city's 45,000 Muslim population.[8]

The Palestinian Christian community was heavily affected by the conflict between the Palestinian national and Zionist movements. The Arab-Israeli war of 1948 resulted in a mass exodus of Palestinian Christians, 50,000–60,000 of the 726,000 of those who were forced to leave their houses in Palestine were Christians. Many of the Christian refugees eventually found their way to the Americas and Australia. The Christian population of Jerusalem provides a specific example of the catastrophic effects of the 1948 war and the prolonged conflict on Arab Christians. In 1944, the Christian population of the city was estimated at more than 29,000. By the end of the 1990s, it numbered less than 10,000, and is estimated at 50,000 today.[9] The same is true of Jaffa – only 3,000 Arabs, Muslims, and Christians are left of a pre-1948 population. Christians constituted a quarter of the city's inhabitants (17,000 out of a total of 71,000) after its occupation by Israeli forces.[10] According to Sabella, by the end of the Mandate, while Palestinian Christians numbered 156,000, only 34,000 remained within Israeli territory.[11]

The Druze of Palestine counted around 15,000 people, constituting no more than 1% of the total population of Palestine. They were overwhelmingly rural geographically, socially peripheral and traditional. In general, the Druze peasant population was led by several Hamulas (clans)[12], the most prominent of them were those of Tarif of the village of Julis, the Mu'adi of Yarka, and Khayr of Abu-Snan.[13] The geographical distribution of the Druze population did not change during the Mandate period or after the establishment of the State of Israel. The history of the Druze during the Mandate was that of notable families who controlled their society and their lands.

Passivism and activism: Druze and Christians within the public sphere

Comparison between Christians and Druze in Mandatory Palestine is not the issue of this article. But it is still necessary to address it briefly. It is obvious that the Christians were more involved and integrated in the Palestinian national movement during the Mandate, as well as in its civil administration. As opposed to the Druze passivism, Christians increasingly and consistently showed active participation in the national civil struggle of the Palestinian society. The Christians' activism versus the Druzes' passivism should be attributed to the urban social background of the Christians, in addition to their acquisition of modern education. They were directly affected by the demographic growth and economic empowerment of the Jewish *Yishuv*. The Christians' activism came to be expressed through the political sphere, cultural activities, journalism, and civil society.

Prior to the establishment of the State of Israel, Christians played a prominent and disproportional role in the Palestinian nationalist movement in Mandatory Palestine and Arab society, liaising with the British authorities on behalf of the Arab populace and representing the Arab-Palestinian position to the Western powers. Christian intellectuals were particularly active in the struggle against the Balfour Declaration. The Muslim-Christian Associations (MCA) created in its wake constituted around 20% of all the members of the latter in the large cities.[14] Despite only comprising 25% of the population in Jerusalem, Christians held 33% of the seats in the MCA leadership committee in the city. This figure is particularly striking in view of the fact that the Christian Palestinian population at the time constituted no more than 10% of the total populace.[15]

Following the end of the First World War and the disintegration of the Ottoman Empire, Muslim-Christian societies (*Al-Jama'iyat al-Islamiyya al-Mesihiyya*) were composed mainly of the *Ayan* social class. These societies rose against the Zionist enterprise and the establishment of the Jewish national home, as promised in 1917 by the British Foreign Secretary, Lord Balfour.[16]

These societies demanded autonomy and independence for Palestine under the patronage of Greater Syria, through participation in international conferences such as that in Versailles and opposition to the Balfour Declaration through demonstrations and political meetings. They also called for political and national unity between the Christians and Muslims in Palestine against the Zionist threat and British colonial rule and demanded that Palestine be part of Syria.[17]

The majority of Arab members of both the Palestinian Communist Party (PCP, founded in 1923) and the League for National Liberation came mostly from urban centres. These were members of either of two social and religious groups; while Christian members were those with urban social background, educated, and constituting the leadership echelons, Muslims constituted echelons of junior members and organised workers in the new industrial economy.[18] Haifa and Jaffa, the less traditional cities on the coast, witnessed intensive urbanisation and the development of a modern economic structure. Hence, the socioeconomic dynamics in the two cities was the meeting point between the revolutionary educated class and the urban workers. The PCP and later the League for National Liberation constituted a modern political framework for new social classes not represented among the traditional Palestinian elite during the British Mandate.[19] Traditionally, Greek Orthodox Christians were most prominent in both the Communist and Arab nationalist movements, not only in Palestine, but generally in all of the Fertile Crescent.

Similar to other historical parts of the Middle East, communism in Palestine applied to social classes of peasants, proletariats, and students. The adoption of communism found powerful echoes among urban middle classes and laid the foundation for the growing integration of educated Christians within the political leadership of the Communist party. The new social milieu that was drawn to Communism and Marxism included many educated middle-class Christians; among them was a distinct social group composed of young, Christian-Orthodox, the majority of who were from Haifa.[20]

Merav Mark suggests three processes that might explain the harmonious meeting between communism and Orthodox Christians in Palestine. In addition to what is called by her the Russian-Arab connections and the anti-clerical sentiments in the community, a third reason for the success of communism was the unique geopolitical situation that resulted from the war in 1948.[21]

Christian activists, most of whom were Orthodox, were at the centre of the split in the ranks of the Palestinian Communist Party in 1943 due to the controversy within the party the solution of the conflict between the Palestinian and Zionist national movements. In September 1943 they concentrated on the establishment of a new political movement called the National Liberation League. Of the eight founding members of the movement, at least seven were Christians, most of them from the Haifa area.

In 1946, the new movement published its political platform, which may be summarised in three main points: the abolition of the British Mandate and the withdrawal of all foreign forces from Palestine; the establishment of a secular, democratic, and egalitarian Palestinian state that would grant equal status to all its citizens; and finally, the movement drew its inspiration from the universal model of Marxism. The new movement emphasised the difference between Judaism and Zionism. While Zionism was described as a movement that served Western imperialism, the movement emphasised the moral obligation to respect the rights of the Jews living in Palestine.

One important issue that should be discussed here, if only briefly, was the nationalisation of the local Orthodox community against the foreign clerics.[22] The struggle for the Palestinianisation of the Orthodox Church was supported by the Palestinian political leadership, in line with the aspirations of the new educated elite, which was trying to replace the clerical elite, by basing its social and intellectual authority on modern education and nationalism. But the dreams of an independent Palestinian Orthodox Church never materialised. The outbreak of the Arab Revolt (1936–39) changed the priorities of the Palestinian national leadership, and communal matters became less important than the common anti-imperialist efforts directed against Zionism and the Mandatory government.[23]

Assessing the political and ideological views of non-elite classes among Palestinian Christians during the mandate is impossible, given the absence of documentation. Still, elitist classes and prominent notables in general supported the National Party established by the Nashashibi faction. There are two common explanations for Christians' support of the Party. The first is due to the fact that a major part of the Arab officials in the mandatory government were Christians; working with the government was consistent with the conciliatory approach adopted by the Nashashibi faction. Second, supporting the Opposition (*al-Mu'arada*) was, to a certain extent, a reflection of growing fears among Christians of the increasing Islamisation of the Palestinian national struggle against Zionism.[24]

There is no dispute that the Grand Mufti, Hajj Amin al-Husseini, had integrated religion and politics and did not hesitate to use Islam as a tool for mobilizing the Arabs in the struggle against Zionism and the British.[25] Islamisation could partially explain Christian elite members' inclination to the opposition given the fact that some important Christian personalities remained loyal to the Mufti, while many Muslims joined the opposition.[26]

The Christians supporting the Nashashibi faction should be seen within the context of the traditional division characterizing the Palestinian social and political elite during the mandate. Furthermore, the fact that most elitist and prominent Christian public figures were on the Nashashibis' side should be attributed to their prestigious social affiliation more than to religion-related considerations.

Struggling and resisting Zionism and the Mandate by mobilizing religious symbols, terminology, and holy places, as indicated by Haiduc-Dale, did not lead to sectarian strife or violence between Muslims and Christians; but it was a significant shift for Palestinian Christians.[27]

British policy towards the Druze continued the Ottoman heritage, which considered the Druze a part of Islamic collectivism. The mandatory authorities' refusal to recognise the Druze as a separate religious community was part of its policy of maintaining the status quo, given the fact that there was no imperial interest in recognizing the Druze as an independent community (similar to French policy in the Lebanon). The Shiite community was recognised as a separate religious group, in order to limit the expansion of the Syrian Great Revolt to southern Lebanon. Therefore, the Druze in Palestine were regarded as a minority within the larger population of Palestinian Sunni-Muslims. Consequently, the Druze were obliged to use the Sharia court system.[28] Furthermore, by establishing the Supreme Muslim Council (SMC), in 1922, the Druze *waqf* and holy shrines were subordinated to the former. In addition, the grand mufti was authorised to approve all appointments to governmental and official positions for the Muslim millet (which included the Druze community).[29]

Druze politics during the British mandate was dominated by the leading families, especially the Tarif family, whose efforts were directed to achieving formal recognition of the Druze as a separate community. These efforts were supported by the other two sides of the triangle: the Kheyr and the Muadi families. Already by the early 1920s, Sheikh Tarif had convinced a large number of leading families to sign a petition calling on the mandatory authorities to recognise the independence of the Druze community.[30] It would be misleading to consider this as community politics, rather than the leading families' politics, striving to achieve representative positions, control over *waqfs* and holy places, and social prestige. Hence, struggling for recognition was not driven by motivation to empowering the community. It was aimed at strengthening the status of the leading families.

Kais Firro has developed an entire historical thesis around the shrine of the prophet Shua'ib, according to which the State of Israel worked to cultivate the religious and social cult of the tomb of the Prophet Shuaib, in order to place the Holy Sepulchre at the centre of the Druze identity formation, according to the Zionist model. It is obvious that the state of Israel spared no efforts to crystallise a Zionist duplicated-model of Druze identity[31] around the shrine of the prophet Shuaib. However, the cultivation of the Shuaib cult was initiated by Tarif religious leaders, driven by the pronounced goal of empowering the family's religious and social prestige.

A review of the history of the Tarif family during the Mandate period actually undermines this thesis. The Tarif family's political and religious activities during the Mandate period focused on two main goals: on the one hand, achieving recognition of the Druze as a separate community, and on the other, gaining control of the tomb of the Prophet Shuaib. Sheikh Tarif and Sheikh Amin Tarif acted consistently to gain control of the tomb of the prophet Shuaib. This can be seen from petitions submitted to the High Commissioner. In addition, Sheikh Amin tried to enlist the support of Syrian Druze leaders to promote this goal.[32]

The death of Sheikh Tarif Muhammad Tarif in 1928 sparked an argument among the Druze leadership in Israel regarding the identity of his successor. During this period, an opposition led by the Khir family sought to replace the Tarif family and place its sons in the positions of spiritual leaders of the community and the *kadi*. Another goal was to undermine the family's control of the assets of the Druze Waqf, headed by Maqam Nabi Shuaib.

However, the superior power of the Tarif family blocked this attempt and the Sheikh Amin Tarif was appointed spiritual head of the community in Israel. This was due Britain's desire to preserve the status quo – Sheikh Amin's ties with the Druze leadership in Lebanon and Syria, his religious status, and his ability to use Maqam Nabi Shuaib and other holy sites as a venue for religious meetings under his leadership.[33]

In view of the intensification of the conflict at the beginning of the twentieth century, the Druze generally chose a neutral position. This position stemmed from their being a relatively weak community, lacking national leadership and aspirations, and their perception of the conflict as a religious one that did not concern them. This was also expressed in a letter published by Druze dignitaries following the events of 1929.[34]

The Great Arab Revolt: the breaking point of the Palestinian national movement

Although the Arab Revolt was sparked by the death of Shaykh 'Izz al-Din al-Qassam in 1935, it did not ultimately lead to the Islamisation of the rebellion, at least not in the stage of civil disobedience.[35] By the same reasoning, the fact that the great majority of the rebellion's leaders were Muslims or traditional Muslims did not lead to Islamizing the rebellion that was in the first place of national character, anti-imperialist, and anti-Zionist. Instrumentalizing Islam as a means of national struggle did not Islamise the 1936–39 revolt.

Internal Palestinian violence was mainly driven by social, militant national and factional motivations. Hence violence was directed against riches, urban middle-class, people accused of cooperation with the British authorities and certainly against individuals and families identified as anti-Husseini. The militarisation of the revolt, the transformation of the centre of gravity of the revolt from the city to the countryside, underwent two transformations that had a profound impact on the internal social and political dynamics of Palestinian society. Rashid Khalidi has described the internal social dynamics of the violent stage of the rebellion as a sort of mistrust between the military field commanders and cadres and the Palestinian political leadership; There was deep mistrust between the nominal Palestinian political leadership grouped together in the Arab Higher Committee and many of those who were actually involved in the armed resistance to the British.[36] As for the catastrophic results of the revolt described by Khalidi:

By the end of the revolt, existing political divisions within the Palestinian polity had become envenomed, leading to profound rifts between the majority supporting the revolt and a minority that had become alienated from the leadership: the consequence was assassinations, infighting, and further weakening of the Palestinian position.[37]

Mustafa Kabha states that the rebellion suppressed social processes, especially that of urbanisation along the coastal plain; consequently, many villagers who migrated to the city in the early 1930s began returning to their villages after the outbreak of the revolt. These were mainly Islamist or communist activists who became the hard core of the rebellion.[38] Kabha concludes:

> Their takeover in the name of the nation's struggle over the population first in the countryside areas, and in 1938 also in the cities, created tension and caused friction on the basis of class. The rise of young leaders, any education, was not a positive development for the important urban families or even for the rural affluent families. This takeover was also characterized by violent activity; the representatives of the new forces began to launch revenge attacks, on class and personal grounds against the upper echelons.[39]

Historical wisdoms presented by these two scholars may serve us in analyzing the ramifications of the revolt against Druze and Christians as part of the Palestinian social fabric in Mandatory Palestine. The trend towards Islamisation that increasingly marked the Palestinian national struggle after the events of 1929 led many Christians to abandon it. One of the first signs of this shift can be found in a letter Khalil Sakakini – a prominent Palestinian writer – sent to his son in December 1932:

> It doesn't matter how high my status is in science and literature, how genuine my patriotism is, how much I do to revive this nation … as long as I'm not a Muslim, I'm nothing or less than nothing. If you want to be worth something, be a Muslim and then they'll let you live in peace.[40]

The conspicuous Islamisation of the Arab revolt, precisely in its military stage, alienated many Arab Christians from its ranks, despite the Mufti's attempts to unite Christians and Muslims under his leadership. The bourgeois and urban status of many Christians also contributed to their limited participation in the revolt. As the centre of gravity of the armed struggle shifted to the countryside, the rural rebels directed their ire at urban residents. The fact that many Christians were traders and clerks also made them the target of repeated attacks, perceived as fuelled by sectarian motives.[41] The increasing Islamisation of the Palestinian national struggle after the 1930s prompted many educated Christians to turn their backs on the traditional leadership and to seek a radical solution within the communist movement, many leading members of the communist 'League of National Liberation' being Christians.[42] The League called for the establishment of an independent, democratic, secular state in Palestine that would protect and ensure equal individual civil rights to Jews and Arabs alike, thereby guaranteeing Arab Christian integration within the public sphere on the basis of cross-cultural and universal values.[43]

The Palestinian movement under the Mufti also regarded the Islamic holy sites in Jerusalem as a weapon for enlisting support, both internally and externally – i.e., in relation to the Arab and Islamic space. Two events in particular signalled the process of the Islamisation of the Palestinian national struggle during this period – the riots of 1929 and the revolt of 1936. These demonstrated that Christians were gradually excluded from the national movement. The urban, bourgeois status of Palestinian-Christians accounted for their minimal participation in the revolt; moreover, the centre of gravity of the armed struggle shifted to rural areas, the rebels there imprinting their stamp on the urban residents. The fact that many Christians were also traders and clerks, made them a target of repeated attacks at the hands of the rebels – this being perceived as an essentially sectarian issue.[44]

However, the political intellectualisation and instrumentalisation of religion were not the sole contributing factors that led to the growth of the trend towards sectarianism within the Palestinian nationalist movement. Just as sectarianism was an outcome of the socio-economic dynamics that drove Palestinian society, so it was also umbilically linked to the political patterns of behaviour of the elite. During the Mandate period, the Palestinian elite was split into two factions – the Husseinis, who ruled the Supreme Islamic Council, and the Nashashibis, who were excluded from it. In an effort to strengthen their political position and challenge the official nationalist discourse led by Haj Amin al-Husseini, which emphasised national unity between Muslims and Christians, two of the Mufti's opponents – Sheikh Suleiman al-Farouki and Sheikh Asaad al-Shuqayri – convened a 'National-Islamic Council' and initiated the establishment of organisations known as the Nationalist-Islamic Associations.[45] The two subsequently sought to promote their political status as a rival force to the Mufti by raising a new agenda – namely, the struggle against the non-proportional representation of Christians in the governmental administration and their control of the Palestinian municipal economy. Their public relations campaign called for a boycott of Christian stores and trade with Christians – a move that was felt primarily in Jerusalem and Jaffa.[46]

The internal mechanisms driving Palestinian politics and the social dichotomy between minority groups of the educated, affluent Christian middle class and the poorer, less-educated urban Muslim majority formed fertile ground for the emergence of political sectarianism and its expansion into violent conflict in the 1930s.[47]

In 1933, there was friction between Al-'Assa, editor of the newspaper *Filastin*, and Farouki, editor of the newspaper *Al-Jama'a al-Islamiyya*. The tension between the two took on personal and religious form, which was expressed in the publication of articles in the two newspapers against each other. The British police were on guard in Jaffa because there was fear that the conflict would escalate into riots between young Christians and the Muslim community.[48]

Laila Parsons's analysis of Druze political activity during the revolt shows how pivotal this period was in the formation of Druze loyalties and behaviour patterns, with both Palestinian rebels and the *Yishuv* vying for Druze support during the uprising's early months. At this time, some Druze (mainly Muslims) supported the rebellion, while others took the side of the Jews. However, according to Parsons, "The majority of Druze adopted a neutral position", trying to "stay as uninvolved as possible in the hope that the troubles would pass them by and that they would be able to carry on with their normal lives".[49] Nevertheless, some rebel groups attacked individual Druzes and whole villages, because they saw the lack of Druze involvement in the uprising as a sign of betrayal; in other cases, attacks were directed against individuals who were accused of collaborating with the Jews or with the Mandatory authorities. At the beginning of the uprising in April 1936, the leaders of the revolt called on the Druze to join them. The commander of the revolt in the north issued a flyer emphasizing the Druze's loyalty to the Arab struggle.[50] Upon the outbreak of the revolt, some Druze fellahin joined the ranks of the rebels and quite a few Druze sources who sympathised with the Palestinian national movement, as well as those who demonstrated a hostile attitude towards it, mentioned names of several Druze fellahin who were among the rebels.[51]

But what happened in Palestinian society as a whole also occurred among the Druze themselves; that is, there were Druze who joined the rebels and there were Druze who joined the peace associations that cooperated with the British.

The anarchistic militarisation of the uprising, the loss of control of the political leadership over the uprising and the growing Islamisation among the groups of fighters led to a series of murderous attacks on the Druze communities between 1936 and 1939.

The chronological review presented by Raja Faraj shows that the murderous attacks on the Druze villages multiplied from the end of 1938, and included mainly those on the Carmel mountains, collecting protection fees, killing Druze who were accused of collaborating with the Jews, stealing cattle, and more. This wave reached its peak with the assassination in 1939 of Sheikh Hassan Khanifas, one of the most prominent and well-known Druze from Shfaram.[52]

The fear of escalation led to the immediate intervention of Palestinian institutions of reconciliation. Following a mandatory court decision to sentence to death Muslim rebels who were convicted of killing Druze peasants, Muslim and Druze notables went into action to avoid implementation of the sentence. The fear was that if the execution were carried out, acts of Muslim revenge and retaliation would follow. A committee was formed in order to achieve a *sulha* (reconciliation). The arrival of a delegation from Syria headed by Abd al-Ghaffar al-Atrashi was an indication of the nature of the escalation. By early 1940, the Druze and Muslim committees reached a *sulha* agreement, under the auspices of the mandatory authorities. This put an end to two years of one of the several inter-communal conflicts that broke out between 1938–39.[53]

The arrival of Druze volunteers from Syria and Lebanon aroused deep concern among the Zionist leadership; accordingly, two chiefs from the Abu-Rukun family, Hasan and Zayed, were sent on a mission to convince the Druze leaders of Lebanon and Syria to stop the stream of volunteers. These appeals fell on attentive ears in the case of the Junblati faction's leader al-Sitt Nazirah Junblat. The suspicious and even hostile attitude of al-Sitt Nazirah to the Muslims was most evident during the revolt. She was strongly opposed to the Druze-Lebanese volunteers joining the rebellion movement – "to be [hand] in hand with the government and the Jews because the end was destruction and destruction for Muslims".[54] Works that come from a political point of view, such as that by Zaid Naffa, try to glorify the Druze participation in the uprising.[55] Still, most Druze who took part in the uprising acted individually and no communal efforts were made in favour of the rebellion or the rebels.

In fact, Druze conscription goes back to the 1936–39 revolt. Druze historian Kais Firro sums up the historical impact of the revolt on the Druze community thus:

> Although the Druzes within Israel maintained an attitude of indifference toward the conflict, their particularism and the impact of the events of the years 1936–1939 were later made use of by the Israel authorities to gain the loyalty of the Druzes to the new state.[56]

The Zionist movement – and subsequently the State of Israel – thus construed the revolt as a traumatic event that threatened Druze existence. In the wake of the murder of five Druze peasants by Palestinian rebels, Abba Hushi, a powerful Zionist leader, stated: "The massacres … have lit the flame of revenge in the hearts of the Druzes and if only someone could exploit this, the outcome would be significant".[57] Therefore, the revolt was manipulated to form the historical background for promoting an alliance between the Druze and the Jewish State as two persecuted minorities fighting Arab-Muslim oppression.

The basic assumption in Israel's strategy towards the Druze has not changed since the 1930s and has continued to be based on the idea of a League of Minorities. The Druze were considered non-Arabs and haters of other Muslims who could be used against those around them. As Aharon Chaim Cohen wrote in 1937, "This is the way for us: to create visiting points within the dark Arab sea which surrounds us".[58] Or as Kais Firro called it in his book, *The Druze in the Jewish State*, the Druze were a knife in the back of Arab unity. This line of thought had a practical translation: the Druze recruits were separated within the minorities unit. The French and British used the same practice in the Troupes Specials in Syria and Lebanon, and the British with the Iraqi Levies.

Yitschak Ben-Zvi, Israel's second president, gave this 'Druze policy' an ideological and conceptual dimension. He referred to

> the old tradition connecting the Jews with the Druze, whether ancient history or nothing but a product of tradition and late acceptance. I mean the holy places. One of the greatest and most praised personalities of their days is Shuaib or Yitro, Moshe's father-in-law.

The second is related to Zionist theorisation of Druze history as a 'persecuted minority group'.

> This nation has suffered so much from the persecution of Muslim and Christian fanaticism for centuries. It has no irredentism, neither near nor far. One should consider this friendship rooted in ancient tradition and similar fate worthy and deserving the cultivation and strengthening of historical ties.[59]

This notion of mobilizing the Druze against their Arab-Muslim neighbours has always accompanied Zionist political strategy. Two examples are worthy of note. In 1939, the Zionist movement developed a plan to transfer the Druze village populations in the Galilee and the Carmel Mountains to the Hauran Mountains. This population transfer would be organised and financed by the Zionist movement. Abba Hushi was given the mandate to negotiate on behalf of the Zionist movement with the Druze leader Sultan al Atrash, to convince him to support the plan and cooperate in carrying it out. Were the peasants to settle there, the Zionist movement would help each of them to purchase a piece of land. Three decades later, right after the 1967 war, Yigal Allon, one of the Labor leaders, suggested using the disruption resulting from the war to create a Druze buffer state between Israel and Syria in the Golan Heights and the Hauran Mountains. This state would be sponsored and armed by the Israeli government and would serve as a front line in the struggle against the Arab threat.[60]

It is doubtful if one can relate to the 'Christian policy' of the Zionist movement. But it may be argued that as early as the second half of the 1930s, and against the backdrop of the Arab Revolt, a Zionist 'Druze policy' began to crystallise, with the clear aim of separating the Druze from the Palestinian-Arabs, channelling a Druze doctrinal particularism into a separatist trend like the Zionist model. This trend is reflected at both levels of the discourse and practice, especially in the alliance with Druze families, the transfer plan, and later in the recruitment project.

The plan, which was described by Hillel Cohen as a key document, rested on three main strategies. First, supporting opposition forces and creating an alternative leadership; second, deepening fissures within Palestinian society; and third, launching a propaganda machine to publicise the economic advantages of Zionism.[61]

The execution of this plan was assigned to Chaim Margalit Kalvarisky, head of the Zionist Executive's Arab Department. As far as Arab-Christians were concerned, the plan strove to create "provocation of dissension between Christians and Muslims".[62] But the main focus of Kalvarisky's strategy was the Muslim effendis and the social elite. The only way to win over their sympathy was to emphasise the economic benefits they would receive from the establishment of a Jewish state. Although driving a wedge between Muslims and Christians lay at the heart of the plan, the Muslim social elite remained the primary objective of it.[63] Kalvarisky led the efforts to establish Muslim-National Associations, with the clear aim of creating a counterweight to the Muslim-Christian Associations, which were considered as the hard kernel of the Palestinian national movement.[64] The Muslim-National Associations were headed by public personalities who were known as oppositionists to al-Haj Amin al-Husseini. Their activities challenged his leadership as well as the Palestinian national unity in the name of Islam and Muslim interests.

Demographic, socio-economic, and cultural differences between Druze and Christians may explain the deep gaps between the two communities in their levels of participation in the Palestinian national struggle. Yet neither group played a significant role in the violent revolt against the British. According to Porath's list of rebel commanders, only 1.5% were Christians. In comparison with the percentage of Arab Christians within the Palestinian population (approximately 9%), and in comparison to the constructive role they played in the composition of the Muslim-Christian Associations, they were under-represented among the rebel leaders and within the military activism of the rebellion.[65] Haiduc-Dale counts only three Christians among the revolt's local officers.[66] The Christians' contribution to the Palestinian national struggle was prominent in the fields of politics and journalism.[67]

Some Christians and Druze were convinced that they were targeted because of their religious identification. But attacks against Christians and Druze should be seen within the wider context of the internal conflicts and schisms that dominated the Palestinian arena during the revolt. Violence against Christian and Druze individuals was not more violent or cruel than that directed against urban Muslims or against people identified with the Nashashibis. Haj Amin went to lengths to maintain good ties with elite Christians. Furthermore, he was active in ending sectarian tensions and divisions between Muslim and Christians.[68] Despite that, Christians, particularly in the cities, were exposed to repeated attacks by the rebels.

To conclude this point of discussion, it is beyond any doubt that Christians were more active and more prominent within the Palestinian national movement. This applied also to the 1936–39 revolt, where Christians played an important role in perpetuating the general strike. But when it comes to the Palestinian armed struggle, their role was minimal. It seems that the Christians' non-violent participation in the Palestinian national struggle was due to their social configuration as urban and bourgeoisie classes.

Conclusion

The mobilisation of religion as a recruiting mechanism in the service of the national struggle was not unique to the Palestinian national landscape. The Turkish national movement, despite its emphasis on secularisation, did not hesitate to use Islam or religious tradition as a means of control. The Nasserist regime, which expanded the institutionalisation of secular Arabism, at the same time utilised Islam, whether as a tool of control or for the sake of legitimizing Arabism. The Zionist movement followed the same path and did not hesitate to use symbols and religious texts to mobilise the masses. In the same vein, the Palestinian national movement, in view of the intensity of the threats posed by Zionism and the Mandate, also found in Islam an effective means of mobilizing the masses, of forging Arab and Muslim solidarity, and first and foremost, creating the motivation for the armed struggle against the *Yishuv* and the British.

Islamisation, in the sense of stimulating religious enthusiasm, wasn't the sole explanation of the modest participation of groups such as the Christians and the Druze in the Palestinian national struggle, especially during the revolt. Indeed, the Islamisation of discourse and struggle created alienation. But the modest extent of Christians and Druze participation should be seen in the wider social and political context that does not refer only to them. The same undoubtedly refers to the middle class in large cities, for example. This low participation was a consequence of structural weakness that accompanied the Palestinian national movement because of the Mufti's factional approach, internal schisms, and the absence of a cohesive national program. Is was also a result of the inability of the Palestinian national movement to channel local loyalties into a common national denominator. The Palestinian national movement failed to establish a national dialogue that would lead to internal political and social cohesion, just as it failed to create a mechanism for bridging existing gaps between the city and the village, between different religious groups, and especially between the two rival Muslim factions. Determining participation in the 1947–48 war as a measure of loyalty to the Palestinian national movement is a fundamentally false assumption, because Palestinian society as a whole could not mobilise its human resources for the war effort at the most fateful hour of its history. The low level of Christian and Druze participation in the 1936–39 revolt was in fact an indication of a structural crisis within the Palestinian national movement rather than an issue of the loyalty of minority groups.

Notes

1 Yehoshua Porath, *The Emergence of the Palestinian Arab National Movement, 1918–1929,* London: Frank Cass, 1974; idem, *The Palestinian Arab National Movement: From Riots to Rebellion, 1929–1939,* London: Frank Cass, 1977; also Laura Robson, *Colonialism and Christianity in Mandate Palestine,* Austin, TX: University of Texas Press, 2012, p. 151.

2 Noah Haiduc-Dale, *Arab Christians in British Mandate Palestine: Communalism and Nationalism,* Edinburgh: Edinburgh University Press, 2013, pp. 8–9.

3 Itamar Radai, The Rise and the Fall of the Palestinian-Arab Middle Class under the British Mandate, *Journal of Contemporary History* 51/3, 2016, pp. 4–5.

4 Abd al-Qadir Yassen, *al-Sahafa al-Arabiya fi Falistin, [Arab Journalism in Palestine]al-Mawysua al-Falestinia.* Damascus: *Hayaat al-Mawsuaa al-Falisinya,* II, pp. 430–2.

5 Mustafa Kabha, *Journalism in the Eye of the Storm,* Jerusalem: Yad Ben-Zvi, 2004, p. 15 [Hebrew].

6 Daphne Tsimhoni, The status of Arab Christians under the British Mandate in Palestine, *Middle Eastern Studies* 20/4, 1984, pp. 168, 185.

7 Yosef Vashitz, *Arabs in Eretz Yisrael.* Tel Aviv: Merhavia, 1947, p. 142 [Hebrew]; Don Peretz, Palestinian social stratification: The political implications, *Journal of Palestine Studies* 7/1, 1977, pp. 51–2.

8 Itamar Radai, The Collapse of the Palestinian Arab Middle Class of 1948: The Case of Qatamon, *Middle Eastern Studies* 43/6, 2007, p. 962; idem. *A Tale of Two Cities,* Tel Aviv: Tel Aviv University Press, 2015, p. 170 [Hebrew].

9 Bernard Sabella, The Emigration of Christian Arabs: Dimensions and Causes of the Phenomenon, in *Christian Communities in the Arab Middle East: The Challenge of the Future,* edited by Andre Pacini, Oxford: Oxford University Press, 1998, p. 135.

10 Radai, *A Tale of Two Cities,* pp. 170, 241.

11 Bernard Sabella, *Palestinian Christians: Historical Demographic Developments, Current Politics and Attitude Towards Church, Society and Human Rights.* Sabella Survey on Palestinian Christians in the West Bank and Israel, p. 8: www.fosna.org/files/fosna/events/SabeelSurveyPalestinianChristians.pdf

12 *Hamula* is a name given to a group of people who claim descent from a common ancestor. In Arab Villages, during the Ottoman and British periods, each *hamula* occupied a special quarter (*hara*), its members held ownership over common land (*Mush'a*). *Hamula*s lost their economic and social functions following lands confiscation, social and economic changes generated by the state of Israel. Nonetheless, *hamulas* still played a significant political role, especially in local municipal elections. Majid al-Haj, The changing Arab kinship structure: The effect of modernization in an urban community, *Economic Development and Cultural Change,* 36/2, 1988, pp. 237–58.

13 Kais Firro, *The Druzes in the Jewish State,* Brill: Leiden, 1999, p. 21.

14 Porat, *The Emergence,* p. 24.

15 Haiduc-Dale, *Arab Christians in British Mandate Palestine,* p. 42.

16 Bernard Wasserstein, *The British in Palestine: The Mandatory Government and the Arab-Jewish Conflict 1917–1929,* 2nd edition, Oxford: Basil Blackwell, 1991, pp. 14–16.

17 Bayan Nuwayhid al-Hut, *al-Qiyadat wa al-Muasasat al-Siyasiya fi Falastin [Political Leaderships and Institutions in Palestine],* Beirut: Muassast al-Dirasat al-Falastinya, 1981, pp. 82–3.

18 Ilana Kaufman, *Arab National Communism in the Jewish State,* Gainesville, FL: University Press of Florida, 1997, p. 25.

19 Ibid., p. 26.

20 Merav Mack, Orthodox and communist: A history of a Christian community in Mandate Palestine and Israel, *British Journal of Middle Eastern Studies* 424, 2015, p. 395.
21 Ibid., pp. 393–4.
22 Robson, *Colonialism and Christianity*, pp. 86–90.
23 Mack, Orthodox and Communist, p. 393.
24 Haiduc-Dale, *Arab Christians*, pp. 69–70.
25 Ibid., p. 69.
26 Ibid., pp. 69–70.
27 Ibid., p. 90.
28 Amir Khnifess, Israel and the Druze Political Action, PhD diss., SOAS, University of London, 2015, p. 77.
29 Porath, *The Emergence*, p. 174.
30 Khnifess, Israel and the Druze, p. 78.
31 Kais Firro, Reshaping Druze Particularism in Israel, *Journal of Palestine Studies*, 30/3, 2000, pp. 42–8.
32 Raja Farag, *Mawqif al-Shaykh Amin Tarif* [*The Attitude of Shaykh Amin Tarif*], *al-Kalimah* (*Daliat El-Karmel*), 20 August 1990, pp. 8–9.
33 Kais Firro, Druze *maqamat* (Shrines) in Israel: From ancient to newly-invented tradition, *British Journal of Middle Eastern Studies* 32/2, 2005, p. 227.
34 Rami Zeedan, *The Arab Battalion: The History of the Minorities' Unit in the IDF, 1948–1956*, Ben-Shemen: *Maarachot*, 2015, pp. 25–7.
35 Rashid Khalidi, *The Iron Cage: The Story of the Palestinian Struggle for State-hood*, London, UK: Oneworld Publications, 2007, pp. xxiii–iv.
36 Ibid., pp. 112–13.
37 Ibid., p. 108.
38 Mustafa Kabha, *The Palestinians: A People Dispersed*, Ra'anana: The Open University of Israel, 2008, pp. 33–4 (Hebrew).
39 Ibid., p. 34.
40 Khalil al-Sakakini, *Yawmiyat Khalil al-Sakakini* [*Diaries of Khalil al-Sakakini*] Ramallah: Khalil Sakakini Cultural Center, 2005, chapter 4, p. 387 [Arabic].
41 Haiduc-Dale, *Arab Christians*, pp. 140–1; Fuad Farah, *al-Hijarah al-Hayya* [*The Living Stones*], Nazareth, 2003, pp. 82–3.
42 Yehoshua Porath, '*Usbat al-Taharrur al-Watani* [National Liberation League] 1943–1948, *Asian and African Studies* 4, 1968, pp. 1–5.
43 Ilana Kaufman, Communists and the 1948 War: PCP, Maki and the National Liberation League, *Journal of Israeli History* 33/2, 2014, p. 117.
44 Farah, *al-Hijarah al-Hayya*, pp. 82–3.
45 Emil al-Ghuri, *Falastin Abr Sitin Am* [*Palestine During Sixty Years*] Beirut: Dar al-Nahar, 1972, pp. 218–9.
46 Ibid., pp. 219–23.
47 Ibid., pp. 223–5; the most violent-sectarian event referred to by al-Ghuri was the assassination of Michel Mitri, the head of league of Arab workers at Jaffa, in July 1935. This event came against the background of incitement against Christians.
48 The Central Zionist Archive (CZA), S90/2053/2, End of the Polemic between Isa al-Isa and al-Faruqi, 16 March 1933.
49 Laila Parsons, *The Druze between Palestine and Israel, 1947–1949*, Basingstoke: MacMillan Press Ltd., 2000, p. 28.
50 Raga Farag, *The Relationship Between the Druze and Jews*, Yanouh, 2002, p. 55 (Hebrew).
51 Ali Nasib Falah, *Duruz Falastin fi Thawrat Am 1936* [The Druze of Palestine During the 1936 Revolt] n.p.1996, pp. 19–21; *Ahmad Ali al Qadamani, Lamha an al-Arab al-Druz Qabl wa Baad Qiyam Dawlat*, Israel, [A Profile of the Arab-Druze before and after the Establishment of the State of Israel] *al-Itihad*, Haifa, 18 June 2010.

52 Farag, *The Relationship Between*, pp. 63–9 [Hebrew].
53 Firro, *The Druzes*, pp. 29–30.
54 See the report by Sheikh Zaid Abu Rachan sent by Abba Hushi to the Druze villages in Lebanon in 1936; CZA, 25/9165; 4 October 1936.
55 Said Naffa, *Al-Arab al-Duruz wa al-Haraka al-Wataniya al-Falastiniya Hata 1948* [*The Arab-Druze and the Palestinian National Movement up to 1948*], 4th edition, al-Quds: Matbaat al-Risalah al-Maqdisiya, 2010, pp. 81–9; pp. 127–40.
56 Kais M. Firro, *A History of the Druze*, Leiden: Brill, 1992, p. 363.
57 Firro, *The Druzes*, p. 27.
58 A.H. Cohen, On the fate of our relationship with the Druze nation, CZA 25/6638, 2 November 1937.
59 I. Ben-Zvi, Druze Settlement in Israel, *Archaeological, Historical and Geographical Studies*, 1953, p. 209 (Hebrew).
60 Shimon Avivi, *Copper Plate: Israeli Policy towards the Druze 1948–1967*, Jerusalem: Yad Ben-Zvi, 2007, pp. 363–5 (Hebrew).
61 Hillel Cohen, *Army of Shadows*, Berkeley: University of California Press, 2008, pp. 17–18.
62 Ibid., p. 17.
63 Ibid., p. 19.
64 Ibid.
65 Porath, *Palestinian Arab*, p. 269; Haiduc-Dale, *Arab Christians*, p. 150.
66 Ibid., p. 150.
67 Ibid., p. 149.
68 Ibid., pp. 152–3.

8 A troubled bond

The Palestinian-Arab national movement and the Arab states

Avraham Sela

This chapter addresses the intricate relations that developed between the Palestinian Arab national movement and the neighbouring Arab countries during the British Mandate. It explains how the growing Arab-Muslim identification with the Palestine Question (*qadiyyat filastin*) namely, the Zionist threat to the Arab nature of Palestine and the anguish of its Arab population, turned into a prominent cultural and political issue among the Arab and Islamic peoples.

In addition to other formative processes of the inter-war years, primarily the making of new Arab states over the wreckages of the Ottoman Empire, this period witnessed a growing involvement of the Arab fledgling states in the intensifying Arab-Jewish conflict in Palestine. The domestic-regional nexus concerning the Palestine Question became a pivotal factor in inter-Arab rivalries and competition for regional leadership, while indirectly accelerating Pan-Arab and Pan-Islamic tendencies. By the late 1930s, the Palestine Question became a prominent political factor on both domestic and regional levels.

The literature on the Palestine conflict during the Mandate has largely taken the politics of Arab involvement in this matter as a manifestation of pan-Arab sentiments, rarely explaining the social and political driving forces that shaped the development and nature of the relations between the Arabs of Palestine and those of the Arab states.[1] This chapter thus seeks to identify those forces and to analyze their impact on the parties concerned; the increasingly violent Arab-Jewish conflict over Palestine; state formation and social and political dynamics; and the emergence of a regional Arab political system marked by both inter-state competition and shared Arab-Muslim identity.

It analyses, first, the bottom-up diffusion of interest in the Palestine Question, from societal to the domestic political level, up to its adoption by the state as an official interest, which by the late-1930s turned into a primary collective Arab concern. It concludes by highlighting the growing tension between the Palestinian national leadership and the Arab states during WWII, and the latter's institutionalised patronage of the Palestine Question following the foundation of the Arab League (AL) in 1945.

Palestine in Arab-Islamic consciousness: the domestic-regional nexus

The Palestinian-Arab perspective

From the outset, the organised political resistance of the Palestinian Arabs against the Zionist enterprise included persistent efforts to mobilise the Arab and Muslim peoples for preventing the realisation of Zionist aspirations in Palestine. The contours of these efforts were shaped primarily by the growth of the Zionist enterprise in Palestine, the British Mandate's policy and the emergence of newly established political entities by Britain and France that coincided with, and effectively contrasted the rapidly expanding ideology of Pan-Arab nationalism.

Early Palestinian-Arab efforts to mobilise outside support for their cause focused on Arab and Muslim unofficial associations. Appealing to their religious sentiments, these efforts propagated the imminent Zionist threat to the mosques of *al-Haram al-Sharif* (Temple Mount) in Jerusalem coupled by a broad fund-raising campaign for renovating this primary holy site for Islam. Conducted throughout the Hijäz, Iraq, India and Egypt, the Palestinian efforts corresponded with the rise of nationalism and defiance toward Western colonialism in the Arab and Muslim countries.

The living spirit behind this effort was al-Haj Amin al-Husseini, whose dual prestigious positions as the Mufti of Jerusalem and President of the Supreme Muslim Council (SMC), added further effect to this project. His religious positions and fundraising activities enabled Haj Amin to build a broad network of connections with senior nationalist and religious figures across the Arab and Muslim world, from India to the Maghreb. His personal identification with the project of glorifying and defending al-Haram al-Sharif entailed – if not originally aimed at – the enhancement of his own status as a prominent Arab and Muslim leader. The Mufti's long-term project was augmented by his personal involvement in Pan-Islamic and Arab national affairs. In addition to participating in the debates on the Caliphate question and taking part in the Islamic congresses held in Cairo and Mecca in 1926, he maintained political ties with leading Syrian Pan-Arab figures, and organised material and political support for the Syrian revolt of 1925. By the late 1920s, the Mufti had become the most influential Palestinian-Arab leader and the one personifying the Palestine Question.

In late August 1928, the completion of the renovation of *al-Haram al-Sharif's* mosques was celebrated in Jerusalem in the presence of Emir `Abdallah and other non-Palestinian Arab notables. The eruption that same month of a dispute over the Jewish right of prayer at the Wailing Wall was a golden opportunity for the Mufti to accelerate his quest for imbuing the struggle against Zionism with an overall Islamic meaning. On 1 November, Muslim figures from Palestine, Syria, Lebanon and Transjordan gathered in Jerusalem under the auspices of the SMC in support of the struggle for the Muslim holy places.

The yearlong dispute over the Wailing Wall enabled the Mufti to enhance the propagation of the Palestine Question as a national Arab and Islamic concern. The culmination of the Wailing Wall dispute in countrywide riots in August 1929 – the most violent and widespread since the beginning of the Zionist enterprise – reverberated across the neighbouring Arab countries with manifestations of solidarity and noticeable response by social organisations to requests of financial aid for Arab casualties. In Egypt, Islamic associations collected money for Arab victims of the riots and, by propagating solidarity with the Arabs of Palestine, they exploited it to strengthen their own domestic influence. In the following years, particularly the Muslim Brothers (MB) forged close links with Haj Amin al-Husseini, which led to close cooperation between them during the Arab Revolt of 1936–39.

The Arab and Muslim responses to the 1929 riots incentivised the Mufti to intensify the use of the Arab-Jewish religious aspects of the conflict over Palestine. This became necessary in view of Britain's deeply frustrating response to the riots. In contrast to the Passfield White Paper of October 1930, which imposed strict limitations on Jewish immigration and land sales to Jews, intensive Zionist lobbying in London resulted in PM MacDonald's letter to Weizmann in February 1931, which practically reversed the new White Paper. The Arab Executive Committee (AEC) rejected the PM's letter, concluding that the Arabs of Palestine should cease relying on Britain for ensuring their national and economic well-being and, instead, put their trust in the Arab and Muslim world.[2] Henceforth, the Palestinian Arab national movement increasingly adopted organised disobedience – with certain groups preparing for armed struggle – and, at the same time, seeking Pan-Islamisation and Pan-Arabisation of the Palestine problem.[3]

The Mufti convinced leading Muslim figures – such as Muhammad Ali, leader of the Indian Caliphate Committee – to testify before the commission of inquiry set up by the League of Nations to examine the issue of Jewish and Muslim rights at the Wailing Wall. His major achievement, however, was the General Islamic Congress, which he convened in Jerusalem in December 1931, with unofficial Islamic and Arab delegates from 25 Muslim countries. Although no official representatives attended the meeting other than Yemen's delegate, the Congress attested to the Mufti's success in inculcating an all-Islamic/all-Arab concern for the Palestine Question. Despite strong opposition by Egypt's religious establishment and King Fu'ad, and the boycott of the congress by the Mufti's Palestinian rivals, it was a major success.[4]

The broad Muslim representation, with highly reputable Islamic and Arab national figures attending, the congress constituted primarily a demonstration of Islamic solidarity with the Palestine Question. The congress's resolutions indeed adopted the SMC's agenda, including: the establishment of an Islamic university in Jerusalem; applying a strict boycott of the Jewish community products by all the Muslim countries; extending financial aid for preventing sales of Arab lands to Jews; and protesting against the Mandate's policy.

None of these resolutions, however, was implemented apart from the last one. The congress thus failed to counterbalance the international Jewish support for the Zionist movement by establishing an international Islamic front providing financial and political support for the Palestinians.[5]

Haj Amin's political achievement further deepened the internal divisions that dominated the Palestinian political arena throughout the Mandate. Though all political factions resisted the Zionist enterprise, they differed over the question of cooperation with the government.[6] Contrary to the Opposition factions led by the Nashashibi clan supported cooperation with the government, the Husseini clan and its supporters who dominated the Palestinian political arena, dictated a policy of strict boycott of the Mandatory government (although inconsistent with Haj Amin's position as President of the SMC). In addition, they persistently demanded independence for Palestine as an Arab state. From the late 1920s, these rival factions aligned along with the main Arab regional divisions – the Opposition leaders established close relations with the Emir ʿAbdallah of Transjordan, while the Husseinis allied with Ibn Saʿud and Egypt in addition to their supportive networks of unofficial Syrian, Iraqi, Lebanese and Egyptian organisations.

The Arab states and the Palestine Question: the domestic perspective

Between the two world wars, Arab societies in the Levant and Mesopotamia increasingly espoused the Palestinian-Arab resistance to the Zionist enterprise and the British Mandate as an integral part of their own struggle for liberation from Western colonialism. Thanks to geographical proximity and traditional social networks with Palestine, these societies perceived Zionism not only as an extension of the European imperialist invasion of the Arab homeland. Zionism's colonial-settler nature and unhidden intention to establish a Jewish state over Palestine depicted the Zionist enterprise as a formidable threat to the Arab-Muslim nature of Palestine. Seeing Palestine as an indispensable link between the east (*mashriq*) and the west (*maghrib*) of the Arab homeland, Arab nationalists perceived Zionism as a threat to pan-Arab unity. Resistance to Zionism and its enterprise in Palestine thus became increasingly conceived as a national as well as a religious duty, and success in this effort as a prerequisite for the realisation of the envisioned Arab national unity.

The growing public interest in the Palestine Question was a result of the rapid social changes and processes of modernisation – especially urbanisation, expanded education and politicisation of the masses. The emergence of state education systems played a discernible role in the political socialisation of the younger generation, instilling common values of Pan-Arab national identity, independence from foreign domination and an awakening (*nahda*) to a new era of rejuvenated Arab grandeur. These processes had an increasing impact on the changing political sphere, indicated by the rise of modern social movements and populist parties that reshaped collective identities and challenged the existing social and political order.

By the late 1930s, the combined impact of these processes had resulted in a growing domestic instability due to social contention, intertwined with resistance to the continued foreign domination, accompanied by a defiance of the legitimacy of the latter's indigenous allies represented by the traditional notable elites. Increasingly shaped by an emerging urban middle class, politics in the fledgling Arab states assumed a markedly radical nature, saturated with a romantic, populist and chauvinist discourse of identity directed against the Western 'others' – colonialism, Zionism and Arab public figures perceived as insufficiently faithful to national and pan-Arab objectives. The twin processes of politicisation and nationalisation of the masses thus accounted for the Islamisation of nationalism, turning politics into the art of stirring public sentiments. Opposition groups employed Arab nationalist and Islamic rallying myths and symbols as effective means of mobilizing political support, dragging the ruling elites to adopt this discourse as a strategy of survival.[7]

The character traits of domestic Arab politics were particularly prevalent in the newly established political entities in the Fertile Crescent, which suffered the typical weaknesses of post-colonial states: a lack of distinctive political and territorial identity, ineffective institutions and bureaucracy; a highly fragmented population along ethno-religious and socio-economic lines and scarcity of economic resources. In addition, their newly established boundaries cried out for recognition by their neighbours, especially in view of the challenge posed to them by the Hashemite rulers' ambitions of regional unification under their thrones.[8] Supra-state Arab nationalist and Islamic movements that consistently challenged the legitimacy of the newly established Arab states further aggravated the destabilizing domestic conditions. As a result, the Arab ruling elites came under pressure to adopt a nationalist anti-colonial discourse committed to the Palestine Question and resistance to Zionism as the ultimate proof of their patriotism.

The intensifying conflict in Palestine triggered strong emotional identification among Arab neighbouring societies with their distressed Palestinian brethren. Thanks to its heavily loaded symbolism, the Palestine cause became a primary rallying issue in domestic politics. Indeed, political groups and social movements lost no opportunity to demonstrate in public their solidarity with and material support for the Palestinian Arabs as a means to advance their own stature in their respective communities. In this context, the length and intensity of the Palestinian Arabs' Revolt (1936–39) were crucial in triggering broad manifestations of solidarity in the neighbouring Arab states with the Palestinian Arabs in the neighbouring Arab states. With or without direct appeals from the Palestinian leadership, Pan-Arab nationalists in Iraq, Syria, Lebanon and Transjordan, and Islamic groups in Egypt organised demonstrations in their cities, published articles in the press and collected donations, dragging their governments into the fray.[9] The official responses of individual Arab states soon took the form of inter-Arab competition and/or joint action for the sake of Arab Palestine.

Egypt's gradual movement toward official adoption of the Palestine Question is a typical example – albeit late, compared to the Fertile Crescent states – of this dynamic, underlining the close interrelationship between the Palestine Question and inter-state Arab politics. Although public interest in the Palestine Question was apparent already in the late 1920s, it was not until the late-1930s that Egypt became officially involved in the inter-Arab deliberations concerning Palestine. The turning point in this process was Egypt's response to the Peel Commission's recommendation of establishing a Jewish state in a part of Palestine. This was indicated by Nahhas's decision to adopt the Palestine Question as an official policy, after more than a year of deliberate restraint.

Since the beginning of the strike and rebellion in Palestine, PM Nahhas Pasha repeatedly communicated through diplomatic channels his concerns about those events, requesting Britain to alter its policy in Palestine and stressing the destabilizing effect of the events there on his government. The Peel Commission's recommendations and the resumed Arab revolt in Palestine in 1937, however, intensified the domestic pressures on the government to follow the Iraqi example and extend material support to the Palestinian rebellion. During the Palestinian revolt, the Muslim Brotherhood, which the Egyptian government employed as a springboard for direct involvement in the inter-Arab arena, accounted, more than any other political group in Egypt, for placing the Palestine Question high on the public agenda.[10] In July 1937, Nahhas told the British ambassador in Cairo that Egypt could not stand aloof anymore in view of the possible establishment of a Jewish state on its borders, which might seek a territorial expansion into Sinai.[11]

The Palestine Question occupied a central place in the first speech delivered by the Egyptian FM in September 1937, on Egypt's acceptance as a UN member state. Stressing his country's sense of fraternity toward Palestine based on historic, cultural, and geographical ties, the minister rejected the latter's partition and advocated the establishment of an independent, unitary Palestinian state. Egypt's involvement in the Palestine Question accelerated due to the domestic political turmoil that ensued following the dismissal of Nahhas's government by King Farouq in late 1937. Their mutual hostility, coupled by political instability, intensified the competition in propagating support for the Palestine cause by all Egyptian parties.

In October 1938, Egypt upgraded its involvement in the Palestine Question by hosting the semi-official Parliamentary Conference of the Arab and Islamic States in Cairo, attended by senior staff members of the royal court and ministers in the government. The conference clearly represented an Egyptian effort to assert a leading role in the Arab-Muslim effort on behalf of Palestine, which would best serve its quest for Pan-Arab leadership. Furthermore, on the eve of the conference, Egypt demanded that Britain treat her as an official partner in every negotiation concerning Palestine.[12]

Inter-Arab politics and the Palestine Question

From the mid-1920s, the relations between the ruling elites of the newly established Arab entities in the Fertile Crescent were infused with rivalries and competition for regional Arab leadership even before attaining independence. A major cause of inter-Arab tension was the long-lived rivalry between the House of Sa'ud of Najd and the Hashemites from the Hijaz. This rivalry culminated in the conquest of the Hijaz in 1925 from King Hussein Ibn 'Ali, father of the then King Faysal and his brother, the Emir 'Abdallah, who in 1921 had been appointed by Britain as semi-autonomous rulers over Iraq and Transjordan, respectively. Both Hashemite rulers adopted revisionist visions of regional Arab unity under their individual thrones.

The Hashemites in Iraq upheld the idea of unifying the Fertile Crescent as a necessary measure for bolstering their rule over the Sunni minority of Iraq by integrating the Sunni populations of Syria, Lebanon, Palestine, Transjordan and the Hijaz. The Emir 'Abdallah's quest for unifying 'Greater Syria' (*bilad al-sham*) under his throne – largely overlapping his brother Faysal's ambition – was motivated by his frustrating rule over a thinly populated piece of desert with no historic significance – hence his quest for Jerusalem and Damascus. The two visions not only collided with the regional order shaped by the colonial Powers, but they also ran up against the fierce resistance of the Saudi monarch and, from the mid-1940s, of Egypt, Syria and the Lebanon also.

Both Hashemite rulers established close relations with minority groups in the desired territories and made repeated attempts in lobbying the British government to support their territorial aspirations by integrating Palestine to their realms in return for alleviating the latter's burden of governing this disputed country. Attentive to the British commitment to support the creation of a Jewish national home in Palestine, the Hashemite rulers were willing to allow a limited rate of Jewish immigration and an autonomous status to the Jewish community within the regional Arab union they envisioned. 'Abdallah's efforts in this direction began in the early 1920s by approaching the Zionist leaders in an attempt to attain their consent to his aspirations in Palestine, which he persisted in until 1948. Similarly, in the wake of the 1929 Wailing Wall riots in Palestine, King Faysal submitted to the British government his proposal, which aimed to contain the Palestine problem and advance his aspirations for Pan-Arab unity by winning British support for his ambitions. Faisal's program offered to divest Britain of its role in the Palestine quandary, allay Palestinian fears at the prospect of a Jewish majority emerging in Palestine, and enable limited Jewish immigration based on a narrow interpretation of the Balfour Declaration by which the Jews were to remain a permanent minority in Palestine.[13]

The troubled bond: the Palestinian-Arab leadership and the Arab states

Despite their critical need of outside support from other Arabs and Muslims, Palestinian nationalists have traditionally perceived that support as fulfilling a duty rather than a matter of favour, or choice on the part of the Arab states. Identified mainly with the Husseinis and their allies of the *Istiqlal* Party, this approach persisted throughout the Mandate and beyond, in disregard of the particular interests of the Arab ruling elites or their obligations once they attained independence. Hence, the Hashemite rulers' willingness to accept some attributes of Jewish autonomy in Palestine – from the Faysal-Weizmann agreement in 1919 to 'Abdallah's tacit agreement with the Zionists on the partition of Palestine – turned into a historic indictment against them by Palestinian and other Arab nationalists.[14]

Theoretically, the more independence and political power the Arab ruling elites came to wield, the more influence they could exercise in support of their Palestinian brethren. Practically, however, independence and sovereignty entailed prioritizing one's particular interests, which did not always coincide with the Palestinians' interests and at times even collided with them.[15] Ideologically and rhetorically, all Arab politicians agreed on the need to defeat the Zionist enterprise and demonstrated their commitment towards the Palestine Question. In practice, the Arab governments shaped their policies according to their own particular interests and constraints while employing the Palestine Question for gaining political advantage in their domestic and regional arenas.[16]

The regionalisation of the Palestine Question

The collective involvement of the Arab states in the Palestine Question came in response to the entanglement of the Palestinian-Arab general strike declared in April 1936 by the Higher Arab Committee (HAC). As the strike went on for months without any political achievement, while causing heavy economic losses, the hastily established HAC, headed by Haj Amin al-Husseini, fell into deep internal division and effectively lost its ability to call off the strike. Parallel to appealing to the Arab governments to use their influence with Britain to accept the Palestinian national claims,[17] the HAC endeavoured to mobilise popular support in the Arab states, largely through sympathetic opposition groups, disseminating false information about the atrocities suffered by the Palestinian Arabs, including massacres of women and children and desecration of mosques.

Despite intensive efforts by the HAC to press the Arab governments into openly supporting their strike, the latter responded with calculated caution according to their own interests. Syria's leading National Block demonstrated its support for the Palestinians' struggle while secretly advised the HAC to stop the strike and the violence, lest they undermine the Franco-Syrian negotiations on independence.[18] Egypt refused to be involved in the

Palestinian turmoil lest it affect its negotiations for a new treaty with Britain and blocked Palestinian agitation on its soil. Iraq and Saudi Arabia too demonstrated caution in approaching the matter, primarily in order to avoid negative responses by Britain.

The official diplomatic involvement of the Arab monarchs in ending the strike's impasse began with the Mufti's appeal to Ibn Sa`ud to lobby the British government on the HAC's behalf. While the British refused to discuss the HAC conditions, they welcomed the Saudi approach as a preferable alternative to suppressing the revolt by force. The following Arab diplomatic efforts by Iraq's FM Nuri al-Sa`id and the Emir `Abdallah revealed the Arab rulers' individual interest in reaping the prestige of mediating a solution to the dangerous political standoff between Britain and the Palestinians. At the same time, having nothing to offer the HAC other than Britain's intent to appoint a royal commission to inquire into the causes of the revolt, these monarchs were concerned lest their individual efforts end in failure. Therefore, they preferred to issue a joint appeal to the HAC to call off the strike. The inter-Arab diplomatic competition for ending the strike revealed a parallel alignment of the Palestinian factions: whereas the Mufti preferred Ibn Sa`ud and the Egyptian government as mediators and opposed the Emir `Adballah's involvement, the Opposition faction insisted that he participate in the joint Arab call to stop the strike.

Organizing nonofficial support also proved problematic as attested by the arrival in northern Samaria of an Arab volunteer unit headed by Fawzi al-Qawuqji in August of 1936 in support of the revolt. The force was largely recruited and equipped by Iraqi nationalists and veterans of the 1925 Syrian revolt and was loosely coordinated with the HAC. King Ghazi, PM Yassin al-Hashimi, and the Iraqi military unofficially supported the volunteer force both financially and militarily.[19]

Comprising Iraqi, Syrian, Palestinian and Lebanese volunteers, including veterans of the 1925 Syrian revolt and Iraqi military officers, the force's echelons represented an unofficial network of activists who saw their fight in Palestine as an indivisible part of the Arab nation's struggle for independence. Qawuqji's attempts to consolidate a centralised command of the rebel groups in Palestine under his authority as the Commander of the Arab Revolt in Southern Syria, contradicted the HAC's distinctive Palestinian nationalism. Moreover, by ignoring the Mufti and associating himself with the Palestinian Opposition, Qawuqji triggered the Husseinis' hostility. In reaction, the latter disseminated rumours about his collaboration with British military agents and inclination towards the Nashashibis. In October 1936, following the Arab monarchs' call on the Palestinians to stop the strike and revolt, the Mufti asked the volunteer force to leave Palestine. Qawuqji agreed, but promised to return and resume his fight if the truce did not lead to British acceptance of the rebellion's demands.[20]

The Arab strike indeed failed to attain its goals and in view of the Peel Commission's recommendations, it even backfired. Moreover, the apparent success of enlisting the Arab monarchs' collective weight for mediating the HAC conflict with the British government heralded a gradual erosion of the Palestinian leadership's control over their own case. The Arab monarchs were by no means willing to support their Palestinian brethren at the cost of embarrassing Britain. In November 1936, the Arab monarchs intervened once again, in response to the HAC's boycott of the Royal Commission due to the government's issue of the semi-annual quota of Jewish immigration permits. Perceiving themselves accountable to Britain, the Arab rulers pressured the HAC to testify before the Commission. Following weeks of stalemate, the HAC eventually succumbed.[21]

The Palestinian leadership experienced another disappointment with the Arab states' responses to its call to take action against the partition of Palestine into a Jewish state and an Arab state under the Emir 'Abdallah, as recommended by the Peel Commission. Apart from 'Abdallah, who had every reason to be satisfied with these recommendations, other Arab states contented themselves with official protests against them. Typically, Iraq set the tone by presenting to the League of Nations its official opposition to the partition of Palestine.[22] The Syrian government and Ibn Sa'ud followed suit. However, the Egyptian government gave publicity to its opposition to partition only two months later, under heavy domestic and regional public pressure to actively support the Palestinian-Arabs' attitude.

The Arab official involvement in ending the strike was a major factor in internalizing the perception among British Foreign Office officials that the Palestine Question had become a regional Arab matter that could affect the British interests in the Arab and Muslim countries.[23] In view of the Italian and German agitation in the Arab countries, that perception became a cornerstone of Britain's Mandatory policy in the following years.

Defying the Arab states

Disappointed by the Arab responses to Britain's partition plans, the HAC turned to an intensive effort to consolidate a broad Arab *public* resistance to the establishment of a Jewish state in part of Palestine. The Palestinian effort to recruit primarily radical Arab nationalist and Islamic organisations as potential pressure groups on their governments was often conducted in defiance of the Arab governments' restrictions. As of late 1936, the Mufti's efforts to convene an all-Arab conference in support of the Palestinian cause failed, mainly due to Egyptian and Saudi opposition. However, the broad Arab resistance to the partition of Palestine paved the road to convening an Arab National Congress in Bludan, Syria, on 8 September 1937.

Sponsored by the HAC and leading Syrian nationalists, the Bludan congress was mostly attended by non-officials from Syria, Palestine, Lebanon, Iraq, Transjordan, and Egypt. Among the participants were also prominent Arab nationalists and formerly high-level officials. The congress adopted the HAC's proposals, stating that Palestine was an indivisible part of the Arab world and calling for opposing its partition and the establishment of a Jewish state on its soil. It also called for the prohibition of immigration and land sales to Jews and the abolition of the British Mandate and its replacement by an Anglo-Palestinian treaty in the format of the Anglo-Iraqi one. In addition, the conference decided to establish propaganda offices in the Arab capitals, London and Geneva and to boycott the Jewish economy.[24]

The Bludan conference was an impressive popular Arab demonstration of solidarity with the Palestinians, which encouraged the resumption of the Arab rebellion in Palestine. The Mandatory government responded by adopting harsh suppressive measures, including the outlawing of the HAC, the arrest and exile of some of its members and other leaders, and the dismissal of Haj Amin al-Husseini from his position as president of the SMC. As a result, the Palestinian political centre headed by Haj Amin al-Husseini and hundreds of his entourage fled the country and found refuge in Lebanon where they established their headquarters that coordinated the transfer of Iraqi, Syrian, Saudi and Lebanese financial and military aid to the rebel groups in Palestine, until the rebellion finally ended in late 1939.[25]

The Mufti's forced exile ostensibly opened new political opportunities for reinvigorating the armed rebellion in Palestine with increased popular support of non-governmental organisations as well as Italian financial aid and German arms smuggled through Iraq.[26] However, by late 1938 the rebellion had turned into bloody infighting between the rival Palestinian factions, resulting in long-term blood feuds and vengeance accounts between the Nashashibis, who collaborated with the government's repression of the rebels and their Husseini supporters.[27]

The intensified Arab revolt and the growing manifestations of the Arab states' resistance to partition of Palestine indeed forced Britain to retreat from this policy and seek another outlet from the Palestine impasse. Thus, British interests first coincided with, and later deliberately involved the Arab states in the Palestine Question as a means to alleviate the burden of Palestinian-Arab resistance to its policy. By early 1939, as the Arab revolt had weakened and war in Europe seemed imminent, Britain sought to minimise Arab alienation toward its policy in Palestine and ensure close cooperation with the Arab states as a crucial component of its interests in the Middle East.[28] Britain thus called for a Round Table Conference on Palestine in London with the aim of reshaping its policy on this issue. Hoping to enlist the Arab states' support for moderating the Palestinian leadership's attitude in accordance with its own imperial interests, the government invited to the conference, in addition to Palestinian-Arab and Zionist representatives, also delegates from Egypt, Iraq, Saudi Arabia, Yemen and Transjordan.[29]

The extent to which the Palestine Question had now become a collective Arab concern was demonstrated by the preliminary consultations of the Arab delegations (except Transjordan's) in Cairo to shape a unified Arab position. Held under the auspices of the Egyptian royal court and government, the meeting demonstrated not only Egypt's regional leadership, it set a precedent of collectively discussing a joint Arab policy on the Palestine question. Furthermore, this forum set a precedent of adopting the HAC positions: no direct negotiations with the Jews, effectively thwarting Britain's intention of conducting 'round table' talks; insistence that Palestine must be an independent and unitary state; and acknowledging the HAC's veto power on the Palestine Question.[30] The composition of the Egyptian delegation in the February 1939 London talks indeed reflected Egypt's Pan-Arab aspirations and the growing involvement of the royal court in shaping this line of foreign policy.[31]

The Arab consultations in Cairo, as well as the talks in London revealed the gap between the Arab states' and Jamal al-Husseini, the Palestinian representative concerning the British proposals. The Arab States' delegates tended to accept Britain's proposals for *limiting* Jewish immigration and land sales, guarantee a semi-autonomous status to the Jewish community in areas where they constituted a majority, and the postponement of any decision on the future status of Palestine for five to ten years from the country's return to stability. The Husseini leadership, however, rejected any continuation of Jewish immigration and land sales to Jews and insisted on independence within three years.[32]

The White Paper of May 1939 stated Britain's intention to continue consulting with the Arab states concerning Palestine, a principle that it fully adopted in the post-World War Two diplomatic efforts to resolve the Arab-Jewish conflict over Palestine. The new policy formulated in the wake of the futile conference in London indeed imposed severe restrictions on Jewish immigration and land acquisitions – effectively sentencing the *Yishuv* to a permanent minority status – albeit leaving the future of Palestine as an independent Arab state uncertain.

The Mufti in Iraq, 1939–41

Contrary to the Egyptian and Iraqi advice to accept the White Paper as a temporary arrangement toward a Palestinian state, the HAC rejected it while trying to keep the rebellion going. The Arab states, save Transjordan, acquiesced reluctantly with the HAC decision while some, especially Iraq, persisted in their efforts to extract a clear British commitment regarding the timetable of implementing the constitutional component of the White Paper. Iraq's attempt to take advantage of the Allies' dire military condition from early to mid-1940 for attaining further concessions on behalf of the Palestinian-Arabs reflected its particular interest in balancing between domestic anti-British tendencies and the regime's loyalty to Britain.

Whereas the pro-British Regent and PM Nuri al-Sa`id wanted to declare war on Germany, the fiercely anti-British nationalists and the military strongly opposed such a motion without substantial British concessions on Palestine. Nuri al-Sa`id's need to justify a declaration of war on Germany was indeed acute due to the anti-British sentiments in Iraq, which had been intensified by the arrival in October 1939 of the Mufti and a few hundreds of his followers. Forced by tightened French control in Lebanon once the war in Europe erupted, the Mufti and his staff opted for Iraq as their alternative territorial basis for conducting the Palestinian national struggle.[33]

In the course of 1940, as a FM in Rashid 'Ali al-Kaylani's government, Nuri al-Sa'id and senior Palestinian figures, including Jamal al-Husseini and Musa al-Alami, were involved in contacts with British emissaries over a solution to the Palestine Question within a federation of Iraq, Transjordan, and Palestine. Later that year, at Britain's toughest moment in the war, Nuri al-Sa'id went as far as suggesting that Britain take immediate steps toward Palestinian independence, in return for the Mufti's support of Britain and active Iraqi participation in the British war effort. It is not clear whether the Mufti had given his consent to these suggestions and in any case, the British cabinet rejected them.[34]

The Iraqi pan-Arab nationalists and army leadership – mostly ardent anti-British – received the Mufti with enthusiasm as a symbol of Arab-Muslim resistance to Britain. Thanks to generous funding by the government, the Mufti fostered close relations with ultra-nationalist Iraqi politicians and the pro-German clique of senior military officers known as the 'Golden Square,' establishing himself as an influential centre of power. He purchased a newspaper, which disseminated anti-British and pro-German propaganda, developed high-level contacts with the German government, and most of all, engaged in mobilizing, training and equipping Syrians and Palestinians assigned to resume the revolt in Palestine.[35] Although the Mufti's anti-British activity and political interference in Iraqi politics were embarrassing for the pro-British Regent and PM Nuri al-Sa'id, the latter were too weak to restrict his freedom of action.

Assuming that the war would end with German victory, since his arrival in Iraq, the Mufti strove to conclude an Arab-German alliance against Britain and the Jews. Presenting himself as the 'Grand Mufti of Palestine' and the leader of the 'Arab nation', he sought to extract from Hitler a commitment to support the independence of all Arab countries, including Palestine, recognise the Arabs' right to unity and to determining the fate of the Jews living among them, including the Jewish national home in Palestine. The German response to the Mufti's proposals, however, fell short of his expectations, reflecting the lack of clear vision about the post-war status of the Arab states.[36]

The Mufti's anti-British activity and contacts with the Germans caused tension with PM Sa'id and the Regent, whose public position reached a low point due to their unpopular decision to cut off Iraq's diplomatic relations with Germany, as stipulated by the Anglo-Iraqi Treaty of 1930. With the advent of Rashid 'Ali's government in March 1940, the Mufti became a prominent actor in a trilateral coalition, together with Kaylani and the 'Golden Square' colonels. Their pro-German policy led to the April 1941 revolt and the declaration of war against Britain, which the Mufti inspired and coordinated with Germany, forcing the Regent, Nuri Sa'id and other Hashemite figures to flee the country. Britain's suppression of the revolt by force resulted in the dispersal of the Palestinian national leadership, the arrest and exile of many by the British authorities, and the escape of others to neighbouring Iran and Turkey. The Mufti eventually found refuge in Germany where he maintained close collaboration with the Nazis against the Allies until the end of the war.

The Mufti's active involvement in the anti-Hashemite coup in Iraq and his collaboration with Nazi Germany left bitter residues among the Iraqi Hashemite leaders and the British. Although the latter refrained from settling accounts with him as a war criminal lest it might harm their interests in the Arab and Muslim world.[37] Whereas the Palestinian infighting during the revolt would deprive the Mufti of the Opposition's cooperation at the most fateful struggle to come with the Yishuv, his wartime politics in Iraq and collaboration with Nazi Germany won him the deep hostility of the Iraqi Hashemites and British decision makers. In hindsight, the Mufti's wartime activities entailed disastrous implications for his post-World War Two efforts to assume the effective leadership of the Palestinian struggle toward the end of the Mandate.

The Arab League and the Palestine Question: from patronage to appropriation

The creation of the Arab League (AL) in March 1945 opened a new chapter in the relationship between the Arab states and the Palestinian-Arabs. Henceforth, the AL took over the shaping and implementation of Arab policy on Palestine, practically establishing a patronage over this issue. The collective Arab patronage, soon to become an appropriation of the Palestine cause, represented its member states' domestic and regional stakes in this matter on the one hand, and on the other, the grave political weakness of the Palestinian national movement during World War Two and after.

Contrary to the Hashemites' visions of regional unity or federation, the AL's Pact represented a loose framework aimed at maintaining the regional status quo of equal and independent Arab states. Whereas the AL effectively shunned aside the vision of Arab unity, in the following years the Palestine Question topped its agenda, turning into a touchstone of its image as a symbol of Arab unity. The AL's occasional meetings became an arena of inter-Arab competition for regional leadership in which the Palestine Question played a pivotal role. This was largely the result of Iraqi determination to compensate itself for the loss of Arab leadership to Egypt by conducting extreme policies on Palestine and dragging other member states to follow suit.

The AL Pact included a special annex on Palestine, underlining its right to be independent like other AL member states. Due to British pressures, however, the AL allotted to the Palestinian delegate only the status of an observer whose participation was limited to discussions on Palestine. That Palestine, of all other colonised Arab territories, won such a special status was admittedly due to the Zionist threat to its Arab nature.[38] In response to the special annex, the Palestinian-Arab parties reproached the Arab states for their insufficient commitment to their cause. Specifically, they deplored basing the claim for Palestinian independence on the Treaty of Lausanne and League of Nation's Charter, which could be interpreted as a tacit recognition of the British Mandate over Palestine and the Balfour Declaration.[39]

The Arab states appeared united, rhetorically and diplomatically – often despite disagreement with the Palestinian representatives – as manifested at the London Conferences convened by Britain in September 1946 and February 1947, and the United Nations' deliberations in May 1947. However, inter-Arab and intra-Palestinian conflicts, prevented effective implementation of the AL projects aimed at alleviating the Palestinians' plight. These included: diplomatic lobbying in Britain and the US; 'rescuing' Arab land from sale to Jews; applying a total boycott against the Jewish economy in Palestine; and preventing Jewish immigration to Palestine through the Arab states.[40]

The Arab states' selfish interests typically shaped the implementation of those projects. Iraq initiated the propaganda bureaus – and funded the lion's share of their budget – established as of mid-1945 in London, Washington and other capitals, with their headquarters in Jerusalem. Iraq was also the main donor for helping the Palestinian rural sector reduce land sales to Jews. However, Iraq refused to let the AL – or the HAC – to control these funds and instead entrusted them to Musa Alami, whose pro-British reputation ensured Britain's tacit endorsement of these projects. Both of these projects suffered from insufficient funds, inter-Arab discords over their control and, concerning help to the Palestinian rural sector, also delayed decision-making, rendering it useless once hostilities erupted in late 1947.

As of January 1946, the Arab states were more efficient in boycotting the Jewish economy, which had long been called for but previously implemented only partly by the Palestinian Arabs. The AL neither thoroughly studied the implications of the boycott nor did it set clear regulation for its implementation. It derived from selfish considerations, primarily of Iraq and Syria, of bolstering their national economies – hence their leading role in expanding the boycott while Lebanon and Egypt lagged behind. Transjordan could not implement the boycott at all because of its economic unity with Palestine. Despite its loose enforcement, the boycott reduced considerably the trade exchange between the Arab states and the *Yishuv*,[41] while claiming discernible costs by the Palestinian Arabs due to its indiscriminate implementation. Indeed, whereas the HAC initially welcomed the Arab boycott, hoping it would deal a deathblow to the Jewish community in Palestine, its representatives soon complained before the AL forums about the heavy losses incurred by the Palestinian-Arab economy.[42]

By the time Haj Amin arrived in 1946 in Egypt after a long exile in Europe, the AL's collective patronage over the Palestine cause had failed to resolve the deep intra-Palestinian divisions. In June 1946, the AL established a new Palestinian-Arab national representative body under the name the Higher Arab Institute (HAI), reaffirming the Mufti's leadership as well as the Husseinis' domination in this body. Indeed, none of the Arab governments could overlook al-Haj Amin, who enjoyed a tremendous popularity among the Arab peoples as a saint and national hero of the Arab struggle against Western imperialism and Zionism. Practically, however, the Arab governments distanced him from any influential position on matters related to Palestine, especially financial and military resources.

The inter-Arab divisions on Palestine came to the fore following Britain's announcement in September 1947 of its intention to relinquish the Mandate and withdraw from Palestine, and especially in the wake of the UN approval of the partition of Palestine and establishment of a Jewish state, which ensured that an Arab-Jewish confrontation was inevitable. While the AL continued to shape collective diplomatic and military responses, Arab rulers rushed to ensure their own particular interests in this matter. King 'Abdallah reached a secret understanding with the Zionists on peaceful partition of Palestine and the annexation of its Arab part to his kingdom whereas Syria embarked on organizing a force of volunteers under its own control so as to prevent King 'Abdallah from military takeover of parts or all of Palestine once the Mandate ended.

In December 1947, faced with intensifying Arab-Jewish hostilities in Palestine, the AL adopted Syria's plan of sending volunteers from the Arab neighbouring countries to help the Palestinian-Arabs to resist the much stronger and better organised Jewish militias. The AL plans first overlooked the Mufti who insisted on limiting the Arab states' involvement to merely providing him with armament and funds. Eventually, the AL Military Committee agreed on sharing the battleground between the AL-sponsored 'Army of Deliverance' under Fawzi al-Qawuqji's command and the Mufti's loyalist militia. The mutual hostility between them, however, doomed the unofficial war effort. By mid-April 1948, following a series of military defeats of both forces and the collapse of the Palestinian-Arab society, the Palestinian leadership lost whatever limited control of events it had ever exerted before.

Conclusion

Until the early 1930s, with most Arab states still lacking independence, the Palestinian-Arab leadership appealed for support from Arab and Muslim societies. By the late-1930s, it shifted to enlisting the Arab states' support through mobilizing their political opposition groups in defiance of the official policy, which culminated in the Mufti's personal involvement in the 1941 anti-Hashemite coup in Iraq.

The Palestinian approach deepened the gap between the Palestine Question as a sacrosanct Arab national and Islamic value, and the Palestinian-Arab body *politik* seen increasingly as risking the Arab states domestic stability. This two-level approach assumed far-reaching political significance due to the desperate need of Arab ruling elites for domestic legitimacy, inter-Arab competition for regional leadership, and particular international obligations.

The result was a built-in discrepancy between rhetoric and practice in handling Palestine by the Arab governments, which culminated in the last month of the Mandate with the collapse of the unofficial war effort and the growing flow of Palestinian Arab refugees into the neighbouring countries. At this stage, too late to prepare for an effective military intervention and pressured by their own peoples, the Arab governments opted for a hasty joint invasion of Palestine.

Notes

1 For an exception, see Michael Eppel, The elite, the *Effendiyya*, and the growth of nationalism and pan-Arabism in Hashemite Iraq, 1921–1958, *International Journal of Middle East Studies* 30/2, May 1998, pp. 227–50.

2 Yehoshua Porath, *The Palestinian Arab National Movement, 1929–1939: From Riots to Rebellion*, London: Cass, 1977, p. 34.

3 Avraham Sela, The "Wailing Wall" riots (1929) as a watershed in the Palestine conflict, *The Muslim World* Vol. LXXXIV, 1-2, January-April, 1994, pp. 71–81.

4 Martin Kramer, *Islam Assembled: The Advent of the Muslim Congresses*, New York: Columbia University Press, 1986, pp. 133–4, 141; Uri M. Kupferschmidt, *The Supreme Muslim Council; Islam Under the British Mandate for Palestine*, Leiden: Brill, 1987, pp. 211–12; `Abd al-`Aziz al-Tha`alibi, *Khalfiyyat al-mu`tamar al-Islami fi al-Quds* [*Background of the Islamic Congress in Jerusalem*], Beirut: Dar al-gharb al-Islami, 1987, pp. 43–5, 58–62, 112–15.

5 Yehuda Taggar, *The Mufti of Jerusalem and Palestine: Arab Politics, 1930–1937*, New York: Garland, 1986, p. 175; Taysir Jbara, *Palestinian Leader Hajj Amin al-Husayni: Mufti of Jerusalem*, Princeton: Kingston, 1985, pp. 111–13; Kupferschmidt, *Supreme Muslim Council*, p. 196.

6 Issa Khalaf, *Politics in Palestine: Arab Factionalism and Social Disintegration, 1939–1948*, Albany: SUNY Press, 1991.

7 Elie Kedourie, Religion and nationalism in the Arab world, in Elie Kedourie (ed.), *Islam in the Modern World*, London: Mansell, 1980, pp. 54–5; Ernest Dawn, The formation of Pan-Arab ideology, *International Journal of Middle East Studies* 20/1 1988, pp. 67–91; Bernard Lewis, *The Middle East and the West*, London: Weidenfeld & Nicolson, 1963, pp. 59–60, 82–3.

8 Clifford Geertz, *The Interpretation of Cultures*, New York: Basic Books, 1973, pp. 234–54; Albert Hourani, Independence and the imperial legacy, *Middle East Forum* 42/1, Winter 1966, pp. 5–27.

9 `Awatif `Abd al-Rahman, *Misr wa-filastin* [*Egypt and Palestine*], Kuwait: al-`Arabi lil-nashr wal-tawzi`, 1980, pp. 264–6.

10 Ibid., pp. 107–9; Israel Gershoni, The Muslim Brothers and the Arab Revolt in Palestine 1936–39, *Middle Eastern Studies* 22/3, July 1986, pp. 368–70.

11 Trefor E. Evans (ed.), *The Killearn Diaries, 1934–1946: The Diplomatic and Personal Record of Lord Killearn (Sir Miles Lampson), High Commissioner and Ambassador, Egypt*, London: Sidgwick and Jackson, 1972, pp. 83–4.

12 James Jancowski, The government of Egypt and the Palestine Question, 1936–1939, *Middle Eastern Studies* 17/4 October 1981, pp. 434–6; Mahmoud A, Goma'a, *The Foundation of the League of Arab States: Wartime Diplomacy and Inter-Arab Relations 1941–1945*, London: Longman, 1977, pp. 45–8.

13 Neil Caplan, *Futile Diplomacy: Early Arab-Zionist Negotiation Attempts 1913–1931,* London: Frank Cass, 1983, pp. 83, 221–4.

14 Eliyahu Sasson to Ben-Gurion, July 3, 1944 on his meeting with Nuri al-Sa'id on June 29, 1944, *CZA*, S/25, 5633; Anis Sayigh, *Al-Hashimiyyoun wa-qadiyyat Filastin* [*The Hashemites and the Palestine Question*], Beirut: al-maktaba al-'asriyya, 1966.

15 Gilbert MacKereth (Damascus) to Anthony Eden, 25 October 1937, in Michael G. Fry and Itamar Rabinovich (eds), *Despatches from Damascus: Gilbert MacKereth and British Policy in the Levant, 1933–1939,* Tel-Aviv: Dayan Center, Tel-Aviv University, pp. 171–3.

16 Elie Kedourie, Arab unity, then and now, in *Islam*, p. 79.

17 Halting Jewish immigration and land sales to Jews and the establishment of an elected national government.

18 MacKereth to High Commissioner, Palestine, April 22, 1936 in Fry and Rabinovich, *Despatches,* p. 150.

19 Kazim Z. 'Abboud, (ed.), *Min awraq al-malik Ghazi* [*King Ghazi Papers*], Baghdad: Sharq gharb lil-nashr, 2010, pp. 105–6; Laila Parsons, *The Commander: Fawzi al-Qawuqji and the Fight for Arab Independence 1914–1948*, New York: Hill and Wang, 2016, pp. 116–117.

20 Porath, *Riots,* pp. 188–192; Parsons, ibid., pp. 133–6.

21 Ibn Sa'ud's letter to the HAC, in 'Issa Sifri, *Filastin al-'arabiyya bayn al-intidab wal-sahyuniyya* [*Arab Palestine between the Mandate and Zionism*], Jaffa: n.p., 1937, pt. 2, p. 180.

22 Iraq was later willing to consider the cantonisation of Palestine, see Yehoshua Porath, *In Search of Arab Unity, 1930–1945*, London: Frank Cass 1986, pp. 166–7.

23 Elie Kedourie, Great Britain and Palestine: The turning point, in *Islam*, p. 114 ff; Michael J Cohen, *Retreat from the Mandate: The Making of British Policy, 1936–45*, London/New York: Paul Elek, 1978, pp. 39–42, 46–7.

24 Elie Kedourie, Bludan, p. 25; Akram Zu'aytar, *Yawmiyyat Akram Zu'aytar: al-haraka al-wataniyya al-filastiniyya, 1935–1939* [*Akram Zu'aytar Diaries; the Palestinian National Movement, 1935–1939*], Beirut: Mu'assasat al-dirasat al-filastiniyya, 1980, pp. 316–27.

25 Eliyahu Sasson, *Ba-Derekh el ha-shalom* [*On the Road to Peace*], Tel-Aviv: Am Oved, 1973, pp. 76, 79–85; Kedourie, *Great Britain*, p. 155.

26 Lukasz Hirszowicz, *The Third Reich and the Arab East,* London: Routledge & Kegan Paul, 1966, p. 52.

27 Porath, *Riots,* pp. 249–60.

28 Ibid., pp. 277–81.

29 Syria and Lebanon were not invited due to French opposition.

30 Porath, *Riots,* pp. 283–4.

31 M. Hussayn Haykal, *Mudhakkirat fi al-siyasa al-Misriyya* [*Memoirs in Egyptian Politics*], pt. II, Cairo: Matba'at Misr, 1953, p. 132.

32 Shuqayri, *Arba'oun 'ama fi al-hayat al-'arabiyya wal-dawliyya* [Forty Years in Arab and International Life], Beirut: Dar al-nahar lil-nashr, p. 190; Porath, *From Riots,* pp. 285–6; *Taqrir lajnat al-tahqiq al-niyabiyya fi qadiyyat Filastin* [*Report of the Parliamentary Committee of Inquiry on the Palestine Question*], Baghdad: n.p., 1949, pp. 5–6, 52.

33 Geoffrey Warner, *Iraq and Syria 1941,* London: Davis-Poynter, 1974, p. 35.

34 Warner, ibid., pp. 28–31; Michael Eppel, *The Palestine Conflict in the History of Modern Iraq: The Dynamics of Involvement, 1928–1948*, London: Frank Cass,

1994, pp. 96–7; Gavriel Cohen, *Ha-cabinet ha-Briti ve-she'elat Eretz-Israel, April-Yuni 1943* [*The British Cabinet and the Palestine Question, April-June 1943*], Tel-Aviv: Tel-Aviv University, 1976, pp. 13–14.

35 Al-Sabbagh, Salah al-Din, *Fursan al-`urouba fi al-`Iraq* [*The Knights of Arabism in Iraq*], Damascus: *al-Shabab al-`Arabi*, 1956, pp. 271–3; Eppel, *Palestine*, pp. 104–7.

36 Warner, *Iraq and*, pp. 35–8.

37 For British considerations see Michael J Cohen, *Britain's Hegemony in the Middle East, 1917–56: Changing Strategic Imperatives*, London: Valentine Mitchell, 2017, Chapter 9.

38 Jami`at al-duwal al-`Arabiyya [League of the Arab States], *al-mahadir al-khitamiyya li-jalsat dawr al-ijtima` al-`adi al-thani li-majlis al-jami`a* [Final Protocols of Meetings of the League Council's Second Regular Session]. October 31-December 14, 1945, Cairo: 1949, Session 2, November 5, 1945, p. 22.

39 Memorandum by the Committee of Arab Palestinian parties, April, 1945, Israel State Archives, *(ISA)*, 65/5, 3545.

40 Goma'a, *The Foundation*, pp. 223–4.

41 Taqrir lajnat al-jami`a al-`Arabiyya li-muqata`at al-muntajat al-Sahyuniyya [Report of the AL Committee on the boycott of Zionist products], 1 January 1946–30 September 1947 in Jami`at al-duwal al-`Arabiyya, *Madabit jalsat dawr al-ijtima` al-`aadi al-sabi`* [Protocols of the Seventh Regular Session's Meetings], October 15, 1947, Cairo: 1948, pp. 100–101; *Haaretz*, 14 May 1947; *Ha-Boker*, 17 June 1947.

42 *Al-mahadir al-khitamiyya li-jalsat dawr al-ijtima` al-`aadi al-thalith li-majlis al-jami`a* [Final Proceedings of the Third Regular Session of the League Council], March 30, 1946, p. 42, Cairo: 1949; *Jami`at*, ibid, Seventh Session, October 15, 1947, p. 78, 108. See also a host of complaints by Palestinian chambers of commerce to the HAC, January-March 1946, *ISA* 65/5, 3055.

Part III
Zionist perspectives

9   Zionism as a blessing to the Arabs
History of an argument

Hillel Cohen

This chapter explores the history of the argument according to which Zionism was a blessing to the Palestinian Arabs. From its outset, this perception was a key element in the Zionist case, developed throughout the mandate period and to some extent persists until the present. The idea behind this argument is that the positive effects of Zionism would not be limited to the Jews only, but would encompass all of the inhabitants of Palestine and even of the entire Middle East. As we shall see in the conclusion, some thinkers went even further and spoke of Zionism as a blessing for the whole world. This concept stands in contrast to the Zionist approach that focused on the Jewish people only, and believed that it was better to evacuate ("transfer") the Arabs of Palestine in order to establish a homogenous Jewish state. Whereas the idea of transferring the Arabs has been discussed at length in the literature by supporters and opponents,[1] the idea of Zionism as a blessing to all has received less attention.

I will attempt to analyse this concept by focusing on the following: a) the internal Zionist debate; b) Arab responses; c) Western responses; and d) developments in the Zionist discourse. I will conclude with a discussion of the political, ideological and moral motivations that led to the crystallisation of this thesis. This will throw light on the diversity within the Zionist movement, Arab opposition to the concept and the tension between the Zionists' self-image and the reality on the ground. I assume that at least some of the Zionists who promoted this argument truly believed in it, i.e., they did not invent it only for the purpose of public relations, or propaganda.

The 'blessing' thesis – first phases

In the utopian novel *A Journey to the Land of Israel 2040* (1892) by Elhanan Lewinsky, the narrator is a Jew who arrives in the holy land with his wife to spend their honeymoon there, as was the custom among Jews at that time. The country they tour lies on both sides of the Jordan River, its northern border the Euphrates. It is economically flourishing, the towns are well designed and aesthetic, with an overwhelming Jewish population. The land is redistributed every jubilee among all classes to prevent the accumulation of property by individuals. The state lives in peace with its neighbours except for minor border incidents with Bedouin tribes. 'Gentiles' are mentioned in the book but they are not part of the landscape. The word 'Arab' is mentioned only in the context of Arab coffee or architecture. Arabs are not mentioned and not seen. It is unclear where they have gone? But it is clear that the utopia is of a Jewish state with (almost?) no Arabs.[2]

Lewinsky was a Zionist activist, writer and educator. A decade later, the founder of political Zionism, B.Z. Herzl, published his utopia entitled *Altneuland* – the old-new land. In this novel, the tourists Löwenberg and Kingscourt arrive in Palestine twice. In their first visit, at the beginning of the twentieth century, they see an under-developed, backward, depressing country. In 1923, they face a totally different experience. The country is vital culturally and politically, flourishing economically, and is ruled in justice. As opposed to Lewinsky's utopia, Herzl's tourists, on their second visit, have an opportunity to discuss the situation with an Arab inhabitant of the country, a Muslim engineer named Rashid Bey. Rashid was involved with the New Company that had been established by the Jews in order to develop the country, and is defined in the book as a second-generation friend of the Jews: his father was one of those who grasped immediately that Jewish immigration could only be beneficial to all.[3]

The huge gap between their first and second visits led Löwenberg and Kingscourt to ask Rashid: "What happened to the old inhabitants of the land who possessed nothing – the tenantry?":

> Those who had nothing could only gain. And gain they did: employment, better food, welfare. There was nothing more wretched than an Arab village of *fellaheen* at the end of the nineteenth century.... Today things are changed indeed ... people are far better off than before; they are healthy, they have better food, their children go to school,... The Jews have brought us wealth and health; why should we harbour evil thoughts about them?[4]

Rashid's answer contains the basics of the blessing concept. The local population is in a poor condition in the fields of health, nutrition, education and employment. The European Jews feel these needs and improve the lives of the natives.

This utopian novel was written by Herzl, not by Rashid Bey, and the words that were put in the mouth of the latter expressed the hopes of the Zionist leader, albeit they also betrayed his fear that it might not be so.

In one of his rare interactions with a Palestinian Arab, when faced with a sombre response to Zionism by an Arab leader, Herzl dismissed his arguments, again, by using the same concept. Yousef Ziaa al-Din al-Khalidi, a Jerusalemite thinker and politician, wrote Herzl a letter in which he empathised with the suffering of the Jews and acknowledged their history in the holy land, but advised Herzl that "the Jews would do better to go somewhere else", because the land was already inhabited. Herzl responded on 19 March 1899:

> In allowing immigration to a number of Jews bringing their intelligence, their financial acumen and their means of enterprise to the country, no one can doubt that the well-being of the entire country would be the happy result.... Do you think that an Arab who owns land or a house in Palestine worth three or four thousand francs will be very angry to see the price of his land rise in a short time? [...] That will necessarily happen with the arrival of the Jews.[5]

Herzl used this theory as a tool to ignoring the claims of al-Khalidi, and pretended to know better than the Jerusalemite leader what were the needs of his community and his country. In this he followed the path of Western colonialism in general.[6] A few Zionist activists who were already in Palestine had a more nuanced approach. A prominent figure among them was Yitzhak Epstein (1863–1943) of the first *Aliya*, who settled in Palestine in 1896 and advocated Jewish-Arab co-existence. In 1907 he published his paradigmatic article 'A Hidden Question' in which he referred to the blessing concept:

> Indeed, the Jewish *Yishuv* has already bestowed considerable bounty on the country's inhabitants: the condition of the cities and villages near the settlements has improved, hundreds of craftsmen – masons, builders, painters, [and] donkey and camel drivers-and thousands of workers find employment in the settlements, commerce has grown, and the demand for dairy products and garden produce has increased.... But all of this will not compensate for what we have subverted.... How strong is the envy of people who have been swept off their land.[7]

Epstein noticed that the general improvement in the wellbeing of the Arabs did not bring about Arab support of Zionist settlement. In addition, the eviction of tenants from land purchased by the Jews evoked strong anti-Zionist sentiment among them. In other words, that the harm caused to the Arabs was greater than the benefit. Hence, he believed that the Zionists should settle only on waste lands purchased by them, and that they should purchase parcels inhabited by Arabs only with the explicit precondition of "leaving them on the estate and bettering their condition by instituting improved agricultural methods.... As enlightened owners we will devote a certain sum to the betterment of the tenants, because what is good for them is good for us".[8]

In 1921, that is more than three years after the Balfour declaration and the occupation of Palestine by the British army and a few months after the May 1921 Arab attack on Jews in Jaffa and elsewhere, Epstein published his article, 'A Question that Outweighs All Others'. In it, he urged the Zionist leadership to take immediate steps towards reconciling the Arabs. Again, he focused on the advantages of Zionist settlements for the Arabs, and emphasised that these advantages should be institutionalised, rather than remain a by-product of Zionist activity. He suggested the establishment of an organisation that would take responsibility for relations with the Arabs, which would be active in three fields: 1) national – to support Arab nationalism and use Jewish influence worldwide in that direction; 2) economic – to provide loans in reasonable terms to the Arabs as well as medical treatment; 3) social – to strengthen social and cultural ties between Jews and Arabs.[9]

Zionist critics of the 'blessing' thesis

The pro-active approach of Epstein, and his demands of the Zionist movement were not accepted by all Zionist settlers. Moshe Smilansky (1874–1953) – another farmer and educator of the first *Aliya* – who was involved in purchasing land from the Palestinian Arabs, supported co-existence and fairness in relations with the Arabs. But he attacked Epstein's proposals fiercely. In an article published in the socialist magazine *Ha-Poel Ha-Tza'ir* [The Young Worker] he rejected the claim that the Arabs of Palestine were a nation, since a country could not be the homeland of two nations. Since Palestine belonged to the Jews it could not also belong to the Arabs. He argued that the Arabs had no collective rights to the country because they had not developed it. Smilansky stressed that Zionists settlers should not behave cruelly to the local population, but at the same time they should not invest in developing Arab society, economics and agriculture, and should not expect the Arabs to agree that Jewish immigration would be beneficial for them.[10]

He argued further that this was not only because of the Zionists' limited resources and the need to prioritise Jewish settlement, but because developing Arab culture and consciousness would be harmful, "like a person who finds a frozen snake and warms it in his lap". He emphasised that such policy would not decrease Arab hatred of the Zionist project.

> Holy naiveté! If their nationalism is so sacred to them that they are ready to shed their blood for it, would not they use all cultural means that we give them in order to enhance their national existence? And who will be their adversaries if not we?

He concluded: we have to employ only Jews so the Arabs would not develop economically; to improve our agricultural techniques but not theirs; to enhance our education system so our kids would be stronger than theirs.[11] However, he added, when we Zionists become stronger and the majority in the country, and the Arabs asked for our advice – when there would be no risk in educating them, because we will be stronger – then we will be equal and make peace as equals.[12]

The sentiment that it was better to leave the Arabs in their backwardness was also expressed by others throughout the following decades – Zalman

Levontine, a prominent Zionist banker and one of the founders of the town of Rishon Le-Tzion, wrote in 1904:

> when I visit one of our colonies and see our kids study in school, and then pass through Arab villages and see their kids herd the sheep or throwing dirt at each other – then I am very satisfied. I think to myself: we have a wide range of action as long as the natives are uneducated. But once they build schools and their kids would study, get educated and grew up – then what will be with us?[13]

Menahem Ussishkin, the head of the Jewish National Fund (JNF) expressed similar concerns, from a different perspective:

> As the country develops, the inhabitant feels better, as he deepens his roots, as there are hospitals and schools and roads and housing and people are exempted from army service and there are less taxes – as this happens the willingness to sell the land and leave it to others decreases ... and we can see this on a daily basis in the country... from the day the British flag flew in the country and secured order, peace, rest, and the development of the country, and on the other hand the Jews arrived with great excitement and large sums and started to develop the country in different ways, since that day the land of Israel ceased to be the country we used to think of as easy to purchase.[14]

At the Zionist Congress of 1937 David Remez of the labour movement stated:

> We strengthen them in all fields, and first of all financially. We serve as their example in organisation. We increase the level of their education and the standard of living ... our money turn into weapon in their hands.[15]

The 'blessing' theory: the official Arab response

Zionist thinkers agreed that the Arabs would benefit from Jewish settlement in Palestine, and debated whether there was a Zionist interest in aiding the Arab population and whether the benefits bestowed on them would change their political behaviour. Ze'ev Jabotinsky, in his definitive essay 'The Iron Wall' (1923) was clear about the latter point:

> To imagine, as our Arabophiles do, that they [the Arabs] will voluntarily consent to the realisation of Zionism in return for the moral and material conveniences which the Jewish colonist brings with him, is a childish notion ... it means that they despise the Arab race, which they regard as a corrupt mob that can be bought and sold and are willing to give up their father-land for a good railway system. There is no justification for

such a belief.... Every native population in the world resists colonists as long as it has the slightest hope of being able to rid itself of the danger of being colonised.[16]

Indeed, the Arabs' rejection of Zionism had nothing to do with its anticipated blessings.[17] The Arabs voiced two main arguments: first, that the Arabs did not need the Zionists in order to improve the standards of living in the country; and, second, that Zionist immigration and settlement was wrong, regardless of the economic benefits they might bring with them.

Immediately after the First World War, Arab nationalists demanded that the British Foreign Office abolish the Balfour Declaration. They argued that Palestine was a fertile country and could be developed by its current inhabitants. Massive immigration of foreigners, they argued, would not bring about prosperity to Palestine but rather would make the country into a scene of constant conflict.[18]

Winston Churchill, the Colonial Secretary, heard this Arab response during his visit to Palestine in 1921. After hearing from the delegation of the Jewish National Council that "a Jewish renaissance in this country can only have a strong and invigorating influence upon the Arab nation" and that "the two brother nations, Jews and Arabs, working together in peace and harmony, are destined to bring about the cultural and economic revival of the awakening people of the Near and Middle East", he received the response of Musa Kazim al-Husseini, former mayor of Jerusalem and head of the Palestinian Arab Executive, who wondered how one could believe that the Zionists would contribute to the prosperity to Palestine. Referring to the protocols of the Elders of Zion, he wrote in a memorandum given to Churchill: "Jews have been among the most active advocates of destruction in many lands, especially where their influential positions have enabled them to do more harm". He added:

> Since Palestine opened its doors to them its trade has gradually drifted into their hands. They depreciate the value of land and property and at the same time manipulate a financial crisis in order that landlords under the stress of need, should sell out at ruinous prices. Can Europe then expect the Arabs to live and work with such a neighbour? Had not England better find a country for them in the vast uninhabited regions of her great Empire?[19]

Churchill ignored Husseini's arguments and stressed:

> We think it will be good for the world, for the Jews and good for the British Empire. But we also think it will be good for the Arabs who dwell in Palestine, and we intend that it shall be good for them, and that they shall not be sufferers or supplanted in the country in which they dwell or denied their share in all that makes for its progress or prosperity.[20]

One should not assume that Churchill necessarily believed in what he stated. Not only had he published a year earlier an article in which he blamed the Jews for the atrocities committed by the Bolsheviks, he also believed that the Jews took it for granted that the local [Arab] population would be "cleared out to suit their convenience".[21] But he did not share these beliefs with his Arab interlocutors.

A more detailed Arab argument against Zionism as a blessing to the Arabs was presented to the American Congressional Committee on Foreign Affairs, during its hearings regarding the Balfour declaration on April 18–21, 1922.[22] Fuad Shatara of the Palestine National League was one of two Palestinian Arabs who presented the anti-Zionist case before the committee.

> The claim that the Zionists will make an oasis out of barren Palestine is both erroneous and misleading. Palestine has more than 70 inhabitants per square mile, whereas the United States, with its rich natural resources, has only about 35 per square mile. There is more justification for admitting the overcrowded Japanese to colonize Texas. The Jew is not, instinctively, a farmer, and the Zionist colonies in Palestine were mostly built by non-Jewish labor and [...] are still not self-supporting.... Palestinians are not as backward as the Zionists portray them. They are entitled to a chance to build their own homeland under a just and helpful administration.[23]

Selim Totah, a law student, having recently immigrated to the US, was the second Palestinian Arab whom the Congressional committee invited. He stated:

> The natives cultivated the land there. We have intelligent law-abiding people and can develop the country if given a chance.... Now ... there come the Zionists to deprive us of the first instance where we have a chance to assert ourselves and see what we can do if not hampered.[24]

But the Committee was not impressed by the Arabs' arguments.[25] Its report stated:

> Palestine, the ancient homeland of the Jew, is to-day a comparatively sterile country.... What was once the country of milk and honey has become, through misrule and oppression, a devastated and sparsely settled land.... We of America should be glad to give our moral support to a project which is based upon justice and humanity. To give this recognition to so laudable an endeavour of a people seeking to create a haven of refuge for the oppressed and homeless of their race is to act in consonance with the loftiest American ideals... Leaders of the Jewish people here and abroad ... anticipate the eventual creation of an enlightened state which shall be a center of Jewish culture, *a blessing to humanity*

[emphasis mine] and the Jewish race, in that ancient land which was given by Jehovah to Abraham.[26]

Notwithstanding British and American support of the 'blessing' concept, the Arab leadership rejected it unreservedly. Thus, Zionist thinkers were forced to explain to the international community and to themselves why the Palestinian Arabs did not understand the blessings of Zionism and why they attacked the *Yishuv* politically and militarily.

The 1920s: from capitalist benefit to socialist awakening

The first Arab mass attack on Jews under British rule took place in April 1920, in Jerusalem. It generated heated discussions among the Zionists. A few weeks after the disturbances, the Jewish National Committee (*ha-Vaad ha-Leumi*) established a 'Committee for our Relations with the Arabs' to discuss what could be done to reduce inter-ethnic tensions in the country. The committee was composed of veteran and native Jews, most of them with well-established social and economic relationships with the Arabs. At its first meeting, Yosef Eliahu Shlush of the veteran Mugrabi family of Jaffa, proposed the creation of a special fund for loans to Arabs, and the establishment of a Zionist newspaper in Arabic. The latter idea was not new; since the 1908 Young Turk revolution a few Zionist activists had been arguing that such a newspaper would make the Arabs aware of the advantages of Jewish immigration. The industrialist Isaac Hayutman, one of the founders of Tel Aviv, added that the *Yishuv* should employ educated Arabs as teachers and journalists in its institutions. Meir Dizengoff, who would be elected as mayor of Tel Aviv in 1921, who had been involved in purchasing land from Arabs since 1904, emphasised the necessity of joint economic projects with local Arabs. "If anyone from outside comes to investigate the situation they would find out that actually we had in mind only our own interests and we do not consider the vast Arab population which dwell in the country". He added that helping the Arabs would be good not only for relations between Jews and Arabs in Palestine, but also for the Zionists' public relations.[27]

It is worth noting that all the members of this committee were from a non-socialist (sometimes anti-socialist) background. The labour movement which was in the early 1920s emerging as the leading power of the *Yishuv*, had a more complex attitude to the benefit theory, especially in the light of their call for 'Hebrew Labour', i.e. when possible, the replacement of Arab workers by Jewish. David Ben Gurion, the Secretary-General of the *Histadrut* (the *Yishuv*'s Labour Union), was at pain to explain how Arab workers would benefit from Zionism – despite its policy of Hebrew Labour: this policy might harm a number of Arab workers, but, he added: "ultimately it would improve the economic situation of Palestine as a whole, create new and better jobs in the Arab sector as well and thereby benefit the Arab workers".[28] In other words, although Zionism would create some inconvenience to Arab workers initially, in the long run they would benefit from it as well.

When explaining Arab resistance to Zionism despite its blessing, Socialist Zionists used a class analysis. "The peasant is interested in the expansion of employment and industry in the country and the improvement of the workers' lot, which by necessity results from Jewish settlement and immigration. Thus the peasant is not opposed to [Jewish] immigration". This was claimed by Yitzhak Ben Zvi, labour activist and later Israel's second president. The opposition to Zionism, he argued, "was by a tiny stratum of *effendis*, landlords, who were afraid that the Zionist socialists would push the fellahin and the Arab masses to demand their rights and bring an end to the system of exploitation from which the effendis are the beneficiaries".[29]

This approach was dominant among Zionist labour parties well into the 1930s. At the *Histadrut* Congress in 1934, Yaakov Hazan of *Hashomer Hatzair* put it as an axiom: "We always knew that the Zionist project shares interests with the masses of the Arab workers and contrasts the interests of the feudal, reactionary landlords, the clerics and the usurers".[30] The outbreak of the Arab revolt in 1936 – although most of its participants came from the lower classes – did not bring about a change of the discourse. The Zionist labour delegation that headed to the planned anti-Nazi Olympic games held in Barcelona in July 1936, published a leaflet which pointed out that the Jews were returning to Zion in order to build a free homeland together with the Arab workers and for the sake of both peoples. It continued: "But the Arab effendis and the agents of the reactionary forces, could not watch the resurrection of Israel and the revival of the Arab fellah and worker, therefore incited the masses against us by lies and defamation".[31]

During the first 15 years of the British Mandate, Zionist civil circles (i.e. liberals) were trying, with the coordination of the Zionist Commission, to establish ties with Arab landlords and *effendis* (people like Herzl's character, Reshid Bey's father), in order to strengthen the opposition to the leadership of the Mufti Hajj Amin al-Husseini, the Palestinian Arab leader.[32] For its part, the labour movement advocated an alliance with the Arab workers against the *effendis*. Each party chose its interlocutors according to its ideology, and presented the 'blessing' of Zionism according to its worldview. Labour spoke about social revolution and an end to the exploitation of the masses by the urban elites. The liberals emphasised the development of industry and commerce.

Ben Gurion's proposal rejected: a conditional blessing

The rise of the Labour party to the hegemony of the Zionist movement, and in particular, the election of David Ben Gurion and Moshe Shertok to the Zionist Executive in 1933, initiated a new Zionist effort to reach an agreement with the Arabs. The two leaders began political negotiations with Arab personalities in Palestine and beyond, and put aside ideas about class alliances. Their counterparts were Arab politicians of middle or upper-class backgrounds.

A key Arab figure in these talks was Musa al-Alami, son of a prominent Jerusalemite Muslim family, who served as a senior official in the Mandate government. As Ben-Gurion recalled in his *My Talks with Arab Leaders*, they met first at Shertok house in Jerusalem in April 1934. Ben Gurion presented his view that Zionism was "bringing a blessing to the Arabs of the country and therefore they had no reason to oppose us".[33] Another person whom Ben Gurion met, in the summer of 1934 was the Palestinian leader of the pan-Arab Istiqlal party, Awni Abd al-Hadi. Ben Gurion recalled:

> Both Dr. Magnes and I tried to prove to him that the settlement of the Jews was a blessing to the Arab *fellahin* in the coastal valley and in other areas; their farms had developed, yields had increased, working methods had been improved, and their income was much larger than it had been previously.[34]

However, what seemed to Ben Gurion to be an obvious fact was rejected by his interlocutors. "That assumption was shattered", recalled Ben Gurion. "Musa Alami told me that he would prefer the land to remain poor and desolate even for another hundred years, until the Arab themselves were capable of developing it and making it flower". Al-Aami went on to present the pessimistic feeling among the Arabs that

> they were being gradually ousted from all the important positions, the best parts of the country were passing into Jewish hands ... the national budget was expended on defence, for which the Arabs had no need ... and all for the sake of the Jewish National home.[35]

Ben Gurion felt that "as a patriotic Arab he had every right to this view",[36] but he tried to find other ways to persuade the Arab leadership to accept the Zionist project. The idea he had in mind was for the Arabs to consent to a Jewish state on both sides of the Jordan River, in return for Zionist "support of the establishment of an Arab federation in the neighbouring countries and an alliance of the Jewish State with that federation".[37]

The change in Ben Gurion's approach was at two levels. First, his decision to negotiate with the *effendis*, whom he had described for years as the oppressors of the Arab masses; and to reframe the concept of 'blessing' as a political-national gain, rather than a socio-economic one. These changes were explained by him at the Histadrut Congress of 1937: "I still believe in the alliance between us and the Arab worker", he declared, "but I would not say today that the only way to reach understanding is through the Arab worker.... We cannot decide who would represent the Arab people, nor wait until the workers talk in the name of the people". The 'blessing', he added, cannot be on the economic level only. "A '[pro-] Jewish Orientation' among the Arabs would be possible if we, and the supporters of this orientation, were able to prove that there is a blessing in cooperation with the Jews not only economically but also politically".[38] However, the negotiations he conducted with *Al-Alami* and with Arab leaders from neighbouring countries failed. They rejected the idea of a Jewish state and the alleged benefits that would accompany it.

The rejection of the 'blessing' thesis – on both economic and political grounds – was expressed at the time in a booklet *The Palestine Arab Cause*, published by *Tawfiq Canaan*, a Palestinian physician and ethnographer. Based on British reports he argued: "The [Zionist] immigrants have come into Palestine in excess of the economic absorbing power of the country". He next quoted from the constitution of the Jewish Agency:

> The land acquired shall be held as the inalienable property of the Jewish people... in all the works or undertaking carried out or furthered by the Agency it shall be deemed to be a matter of principle that Jewish labour shall be employed.[39]

The message was clear: Jewish immigration was about control, not only in the economic but also the political sphere. He continued, allegedly citing the Zionist thinker Ahad Ha-Am, the goal of Zionism was to "rule over it (Palestine) and manage all its affairs in its own way, without regard to the consent or non-consent of its present inhabitants".[40] From the Arab perspective, the claim that Zionism was a blessing rang hollow.

Although Zionist leaders were aware of the Arabs' rejection of the 'blessing' concept, Zionist officials continued to emphasise it up until 1948 (and in different ways, even up to the present day). In March 1946, the Jewish Agency submitted a special memorandum to the Anglo-American Committee of Inquiry, in which it presented in detail the positive effects of Jewish immigration on Arab health and sanitation (thus also on population growth), agriculture, industrialisation, wages, and education.[41] In July 1947, the *Histadrut* submitted to the United Nations Special Committee on Palestine a survey of its activities among the Arabs, which also highlighted the benefits of Zionist socialism for the Arabs.[42] Both reports were public relations efforts, directed at international bodies.

In December 1947, just after the UN partition plan was approved by its General Assembly, and following the outbreak of violent Arab resistance to it, the Jewish National committee made a final, desperate effort to assuage Arab opposition. It published the following proclamation to the Palestinian Arabs:

> Arabs! The Jewish National Committee sends you words of peace.... The Jews are willing to build their state, in the borders designated to them by the UN resolution, with economic partnership and full, trusty friendship. The Jewish enterprise brought with it prosperity and enriched the whole of the country in the past and will remain a source of continued blessing,

to both Jews and Arabs. Do not listen to those who incite the public and accept our outstretched hand for peace.[43]

As in previous years, the Palestinian Arabs – not necessarily as individuals but as a political collective – were not convinced and rejected the 'blessing' brought by Zionism.

Conclusion

The argument that Zionism brought a blessing to the Arabs was as old as Zionism itself. During the mandate period this argument was developed and diversified along ideological lines. Why did the Zionists insist on presenting their movement as a blessing to others? Why was it so important to them? One possible answer is that because it was true. It is hard to ignore the fact that Jewish immigration brought significant improvements in certain aspects of the lives of the Palestinian Arabs. As with colonial projects elsewhere, this argument had its factual value also in the unique Zionist case.

But there were two additional, major reasons for the repeated discussion of it. One was external – British support of the Zionist project, especially in the fields of land acquisition and Jewish immigration, was conditioned on the ability of the country to absorb more inhabitants without harming the indigenous Arab population (although this did not prevent Weizmann from demanding that Jewish capital be used exclusively for the employment of Jews).[44] The second reason for voicing this argument was internal and had to do with the self-image of the Zionist movement. Most Zionists truly believed in their own high morality, and did not have any intention of harming the Arabs of Palestine. When analyzing the situation, they preferred to focus on the positive results of their coming to the country – positive also from the Arab perspective – and to keep their pure self-image, rather than to deal with the concrete Arab claims. This is true for those who believed that Zionism was bringing economic benefits, as well as to those who believed that it had a spiritual role in the Middle East.

Most Zionist thinkers focused on the socio-economic benefits to the Arabs, or at the political level. But there were others who concentrated on the moral and spiritual aspects. The Ashkenazi chief rabbi of Palestine, Avraham Isaac Hacohen Kook, who is considered the spiritual father of religious Zionism, believed that the Land of Israel was granted to the Jewish people by God, and emphasised that the return of the sons of Israel to Zion and the re-establishment of "our house of life" would bring light and salvation "not only to us but also to all those who – because of the blindness of their spiritual eyes – think that we harm them". In other words, the Arabs would understand that the return of the Jews would not cause them any harm but on the contrary, bring salvation to all nations including them.[45]

The philosopher-theologian Martin Buber's approach was, in a sense, similar to that of Kook – the attachment of the people of Israel to Zion could not be considered egoistic nationalism, he wrote, because it was part of a universal mission. "Zion means memory, demand, destiny; the very base of humanity's messianic building". He emphasised that the process of the Jewish return to Zion was not for the sake of Jews only, "but might be a meaningful truth towards the solution of the faith crisis not only in Judaism but for Humanity as a whole".[46] As we have seen, the US Congress had a similar view.

Perhaps Moshe Shertok's lecture of May 1940 on the history of Zionist activity *vis a vis* the Arabs best describes this phenomenon:

> Arab resistance puts Zionism into a terrible distress. It makes us restless. It puts a tragic question-mark in regard to our future.... The Zionist movement ... did not take into account the political and national elements, the racial instincts that play a role here.... It is strange that Zionism ... stripped Arab society of its emotional world and the desires and instincts which operate within it ... we tried to ... present [the] ... Arabs ... as mere persons, without taking into consideration the specialities of the spirit and the experiences of being Arab.[47]

Thus, Shertok suggested a psychological explanation for what motivated Zionists to believe in the blessings they brought to the Arabs. No wonder the Arabs rejected this notion. Ben Gurion fully understood it. Nevertheless, the argument regarding the blessings that Zionism brings to the Arabs is still part of the Zionist discourse, until the present day. It can be considered a legacy of colonialism and of the mandate period.

Notes

1 Israel Shahak, A history of the concept of 'transfer' in Zionism, *Journal of Palestine Studies*, 18/3, 1989, pp. 22–37; Nur Masalha, *Expulsion of the Palestinians: The Concept of "Transfer" in Zionist Political Thought, 1882–1948*, Washington DC: Institute for Palestinian Studies, 1992; Chaim Simons, *A Historical Survey of Proposals to Transfer Arabs from Palestine 1895–1947*, Gengis Khan Publishers, Internet edition 2004; Benny Morris, *The Birth of the Palestinian Refugee Problem Revisited*, Cambridge: Cambridge University Press, 2004, pp. 39–64.
2 The absence of the Arabs is so manifest to the degree that readers believed that all the inhabitants of the future Jewish state would be Jews. See Baruch Ben Yehuda, *Historia shel Ha-Tziyonut [History of Zionism]*, Tel Aviv: Ahdut, 1942, (in Hebrew), p. 301.
3 Theodor Herzl, *Altneuland* (trans. Paula Arnold), Haifa: Haifa Publishing Company, 1960 [orig. 1904], pp. 95–8.
4 Ibid., p. 100, also Glenn Bowman, A place for Palestinians in the Altneuland: Herzl, anti-Semitism, and the Jewish state, in *Elia Zureik, David Lyon, Yasmeen Abu-Laban* (eds), *Surveillance and Control in Israel/Palestine*, London: Routledge, 2010.
5 Quoted in Walid Khalidi, *From Haven to Conquest*, Washington: Institute for Palestine Studies, 1971, pp. 91–3; for background and analysis of Herzl's views on this see Derek J. Penslar, Herzl and the Palestinian Arabs: Myth and counter-

myth, *Journal of Israeli History* 24/1, 2005, pp. 65–77; also Joseph Nedava, Herzl and the Arab problem, *Forum on the Jewish People, Zionism, and Israel* 27, 1977, pp. 64–72, 106.

6 On the relations between Zionism and the Western colonialist project see Abdul-Wahab Kayyali, Zionism and imperialism: The historical origins, *Journal of Palestine Studies* 6/3, 1977, pp. 98–112.

7 Yitzhak Epstein, She'ela Naálama [Hidden Question], *Ha-Shiloah*, 17, 1907, pp. 193–206. The English translation of Hidden Question, is from Alan Dowty, "A question that outweighs all others": Yitzhak Epstein and Zionist recognition of the Arab issue, *Israel Studies* 6/1, 2001, pp. 34–54.

8 Ibid., p. 48.

9 Yitzhak Epstein, A Question That Outweighs All Others, *Doar Ha-Yom*, 17 August 1921 (in Hebrew).

10 Heruti [Moshe Smilansky], Issues From the *Yishuv, Ha-Poel Ha-Tza'ir*, (shvat-Adar I 5668 [1908]), vol. 4–5, pp. 5–10 (in Hebrew).

11 Ibid., pp. 7–8.

12 Ibid., p. 8

13 Zalman D. Levontine, *Le-Eretz Avotenu* [*To our Ancestors' Land*], Tel Aviv: Masada, 1924 (in Hebrew), vol. 2, p. 67.

14 Menahem Usishkin, The land requires its redemption, speech at the 19th Zionist Congress, 22 August 1935, *Hakongres ha-Tziyoni ha-Yod-Teth*, Jerusalem: The Zionist Organisation, 1937 (in Hebrew), p. 128–130.

15 *Hakongres ha-Tziyoni ha-Esrim* [*The 20th Zionist Congress*], Jerusalem: The Zionist Organisation, 1937 (in Hebrew), p. 56.

16 Published originally in Russian in *Rassvyet*, 4 November 1923; for online English version see www.jewishvirtuallibrary.org/quot-the-iron-wall-quot

17 On Arab rejection of Zionism in the late Ottoman period see Neville Mandel, *The Arabs and Zionism before World War* One, Berkeley: University of California Press, 1976.

18 A letter by Palestinian Arab leaders to the British Foreign Office, 12 December 1918, quoted in Bayan Nuweyhed al-Hut, *al-Qiyadat wal-Mu'asasat al-Filastiniyya fi Filastin 1917–1948* [*The Palestinian Leadership and Institutions in Palestine 1917–1948*], Beirut: Dar al-Huda, 1986, pp. 712–14.

19 Official Report: Deputation of Representatives of the Jewish Community, With Replies by Mr. Churchill, his speech at the Hebrew University site, and a minute by Sir Herbert Samuel on the memorandum of the Haifa Congress, 28 March 1921, in CAB 24/126, appendix 23; pp. 145–6, British National Archives, (NA).

20 Ibid.

21 Michael J Cohen, "The Churchill-Gilbert symbiosis: Myth and reality", *Modern Judaism* 28/2, 2008, pp. 207, 212.

22 US Government, *Establishment of a National Home in Palestine: Hearings before the Committee on Foreign Affairs, House of Representatives, April 18–21, 1922* Washington: Government Printing Office, 1922.

23 Ibid., pp. 163–4

24 Ibid., p. 166.

25 On the Western perception of Palestine at the time see Lodewijk van Oord, The Making of Primitive Palestine: Intellectual Origins of the Palestine-Israel Conflict, *History and Anthropology* 19/3, 2008, pp. 209–228.

26 "National Home for the Jewish People in Palestine", Report No. 1038 of the Hearings before the Committee on Foreign Affairs, House of Representatives, April 18–21, 1922. Appendix of *Establishment of National Home*, Washington: Government Printing Office, 1922.

27 Zionist Commission to M. Ushishkin, 4 May 1920, file L4/1001, Central Zionist Archives (CZA).

28 Zachary Lockman, *Comrades and Enemies: Arab and Jewish Workers in Palestine 1906–1948*, Berkeley: University of California Press, 1996, p. 88.
29 Ibid., pp. 60–1.
30 *Davar*, 9 August 1935.
31 Ibid., 21 July 1936.
32 For detailed analysis of this activity see Hillel Cohen, *Army of Shadows: Palestinian Collaboration with Zionism 1917–1948*, Berkeley: University of California Press, 2008, Chapters 1–3.
33 David Ben Gurion, *My Talks with Arab Leaders*, New York: The Third Press, 1972, p. 15.
34 Ibid., p. 19
35 Ibid., pp. 15–16.
36 Ibid., p. 15.
37 Ibid., p. 16
38 The Congress meetings, supplement to *Davar*, 30 April 1937, pp. 29–30.
39 Tawfiq Canaan, *The Palestine Arab Cause*, Jerusalem: The Modern Press, 1936, pp. 8–9.
40 Ibid., p. 15. It is not clear which Ahad Ha-Am article Canaan took this quote from.
41 Jewish Agency for Palestine, *Memorandum on Influence of Jewish Colonisation on Arab Development in Palestine, Submitted to the Anglo-American Committee of Inquiry*, Jerusalem, March 1946.
42 Memorandum in file TT 39/7, Israel State Archives (ISA).
43 *Davar*, 4 December 1947 (and other Hebrew newspapers of that date)
44 Michael J Cohen, *Britain's Moment in Palestine*, London: Routledge, 2014, pp. 166–7.
45 A. Y. HaCohen Kook, Introduction, in Reuven Gafni, *Our Historical-Legal Right to Eretz Israel*, Jerusalem: Tora va-Avoda, 1933 (in Hebrew), pp. 1–2.
46 Quoted in Shalom Ratzabi, *Anarchizem Be-Tzion: Bein Martin Buber le-A.D. Gordon [Anarchy in "Zion", Between Martin Buber and A.D. Gordon]*, Tel Aviv: Am Oved, 2011, pp. 40, 46.
47 Shertok's lecture, file S25/22201, pp. 2–4, CZA.

10 Jewish immigration

The base of the Palestine triangle

Aviva Halamish

The history of Palestine under the British Mandate is essentially a demographic race between the indigenous Arabs, constituting the majority of the population and the Jewish minority. By the end of World War One, about 56,000 Jews and about 600,000 Arabs lived in what would soon be Mandatory Palestine, a ratio of 1:11. In 1931, the Jews constituted around 17 percent of the total population (some 175,000 out of almost 1,036,000), and on the eve of World War Two, they numbered 450,000 – approximately one-third of the country's population. The same proportions remained at the outbreak of the 1948 War: about 600,000 Jews and twice as many Arabs – Muslims and Christians. While the Arab population grew (roughly nine-tenths) almost exclusively due to natural increase, the main source for the growth of the Jewish population was immigration.

My main contention is that Jewish immigration was the most significant factor in the history of Mandatory Palestine and in the shaping of relations between the three sides of the Palestine triangle. Immigration constituted one of the three main issues around which the conflict in Mandatory Palestine revolved; the other two were the establishment of institutions of representative self-government and the acquisition of land by Jews. For Arabs and Jews alike, Jewish immigration was a crucial issue with no room for compromise.

The principal goal of the Zionists between the world wars was to increase the Jewish population of Palestine, in order to attain a Jewish majority and form the basis for a sovereign Jewish state. During most of the 1920s, they felt no need to hasten Jewish immigration to Palestine because the pushing forces in Europe were weak, the economic absorptive capacity of Palestine was low, and the political future of the country was not on the immediate agenda. But in the 1930s, two factors caused the Zionists to sense urgency in the Palestine arena. First, the Zionists appreciated that with all of the regional turmoil, the moment of determining the country's political fate was approaching, and it became imperative to create a Jewish majority, or at least, a Jewish critical mass in the country. Second, towards the end of the decade, with war looming, the demographic factor was deemed crucial for the ability of the *Yishuv* to defend itself. As one of the Jewish witnesses told the Peel Commission: "There is safety in numbers", and "if we are kept in a state of permanent minority, then it is not a National Home, it may become a death-trap".[1]

The guiding principle of Zionist policy during most of the Mandate was cooperation with Britain, the Mandatory power and Zionism's only ally. The Zionists understood that the British provided an umbrella for the development of the National Home. The Zionist Organization refrained from generating a crisis around any issue, including immigration, so as not to destroy the basis of the cooperation with the Government. However, at the same time, the Zionists refused to compromise on the issue of maintaining immigration under all circumstances, even in periods of security tensions and decisive political decision-making. The issue of immigration was so crucial to the Zionists, that the option of imposing an arbitrary ceiling on Jewish immigration, raised by the Peel Commission in 1937, was one of the key factors behind the decision of the twentieth Zionist Congress (1937) to accept the idea of partitioning Palestine, and establishing a sovereign Jewish state in only a part of it.

What the Arabs most desired was national independence, and they were concerned lest they become a minority under Jewish domination in their own country. They complained that Jewish immigration not only threatened their status as the majority in the country but also harmed them economically. From the very beginning of the Mandate, the Arabs consistently called for the immediate cessation of Jewish immigration. This demand remained a central issue, together with their demands for the establishment of a democratic government, and the prohibition of the sale of Arab lands to Jews. As early as in 1921, the Palestine Arab delegation to London demanded the cessation of Jewish immigration until a national assembly could be formed.[2] In their eyes, the Jews were not refugees seeking shelter, but settlers intent on taking possession of their land, with the goal of achieving sovereignty.[3]

The fear of the Arabs that the Balfour Declaration would bring massive Jewish immigration to Palestine was already manifested during the British military regime (1918–20), despite the ban imposed by the Military on Jewish immigration (which allowed in only former residents of the country). The report of the inquiry into the 1921 'disturbances', conducted by a committee headed by the Chief Justice of Palestine, Sir Thomas Haycraft, stated that the root of the trouble was the Arab fear of a steady increase of Jewish immigration, which would ultimately bring about their political and economic subjection.[4] It is worth noting that the main target of Arab animosity on the first day of the May 1921 events was the Jewish Immigrants' Hostel in Jaffa. The Haycraft Commission concluded that "the primary cause of the 'disturbances' was Arab discontent over the political and economic consequences of continued Jewish immigration, as well as a perceived pro-Jewish bias by the Mandatory authorities".[5]

For their part, the British authorities, whose main concern was to ensure law and order, tried to navigate between their various obligations to the Jews and the Arabs, while preserving British interests. Their attitudes and policy regarding Jewish immigration changed according to events and developments in the country, the region, and the world. Until the eve of World War Two, Britain was committed to the Balfour Declaration (1917) which promised to facilitate the establishment of a National Home for the Jewish people in Palestine, and to its undertaking of 1922, to enable the Jewish community in Palestine to increase its numbers by immigration, according to the economic absorptive capacity of the country.[6]

Once the Balfour Declaration was incorporated in the League of Nations Mandate for Palestine, it assumed the status of an international document.[7] The council of the League made Britain 'responsible for placing the country under such political, administrative and economic conditions as will secure the establishment of the Jewish National Home'.[8] In this respect, the Palestine Mandate differed from other type 'A' mandates.[9] The Mandate for Syria and Lebanon, for instance, directed the French to frame an organic law within a period of three years of the coming into force of the mandate, in agreement with the native authorities, and to take into account the rights, interests, and wishes of the population inhabiting these countries. The French also had to enact measures to facilitate the progressive development of Syria and the Lebanon as independent states.[10] Such clauses were absent in the Mandate for Palestine, as their implementation would have frustrated the preferential undertaking of the Mandatory power, namely facilitating the establishment of a Jewish National Home.

The three sides of the Palestine triangle were fully aware that the goals of self-government based on a legislative council reflecting the demographic composition of the population in Palestine, and the realisation of the Jewish National Home, were irreconcilable. It was taken for granted that an Arab majority in such a body would put an end to Jewish immigration. In 1937, the Royal [Peel] Commission made it clear that, "a national self-government could not be established in Palestine as long as it would be used to frustrate the purpose of the Balfour Declaration".[11] It admitted that the British could not concede both the Arab claim to self-government *and* secure the establishment of the Jewish National Home.[12] At that point (1937), Britain's attempt to resolve the contradiction between its obligations to the Arabs and the Jews was seen as involving a choice between two courses of action: either terminating the Mandate and establishing a Jewish state in part of Palestine (while annexing the Arab part to Trans-Jordan), or putting a 'political high limit' on the volume of Jewish immigration.

Britain adopted the latter option in two stages. In July 1937, it published a White Paper setting the number of Jewish immigrants at 1,000 a month, pending an adoption of an alternative solution to the conflict.[13] In its White Paper of May 1939, on the eve of World War Two, Britain officially abandoned the first option raised by the Peel Commission – partition – and announced its intention to establish within ten years an independent Palestine State, in which Arabs and Jews would share government in a way that safeguarded the essential interests of each community. The government declared that its obligation under the Balfour Declaration regarding the Jewish National Home in Palestine had been fulfilled. It substantiated its claim by citing the fact that more than 300,000 Jews had immigrated to Palestine, and the Jewish population had risen to some 450,000, nearly one-third of the entire population of the country.[14]

As to the future, the government stated:

> Jewish immigration during the next five years will be at a rate which, if economic absorptive capacity permits, will bring the Jewish population up to approximately one third of the total population of the country. Taking into account the expected natural increase of the Arab and Jewish populations, and the number of illegal Jewish immigrants now in the country, this would allow of the admission, as from the beginning of April this year [1939], of some 75,000 immigrants over the next five years.[15]

The statement stipulated further that after five years, no further Jewish immigration would be permitted without the Arabs' consent. Furthermore, after five years, there would be no justification to facilitate further the development of the Jewish National Home by immigration regardless of the wishes of the Arab population, and the British would not be under any obligation to facilitate such immigration. World War Two opened a new chapter in the history of Palestine, in which immigration was no longer a central issue in the Palestine triangle.

Jewish immigration to Palestine between the world wars: principles and practice

Under Article 6 of the Mandate, Britain was obliged to ensure that the rights and status of other sections of the population would not be prejudiced by Jewish immigration. For that purpose, Britain introduced the 'economic absorptive capacity' principle as the yardstick for determining the volume of Jewish immigration. The 1922 (Churchill) White Paper stated that for the fulfilment of the policy contained in the Balfour Declaration, "it is necessary that the Jewish community in Palestine should be able to increase its numbers by immigration". However, the new policy added that the immigrants "should not be a burden upon the people of Palestine as a whole, and they should not deprive any section of the present population of their employment".[16]

Economic absorptive capacity was defined as the annual rate at which the country could receive immigrants without causing friction and serious economic disturbance.[17] Immigration regulated by this principle was classified into three main categories: 1) immigrants who bring with them the necessary resources for their absorption; 2) immigrants with no financial means, who come to find work; and 3) immigrants who depend on residents of the country or on immigrants from the first two categories. In fact, in Mandatory Palestine immigrants were classified into four main categories:[18] persons of independent means (Category A, 'Capitalists'); students and persons of religious occupations whose maintenance was assured (Category B); persons who had a definite prospect of employment (Category C, 'Labour'); dependents of permanent residents of Palestine or of immigrants in other categories (Category D). Only immigrants of category C were subject to the economic absorptive capacity principle, as the immigrants of categories A, B and D were not expected to join the labour market. Therefore, until 1937, there was no limit on the number of immigrants in the latter categories.

The Government regulated the immigration of categories A, B and D, and it granted the Zionist Organization partial authority over category C, in return for the organisation's undertaking to guarantee the maintenance of the immigrants during their first year in Palestine.[19] The status of the Zionist Organization in immigration matters was based on the League's and the Mandatory's recognition of the Zionist Organization as the sole representative of the Jewish people in all matters concerning Palestine.[20] Every six months, the Zionist Executive submitted a detailed request for labour certificates, accompanied by a survey, carried out in collaboration with the Mandatory's Department of Migration, of the economic situation in general, and that of the Jewish community in particular.[21] The same Department also made a rough survey of Arab unemployment at that time, and of other economic factors. After considering the request submitted by the Zionist Organization (from 1930, the Jewish Agency), and the recommendations made by the Immigration Authority, the High Commissioner determined the size of the labour schedule.

The Government allotted the Zionist Organization most of the labour certificates for distribution, with directives regarding the age of the immigrants, their employment skills and the ratio of the sexes.[22] As a rule, labour certificates were supposed to be given to people between the ages of 18 and 35, who were capable of physical labour, or experts in specific trades, with a 2:1 ratio in favour of male immigrants. Over time, the government increased its involvement in certificate allocation, at times even dictating the number of certificates to be sent to specific countries.[23] In other words, the Mandatory power dictated the rules of the game, and always had the final say. The Zionist Organization thus had limited authority over immigration, and could never influence its scope.

The Zionist Organization accepted the economic absorptive capacity principle because it believed it to be the lesser of two evils.[24] Replacing this principle with a political yardstick would have brought about the suppression of Jewish immigration under Arab pressure, while free, unlimited immigration would have led to the strangling of the Jewish economy in Palestine. Aware of its limited power, the Zionist Organization never asked for overall control over immigration and accepted that the determination of the scope of immigration was the Mandatory's prerogative.[25]

The Zionist Organization adhered to the economic absorptive capacity principle for an additional reason; it believed that with the help of funds from world Jewry, immigration controlled by the country's economic capacity would bring about the creation of a Jewish majority in Palestine within a foreseeable time. The number of Jewish immigrants in 1935 was 62,000. In 1937, the Peel Commission estimated that if Jewish immigration continued at this rate, the Jewish population would equal that of the Arabs within ten years.[26]

Though the British and the Zionists agreed on the principle of economic absorptive capacity, they differed on how to interpret and implement it. The two main issues of dispute and conflict were: 1) was the absorptive capacity the sole and binding factor in determining the rate of immigration, or might other factors, mainly political, be considered, in order to reduce its volume? And 2) should the economic absorptive capacity be that of the entire Palestinian economy, or only that of the Jewish sector?

Britain's fluctuating immigration policy: economic and other considerations

Jewish immigration was essentially a political issue, and all three sides, the British, the Arabs and the Jews, were unable to relate to it in purely economic terms. Hence, the discussion here focuses on the question what were the decisive considerations in shaping and implementing the Mandatory's immigration policy, and on the discrepancy between official and public statements, and actions in practice.

The first year of the Civil Administration may serve as a microcosm for the entire inter-war period, concerning the interplay of economic and political considerations. On 4 May 1921, a few days after the outbreak of the disturbances in Jaffa, High Commissioner Herbert Samuel ordered the suspension of all Jewish immigration.[27] A month later, on 3 June, he declared that future immigration policy would be ruled by the principle of the country's "economic absorptive capacity" and be limited "by the numbers and interests of the present population".[28] Then, on 14 June 1921, Colonial Secretary Winston Churchill announced in Parliament that although the government supported the principle of Zionist immigration, "the movement would be carefully controlled from the point of view of numbers and character".[29] While the temporary suspension of Jewish immigration was a direct result of the May disturbances, Samuel's decision was, to a great extent, due to his inside knowledge that the Zionist Organization had failed to raise sufficient funds to absorb the immigrants, most of who did not have independent means. He believed that the suspension would assuage both Arabs and Zionists. In January 1922, he wrote to Chaim Weizmann, President of the Zionist Organisation, "if I had not enforced fairly close restrictions on immigration

[...] the Zionist Organization would have had to act in the same direction, and borne the odium itself". Apparently, Samuel did not foresee the Zionist firestorm that the suspension provoked. The timing gave the impression that he had yielded to Arab pressure.[30]

In the years 1922–29, the Government did not have to evoke political considerations in the implementation of its immigration policy; the economic capacity of the Jewish community to absorb newcomers in those years fell short of the political threshold set by the British.[31] In addition, the Jewish community experienced two waves of economic crisis, one in 1923, and the other from late 1925 to the beginning of 1929. At the same time, the Arabs were immersed in their own internal power struggles.[32] Consequently, the massive wave of immigration in the middle of the 1920s (from 1924–26, about 60,000 Jews immigrated into the country) was not met with a violent Arab reaction. Steps taken by the British during the economic crisis of the second half of the decade, such as stopping labour immigration for a while, and raising the amount required for Capitalist visas, were indeed prompted by economic considerations.[33] To the extent that other considerations were involved, they worked in favour of the Jews; for instance, in spite of unfavourable economic conditions in 1926, immigration was not suspended, for fear of undermining Zionist fundraising.[34]

The violent clashes between the Arabs and the Jews in 1929, rather than economic conditions, led to the Government's re-consideration of limiting Jewish immigration.[35] On the eve of John Hope-Simpson's visit to Palestine in May 1930, for the first time, the Government openly invoked political considerations in its immigration policy; the Colonial Office instructed the High Commissioner to suspend the grant of the Labour Certificates for the spring schedule, pending the conclusion of Hope-Simpson's mission.[36] In this case, the arrival of Hope-Simpson was an excuse, and the real purpose of halting immigration was to appease the Arabs and to prevent the renewal of disturbances.

Hope-Simpson arrived in Palestine following the Shaw Commission's recommendation (March 1930), "that His Majesty's Government should issue at an early date a clear and definite declaration of the policy which they intend to be pursued in regard to the regulation and control of future Jewish immigration to Palestine".[37] In his report, Hope-Simpson proposed to extend the principle of 'economic absorptive capacity' from the Jewish sector to the entire population of Palestine, and called for a reduction, even a suspension of Jewish immigration, if the new immigrants were likely to increase the number of Arab unemployed. His recommendations were implemented in the 1930 (Passfield) White Paper, which stated that immigration should be regulated by political, and not only economic, consideration. It has been asserted: "Had it been passed into law it would have effectively curtailed, if not halted completely, the further development of the Jewish National Home in Palestine".[38]

But within a few months, the 1930 White Paper was annulled for all practical purposes by a personal letter written by Prime Minister Ramsay MacDonald to Chaim Weizmann (13 February 1931). The letter, which until 1937 became the authoritative interpretation of the 1930 White Paper, restored the principle of economic absorptive capacity as the yardstick for immigration.[39]

Thus, following the first stage of the Arab Revolt, which erupted in April 1936, William Ormsby-Gore, Secretary of State for the Colonies, announced in the House of Commons on 5 November 1936, that the Government's decision to suspend immigration during the investigation of the Royal Commission "would not be justifiable on economic or on other grounds". The Government's view was:

> if any drastic departure from the immigration policy hitherto pursued were now to be introduced in advance of the findings of the Royal Commission, this would involve an alteration in the existing situation and might be held to prejudice the inquiries of the Royal Commission, which will be directed, among other matters, to the very important question of immigration generally.[40]

The Peel Commission concluded that in addition to economic factors, immigration policy should take into account political, social, and psychological considerations as well, and advised to set a 'political high level' of 12,000 immigrant Jews annually for the next five years. The Commission stated categorically that under no circumstance, should this maximum figure be exceeded in any one year during that period. However, this maximum figure remained subject to the economic absorptive capacity of the country.[41]

Thus, in the long term, the 1930 White Paper proved to be the precursor to a new British policy regarding Jewish immigration to Palestine. In the summer of 1937, Britain formally replaced the principle of economic absorptive capacity with the 'political high level' principle. This aimed at preventing the growth of the Jewish population beyond the existing demographic balance of about one-third Jews and two-thirds Arabs in Palestine. In 1937, this ceiling was set at 12,000 per year. The White Paper of May 1939 raised the number to 15,000, reflecting the rapid natural growth of the Arab population in Palestine.[42]

Originally, Britain interpreted the Balfour Declaration as intended for the Jewish people as a whole, not just for the Jews who already resided in the country.[43] At the same time, its immigration policy detached Palestine from the situation of the Jews in Europe; its policy was based on the premise that immigration to Palestine should not be expected to provide the solution for all Jews who were deprived or persecuted.[44] In 1924, a series of changes in American immigration laws, though not intended to restrict Jewish immigration specifically, practically closed the United States to Jewish immigrants from Eastern Europe. Still, in the second half of the

1920s Jewish immigration to Palestine was slow because both the pushing and the pulling forces of the immigration process were weak. During that period, nowhere in the world were the Jews under acute pressure to leave. As we have seen, in Palestine, the economy went through periods of recession and depression. Thus, the economic crisis in Palestine in the second half of the 1920s, the political instability at the beginning of the 1930s, and a relative lull in the pressure on the Jews in Europe (up to 1933) – all served to reduce the effects of the American closed-door policy on Jewish immigration. In the 1930s, however, with Hitler's ascent to power and the deterioration of the situation of the Jews in Eastern Europe, the implications of the new American immigration policy for the Jews and for Palestine became patently clear.

From 1933 on, Britain granted Jews from Germany (and in 1938–39 from Austria also) a preferential status in immigration into Palestine. However, this favouritism towards German Jews did not lead to an increase in the total number of certificates issued, but instead, made a change in the apportioning of the cake. In other words, the generosity of Britain toward German Jews resulted in diminished immigration opportunities for Jews from other countries.

A few days after Germany's annexation of Austria (the *Anschluss*, 12 March 1938), President Franklin D. Roosevelt, invited European and South American states to a conference in Evian on the issue of German refugees. Britain agreed to take part, only after being assured that 'no country would be expected or asked to receive a greater number of immigrants than is permitted by its existing legislation'. There was a silent Anglo-American understanding that Palestine would not be raised at the conference as a potential destination for the refugees.[45] About a year later, the 1939 White Paper set up a special quota for refugees, but this was done not by raising the total immigrant quota, but by including the allotment within the number set [at] "a rate which [...] will bring the Jewish population up to approximately one third of the total population of the country". In other words, first, Britain decided that in the following five years, 75,000 Jews would be allowed to enter Palestine; and then, it announced that 25,000 of them would be allotted to refugees, "as a contribution towards the solution of the Jewish refugee problem".[46]

The small number of immigrants that were actually allowed into Palestine stands in contrast to the high-sounding declaration made in that document:

> But above all, His Majesty's Government are conscious of the present unhappy plight of large numbers of Jews who seek a refuge from certain European countries, and they believe that Palestine can and should make a further contribution to the solution of this pressing world problem.[47]

The 1939 White Paper was composed under the shadow of an imminent world war; it aimed to appease the Arabs in Palestine and in neighbouring countries, to ensure their support in the event of a war. It was clear to the British that the most important measure they could take to achieve this goal was to meet Arab demands concerning Jewish immigration.[48] However, as stated in the White Paper, an abrupt halt to further Jewish immigration, "would damage the whole of the financial and economic system of Palestine and thus affect adversely the interests of Arabs and Jews alike. Moreover, [it...] would be unjust to the Jewish National Home".[49]

Assessing the economic absorptive capacity of Palestine

As noted, the principle of economic absorptive capacity was intended to ensure that Jewish immigrants would not become a burden on the people of Palestine as a whole, and not deprive any section of the present population of their employment. The main issue in dispute between the Zionists and the British remained how to apply this principle, whether the basis for the calculations was Palestine as a single economic unit or only the Jewish sector's economy.[50] In other words, should the calculations take into account the absorptive capacity of the Palestinian economy as a whole or just that of the Jewish sector?

The Jewish economy was more developed and advanced than that of the Arabs,[51] and its capability to absorb immigrants as a closed economic unit was greater than that of the Palestine economy as a whole. Zionist organisations and institutions consciously worked to develop a separate, autonomous, and self-sufficient Jewish economy, employing only Jewish labour, with the purpose of encouraging the growth of the Jewish population. They strove to detach the link between Jewish immigration and unemployment among the Arabs, and demanded that the number of new Jewish immigrants allowed in be determined according to the situation of the Jewish economy alone, plus their share in public works carried out by the Government and the municipalities.

While the Zionists adopted the notion of a separate Jewish economy, and the Arabs advocated the 'single economy' approach, the British, after a period of trial and error, at the beginning of the 1930s sorted the jobs in the Palestine labour-market into three types:

1   Jobs dependent on Jewish capital, which would not have been invested unless Jews were employed in them. The British were fully aware that Jews invested capital in Palestine to create jobs exclusively for Jewish workers, to increase the Jewish population – and not for providing employment for the country's Arab residents.[52] Therefore, they viewed the immigration of Jewish labour as justified, even at a time of Arab unemployment, provided that the newly-imported Jewish labour was assured work of a permanent nature in enterprises set up specifically for this purpose.[53]

The Government also recognized the right of the Jews to apply the principle of exclusive Jewish work in all the works or undertakings carried out or furthered by the Jewish Agency, as long as this policy did not result in displacing Arab labour or aggravating existing unemployment.[54]

2   Jobs in public and municipal works. The Government recognized the right of the Jews to get their due share of those jobs, taking into account Jewish contributions to public revenue, which were proportionally higher than their percentage of the general population.[55]

3   Other types of work, which were subject to other considerations, including, in this type as contrary to the others, Jewish and Arab unemployment. In 1930, Hope-Simpson argued that it was wrong, 'that a Jew from Poland, Lithuania, or the Yemen, should be admitted to fill an existing vacancy, while in Palestine there are already workmen capable of filling that vacancy who are unable to find employment". Implementing his approach would have meant that no Jewish immigration would be allowed as long as there remained unemployed Arabs. However, in Mandatory Palestine, it was difficult, even impossible, to obtain reliable data on Arab unemployment.[56] Albert Hyamson, the chief immigration officer, pointed out that Arabs were 'awaiting' employment rather than seeking it.[57]

In practice, the British prohibited the entry of Jewish workers to replace employed Arabs, but approved immigration even when there were unemployed Arabs. In the early 1930s, when immigration was slow, and the Jewish economy was afflicted by unemployment, the issue of Arab unemployment was rarely raised in British-Zionist deliberations on immigration. However, once the economy recovered, and during the years of relative prosperity, full employment, and even shortage of Jewish workers in the Jewish economy, figures of Arab unemployment were introduced into the Government's calculations in determining the volume of Jewish immigration. In April 1934, the British Cabinet decided not to let in new Jewish immigrants for carrying out work that could be done by unemployed Arabs.[58] This was one of the first signs of the British move to replace the principle of economic absorption capacity by political-demographic considerations, aimed at preventing the creation of a Jewish majority in Palestine.

It is widely accepted that in shaping its immigration policy, Britain related to the absorption capacity of the Jewish community alone, rather than treating the Palestinian economy as a monolith,[59] hardly considering the condition of the Arab labour market.[60] It is also agreed usually that if the economic absorption capacity principle had been applied to the whole of Palestine, no Jewish immigrants would have been allowed into the country.[61]

The impact of Jewish immigration on the Palestinian Arabs

The three sides of the Palestine triangle differed in evaluating the economic impact of Jewish immigration on the Arab economy, and there are conflicting estimates of the overall impact of Jewish immigration on the well-being of the

Arabs. The British attributed the growth of the Arab population in part to the influx of Zionist capital.[62] The Jews insisted that their National Home never injured the Arabs, but to the contrary, had contributed significantly to the growth of the Arab economy.[63]

In contrast, the Arabs claimed that Jewish immigration did harm them. Some recognised the economic value to the country of a reasonable number of Jewish residents. However, as a prominent Arab public figure was quoted in the Peel Report, "Who that wants salt empties the whole cellar into his plate?"[64] As a rule, the Arabs denied that they benefitted from Jewish immigration, claiming that they were better off before the days of the British occupation.[65] When David Ben-Gurion, then a member of the Jewish Agency Executive, expounded on the impetus of development brought to Palestine by the Jews, and repeated the claim that they had also benefited the Arabs, the Palestinian politician, Musa Alami, replied that he would prefer Palestine to remain desolate for another hundred years if necessary, until the Arabs themselves were able to develop the country.[66] Thus, in assessing the Arab attitude, psychological aspects cannot be ignored in comprehending their position; it is clear that they considered Jewish immigration as economically, as well as politically, harmful to their interests.

In summary, Jewish immigration had a mixed economic impact on the Arabs. Evidently, it brought great advantage to Palestine as a whole; however, the Peel report asserted that the direct benefit to individual Arabs was negligible. The Report stated that in the late 1920s (a period of general economic depression), "everywhere among the Arab people, the Zionist movement was regarded as the cause of the economic problems of the country".[67] Nevertheless, the Report did conclude that "broadly speaking, the Arabs have shared to a considerable degree in the material benefits which Jewish immigration has brought to Palestine".[68] The Report also found that Jewish immigration actually increased the economic absorptive capacity of the country as a whole.[69] To illustrate the general beneficent effect of Jewish immigration on Arab welfare, the Report pointed to the fact that the increase in the Arab population of Palestine was marked mostly in urban areas affected by Jewish development.[70] However, periods of economic depression or expansion within the Jewish community did not overtly affect the Arab population.[71]

Conclusions

In the interwar years, Mandatory Palestine was an arena for a demographic race between Arabs and Jews, with the British Mandatory government serving as a sort of referee. The Jews were striving to become the majority in the country via immigration, and to establish a Jewish state; the Arabs aspired to protect their status as the majority by curtailing Jewish immigration and achieve national independence; the British, although enabling Jewish immigration to change the demographic ratio between the two communities, were determined not to let the Jews become the majority.

The British included political considerations in their Palestine immigration policy well before they officially abandoned the economic absorptive capacity principle. The application of political considerations in immigration matters had a varying impact on the volume of Jewish immigration. In times of economic depression or slow-down (the mid-1920s, early 1930s, and from 1936 up until the outbreak of World War Two), political considerations precluded a complete stoppage or the imposition of more drastic restrictions. The Government allowed labour immigration in periods of economic downturn for political reasons, even when there was no economic justification for it, in order to avoid a complete halt to Jewish immigration. It was in the period of economic boom (1933–35) that the deviation from the economic absorption capacity yardstick for political-demographic reasons posed a real obstacle to the growth of the Jewish population. During that period, the Government issued fewer certificates than the ability of the Jewish economy to absorb newcomers. This assertion is supported by the high number of illegal Jewish immigrants, who could not have remained in the country had they not found jobs.[72]

In British eyes, the demographic growth of the Jewish National Home was always the underlying cause for the recurrent Arab disturbances – in 1920, 1921, 1929, 1933 and 1936 – viewing them all as violent reactions to Jewish immigration and a threat to Arab national independence. For instance, the Peel Commission stated, with a grain of empathy, that the fast expansion of the National Home from 1933 onwards had exacerbated the Arabs' hate and fear of it: "It is not surprising, therefore, to find, as ship after ship of Jewish immigrants arrives, hailed with unrestrained enthusiasm by the Hebrew Press, the old antagonism growing hotter and hotter, till it bursts again into flames".[73]

The Arab reaction to immigration was caused not only by past events, but also by the belief that further growth of the Jewish National Home might lead to their political and economic subjection to the Jews, robbing them of their majority, and deprive them of future national independence. While the economic figures indicate that the Arab economy also benefitted from the development of the Jewish National Home,[74] it is also evident that the objective indicators did not alleviate the feelings of the Arabs that their status as a majority was under threat. Thus, the three sides of the Palestine triangle differed not only on the measurable economic impact of Jewish immigration on the Arabs; they also disagreed on whether the Arab reaction was based only on objective facts and figures, or also on more subjective parameters.

During most of the interwar period, the British were faithful to their commitment to facilitate the establishment of a Jewish National Home in Palestine in a way that worked for the benefit of the Jews – provided that they did not exceed the proportion of one-third of the total population. Up until 1939, the Mandatory facilitated the growth of the Jewish community, while at the same time it protected the majority status of the Arabs. From the year 1939 on, British immigration policy, served only the latter purpose. It was indeed successful: the proportional size of the two communities in Palestine remained stable until the outbreak of the 1948 war.

In the last decade of the Mandate rule, as a result of world and regional political developments, the centrality of Jewish immigration in the triangular relationship gradually came to an end. The British allowed Jewish immigration to continue after the five-year deadline stipulated by the 1939 White Paper, due to the success of the government's efforts not to exhaust all of the 75,000 certificates allotted by the 1939 policy. Henceforth, they permitted 1,500 Jews to enter Palestine each month.

During the years 1945–48, Jewish immigration, which was mostly illegal served primarily as a tool in the Zionist struggle for statehood.[75] Following the suppression of the Arab Revolt, the crushing of the local Arab leadership and the increased intervention of the Arab states in the affairs of Palestine, the Palestinian Arabs did not have their own representation, but relied almost totally upon the Arab states.[76] Furthermore, in late 1945, the United States became actively involved in the Palestine problem, and at the beginning of 1947 the issue was handed over to the United Nations. Thus, after 1939, and even more so, after World War Two, the Palestine problem ceased to be triangular, and Jewish immigration was no longer the central axis in the country's history.

Notes

1 *Report of the Palestine Royal Commission*, Cmd. 5479 [*Peel Report*], V, 21, London: HMG Stationery Office (HMSO), July 1937. This document, like all official documents issued by the Mandatory Government, was published simultaneously in all of the three official languages of Palestine; the references to this Report will indicate the relevant chapter in Roman numerals, and paragraphs in Arabic numerals.
2 Yehoshua Porath, *The Emergence of the Palestinian-Arab National Movement 1918–1929*, London: Frank Cass 1974, p. 141.
3 Hillel Cohen, *Year Zero of the Arab-Israeli conflict 1929*, Waltham MA: Brandeis University Press, 2015, pp. 255–6.
4 *Peel Report*, III, 18. My emphasis.
5 Report of the Commission of Enquiry into the disturbances in Palestine in May, 1921, with correspondence relating thereto (Disturbances), London: HMSO, 1921, Cmd. 1540.
6 Great Britain, Colonial Office, *Correspondence with the Palestine Arab Delegation and the Zionist Organisation, Presented to Parliament by Command of His Majesty's Government, June 1922*, Cmd. 1700, London: HMSO, 1922.
7 The Council of the League of Nations, The Palestine Mandate, 24 July 1922. The preamble of the Mandate for Palestine also gave recognition to 'the historical connection of the Jewish people with Palestine and to the grounds for reconstituting their national home in that country'.
8 Ibid., articles 1, 2.
9 See The Covenant of the League of Nations, article 22.
10 The Council of the League of Nations, French Mandate for Syria and the Lebanon, 29 September 1923, article 1.

11 *Peel Report*, III, 25.
12 Ibid., XX, 17.
13 Great Britain, Colonial Office, *Palestine: Statement by His Majesty's Government*, Cmd. 5513, paragraph 6, p. 3, London: HMSO, July 1937.
14 Colonial Office, *Palestine: Statement of Policy by His Majesty's Government*, Cmd. 6019, London: HMSO, 1939.
15 Ibid.
16 Cmd. 1700, supra, and Moshe Mossek, *Palestine Immigration Policy under Sir Herbert Samuel*, London: Frank Cass 1987, p. 153.
17 Julius Isaac, *The Economics of Migration*, London: K. Paul, Trench, Trubner & Company 1947, p. 10; for a discussion of the case of the Palestine Mandate, see ibid., pp. 121–7.
18 These are the main categories, though there were a number of additional sub-categories. The letters indicating each category went through some changes during the Mandate period, but the mentioned letters were in use for most of the period under discussion.
19 *The Palestine Gazette*, 15 May 1925.
20 The Council of the League of Nations, article 4. The document recognised a 'Jewish Agency' for that purpose, adding, "The Zionist Organization, so long as its organization and constitution are in the opinion of the Mandatory appropriate, shall be recognised as such an agency". The Jewish Agency was established in 1929, and was composed of Zionist and non-Zionist members on a parity basis. The terms 'Zionist Organization' and 'Jewish Agency' are synonymous for the purpose of the current discussion.
21 Between 1922 and 1924 this mechanism worked on a three-monthly basis.
22 Mossek, *Palestine*, pp. 123–4; *Peel Report*, X, 19
23 Aviva Halamish, Palestine as a Destination for Jewish Immigrants and Refugees from Nazi Germany, in *Refugees from Nazi Germany and the Liberal European States*, Frank Caestecker and Bob Moore (eds) New York: Berghahn Books 2010, pp. 122–50.
24 The principle was accepted by the Zionist Organisation in a letter from Weizmann to the Colonial Office, 18 June 1922, CO733/36/292, British National Archives (NA). See also Mossek, *Palestine*, pp. 59–60.
25 For a detailed and annotated discussion of Zionist immigration policy in the Mandate era, particularly in the 1930s see: Aviva Halamish, *B'Merutz Kaful Neged ha-Zman [A Dual Race against Time: Zionist Immigration Policy in the 1930s]*, Jerusalem: Yad Izhak Ben-Zvi Press, 2006.
26 *Peel Report*, X, 5.
27 Barbara J. Smith, *The Roots of Separatism in Palestine: British Economic Policy, 1920–1929*, Syracuse: Syracuse University Press, 1993, p. 68; Mossek, *Palestine*, p. 17.
28 Smith, ibid., p. 68; Mossek, ibid.
29 Churchill's statement on immigration, 14 June 1921, CO733/13, NA.
30 Mossek, *Palestine*, pp. 17–34, 154, also Michael J Cohen, *Britain's Moment in Palestine*, London: Routledge, 2014, pp. 117–22.
31 ESCO Foundation for Palestine, *Palestine: A Study of Jewish, Arab and British Policies*, I, New Haven: Yale University Press 1947, p. 319.
32 Porath, *The Emergence*, pp. 241–57.
33 Halamish, *A Dual Race*, pp. 23–6. It should be noted that in 1927, the number of Jews leaving Palestine was almost twice as many the number of the newcomers; in 1928, the immigration surplus was only ten. On the economic situation of Palestine and of the Zionist enterprise in the second half of the 1920s from the British perspective see, Michael J Cohen, *Britain's Hegemony in Palestine and the Middle*

East, 1917–56 – Changing Strategic Imperatives, London: Vallentine Mitchell, 2017, pp. 65–74.

34 Smith, *The Roots,* p. 84.
35 Ibid., p. 82.
36 Frederick Hermann Kisch, *Palestine Diary,* New York: AMS Press, 1974, pp. 295–6.
37 Great Britain, *Report of the Commission on the Palestine Disturbances of August 1929,* Cmd. 3530, 1930, pp. 112, 165, London: HMSO. On the Shaw Commission see, Pinhas Ofer, The Commission on the Palestine Disturbances of August 1929: Appointment, Terms of Reference, Procedure and Report, *Middle Eastern Studies* 21/3, 1985, pp. 349–61.
38 On the Passfield White Paper, and the fluctuation of British immigration policy from 1929–1931, see Cohen, *Britain's Hegemony,* pp. 81–106; cf. The Hope Simpson *Report on Immigration, Land Settlement and Development,* Cmd. 3686, London: HMSO, 1930. The Passfield White Paper was published as *Palestine: Statement of Policy,* Cmd. 3692, London: HMSO, 1930.
39 Great Britain, Palestine: *Letter by the Prime Minister to Dr Chaim Weizmann, Middle East,* No. 39, February 1931 [hereafter: MacDonald Letter 1931].
40 *Peel Report,* IV, 20.
41 Ibid., X, 73, 97.
42 Cmd. 5513, para. 6. p. 3, and Cmd. 6019, para. 14 (1), pp. 11–12.
43 MacDonald Letter, 1931.
44 Gabriel Sheffer, 'Political Considerations in British Policy-Making on Immigration to Palestine', *Studies in Zionism* 2/2, 1981, pp. 237–74.
45 Henry Feingold, *The Politics of Rescue: The Roosevelt Administration and the Holocaust, 1938–1945,* New Brunswick: Rutgers University Press, 1970, p. 26.
46 Cmd. 6019, para. 14, pp. 10–11.
47 Ibid.
48 Ronald W. Zweig, 'The Palestine Problem in the Context of Colonial Policy on the Eve of the Second World War', in *Britain and the Middle East in the 1930s: Security Problems, 1935–39,* Michael J Cohen and Martin Kolinsky (eds) London: Macmillan 1992, pp. 206–16. On the 1939 White Paper see J. C. Hurewitz, *The Struggle for Palestine,* New York: W.W. Norton & Company, 1950, pp. 94–111.
49 Cmd. 6019, para. 14, pp. 10–11.
50 Jacob Metzer, *The Divided Economy of Mandatory Palestine,* Cambridge: Cambridge University Press, 1998, pp. 1–13.
51 Ibid.
52 In 1930, John Hope-Simpson referred to the claim "that Jewish capital will not be brought into Palestine in order to employ Arab labour. It will come in with the definite object of the employment of Jewish labour and not otherwise" cited in *Peel Report,* III, 59.
53 *Peel Report,* ibid. This approach was incorporated into Prime Minister MacDonald's Letter to Weizmann in early 1931.
54 MacDonald Letter, 1931.
55 Ibid.
56 Smith, *The Roots,* 75.
57 Ibid.
58 Cabinet 14 (34), 4 November 1934, Cab.23/78, NA.
59 Smith, *The Roots,* p. 76.
60 Ibid., p. 75.
61 Ibid., p. 85.
62 *Peel Report,* V, 23.
63 Ibid., III, 91 and IV, 42.
64 Ibid., III, 17.
65 Ibid., V, 23.

66 Anita Shapira, *Land and Power: The Zionist Resort to Force, 1881–1948,* New York: Oxford University Press, 1992, p. 210.
67 *Peel Report,* III, 53.
68 Ibid., III, 59.
69 Ibid., III, 82.
70 Ibid., V, 32.
71 Smith, *The Roots,* 84.
72 There is no exact data on the volume of illegal immigration in the interwar era. The Peel Commission estimated that between 1932–33 the number of illegal immigrants reached 22,400, *Peel Report,* X, 34.
73 Ibid., III, 84, 76.
74 Ibid., V, 46.
75 Aviva Halamish, *The Exodus Affair: Holocaust Survivors and the Struggle for Palestine,* Syracuse: Syracuse University Press, 1998, pp. 265–7.
76 Yehoshua Porath, *The Palestinian Arab National Movement: From Riots to Rebellion, 1929–1939,* London: Frank Cass, 1977, pp. 302–3.

11 Zionist land acquisition

A core element in establishing Israel

Kenneth W. Stein

Linking people to the land

This chapter reviews the pace, methods and procedures of Jewish land acquisition, the motivation for Palestinian Arabs to sell their lands to Jews, and the futile efforts of the British to stop the sales. The central core of Zionism and Arab opposition to it was land. If the Zionists could buy enough land to create the nucleus for a Jewish state, then their dream would be realised. The geographic nucleus for a Jewish state was in place already by 1939.

To make a modern Jewish state unfold, two physical requirements were necessary: a population and a territory. Immigration and land acquisition made Zionism a reality. Both were oxygen to nation building. For Jews living abroad, transformations in Palestine of successes and setbacks sparked interest and attention. Zionist changes in the Palestine landscape persuaded many to consider a commitment to Zionism and whether to join a dynamic movement. With each person absorbed and each land parcel acquired or redeemed, Zionism's purpose moved to fulfilment. When another Jew settled in Palestine or an Arab sold a land to a Jewish buyer, Zionism continued to breathe. A symbiotic linkage existed between Jewish land purchase and Jewish immigration. In 1939, Chaim Weizmann wrote to Prime Minister Neville Chamberlain "Land was the basis of the [Jewish] National Home; we were not coming to Palestine to remain town-dwellers, but were striving to return to the soil. Land was fundamental to our work".[1]

From 1882 when the modern Zionist chronological clock started ticking, to 15 May 1948 when the state of Israel was declared, the Jewish population in Palestine grew from 25,000 to 650,000; in the same period Jewish land acquisition grew from several hundred thousand dunams (one dunam equals a quarter of an acre) to 2 million dunams. In the period from 1882 to January 1948, 315 Jewish rural settlements were established in Palestine.[2] By 1939, before one-third of world Jewry was destroyed in the Holocaust, a geographic and demographic nucleus for a Jewish state had been established in Palestine; 450,000 Jews and 67% of all the land Jews would purchase were already in

Jewish hands. By the same year, Arabs in Palestine and elsewhere in the Middle East were fully cognisant of the reality that the Zionists were on the verge of creating a state. Arabs saw, knew, and wrote about Zionism on the doorstep of entering the national home. By then and in the decade that followed, Zionists built rural settlements, created urban centres, social, cultural and political institutions, and elements of an infrastructure to support a nascent economy, banking system, and fledgling self-defence forces. Jewish geographic development concentrated primarily on the Jerusalem-Tel Aviv road, along the coastal plain from Gaza to Haifa, from Haifa south through the Jezreel Valley, east to the Sea of Galilee and thence, vectoring north past the Huleh Lake, to the Lebanese-Syrian border. With a few exceptions, the geographical and demographic footprint for a Jewish state did not focus on settling or buying land in the Judean and Samarian foothills, in the upper central Galilee, or south of Beersheba.[3]

The physical growth of the modern Jewish national home began in the years prior to the First Zionist Congress, held in 1897 in Basle, Switzerland, under Theodor Herzl's orchestration. From the 1880s, tens of thousands of Jewish immigrants, primarily from eastern European and Middle Eastern origins, established small settlements in Palestine. Affirming a commitment to build a Jewish State,[4] the World Zionist Organization established financial and land purchasing institutions to aid in the immigration and land purchasing processes. Between 1882 and 1918, 58 small settlements, *kibbutzim, moshavim*, and urban areas were established. Before the 1917 Balfour Declaration, modern Jewish land purchase totalled some 450,000 dunams, one-quarter of the entire total acquired by May 1948. By the time Palestine under the Ottoman Empire fell under British occupation, the Palestine Colonization Association (1891), the Jewish National Fund (1901), the Jewish Colonial Trust (1899) and its subsidiary the Anglo-Palestine Bank (1902), a Palestine Office of the World Zionist Organization (1907) and Jewish land purchasing agents such as Yehoshua Hankin, Arthur Ruppin, and Jacob Thon were engaged in land purchase and settlement, long before political sanction was secured. During and after the war, critically important lobbying achievements were achieved by a host of Zionist leaders among them Nahum Syrkin, Menachem Ussischkin and Chaim Weizmann. Weizmann garnered particular successes at the 1919 Paris Peace Conference, where he secured the inclusion of portions of the Jordan River and the Sea of Galilee inside Britain's Palestine geographic jurisdiction, and in procuring British government sanction of a Jewish Agency recognised as the official Zionist liaison with the budding Jewish community.[5] Enormously valuable for future Zionist operations in Palestine was the inclusion of Article VI of the Palestine Mandate. It stated that the British Administration, while ensuring

the rights and position of other sections of the population are not prejudiced [HMG] shall facilitate Jewish immigration under suitable conditions and shall encourage, in co-operation with the Jewish Agency referred to in Article 4, close settlement by Jews on the land, including State lands and waste lands not required for public purposes.[6]

This served as a standard base line for land purchase and unimpeded immigration. Throughout the next quarter century of governing the Mandate, Britain would from time to time deviate from the intentions of Article 6, threatening to stop and slowing down immigration and land purchase (see below). What never varied from the earliest days of Zionist immigration and land purchase in Palestine was the Zionist leaders' cognisance of the violent opposition the Arab population of Palestine and eventually, elsewhere in the Middle East.[7] But at the same time, Zionist leaders and purchasers remained constantly aware that there were endless sources of Arab sellers willing to part with their lands, parcel after parcel.

Entwined objectives: immigration and land purchase

The politics of Jewish immigration and land purchase in Palestine differed. Both were dependent upon British policy and the availability of funds. With immigration, Zionist politicians had to calculate the availability of potential Jewish immigrants with their ability to navigate away from home to Palestine. With land acquisition, there never was doubt about the availability of Arab land or their willingness to sell their land, or the proximity of a particular area to link to a specific geopolitical or economic objective. With immigration, the Zionist movement had to cope with levels of apathy and downright opposition to Zionism from potential emigrants. Zionism was often challenged by many Jews throughout the world. Many wanted no part of political Zionism or cared little about shouldering what might be a harsh life in Palestine. From 1920 to 1948, Jewish immigration ebbed and flowed according to any number of other variables: Palestine's economy and the changing political opinion of any number of British officials and politicians who fluctuated between pro and anti-Zionist extremes. There were swings in communal tranquillity and civil revolt. These unfolded in the days of sporadic or prolonged communal violence – in 1920, 1921, 1928, 1929, 1933, 1936–1939, and especially from 1945 to the end of the Mandate. The British inevitably placed blame for communal unrest on the shoulders of the developing national home; they repeatedly considered threatening both Zionist essentials. When confronted with a stoppage of either immigration or land purchases, Zionists countered repeatedly with innovative circumventions.

In 1921, within a year after the British civilian administration began in Palestine, Jewish immigration was suspended. Nonetheless, Jews continued to trickle into Palestine. In the British White Paper of 1922, Colonial Secretary Churchill defined Jewish immigration for Palestine according to the highly ambiguous definition of the "economic capacity of the country to absorb new immigrants". The Administration established categories according to whether potential immigrants brought their own funds, would be part of a labour schedule, or came under other limitations. After seven relatively calm years in the British administration, violence erupted in 1929 with hundreds of Jews and Arabs killed. From then through 1934, Britain sent or established in Palestine half a dozen commissions of inquiry (Shaw, Hope-Simpson, Johnson-Crosbie, French, and a Landless Arab Inquiry). These concluded that Jewish immigration and land purchases had aroused Arab anger and were the causes of communal violence. But no real policy changes were made. During these three years, the Zionists sensed that the growth of their enterprise was threatened, and planned accordingly. Land purchase and illegal immigration (*Aliyah Bet*) accelerated where possible. In 1939 British policy changed dramatically. A new White Paper restricted Jewish immigration to 75,000 over the next five years and severely restricted the areas in which the Zionists would be allowed to buy Arab lands. The Zionists remained undeterred. British administrators proved incapable of stopping the Zionists' physical or demographic growth. The Zionists circumvented British restrictions.

The British had promised to facilitate the growth of the Jewish national home while protecting the civil and religious rights of the Arab community. This concept lay at the centre of the Balfour Declaration and of the Mandate. It was an unequal obligation from the outset. Great Britain continually redefined the political trade-offs to try to effect duality, as the politics, tranquillity, and respective strengths of the communities changed, and as British needs in Palestine grew from maintaining the status quo to intervention to avoid periods of unrest. In White Papers issued in 1922, 1930, and 1939, and in the dozens of reports it wrote, it kept on defining the application or the applicability of duality as a policy. But duality failed because the obligation to establish a Jewish national home proved to be incompatible with the protection of the civil and religious rights of the non-Jewish communities. The first statement was a granted right; the second, a statement of bestowed sufferance. Not only were the obligations made and undertaken in unequal portions, the two communities differed dramatically. They diverged in socio-economic composition, political outlooks, educational levels, access to capital, organisations that served respective communal needs, leadership cadres, and capacities to change short term tactics to fit unalterable long-term strategic objectives. The Arabs lacked a diaspora that took an interest in Palestine. Over time, the Zionists established a small but committed number of Jews passionately dedicated to Zionism's growth.

Jewish nation building: Arab sources and motivations for land sales

Britain had greater success in curbing immigration than in stopping Arab land sales. London stopped immigration briefly in 1921, threatened to do so in the 1929–31 period and then actually limited Jewish immigration to a trickle in 1939. It closed Palestine's maritime borders and used the Royal

Navy to prevent illegal immigrant ships from landing on the Mediterranean coast. Britain had much less success in the land sphere. It could not stop Arab willingness or readiness to sell land. Unlike immigrants, land transactions were not visible; they could easily go unnoticed, particularly when it was in the mutual interest of Arab sellers and Jewish buyer to keep transactions private. In the land sphere, Britain either did not have the numbers or trained personnel to thwart subterfuge or interactive cunning. The 1940 Land Transfer Regulations were religiously and actively circumvented by legal ruses of many types. Only in the land sphere, could the Arabs themselves personally say 'no' to Zionism and refuse to participate in a process that ultimately alienated many from their own patrimony. Arab offers to sell emanated from landowners who resided inside and outside the boundaries of Palestine, from large and small landowners alike, from Arab political leaders, well-to-do members of the upper-classes, whether of older or younger generations, from middle class independent owners farming or grazing on their own lands, and peasant classes. All understood the consequences of land sales. The Palestinian Arab press and Arab politicians recognised the implications of complicity in land sales, especially by Palestinian Arabs themselves.

For Zionism's first 50 years, the major source of Jewish land purchases were owners or families with large holdings. Most of the large Arab land areas sold to Jews usually had few Arab peasants working them. For example, in the purchase of the 200,000 dunams of the Sursock lands, there were less than 700 Arab tenants working there or perhaps no more than 5,000 people in total. When the Jewish National Fund (JNF) purchased the Shatta village lands in the Beisan area in 1929–30 from the Ra'is and Abyad families in Haifa, there were 900 Arabs living on 14,000 dunams. In 1929–30, when the JNF purchased 30,000 dunams of land from the Beirut Tayan family at Wadi Hawarith and Wadi Qabbani, lands located south of Hedera, known also as Emek Hepher, there were 1,200 Bedouin families, living there. The Sursocks like other Arab real estate investors bought land for potential asset appreciation. They accumulated large quantities of land in Syria and Palestine primarily from the middle of the nineteenth century forward. When the Ottoman Empire sought to increase revenue for the central government's reply to European pressures to pay its debts, the Sultan's administration instituted the 1858 Ottoman Land Law and 1864 Ottoman Land Registration Laws. Both were meant to generate revenue by having peasants register their own lands. Instead, most peasants, feared rapacious taxation demands and conscription if their names appeared on government rolls. In seeking anonymity, the unwillingness to register their lands made it easier for urban notables, merchants, moneylenders, local Ottoman officials and religious leaders to lay claim to their lands and to expand their holdings.[8] Constantly facing annual debts, these same peasants exchanged traditional rights to work lands for immediate needs: a plough animal, seeds, or funds to make it through a year. Frequently peasants would sell their crop yields in advance of a crop-planting season or in advance of a harvest, and if the harvest did not materialise, either additional peasant indebtedness ensued or rights to land use or ownership in a village was exchanged for debt relief. Families with large areas under their control continued to hold sway in most of the urban areas of Palestine in the latter part of the nineteenth and twentieth centuries. Many evolved into the elite urban families that dominated the Palestinian Arab national movement in the 1920s, and in some cases passed on to their offspring in the 1930s and 1940s.

By the statistics of the 1931 Census for Palestine, 85% of the Arabs were engaged in the rural sector, which meant that buying and selling land had the potential to affect the immediate well-being of significant segments of Palestine's Arab population. Among the Arabs, 440,000 persons were supported by ordinary cultivation, 108,765 of whom were earners and 331,319 dependents. Of the earners, 5,311 derived their livelihood from the rents of agricultural land, or what otherwise were the landowning/political elites, and 63,190 who either cultivated their own land, were agricultural laborers or worked on someone else's land as tenants.[9] Additionally corrosive factors contributed to the Palestinian peasants' persistent impoverishment. Rural devastation form World War One left the countryside in the hill and valley regions despoiled by marching armies.[10] Trees were uprooted, plough animals requisitioned and killed and crops either destroyed, not planted or harvested. In 1926, there was a cattle plague that hurt peasant agriculture. Successively bad agricultural yields in the early 1930s made subsistence even more difficult. Periodic rural violence, particularly in 1936–39 period left peasant farmers at the mercy of bands that terrified the countryside, actually causing a small number of small landowners to sell the lands, take their small financial gains, and leave Palestine. Impromptu terrorist bands requisitioned foodstuffs, seized animals, ruined crops and directly pushed local villagers deeper into the arms of avaricious moneylenders.[11] For centuries, two long-term rural practices enfeebled the economic well-being of Palestine's agricultural classes. Most crippling to peasant agricultural output was the self-imposed village and peasant practice of moving from land parcel to land parcel every two, three or five years. This *musha'* system of land tenure was characterised by every Arab, Zionist, or British land expert as extraordinarily debilitating because the peasant avoided making long term improvements on his lands, and remained perennially dependent on credit sources, often outside of a village, that turned into "monetary exploitations".[12] In February 1930, Heinrich Margulies of the Anglo-Palestine Bank described one example of Arab landlord pressure tactics placed on peasants with *musha'* held lands. Margulies noted that the peasant had no way of knowing the size of his total holding, was tempted by the *effendi*, or intermediaries offering 20 piasters per dunam. They accumulated large areas, which they sold to Jews for about six pounds per dunam. "Those who relinquish their land in this manner often fall victim to poverty, all the more so because the *effendis* chased them from the land in a ruthless and brutal manner".[13]

Massive Arab peasant indebtedness to urban notables and merchants was carried over from Ottoman times until the end of the Mandate. Urban notables, among them merchants, landowners, religious leaders, and others in

Palestinian Arab society applied usurious rates of interests, causing peasants to accumulate and live almost perennially under massive debts, constantly beholden to a well-to-do non-resident Arab debt-note holder. Moneylenders often held promissory notes that showed that the borrower received a larger sum than actually paid to him.[14] Palestinian notables styled themselves paternalistically as caretakers of the peasantry; they controlled the peasant as their sources of credit.[15] More than caretakers, Palestinian property owners who held peasant debt, fashioned themselves as a privileged segment of the notable elite. In 1934, A.L. Tibawi, requested permission from H.M. Foot, the Nablus British district officer of Samaria, to move his tenants off his land without providing them with required monetary compensation. In his petition to the government, which he won, Tibawi argued that the three tenants' income was far less than that cultivated by the hired laborers. And that the

> the tenants not only ceased to contribute their share to the income [from the land], but also failed to pay the government taxes. The tenants' presence threatened his future with serious material loss. Landlords had to maintain a high standard of living which would not be fair to compare to that of the tenants.[16]

Detailed summaries of potential areas available for purchase were usually the first items noted in the monthly JNF reports or protocols of their Directorate meetings. The JNF documentation (from 1922 to 1948) reveals not only the quantity of land available, but also the variety – urban or rural, with or without water access, and geographic location. This allowed critical decisions to be made, based on strategic considerations to meet political preferences.[17] On 26 November 1926, while consummating the final sales agreements of more than 176,000 dunams in the Jezreel Valley the previous year from the Sursock family from Beirut, Yehoshua Hankin, the key land agent working for the JNF at the time, told the assembled that there were three million dunams.[18] Over the next five years, Hankin would be involved in purchasing large tracts of land. From 1929 to 1936, Jews acquired 293,374 dunams, second only to the 368,526 dunams they bought from 1921–25.[19] In the early 1930s, small Arab owner parcels grew as a significant source for Jewish land purchase.[20] Larger estates were no longer as plentiful; Jewish immigration increased and with it came small capital sums, the Arab rural sector suffered a series of terrible crop yields and land prices inched steadily upward. The more the number of small parcels that were acquired, or consolidated by land brokers, the larger the number of agricultural workers, grazers, day laborers or tenant farmers were immediately affected by the purchases. The British realised that more and more rural Arabs were being displaced, and instituted an inconclusive Landless Arab inquiry in 1933.

In the early 1930s, when Jewish land purchases reached their peak, the British implemented laws to prevent Arab peasants from leaving lands without alternative land or monetary compensation, or to vacate lands either before or after a transfer was negotiated or consummated. In 1931, 1932, 1933 and 1936, the administration plugged loopholes in the Protection of Cultivator's Ordinances,[21] and implemented the 1931 Law of Execution (Amendment) Ordinance designed to prevent the eviction of tenants through satisfaction of a mortgage debt, as had occurred a year earlier at the village of Zir'in, near Jenin.[22] On the eve of the 1936–39 disturbances, the Administration was about to implement legislation that would guarantee Arab land-owners a minimum 'lot viable', but the outbreak of violence shelved 'small-owner' protection permanently.

Palestinian Arab political leaders participated in land sales to Jews throughout the Mandate. Of the eighty-nine members elected to the Arab Executive between 1920 and June 1928, at least one-quarter were identified, personally or through immediate family members, as having directly participated in land sales to Jews. Of the forty-eight members of the Arab Executive attending the Seventh Arab Congress in June 1928, at least fourteen had by that date been involved in land sales.[23] Members of the various Palestine Arab delegations to London in 1921, 1929, 1930, and 1939 appear to have been deeply involved in the land-sales process. But for many of the individuals who sold lands, that did not preclude a previous or subsequent hostility to land sales. In the Palestinian Arab community, efforts in 1931–32 to raise funds to buy lands from potential Arab sellers to Jews to avert the sales proved a non-starter. The Mufti of Jerusalem, Hajj Amin al-Husayni in an effort to stifle increased Arab land sales to Jews issued a *fatwa*, invoking religious threats against any Moslem who sold or engaged in selling land to Zionists. Those who did sell their lands were labelled as infidels, not to be accorded the rights of burial in Muslim cemeteries. The threat proved ineffective. In the early 1930s when the British investigated how widespread Arab land sales to Jews had become, in an effort to arrive at the number of Arabs made landless by Jewish purchase, the High Commissioner and his staff were stone walled by Arab notables. Zionists also kept such information from the British, seeking to protect their anonymity, in the hope that they might participate in future sales. Noticeably from the early 1930s on, Palestinian Arab newspapers reported and editorialised, and politicians acknowledged the quickening and debilitating process of Arab land sales to Jews, the increased activity of Arab land brokers. They vigorously criticised the Palestinian leadership for their failure to answer what was seen as a threat to the Palestinian Arabs' future. The press reflected the general anger, despair, and fear, almost daily in the five years prior to the April 1936 outbreak of violence. I have argued how land sales, British dithering, Zionist relentlessness in the land and immigration spheres and Arab political ineptitude contributed to the three years of violence.[24] A single, representative example will be cited here:

We are selling our lands to Jews without any remorse. Land brokers are busy day and night with their odious trade without feeling any shame. In the meantime, the nation is busy sending protests. Where are we going to? One looks at the quantity of Arab lands transferred daily to Jewish hands, [one] realizes that we are bound to go away from this country. But where to? Shall we move to Egypt, Hijaz, or Syria? How could we live there, since we would have sold the lands of our fathers and ancestors to our enemies? Nobody could show us mercy or pity, when we to leave our country, because we would have lost her with our own hand.[25]

The mid-1930s to the end of the Mandate

In the summer of 1936, during the first months of the Arab disturbances, three visiting US Senators (Copeland, Austin, and Hastings) found that "while the Arab High Committee in charge of the [Arab civil] strike is officially demanding prohibition of the sale of land to Jews, some of the prominent Arab leaders active in that Committee are quietly trying to sell land to Jewish buyers".[26] By the middle of 1937, British, Arab and Zionist officials, each independently, had concluded that a Jewish state was already a distinct reality. None of their assessments linked events in Europe with what had unfolded in Palestine during the previous two decades. In July 1937, the Peel Commission Report proposed the partition of Palestine into two states, an economic union between them and an independent enclave for Jerusalem. Jewish land purchases up to that date influenced the British to create a very small Jewish state, one whose borders clearly reflected previous Jewish land purchases.[27] On 30 September 1937, a meeting of prominent Palestinian Arab leaders in Damascus estimated that a Jewish state was at hand. Izzat Darwazzah a co-founder of the Palestinian Arab *Istiqlal* Party who was exiled to Damascus for his involvement in on-going disturbances in Palestine stated:

> There is no boundary to the aspirations of the Zionists. If until September 1937, the Jews spoke about building a National Home in Palestine; today they are already talking about the establishment of a Jewish State in part of Palestine. The Jewish community in Palestine has proven in the last two years of the uprising that they could defend themselves. There is no denial that the Jews had held up quite well in their confrontations with the Arab gangs on the roads, in the orchards, and in the agricultural settlements. There is no boundary to the aspirations of the Zionists.[28]

The next month, the JNF's Josef Weitz, in responding to questions of the JNF leadership, made a full-throated assessment of the land issue, current violence and future purchasing possibilities. Weitz was buoyed by the possibility of a Jewish state coming into being because if partition took place and a Jewish state became a fact, the JNF would be recognised by every Jew for its critical role. He noted that for perhaps one of the few times since the Mandate began, the JNF did not possess excess lands for broadening existing settlements or building new ones. It was capital shortages, there was 'absolute feasibility to acquire further land' in the Galilee, Huleh Valley, Judean and Samarian hills, in the vicinity of Nazereth, Jerusalem, Hulda, Tel Mond, Beisan, in the Jezreel Valley and along the coast from Zichron Ya'akov to Haifa. The land prices had fallen, as a result of the insecurity caused by the disturbances. Some landowners, fearing terror, were fleeing the country and wanted to sell before leaving. Weitz summed up his overview with the assessment that the 'Arabs desire to sell is greater than our capacity to purchase'.[29] At the end of December 1937, David Ben-Gurion, head of the Jewish Agency, convened a small number of Zionist leaders (including Weizmann, Abraham Granovsky, Weitz, Ussischkin, and Epstein [Elath]) who were involved in land purchases. He echoed Weitz's assessment, that land sale possibilities

> were on a scale unprecedented since the World War; if means were available, contracts could be closed for 200,000 dunams … including both in areas inside the projected Jewish and Arab State, and on their borders, with an undertaking on the part of the vendors to complete the transaction in a short time. He stressed the political significance of land purchase at the present time. It was most probable that in the event of partition, the Royal Commission scheme would be modified positively and negatively. Certain areas in Galilee were endangered, and in consequence land purchase now by the JNF had an additional value, above its intrinsic merits.

He referred to it as no less than the "rescue of the homeland".[30] He estimated that whether Britain's partition idea was carried out, or modified positively or negatively, further restrictions on land purchase were to be expected, affecting Arab areas where Jews had no foothold. He stated "it was important to acquire land now on the borders of the projected Jewish state, in regions in which Jewish settlement has not yet taken place".[31] As the transcripts of this and subsequent meetings reveal, Zionist leaders were being offered a variety of locations where purchase could take place, allowing them to choose acquisitions that were strategically important, mostly contiguous to existing Jewish settlements, near important road crossings, water sources, adjacent to industries, and existing or new agricultural lands.

After three years of civilian unrest, which some have termed disturbance, riots or rebellion, Great Britain decided to quell the situation by throttling the growth of the national home. The decision to slow down or stop Zionism's growth had been in the making since 1929–31, when British officials threatened immigration and land transfer restrictions, but did not impose them. In issuing the 1939 White Paper, Britain bought time. Fulfilling the dual obligation was not feasible, at least not without violence. Britain acknowledged that Jews and Arabs had to live apart and that Arab land sales and Jewish immigration enflamed Arab passions. Hence, it issued restrictions to quell Arab anger in Palestine and to avoid further antagonizing Moslem populations in the Middle East and elsewhere where London had strategic presence and interest (Egypt, Jordan, Iraq, Saudi Arabia, India, etc.)

The White Paper contained three parts: 1) the termination of the Mandate within ten years and the establishment of an independent federal Palestinian state[32] in treaty relations with Great Britain; 2) the restriction of Jewish immigration to 15,000 per year for the following five years; and, 3) at the High Commissioner's discretion, the regulation and/or prohibition of land transfers. Under the resulting Land Transfer Regulations, Palestine was divided into three zones: Zone A (63% of the land area) in which any "transfer of land ... save to a Palestinian Arab shall be prohibited"; Zone B (32%) in which such transfer "by a Palestinian Arab, save to a Palestinian Arab, shall be prohibited unless... [there was] approval in writing of the High Commissioner"; and the Free Zone (5%) in which "there will be no restrictions on transfers".[33] According to the document and the accompanying explanatory statement, Zone A "includes the hill country as a whole (the so-called highlands of Judea, Samaria and the Galilee) together with certain areas in the Gaza and Beersheba Sub-Districts where the land available is already insufficient to support the existing population", the inhabitants of which were virtually all Arab. Zone B "includes the Plains of Esdraelen and Jezreel (running eastward from the Haifa Industrial Zone to the Jordan), Eastern Galilee, the (two small) maritime plains (one South of Haifa and the other south of Jaffa) ... and the southern partition of the Beersheba Sub-District (the Negev)" in which, except for the desert Negev region, the population was mixed Jewish and Arab. Finally, the Free Zone included "all municipal areas (24 in number), the Haifa Industrial Zone... and roughly speaking the (central) maritime plain", in which, except for most of the smaller municipalities and that of Jaffa, the majority of the population was Jewish.[34] The Regulations interfered with the free market in land in Palestine. By forbidding certain sales, land prices were forced down and sellers therefore profited less from each transaction. Ultimately, this meant (as HMG had intended) that selling land became less tempting to Arabs because the small land owner no longer profited enough from the sale to pay off his debts. Colonial Office officials noted that in the land sphere, it was its responsibility to "prevent the Arab landowner from parting with his land. He has, in fact, to be protected against himself".[35] High Commissioner MacMichael understood that by taking Jewish buyers out of the market, only a lower price might be available from another potential Arab buyer. But he said "the object of the regulations is to protect not the individual Arab landowner but Arab land as a whole".[36] Unsurprisingly Zionist leaders were appalled, Arab leaders applauded.[37] In a very lengthy letter to the High Commissioner outlining Zionist reasons for opposing the White Paper, Ben-Gurion wrote that it "denied Jews equality before the law and introduced racial discrimination".[38]

Space does not permit the enumeration of how Arabs and Zionists ingeniously circumvented the land transfer regulations. The British wrote a very detailed report on this, using volumes of letters and complaints from Arab politicians and lawyers.[39] The ingenuity and connivance of Jewish buyers and Arab sellers could not be thwarted; transactions were carried out despite legal restrictions to the contrary. Economic motives continue to promote Arab interest in selling lands. From 1940–1948, while Jews continued to buy land according to strategic needs and land brokers continued to ply their trade as they had done earlier, the land transfer restrictions produced new consequences. Because the land transfer process became more uncertain, private buyers gave way to the JNF whose fund raising accelerated in the 1940s, particularly from 1945 forward, largely from American sources. The role of the JNF as a key Zionist institutional player in land acquisition and strategic planning increased. The JNF now bought increasing land areas from Jewish sellers who needed cash for their own purposes. With land transfers more difficult, the costs of lands increased in general. Some potential Arab sellers either held off, waiting for prices to rise, or as brokers, they assembling scattered parcels for the Jewish buyers. With fewer immigrants to settle as immigration restrictions reached a peak, the JNF directed expenditures toward land preparation already in Jewish ownership. In 1947–48, for example, only one-third of the JNF budget was spent on land purchase; two-thirds was dedicated to the preparation of existing lands for newly arriving immigrants. Jews acquired lands from Arabs during the period of restrictions by circumventing, not contravening the law. Legal means were used to purchase land, but perhaps not register it as legally required. Methods of engaging Arab sellers included ruses used in earlier years: debt forfeiture, irrevocable powers of attorney, use of nominal Arab holders in which land was purchased by the JNF, but still held in Arab ownership with a financial lien held over the nominee by the Jewish buyer. Land transferred during this period did not constitute a criminal offense. They were considered legally valid. Since there was no prohibition against Jews buying land from non-Palestinians, the JNF drew up an extensive list of Arab landowners residing outside of Palestine who remained potential buyers. Palestinian Arabs and Arabs in neighbouring states tried to keep Arab lands in Arab hands with the establishment of the *Sunduq al-Umma* [Arab Nation Fund]. These efforts were publicised, but absent funds they were short lived. They worried the JNF, but were ultimately unsuccessful in preventing Arab sales.[40]

At the end of 1945, the Palestine Administration looked into the myriad of ways Arab sellers were circumventing a law meant to protect them, and concluded:

> the remedy lies in the hands of the Arabs themselves. Unless they enter into collusion with the Jews to defeat the spirit of the White Paper, Jews will not be able to enter improperly into possession of the land within a restricted area. If the parties whom the law is designed to defend conspire to evade the law, then it is indeed difficult for the authorities to enforce it and to defend them.[41]

It was estimated that the JNF was

> being inundated with offers from Arab sellers and made isolated contracts for completion of purchases after the war, in full confidence that the Land Transfer Regulations would be repealed, and HMG would not have the time to apply itself to the subject.[42]

The officials were not wrong. On 10 November 1946, Josef Weitz, the JNF's Director of Land and Forestry, one of the top officials involved with Jewish land acquisition, noted that during the previous six years under the land transfer restrictions, the JNF acquired 390,000 dunams, (152,000 from Jews and 238,000 from Arabs). Lands purchased from Jews and Arabs evolved because owners needed cash; the potential for land purchases has not decreased; "it remains *each* year at 250 thousand dunams".[43] Weitz noted that Arab resistance to selling lands to Jews was on the rise as were prices. But he estimated that

> the source of land in the country has not dried up ... the possibility of more purchases still exists [and] it can be concluded that the will to sell in the Arab camp has not decreased. If there were no obstacles set up in our way we could purchase land without restraint.

Conclusions

From the early 1880s to January 1948, Zionists purchased 2 million dunams of land in Palestine or 2023.45km^2.[44] Jewish land purchased was a relatively small percentage of all available registered lands in Palestine, but without them, no viable territorial nucleus for Israel would have existed. These lands were provided by Arab sellers. The whereabouts of those sales are shown in the on-line publication; *Forming a Nucleus for the Jewish State 1882–1947.*[45] From 1908 on, Jewish buyers became interested in creating contiguous areas of Jewish settlement, for reasons of security. Well into the 1920s, there was discussion among Jewish officials about formulating some official plan for land purchase; it evolved as a semi-official focus if not a policy by the aftermath of the 1929 disturbances – especially in view of the death of more than 60 Jews in Hebron, situated a good distance from other settlements. The idea that far flung locations could not be easily protected evolved into a focus on creating contiguous zones. But that was not to the exclusion of strategic acquisitions, near Haifa port, on the border with Lebanon, or from 1943 on, looking to acquire land at the Gulf of Aqaba. In February 1931, for strategic and security reasons, the Jewish Agency sent a directive to all organisations involved in land purchases; it stated that regardless of whether land was purchased near or distant from existing major Jewish land concentrations – the coastal plan, the valley regions from Haifa to Beisan, or in the lower or upper Galilee running along both sides of the Jordan River, north and south of the

Sea of Galilee – Arab tenants, grazers, and agricultural laborers should be resettled on vacant lands when the opportunities presented themselves at distances far from existing Jewish areas.

The land area assigned to the Jewish state by the UN Partition Resolution of November 1947 was 14,900km^2. Thus, Jews had purchased 13.5% of the area that was to be designated as the 'Jewish state'. Further, when the Arab and Moslem states refused to accept the UN Partition resolution, but went to war against Israel in May 1948, the Zionists, now Israelis acquired yet more land during the war of independence, referred to by Palestinians and others as the *nakbah* (disaster). When the armistice agreements between Israel and its Arab neighbours ended the war, Israel controlled 20,500km^2. With this as the arithmetic denominator, the Jews had purchased 9.8% of the land that became the state of Israel. No Arab state was established as a result of the UN Partition resolution and the outcome of the 1948–49 conflict. However, the area of the West Bank of 6 million dunams or 6,070km^2 was annexed by Jordan in 1950, and the area of the Gaza Strip, 360km^2 was administrated by Egypt, both until after the end of the June 1967 War when Israel took control of all of what had been the area of the Palestine Mandate.

They used direct contacts, ruses, subterfuge, brokers, and intermediaries to achieve their purposes. Each side was aware of the other's needs and each understood the immediate implications and consequences of their respective actions. The political solutions to solve the Arab-Jewish conflict with Palestine partitioned into Arab and Jewish states as suggested by the British in 1937 and the United Nations in 1947, evolved as potentially workable outcomes because Arabs and Zionists created facts on the ground. Whether one refuses to acknowledge that Zionist land purchase created Arab landlessness and Arab displacement over time or refuses to acknowledge that Arabs sold their lands willingly to Jews, they both remain irrefutable historical realities. Without Arab land sales, a Jewish state would not have evolved, nor would it have been established.

Notes

1 Remarks by Weizmann to Chamberlain, 2 February 1939, Political Series S25/file 7642, Central Zionist Archives (CZA).
2 Kenneth W. Stein, *Forming a Nucleus for the Jewish State 1882–1947*, August 2019, Center for Israel Education, https://israeled.org/forming-a-nucleus-for-the-jewish-state-1882-1947/ (Israeled). By carefully placing 315 Jewish settlements on a series of successive maps of Palestine, covering the period from 70CE to 1947, coded maps and verbal histories provide clarity on where and over what period of time Jewish nation building took place.
3 A comparison of the UN Partition Plan for Palestine of November 29, 1947 with the map of Jewish settlements substantially mirrors previous Jewish land purchase concentrations, ibid., pp. 32–3.
4 Kenneth W. Stein, Theodor Herzl's Jewish State; Explanation and analysis, June 2010, Israeled

5 Meyer W. Weisgal (ed.), *The Letters and Papers of Chaim Weizmann*, July 1920–December 1921, Volume X, Series A, New Jersey: Transaction Books, Rutgers, and Israel Universities Press, Jerusalem, 1977.

6 Great Britain. *Mandate for Palestine*, July 24, 1922, Israeled.

7 Alan Dowty, A Question that Outweighs All Others: Yitzhak Epstein and Zionist Recognition of the Arab Issue, *Israel Studies* 6/1 Spring 2001, pp. 34–54; Anita Shapira, *Land and Power: The Zionist Resort to Force 1881–1948*, New York: Oxford University Press, 1992, pp. 40–52; Josef Gorny, *Zionism and the Arabs, 1882–1948*, Oxford: Clarendon Press, 1987, pp. 29–39; Arthur Ruppin, The relationship of the Jews to the Arabs, *Der Jude* 3, 1918–1919, pp. 453–7; and Hans Kohn, Concerning the Arab question, *Der Jude* 4, 1919–1920, pp. 567–9.

8 Philip Khoury, *Urban Notables and Arab Nationalism: The Politics of Damascus*, Cambridge: Cambridge University Press, 1983, pp. 26–9; Beshara Doumani, *Rediscovering Palestine, Merchants and Peasants in Jabal Nablus, 1700–1900*, Berkeley: University of California Press, 1995, p. 159. For a more detailed history of the evolution of land ownership, land registration and land use in Palestine, see Stein, *The Land Question in Palestine, 1917–1939*, Chapel Hill: University of North Carolina Press, 1984, pp. 9–34.

9 *Census for Palestine*, 1931, Class I. Production of Raw Materials, Vol 1, Palestine, 1932, p. 289.

10 Kenneth W. Stein, Palestine's rural economy, 1917–1939, *Studies in Zionism* 8/1, 1987, pp. 25–49.

11 Information Center of the Palmach, *The Hebrew Defender, Documents and Personalities in the 1936–39 Riots*, April 1944, Central Zionist Archives, (CZA). For a detailed assessment of the impact of the 1936–1939 violence on the Palestinian rural economy, see Gershon Agronsky, Palestine Arab economy undermined by disturbances, 20 January 1939, S25/10.091, CZA, also Israeled.

12 Yaacov Shimoni, *Arvi'e Eretz Yisrael* [*Hebrew: Arabs of Palestine*], Tel Aviv: Am Oved, Chapter 9; *Census for Palestine*, Vol 1, p. 284; Stein, Palestine's Rural Economy.

13 Mr. Heinrich Margulies of the Anglo-Palestine Bank to Mr. Felix Rosenblueth, the Jewish Agency, 5 February 1930, S25/7619, CZA.

14 *Palestine Royal Commission Memorandum 12: Rural Indebtedness*, Palestine, 1937.

15 Charles Anderson, *From Petition to Confrontation: The Palestinian National Movement and the Rise of Mass Politics, 1929–1939*, unpublished doctoral dissertation, New York University, 2013, pp. 356–8.

16 Abdul Latif Tibawi vs. Tenants Kamil Amrur, Abdul Fattah Amrur, and Abdul Hafiz Amrur, File TR/114/33. Tibawi to Assistant District Commissioner, Nablus, November 16, 1934, Box 3922, ISA.

17 For a detailed review of JNF land purchase decision-making see Kenneth W. Stein, The Jewish National Fund: Land purchase methods and priorities, 1924–1939, *Middle Eastern Studies* 20/4, 1984, pp. 190–205.

18 Minutes of JNF meeting, 22 November 1926, KKL 5, CZA.

19 Stein, *The Land Question*, Appendix 2, pp. 226–7.

20 Ibid. Chapter 6, pp. 174–82.The Palestine Land and Land Registries Department statistics, Box 3784/file 7, ISA and Minutes of the JNF monthly meetings confirm the increase of smaller Arab parcels sold to Jewish buyers.

21 Kenneth W. Stein, Legal Protection and circumvention of rights for cultivators in Mandatory Palestine, in Joel S. Migdal (ed.) *Palestinian Society and Politics*, Princeton: Princeton University Press, 1980, pp. 233–60.

22 See Zir'in Village Land Sales documents assembled by British District Officer, Hilmi Husayni, JN Stubbs and A.N Law, both of the Lands Department in the Palestine Administration, Box 3511/file 1, ISA, Israeled.

23 Stein, *The Land Question*, Appendix 3, pp. 228–39. This list of Arab sellers engaged with Jewish buyers was collected in the early 1980s and has not been updated to include additional names who were mentioned in other sources that has been revealed since 1984, especially names and areas of sale as they appeared in JNF Directorate meeting minutes in the 1930s and 1940s.

24 Kenneth W. Stein, Rural change and peasant destitution: Contributing causes to the Arab Revolt in Palestine, 1936–1939, in John Waterbury and Farhad Kazemi (ed.) *Peasants and Politics in the Modern Middle East*, Gainesville: Florida International University Press, 1991, 143170.

25 *al-Ikdam*, 19 January 1931.

26 William Ziff, *The Rape of Palestine,* New York: Longmans Green, 1938, p. 39; Report of the Senators Mission, *New York American*, 1 October 1936.

27 Stein, *Forming a Nucleus.*

28 Remarks by Izzat Darwazzah, Palestinian Arab political leader, in a meeting of Palestinian and Syrian notables in Damascus, 30 September 1938, CZA, S25/105263; also Israeled.

29 Joseph Weitz, Current problems of the Jewish National Fund in reply to JNF Delegates, October 1937, S25/10250, CZA.

30 Eliyahu Epstein, The political significance of land purchase, 31 December 1937, S25/10250, CZA. Israeled.

31 Ibid.

32 In March 1939, by a vote of 14–1 in favour, with the Mufti of Jerusalem the lone dissenter, the Arab Higher Committee rejected the British government's 1939 offer to create a majority Arab state in Palestine in ten years. See Israeled.

33 Palestine Land Transfers Regulations, Cmd. 6180, February 1940, London: His Majesty's Stationery Office (HMSO).

34 Ibid.

35 Notes, 14 June 1940, CO 733/425/75872, British National Archives (NA)

36 Ibid.

37 Arab reaction to the Land Transfer Regulations as recorded by the Colonial Office, 13 June 1940, CO 733/425/ 75872, NA.

38 Ben-Gurion to MacMichael, 27 February 1940, CO 733/418/75072. NA

39 The Palestine Administration, *Land Transfer Inquiry Committee*, November 1945. Box SF/file 215/1/40 and Box LS 249/file 4, ISA. A copy of the report prepared by British, Jewish and Arab officials may also be found at Israeled.

40 Issa Khalaf, *Politics in Palestine: Arab Factionalism and Social Disintegration, 1939–1948*, Albany: State of New York Press, 1991, pp. 97–101; Remarks by Josef Weitz, Meeting of the Jewish National Fund, July 10, 1945.

41 *Land Transfer Inquiry Report,* 1945, Israeled.

42 Letter from Director of Land Registrations to Chief Secretary of the Palestine Administration, 24 April 1945, Box M397, SF 215/40 Vol.1, ISA.

43 Minutes of a Meeting of those involved in Purchasing Lands for the Jewish National Fund, 10 November 1946, CZA, KKL5.

44 For a highly detailed discussion of who owned what land at the end of the Palestine Mandate, see Kenneth W. Stein, The land controversy: The 94% myth, Israeled.

45 Stein, *Forming a Nucleus, 1882–1947.*

12 The origins of militant Zionism during the British Mandate

Colin Shindler

On 28 January 1944, the *Irgun Zvai Leumi*, or *Irgun* (National Military Organization) decided to stage an armed revolt against the British regime in Palestine. The decision was taken by Menahem Begin and his colleagues while the Allies were still fighting Hitler. Yet paradoxically 'the Revolt' was also anchored in the growing awareness of the enormity of the Holocaust. This contradiction was also played out by other anti-colonial movements – who decided to strike while the imperial power was distracted by the struggle against Nazism.

Begin's decision was also a natural conclusion to an ideological journey – an evolving tradition of militant Zionism, stretching back to Herzl's time. He had inherited the mantle of military Zionism from past advocates of revolt such as Abba Ahimeir, but crucially turned their theory into practice. Jabotinsky's writings were selectively chosen by Begin to fit a political and military agenda. After his death, Jabotinsky was subsequently recast in the role of 'the father of the Revolt'.

Ideological influences on Jabotinsky

The origins of the Zionist Right are to be found in the European Left of *fin de siècle* France and Italy. From *Boulangisme* in the 1880s in France, which promoted a strong nationalist, anti-German policy, backed by monarchists and Bonapartists, to the formation of Edouard Dumont's *Ligue antisémitique de France*, which was prominent during the Dreyfus Affair.

The debate within Marxism during the 1890s, following the deaths of Marx and Engels, established the notion that the nation was the vehicle for social action by the revolutionary Right. Figures such as Georges Sorel developed the ideas of revolutionary syndicalism and his work, *Réflexions sur la violence,* promoted the centrality of working-class violence. This cemented the ideological underpinning of a transition to national syndicalism by socialists such as Gustave Hervé in France and Benito Mussolini in Italy.

It was into this ideological maelstrom that Vladimir Jabotinsky found himself immersed as a student at the University of Rome in 1898. His regular articles for the liberal *Odesskie Novosti* testify to his support for progressive political forces in *fin de siècle* Italy. He associated with left-wing journalists and participated in regular evening discussions with his philosophy lecturer, Antonio Labriola,[1] 'the father of Italian Marxism' and admirer of Spinoza. Yet the transition towards fascism was at its inception. Several of Jabotinsky's lecturers, Enrico Ferri,[2] Vittorio Scialoja, Maffeo Pantaleoni,[3] became to varying degrees supporters of Mussolini's regime in the 1920s.

Jabotinsky's views on World War One

The outbreak of war in August 1914 set in train events that led to the rise of fascism in Italy and the commencement of a new conflagration in 1939. In both 1915 and in 1940, Jabotinsky argued for the formation of a Jewish army whose presence he considered would eventually become a bargaining counter in any negotiations during peace conferences to be held at the war's conclusion in the wake of an allied victory.

Jabotinsky's demand for a Jewish military force in 1915 was tempered by his ambivalence towards the war itself. He had predicted the coming of the war. On 1 January 1912, he wrote:

> First of all in the forefront of the events due to come to Europe is the great war. That war of which the world is so frightened and which at the same time, it expects with such a morbid, painful curiosity. A war in the centre of Europe between two (or more) first rate civilized powers, armed to the teeth with all the grandiose madness of present day technical equipment – with the participation of ground, sea, undersea and air forces. (This will entail the loss) of an incredible number of casualties and such financial losses, direct, indirect and reflected – one gets the impression that there not be enough figures in the mathematical lexicon to count it all.[4]

He argued that what was needed was "a change on the throne of the Hohenzollerns". With a prescience depicting the events of 1917 and 1918, he further commented "what Germany is brewing is a revolution, a revolution on a global scale, designed to move the political axis of the world".

By 1916 Jabotinsky felt that it was a war without purpose. The mass killings at Ypres and other battle sites and the use of chlorine gas by Germany in early 1915 clearly influenced Jabotinsky's thinking. In an article in April 1916, he wrote:

> The war has suddenly poured into the world's cauldron a bucket of some terribly corrosive acid. Not for a long time has humanity been shown so clearly that 'everything is possible'; that principles, agreements, promises, progress, traditions, liberty, humanity are all rot and rust and rubbish. Everything is permissible: you may drown women and children, burn people alive, smoke them out like vermin, turn out tens of thousands

onto the high road and drive them the devil knows where, hang and beat and rape. All these are lessons, they 'stick', they sink into minds and hearts, changing the very tissues of human conscience.[5]

The often inexplicable sacrifices of World War One, it can be surmised, accentuated Jabotinsky's sense of fatalism, which he had documented in his 1910 article, *Homo Homini Lupus* – 'Man is a Wolf to Man'.[6] It encapsulated a Hobbesian view of humanity. Yet Turkey's entry into the war in November 1914 also provided an opportunity for the Jews, not only to form an armed force, a Jewish Legion, to fight not on the Western Front, but in the Middle East instead. And yet his sense of futility about the war coexisted with the advantage it offered the Zionist cause.

Jabotinsky's initial view on the tragedy of the outbreak of war was a studied neutrality – virtually "a plague on both your houses". He later wrote about "the magnetic power of war" as "one of the fundamental and dominant forces of the world".[7]

Turkey's participation in the war was the seminal event which persuaded Jabotinsky to take sides and almost immediately initiate moves to establish a Jewish army. However, he emphasised the crucial point that the existence of a military force was a means to raise national consciousness.

Yet Jabotinsky's singlemindedness antagonised many of his colleagues during the war. He was disparaging about the efforts of major figures such as Nahum Sokolov in Zionist diplomacy, who in his eyes was "not an activist".[8] Significantly, most leading Zionists in London – including Max Nordau who had advocated "a muscular Judaism" – were lukewarm to the very idea of a Jewish military force.[9] In addition to compromising the Zionist movement's neutrality in the war, many feared Turkish reprisals in the fashion that had been visited upon the Armenians – massacre and persecution. English Zionists such as Norman Bentwich[10], Harry Sacher[11] and Leon Simon believed that Weizmann had been seduced by Jabotinsky's "jingoism".[12]

Sacher in particular was hostile to Jabotinsky's modus operandi and believed that his close cooperation with Weizmann had infected him with "cadetism",[13] allying him with the approach of Pavel Miliukov's Kadet party in Russia. The English Zionist Federation indignantly opposed the very idea of a Jewish Legion as did Lord Rothschild, later the recipient of the Balfour Declaration.

All this was in addition to many voices in the anglicised leadership of the Jewish community who felt that a specific Jewish Legion was unnecessary and would set them apart from their fellow non-Jews serving in the British armed forces. After all, Chief Rabbi Herman Adler, an opponent of Zionism,[14] commented in April 1909 that the Jews no longer constituted a nation.[15]

The origins of the Jewish Legion

The idea of a Jewish fighting force was not new. The French Revolution had spawned national legions fighting for the independence of their countries. Many started out under the tricolour of France to safeguard the revolution. Such international armies defeated the Prussians at Valmy and Jemappes in 1792.[16]

One hundred years later, the struggles for national liberation in Europe represented the backdrop to the notion that the Jews had survived two millennia through their national will and less through the practice of Judaism. For Jabotinsky, the Land of Israel was at the core of Jewish history – not Judaism. Therefore, he lauded Bar-Kokhba and the Maccabees, but ignored the Rambam (Maimonides) and the Ramban (Nahmanides). Jabotinsky famously wrote that "in the beginning God created the individual"[17] – essentially a call to action, to take responsibility.

The pogroms of the first years of the twentieth century inevitably coloured his views on the need for a Jewish military force. The killings of 1905 and 1906 took the lives of 3,100 Jews, of whom a quarter were women, with some 1,500 children orphaned. Eighty per cent of these pogroms occurred within 60 days of the publication of the October Manifesto.[18]

Jabotinsky's emphasis on military Zionism delineated the established Left from the ascending Right. As both Brian Horowitz[19] and Yosef Gorny[20] have noted, Jabotinsky's philosophy reversed Zionist priorities – it placed military force before constructivism. It differentiated him from the liberal, left mainstream of the Zionist movement. Writing about the Kishinev pogrom in 1903, he commented that it was "more than a day of grief, it was a day of shame".[21]

Romantic nationalism and militant Zionism

Jabotinsky's views on nationalism and the nation state had been crystallised by seminal episodes such as the French Revolution, the year of revolts – 1848, the Polish uprisings and national movements such as the Risorgimento.

More than 100,000 Poles had fought in Napoleon's *Grande Armée* in the invasion of Russia in 1812. The existence of such military forces influenced those Jews who had begun to think in national terms. Indeed, Adam Mickiewicz, the Polish national poet, proposed the establishment of a Jewish Legion in the 1850s, to liberate Palestine.[22]

Jabotinsky translated Mickiewicz's national ode, *Konrad Wallenrod* as well as Esaias Tegnér's romantic epos *Frithjof's Saga*. Both *Wallenrod* and *Pan Tadeusz,* referred to the tragedy, trial and tribulation of Polish revolts during the nineteenth century. Such poetry influenced Jabotinsky and later Menaham Begin, Yitzhak Shamir and Avraham Stern.

Indeed, contrary to later statements, in the 1930s Menahem Begin proclaimed that he was willing to sacrifice himself for the glory of Poland. Some members of *Betar* believed in 'two fatherlands' – the Land of Israel and Poland.[23]

Jabotinsky was also fond of quoting from Ferdinand Lassalle's drama, *Franz von Sickingen* published in 1859. Based on a revolt against the Papacy during the Thirty Years War, the play illustrated the struggle to unify the Germans.[24]

In 1914, it was the contemporary Polish example which impressed Jabotinsky. Basing his approach on the principle that 'the enemy of my enemy is my friend', Józef Piłsudski, the founder of modern Poland, had travelled to Tokyo to solicit support during the Russo-Japanese war in 1904–05. Even before the outbreak of World War One, the Hapsburgs supported Piłsudski in establishing a Polish Legion, as a means of deterring Russian imperial ambitions. Three companies of Polish riflemen immediately invaded Russian Poland following the formal declaration of hostilities in 1914.

Jabotinsky was also interested in Ukrainian nationalism, which was utilised by Tsarism to eliminate Poland from the map at the end of the eighteenth century. Russia did not recognise the Ukraine, but only '*malaya Rossiya*' – little Russia. In 1897, almost three million Jews lived on Ukrainian ethnic territories, some 28% of world Jewry.

Jabotinsky took pains to puncture Ukrainian claims that Russification was the design of assimilated Russian Jews. Yet his efforts to create good relations between the two peoples ran into the ground with the mass killings of Jews in the Ukraine during the conflict between the Red Army and Ukrainian nationalist forces. In 1922, the proposal to establish a unit of Jewish gendarmes to accompany Ukrainian forces in a new invasion of the Ukraine, was strongly criticised within the Zionist movement – especially by the Left. The idea was that this force would protect Jews from further attacks. Although the invasion never took place, Jabotinsky was subsequently accused of aligning himself with pogromists.[25]

Such national movements in Europe were generally viewed as the ideological domain of the Right. Jabotinsky commented that if Garibaldi had lived 50 years later, the Italian revolutionary would have been ridiculed and labelled as a reactionary. On the eve of World War One, Jabotinsky attacked 'radical Europe' for looking unsympathetically on the cause of those national minorities which did not wish to assimilate in their host countries. Italians in the southern Tyrol and Trento, for example, wished to be connected to the kingdom of Italy.[26]

For Jabotinsky therefore, the Jewish Legion possessed an internationalist pedigree in a nationalist cause. It synthesised a merger between cosmopolitanism and Jewish nationalism.

1917 and after: the rapid move to the right

The tight control of the Russian cultural milieu in the wake of the October revolution and the suppression of the right to express independent views by the Bolsheviks deeply affected Jabotinsky and the Russian intelligentsia in general. This was accompanied by the failed expectations that following the

Balfour Declaration, a state of the Jews was imminent. The subsequent retreat by the British from their ambiguous commitments during the war was a further ingredient of the disillusion which grew during the initial period of the British Mandate. During the 1920s, all this moved Jabotinsky from an essentially non-socialist position to an anti-socialist one. The frustration felt in Zionist circles that their hopes had not been realised pushed Jabotinsky into outright opposition, from a maverick within to a rebel without. He resigned from the Zionist Executive in 1923 and two years later in Paris he established the Zionist Revisionists – 'a back to Herzl' movement.

During the first few years of the existence of the Revisionists, Jabotinsky was able to attract to his standard many Russian Jewish *emigrés*. As with Jabotinsky, the advent of Bolshevism had moved many liberals and social democrats to the Right. Many who arrived in Palestine during the early 1920s, at the end of the third *aliyah* – including some who had seen the inside of Soviet prisons and the incremental suppression of Zionism in the USSR – were aghast at the adulation of the Soviet experiment by labour Zionists in the *Yishuv*.

An opposition group, the *Amlanim*, was established within the non-Marxist *Hapoel Hatzair*. They opposed the visit of Levi Shkolnik (Eshkol), to the Moscow Conference of the Communist Cooperative Movement in 1925, while Zionists languished in Soviet prisons. Despite *Tserei Tsion* representatives meeting Shkolnik in Moscow, a split within the party occurred and figures such as Arieh Altman and Baruch Weinstein, later prominent Revisionists, left *Hapoel Hatzair*.

Another prominent *Hapoel Hatzair* critic of the Soviet state and its treatment of Zionists was the writer Abba Ahimeir, who emigrated to Palestine in 1924 and strongly opposed any suggested merger between *Hapoel Hatzair* and the Marxist *Ahdut Ha'avodah*.

On the tenth anniversary of the October Revolution, Ahimeir wrote several articles such as 'The October Terror'[27] and 'The Creator of the Brest-Litovsk Accord'.[28] This was the precursor to the final move to the Right of Ahimeir and two other intellectuals, the poet Uri Zvi Greenberg and the writer Yehoshua Hirsh Yeivin. In February 1928 they made an unannounced appearance at the Revisionist conference at Nahalat Yehuda and formally joined Jabotinsky. Ahimeir symbolically began to sign his articles *Aba Apostata* after the scholarly and pagan Roman Emperor, Julian the Apostate (361–363).

He challenged conventional thinking on the Left and made a distinction between the Jewish working class in Palestine and the labour movement's intelligentsia: "The worker lives his daily life while the intelligentsia hallucinates about the days of the Messiah through Marx's teachings."[29]

Ahimeir was intrigued by the figure of Boris Savinkov, the Russian social revolutionary, responsible for several killings including that of Vyacheslav von Plehve, a Tsarist Minister of the Interior, in 1904. Originally a minister in Kerensky's government, Savinkov's anti-Bolshevism moved him towards supporting the Whites, most notably Admiral Kolchak.

Unlike the Revisionist leadership, Ahimeir, Greenberg and Yeivin came from deeply Jewish rather than assimilated backgrounds. They quickly emerged as the maximalist wing of the Revisionist movement, essentially opposing Jabotinsky's approach and elevating militancy to a new level – a 'revolutionary Zionism' designed to oppose the British in Palestine and those in the Zionist leadership who still believed in negotiating with Britain. Ahimeir's templates for this approach were the national revolutions of Mussolini, Piłsudski and Ataturk as well as his appreciation of Lenin's singlemindedness in the USSR. Greenberg had eulogised Lenin in a poem on his death in 1924, and was later critical of the freedom of speech in democracies.[30]

Understanding such developments, it was argued, could break the logjam of stagnation in Palestine. It also led Ahimeir to admire Mussolini's fascism. In 1929 Italian fascism was not perceived as overtly anti-Semitic – not until the regime's anti-Jewish legislation in 1938. Moreover, Jews had joined Mussolini's party upon its establishment and Jewish ministers served in his administration.

This transition of political allegiances mirrored others who had earlier moved from the Left to the Right, from Italian revolutionary syndicalism to Mussolini's fascism. In 1926, Ahimeir reviewed *Sozialismus und Fascismus* – the work of Roberto Michels, an intellectual supporter of Mussolini, for a *Hapoel Hatzair* publication.[31] Michels had also made the transition from Left to Right.

The non-conformist Ahimeir also strongly opposed the genteel *gentlemeniut*, [good manners] approach of pro-British Jews in Palestine, as well as the *mopsiut*, the admiration of local Communists and their fellow travellers for the USSR.[32]

Ahimeir's disdain for liberalism and parliamentarianism placed him at odds with Jabotinsky.

Cultivating the youth

Jabotinsky's critical commentaries about the USSR not only chimed with many who had left the Soviet Union, but also with the new arrivals of the fourth *aliyah* from Poland in the mid-1920s. Consisting of the Polish Jewish middle class and a coterie of small businessmen, they also exhibited the Polish fear of and antagonism towards their neighbour to the East. Jabotinsky cultivated them with articles such as *Basta*[33] in which he lamented the absence of the private sector and *We, the Bourgeoisie*,[34] which attacked 'the cult of the proletariat'. Jabotinsky remained loyal to the national revolutions of the nineteenth century while disparaging the October revolution of the twentieth.

During his visit to Poland in February 1927, Jabotinsky was surprised to be feted as almost a secular *wunder-rebbe* figure. In a letter to his wife, Jabotinsky admitted that he was concerned by his reception. "They are beginning to transform me into a myth".[35]

However, Jabotinsky also realised that the sheer numbers of young Jews in Poland offered the possibility of building a stronger and more disciplined *Betar* – an organisation which was more than a Zionist youth group. The background of Polish struggles since the three partitions and final disappearance of independence at the end of the eighteenth century undoubtedly influenced the country's interwar Jewish youth. *Betar* was the only Zionist youth movement to align itself with Polish nationalist groups.[36]

The founder of modern Poland, Józef Piłsudski, had only recently staged a coup in Poland and many Jews looked for a similar strongman who could offer them salvation in Palestine. In 1927 Piłsudski established the National Agency for Physical Education and Military Preparation as a means of centrally controlling military activities and 'curbing that of youth movements of national minorities'.[37] But members of Polish *Betar* involved themselves in the activities of the Agency to utilise such knowledge for Zionist aims.

In the light of all this, Jabotinsky reversed his earlier views about Weizmann and the Jewish Legion. The Balfour Declaration was originally seen by Jabotinsky in 1918 as "the personal achievement of a single individual – Dr Chaim Weizmann – and believed that his name would always be linked to this diplomatic breakthrough".[38]

Ten years later, at a time when he opposed Weizmann's political path and when the nascent Revisionist Zionist movement was in ascendancy, Jabotinsky reworked his understanding of the Jewish Legion. Weizmann was now demoted in his pantheon of Zionist heroes. At the conclusion of his book about the Jewish Legion, published in 1928, Jabotinsky comments that during World War One, the Zionist movement was "broken and paralysed, and was by its nature, completely outside the narrow horizons of a warring world with its warring governments".[39] Now, the existence of the Jewish Legion was, in Jabotinsky's eyes, nothing less than a manifestation of Zionist will and willingness for self-sacrifice.

Youth flocked to Jabotinsky's standard in Poland and he promoted this revised model of the Jewish Legion for them. This also served the purpose of depoliticising *Betar* – while leaving the complex matter of politics *per se* to the grown-ups in the Revisionist movement. Regardless of whether or not this separation was intentional and planned, *Betar* assumed a direction of its own. Led first by Adelbert Bibring, who framed *Betar* in scouting imagery *à la* Baden-Powell, then by Reuven Feldschuh, its ideologist, who fanned the flames of a conflict with the Zionist Left.

At this time, in 1927, Jabotinsky published his novel *Samson*, in Hebrew– a story aimed at Jewish youth. He transformed the Samson of the Biblical narrative, airbrushing God out of the story, into a universal nazarite hero. In a supreme act of self-sacrifice of pulling down the Temple about him, Jabotinsky's Samson states that it is "no longer a defense of God's honour, it is now a man's sacrifice for his people".[40]

While Jabotinsky appeared to the Revisionists as the principled negotiator with the British, to the youth of *Betar*, he encouraged their radical enthusiasm and individualism while praising their militancy, directed against the British. The creation of a political space for his youthful acolytes further allowed them to toy with both authoritarianism and militarism in the Poland of the 1930s. Jabotinsky recognised further that there was a need for this generation to mythologise a figure[41] – even if he had previously been highly critical of Mussolini and the cult of the leader. Therefore, during the last decade of his life, Jabotinsky walked a tightrope of contradictions, reflected in his heading the New Zionist Organisation, *Betar* and the *Irgun*, all with different views, all at the same time in the late 1930s. Daniel Heller has argued that Jabotinsky's writings were overtly transformed into a *pot-pourri* of strategic ambiguity. "Jabotinsky's talent as a political writer rested in his ability to situate his bold, provocative claims within an intricate web of contradictions and conditional clauses".[42]

The rise of the maximalists

For many members of *Betar*, the maximalist wing of the Jabotinsky movement became a magnet to which they were attracted. In their view, Ahimeir and the maximalists argued that Jabotinsky's youth group should become the nucleus of an underground army. His incendiary rhetoric should be fashioned into military deeds. For a few, this meant flirting with fascism.

For Jabotinsky, formed in the social milieu of intellectual Odessa and pre-1914 Italian liberalism, all this was alarming. He recalled a meeting as early as 1925, with "a fascist acquaintance" in 1925 and told him: "And what will you do when your 'genius' dies? After all, you yourselves, know that you can't get geniuses by the dozen".[43] Jabotinsky regarded Ahimeir "as too much a fascist",[44] yet he needed him to impress the youth.

Ahimeir promoted the allure of self-sacrifice and argued that Jews should not rely on "the kindness of nations".[45] He lauded the Decembrists revolt at the end of 1825, influenced by the American revolution, which unsuccessfully opposed the rule of the new Tsar, the authoritarian Nicholas I. He also held up the biblical figure of Nahshon ben Aminadav, the first to jump into the unparted Red Sea – as an example for revolutionary youth.[46]

Ahimeir understood the role of *Betar* as 'a national guard' – a revolutionary vanguard. Nietzsche's *der Wille zur Macht* [will to power], he argued, should take root. Ahimeir further detected the idea of *Betar* in modern Hebrew poetry – Y.L. Gordon, Tchernikovsky, Bialik and Berdichevsky as well as in the hero in Max Brod's *Reubeni, Prince of the Jews.*[47]

Embedded in this situation, Jabotinsky struggled to channel the dynamism of the *Betar* youth into productive channels while challenging the certainty of their radicalism. As the storm clouds gathered and Europe headed towards a second conflagration, Jabotinsky's balancing act became more untenable.

In 1927, Ahimeir had written an article for *Ha'aretz* entitled 'If I am not for myself, who will be for me?'[48] Well-known as a saying of the Talmudic sage, Hillel, he noted that it was also the slogan of the Irish Republican Sinn Fein. In other articles, he argued that parliamentary democracy was just not applicable in many countries and put the case instead for national dictatorship. He viewed the ex-socialist Mussolini as the successor of Mazzini and Garibaldi, and wrote a series of articles, entitled *From the Notebook of a Fascist* for the daily *Doar Hayom*.

When Jabotinsky arrived in Palestine in October 1928, Ahimeir attempted to turn him into a Zionist Duce[49], but Jabotinsky swatted away such fawning. Ahimeir commented: "Our messiah will not arrive as a pauper on a donkey. He will come like all messiahs, riding a tank and bringing his commandments to his people".[50]

In contrast, Jabotinsky continued to express his admiration for the British parliamentary system. Yet Jabotinsky's idea of parliament was one that transcended petty politics. In 1928 he suggested the establishment of 'a professional parliament' to supplement an assembly of elected representatives. This second house, a Senate, would deal with practical matters such as the economy and would involve all thoughtful people. The elected parliament, consisting of political parties, would deal with ideological questions.

These clear ideological differences between Jabotinsky and Ahimeir would be fought out in the struggle to forge the future ideological direction of *Betar*.

Ahimeir the teacher and organiser

Ahimeir's opportunity arose when he was asked to lecture on history to the cadets of the *Bet Sefer le-madrikhim Betar* – the school for future *Betar* leaders. The school had been developed by Menahem Arber, Moshe Rosenberg and Yirmiyahu Halperin – all of whom possessed military experience and had been close to Jabotinsky.

Abba Ahimeir and his colleague, Yosef Katznelson,[51] were able to promote the ideas of revolutionary Zionism through these courses.[52] During the disturbances of 1929, Ahimeir compared those Jews killed in Hebron and Safed to those who had been killed in the massacres of Worms, Nemirov and Proskorov. All were considered martyrs in the task of building the Jewish homeland. Moreover, many *Betar* cadets had experienced killings and mock executions at the hands of both the Bolsheviks and the Ukrainian nationalists.[53] Significantly the famous march to the Western Wall in 1929 was not instigated by the existing *Betar* organisation but by the *Bet Sefer le-madrikhim Betar* (the *Betar* leaders' school).

Brit Ha-Biryonim evolved out of Ahimeir's *Bet Sefer* network, which proceeded to organise demonstrations. There were protests against the visit of the Under-Secretary of State for the Colonies, Drummond Shiels, in October 1930, against the 1931 Census[54] and the inauguration of Norman Bentwich as professor of peace studies at the Hebrew University, in February 1932.

Jabotinsky attempted to divert youth from following *Brit Ha-Biryonim* by advocating the acquisition of military knowledge rather than any actual involvement in military action. In an article which resounded within Polish *Betar*, published in Warsaw in October 1931, Jabotinsky stated:

> If I am told that to shoot is militarism, particularly in the present world which hates militarism and strives for peace – I would not disagree, although I am not certain that the world truly has such peaceful aspirations. I would even concede that it is very sad for us Jews at a time like this to be forced to learn to shoot. But we are forced to it and it is futile to argue against the compulsion of a historical reality.[55]

He advocated the formation of a new Jewish Legion rather than a Jewish underground, which he regarded as "bourgeois impressionism, hysterical and short-sighted".[56] He conspicuously fell silent when confronted with IRA activities[57] – actions that were lauded by Ahimeir and subsequently by Begin and Shamir.

In fact, *Betar*'s leadership in Palestine followed Jabotinsky's vision rather than that of Ahimeir. In seeking to neutralise Ahimeir's influence, Jabotinsky adopted a more authoritarian public stance and pointed out the weaknesses of the democracies in an age of national dictatorships.[58] Jabotinsky's strategy was to outmanoeuvre the maximalist wing of the Revisionists and thereby control the militancy of the young, without eliminating its dynamism. He referred therefore to both Ahimeir and Yeivin as "our teachers and masters",[59] and proclaimed "the necessity of adventurism".[60]

However, Jabotinsky argued, in rejecting "the ideology of the *sansculottes*", for a selective adventurism rather than a blanket one.[61] In contrast, Ahimeir believed that it was the *sansculottes* who created breakthroughs in history and cited the examples of Lenin, Mussolini and Hitler.[62] Ahimeir suggested that Zionists should prepare for "their own 1917".[63]

Revisionist conferences were therefore irrelevant for Ahimeir. The model to be followed was that of the meetings of the Marxist faithful in the Swiss villages of Zimmerwald and Kunterhal, addressed by Lenin in preparation for the inevitable Revolution.[64]

In the summer of 1932, Jabotinsky was brutally clear where he stood on the role for *Betar*, in contradistinction to Ahimeir:

> Adventurism? There are moments when it might bring benefits. An underground? Yes, too. But *Betar* is not and cannot be part either of adventurism or of an underground; yet not anti-adventurism and not anti-underground. *Betar*, as I conceived it, is a school with three 'levels' where youth will learn to control their fists, their batons and all other means of defence; to be able to stand to attention and to march well; to work; to foster beauty of form and ceremony; to scorn all forms of negligence – call it whatever you wish, hooliganism or ghetto mentality; to

respect women and the elderly; and prayer – no matter what religion, democracy and many other things which may seem obsolete, but which are everlasting. This is the type of school that *Betar* has to be. Yes, a school like that, for if not, better that *Betar* not exist at all.[65]

Menahem Begin's interpretation

In 1933, Menahem Begin formally aligned himself with Ahimeir and the Polish Maximalists when he signed a collective letter[66] following the Katowice conference, which removed the Revisionist executive. He felt that "the great permanent revolution in Zionism" had become stuck in the mud since Revisionism had distanced itself from "active resistance". In his early articles, Begin followed the line of Ahimeir rather than that of Jabotinsky, while distancing himself from any solidarity with Mussolini. Begin extolled the virtues of militarism and patriotism[67] and spoke about the '*Betarisation*' of the movement.

At the Revisionist conference in Krakow in January 1935, Jabotinsky made a further attempt to retain the passion of the maximalists while limiting their political influence. However, Begin was highly critical of Jabotinsky's accord with Ben-Gurion in London, recalling that Jabotinsky had been labelled 'Vladimir Hitler' by his opponents. The agreement was finally abandoned by both sides, but Jabotinsky was clearly shocked by the vehemence of his young acolytes.

Begin's upward trajectory in *Betar* was a reflection of this radicalisation of *Betar* and its distancing itself from Jabotinsky and the Revisionists. At the beginning of 1938, Begin, Avraham Stern, then a leader of the *Irgun*, and others published the manifesto of the 'Activist-Revisionist Front'. This was an open assault on Jabotinsky's policies while recognising the debt they owed to him:

> When it was founded and during the first years of its existence, Revisionism was understood by the Jewish masses, especially by the youth, as a revolutionary fighting movement, aiming at national liberation by means of uncompromising military action, both against the external enemy and against the internal traitors and unbelievers. However, in recent years Revisionism has restricted itself to the method of secret diplomacy, which we have mocked so much, in the direction of a completely pro-British orientation. The postulate of mass pressure on the external political factors has been completely forgotten. Within the Jewish people, the party executive has pursued an unceasing policy of seeking peace, thus ignoring the historic chances for a victorious crusade against liquidatory Zionism.[68]

The challenge to Jabotinsky's authority became even more acute when he accepted the leadership of the *Irgun* at the end of 1936, having refused it in past years. He now headed the New Zionist Organisation, *Betar* and the *Irgun* – all with very different political approaches. While Jabotinsky attempted to coordinate these often-warring groups, *Betar* moved away from the Revisionists towards the *Irgun*.

The *Irgun* in turn became more homogeneously nationalist as other Zionist parties dropped out, while *Betar* provided it with a continuous supply of recruits. It began to follow the philosophy of 'Defence through Attack'[69] of Yirmiyahu Halperin, one of the founders of the *Betar* leaders' school. Begin famously opposed Jabotinsky at the third world conference of *Betar* in Warsaw in September 1938 – and won the day in advocating military Zionism and the conquest of Palestine by the armed cadres of *Betar*.

By the end of the 1930s, unbeknown to Jabotinsky, the Polish military were training *Irgun* members near Andrychów and providing it with arms and ammunition. A few months before the outbreak of war in 1939, Aharon Propes, the first member of *Betar*, was sidelined, ousted from the leadership and replaced by Menahem Begin. A second tranche of *Irgun* members, including Yitzhak Shamir, was scheduled to attend the training course. This was abandoned due to the outbreak of war.[70]

The sudden shadow of the Holocaust

With the advent of World War Two, the *Irgun* split over whether or not to participate in the British war effort against Nazism. Which was the real opponent of Zionism, the British crown or the Nazi regime? The commander of the *Irgun*, David Raziel chose Britain – as did Jabotinsky. However, Avraham Stern, his close friend and colleague, cast Jabotinsky in the role of 'Hindenburg'. He believed that Imperial Britain and not Nazi Germany was the central enemy. In Stern's eyes, in 1940 Hitler was a persecutor of Jews and not a liquidator.

He formed the *Irgun B'Yisrael* – known by the British as 'the Stern Gang'. After Stern's death this became *Lehi* (Fighters for the Freedom of Israel). Unlike both Jabotinsky and Stern, Begin was ambivalent in Lithuanian exile and did not immediately align himself. He wanted to see which way the war went before making a decision.

In the summer of 1940 when the invasion of Britain seemed imminent, Jabotinsky's thinking had not changed. He advocated that a new Jewish Legion, based in Canada, should be formed. Under British command, this army would eventually expand to 150,000 men and would possess two air-force squadrons.[71] The inaugural convention for the campaign was due to be held in New York at the beginning of September 1940. Such plans were never realised. Jabotinsky died suddenly of a heart attack in New York on 4 August 1940 at the age of 59. Bereft of an authoritative, mentoring figure, both the *Irgun* and *Lehi* were free to act out their own interpretations of militant Zionism.

During the second half of 1942, Jews in Palestine gradually became aware that the Nazis were carrying out a systematic extermination of all Jews and not simply carrying out a series of random pogroms. On 30 November 1942, three days of official mourning in the *Yishuv* were declared. All work stopped between 12 noon and midnight except for essential tasks connected with the war effort.

The emphasis on the fate of Polish Jewry deeply affected those of its members who had found refuge in Palestine. Since Menahem Begin's arrival in Palestine in early 1942, he had advocated the formation of a Jewish army rather than enlistment in the British armed forces. In his writings for *Ha-Madrikh*[72] under the pseudonym Menahem ben Ze'ev, Begin asserted that the 15,000 members of *Betar* remaining in Poland, together with hundreds of thousands of Jews in occupied Eastern Europe and the Soviet Union, should form the nucleus of a Jewish army which would liberate European Jewry. His awakening to the fate of his generation consequently led to several embittered articles in early 1943 and a more radical interpretation of militant Zionism.[73] Begin blamed Mapai and the Jewish Agency for not doing enough and the British for their indifference and perfidy. However, Begin stated inaccurately that Jabotinsky had predicted the coming of the Holocaust.

The Bermuda conference in April 1943 failed to address the question of Jewish refugees. The crushing of the Warsaw Ghetto Uprising a few weeks later completed the radicalisation of Begin. His accession to the leadership of the Irgun at the end of 1943 separated him further from the official Revisionists under Aryeh Altman, who opposed the use of military might. In effect, the decision to conduct an armed struggle against the British in 1944 reflected Begin's ideological distance from his mentor, the now deceased Jabotinsky. This struggle continued until the end of the British Mandate.

On the declaration of Israel's independence in 1948, Begin announced that the *Irgun* would be transformed into a political movement, *Herut*. This, in turn, became *Gahal* in 1965 and the *Likud* in 1973. Four years later, Menahem Begin, the advocate of military Zionism and opponent of Jabotinsky became Israel's first right wing prime minister.

Notes

1 *Severnyi Kurier* 31 February 1900; *Odesskie Novosti*, 27 April 1900, 4 May 1900, 22 December 1900, 11 January 1901, 8 August 1901, 21 August 1901.
2 *Severnyi Kurier* 18 March 1900; *Odesskie Novosti* 22 March 1900, 3 April 1900, 16 April 1900, 28 May 1900, 22 December 1900, 2 February 1901, 13 February 1901, 1 March 1901, 25 March 1901, 17 June 1901, 19 July 1901.
3 *Odesskie Novosti*, 4 May 1900, 7 July 1900, 1 March 1901.
4 Jabotinsky, Horosko', *Odesskie Novosti*, 1 January 1912.
5 Jabotinsky, Solveig, *Russkie Vedomosti*, 2 April 1916.
6 Jabotinsky, Homo Homini Lupus, *Odesskie Novosti*, 18 July 1910.
7 Vladimir Jabotinsky, *Muse and Muscle: Story of My Life and the Invention of Vladimir Jabotinsky,* Brian Horowitz and Leonid Katsis (eds) Detroit: Wayne State University Press, 2016, p.118.

8 Jabotinsky to Felix Lazar Pinkus, 1 September 1916, *Igrot, September 1914-November 1918* Jerusalem: Jabotinsky Institute, 1995.

9 Jabotinsky, *The Story of the Jewish Legion*, New York: Bernard Ackerman, 1945, pp. 31–2, 59.

10 Jabotinsky, *Avtobiografia: Sipur Yamei [Autobiography: Story of my Life]* Eri Jabotinsky (ed.), Jerusalem: Eri Jabotinsky, 1958, p.144.

11 Harry Sacher to Chaim Weizmann, 3 August 1917, in Jehuda Reinharz, *Chaim Weizmann: The Making of a Statesman,* New York: Oxford University Press 1993, note 66, p. 458.

12 Reinharz, ibid., p.199.

13 Sacher to Leon Simon, 2 September 1917 in Jonathan Schneer, *The Balfour Declaration: The Origins of the Arab-Israeli Conflict,* New York: Bloomsbury, 2010, p. 315.

14 Benjamin J. Elton, *Britain's Chief Rabbis and the Religious Character of Anglo-Jewry 1880–1970*, Manchester: Manchester University Press 2009, pp. 91–7.

15 Geoffrey Alderman, *Modern British Jewry*, Oxford: Clarendon Press 1998, p. 232.

16 Colin Shindler, *The Triumph of Military Zionism: Nationalism and the Origins of the Israeli Right*, London: I. B. Tauris 2006, pp. 78–9.

17 Jabotinsky, *Avtobiografia*, pp. 44–8.

18 *Jewish Chronicle*, 3 November 2017.

19 Jabotinsky, *Muse and Muscle,* p. 9.

20 Yosef Gorny, *Zionism and the Arabs, 1882–1948*, Oxford: Clarendon Press 1987, pp. 176–7.

21 Jabotinsky, *Avtobiografia* pp. 44–8.

22 Michael Graetz, *The Jews in Nineteenth Century France: From the French Revolution to the Alliance Israélite Universelle*, Stanford: Stanford University Press, 1996, p. 244.

23 Daniel Kupfert Heller, *Jabotinsky's Children: Polish Jews and the Rise of Right Wing Zionism*, Princeton: Princeton University Press, 2017, pp. 1–2.

24 Shindler, *The Triumph*, p. 73.

25 Nahum Levin, 'Jabotinsky and the Petliura Agreement', *Jewish Standard*, 9 August 1940.

26 Jabotinsky, 'Reactionary', 1912, Jabotinsky Institute Archives, Tel Aviv.

27 *Ha'aretz*, 8 November 1927.

28 Ibid., 23 November 1927.

29 *Doar Hayom* ,19 November 1928 in Peter Bergamin, D.Phil *An Intellectual Biography of Abba Ahimeir,* Oxford: Mansfield College 2017, p. 141.

30 *Kuntres*, 11 August 1925, 26 August 1926.

31 *Hapoel Hatzair*, no. 6 1926, in Bergamin, *An Intellectual Biography*, p. 95; *Kuntres*, 26 August 1926.

32 Bergamin, *An Intellectual Biography*, p. 129. The Hebrew acronym of the Palestinian communist party was '*mopsi*'.

33 *Rassviet*, 28 June 1925.

34 Ibid, 17 April 1927.

35 Jabotinsky to Joanna Jabotinsky, 27 February 1927, *Igrot 1926–1927*, Jerusalem: Jabotinsky Institute, 2000.

36 Heller, *Jabotinsky's Children*, p. 13.

37 Ibid., p.160

38 Jabotinsky to Jacob Landau, end of January 1918, *Igrot 1914–1918,* Jerusalem: Jabotinsky Institute, 1995.

39 Jabotinsky, *The Story of the Jewish Legion*, p. 182.

40 Rachel Harris, Samson's suicide: Death and the Hebrew literary canon, *Israel Studies* 17/3, Autumn 2012.

41 Jabotinsky to Miriam Langer, 27 August 1930, *Igrot 1930–1931*, Jerusalem: Jabotinsky Institute, 2004.

42 Heller, *Jabotinsky's Children*, p. 11.

43 Jabotinsky, 'The Unknown Race', *Causeries,* Paris 1930.

44 Jabotinsky to Shlomo Gepstein, 10 December 1928, *Igrot 1928–1929*, Jerusalem: Jabotinsky Institute, 2002.

45 *Doar Hayom*, 4 October 1929.

46 *Hapoel Hatzair,* 22 September 1926.

47 Aba Ahimeir, *Revolutionary Zionism,* Tel Aviv: Committee for publishing the writings of Abba Ahimeir, 1965, pp. 21–4.

48 *Ha'aretz*, 15 November 1927.

49 *Doar Hayom*, 10 October 1928.

50 Ibid., 14 October 1928.

51 Yosef Zahavi, *Revolutionary Zionism: From Brit HaBiryonim to Etzel* in Yosef Ahimeir, ed. *The Black Prince: Yosef Katznelson and the National Movement in the 1930s,* Tel Aviv: Jabotinsky Institute 1983, p. 293.

52 Moshe Segal, 'Hashavua l'yad Ha'kotel' (Hebrew, *This week at the Wailing Wall*), in Yosef Ahimeir and Shmuel Shatzky, *Hineinu Sikirikim*, Tel Aviv: Nitzanim 1978, pp. 139–40.

53 *Doar Hayom*, 4 September 1929.

54 *Hamedina* [the state], 25 September 1931, *Ha'uma* [the people], 2 October 1931.

55 Jabotinsky, Afn Pripitshek, *Haynt*, 16 October 1931; *Jewish Herald,* 12 September 1947.

56 Jabotinsky, More on adventurism, *Haynt* 29/31, July 1932; *Hazit Ha'am,* 5 August 1932.

57 Shindler, Jabotinsky and the troubles, *Jerusalem Post*, 20 April 2006.

58 Jabotinsky, Zeyde Liberalizm, *Haynt*, 14 October 1932

59 Jabotinsky to Yehoshua Hirsch Yeivin, 9 August 1932, *Igrot 1932–1933,* Jerusalem: Jabotinsky Institute, 2006.

60 Jabotinsky, On adventurism, *Haynt*, 26 February 1932.

61 Jabotinsky, More on adventurism, *Haynt*, 29/31 July 1932; *Hazit Ha'am*, 5 August 1932.

62 Yonathan Shapiro, *The Road to Power: The Herut Party in Israel*, New York: SUNY Press, 1991, p. 45.

63 *Ha'am*, 14 July 1931.

64 *Hazit Ha'am*, 15 July 1932.

65 Jabotinsky, More on adventurism, *Haynt*, 29/31 July 1932; *Hazit Ha'am*, 5 August 1932.

66 Memorandum of the Polish Maximalists to the Katowice Council 7 April 1933, Jabotinsky Institute archives.

67 Begin, *Hamedina*, 25 October 1934.

68 *Le-Ma'an Ha-Moledet* [*For the Homeland*], 14 January 1938.

69 Yirmiyahu Halperin, *Hamedina*, 12 March 1933.

70 Interview with Yitzhak Shamir, 25 July 2000.

71 Jabotinsky aide-memoire, 10 September 1939, Jabotinsky Institute Archives.

72 Menahem Ben-Ze'ev, *Ha-Madrikh*, September, October 1942, February, June 1943.

73 Ben-Ze'ev, *Herut*, 17 May 1943.

13 Is Zionism colonialism?

Yoav Gelber

Islam recognised Judaism as a religion, not as a nationality. Palestinian Arabs defined Zionism as a colonial movement. Indeed, like other colonial movements, Zionism was a movement of immigration and settlement. Here, however, the similarities end. In all its other characteristics Zionism differed from colonial movements and refuted the allegation and the comparisons. This chapter discusses the divergences.

Jewish identity is incomprehensible to many across the world. The compound (in the chemical sense of the word) of biology (or genetics), religion and peoplehood (or nationality) is unique to Jews and does not exist elsewhere. Throughout history, it has been a source of curiosity, fears and hatred. In modern times the special Jewish linkage between ethnos, religion and nation, as well as the worldwide affiliation of Jews to that part of the Middle East called by them the Land of Israel, have become unintelligible to non-Jews and after the Holocaust also to many Jews and even to some Israelis.

Since the French Revolution, the emergence of the modern nation state aggravated the problem of Jewish identity. Jews were asked and also pondered themselves: if they are part of the nation, why are they different? If they are not part of the nation but a separate entity, why do they live in the country and what should their status be? The mainstream Jewish response in Western and Central Europe was to shed the differences, except religious credo, and become Germans, French etc. of the Mosaic religion. This trend led to assimilation and emancipation and, in the last third of the nineteenth century, stimulated the emergence and expansion of modern anti-Semitism.

In Eastern Europe, assimilation and emancipation were barely an option. Jews could choose between adhering to the traditional way of life, joining movements who sought to correct the world order and build "the world of tomorrow" or, since the last quarter of the nineteenth century, emigrate overseas. Jewish nationalism, of which Zionism was the dominant version, was chronologically the last option, and emerged after the pogroms in Russia and the spread of modern anti-Semitism in Western Europe.

The burden of the complicated Jewish identity has been heavy, and one way of dodging the complexity has been to deny its national element. This line has been taken by liberal, socialist and extreme religious Jews. The denial of Jewish nationality has led to denial of Zionism as a national movement and, subsequently, to the denial of Israel as a nation state of the Jews. In recent years, critics and opponents of Zionism and Israel, like Shlomo Sand, deny not only the national element of Jewish identity but also the biological one. They propagate dubious theories about contemporary Jews being the descendants of Middle Ages' converts rather than the successors of the Jewish people of antiquity and therefore they can't have a legitimate claim to the Land of Israel.[1]

Still, the critics have to face the question who and what Zionists/Israeli Jews are if they are not a nation and have no common ethnic roots. Since the de-colonisation, the simple answer of Israel-baiters is: they are colonialists who settled in a Third World country and dispossessed the natives. For that purpose, the Zionists faked history, invented a non-existent national identity and even appropriated the memory of the Holocaust that should have been universal.

During the Mandate, colonialism was not considered a dirty word and these accusations carried little weight. The almost total disappearance of other national and non-national alternatives in the Holocaust made Zionism a default choice for survivors in Eastern and Central Europe and facilitated the foundation of Israel. However, de-colonisation changed the scene and in the mid-1960s questions about the legitimacy of Zionism and accusations of colonialism against Israel penetrated public discourse, first in the West and subsequently in Israel.

The Six Day War brought the Palestinians back to the political arena. In the eyes of progressive intellectuals and radical youngsters in Western Europe, Israel turned rapidly from an underdog into a conqueror. A point of departure was a massive volume that had been written and edited before the war and came out in June 1967 as a special edition of *Les Temps Modernes*. The contributors to this volume were French, Jewish and Arab (Palestinian and North African) intellectuals who failed to reach a dialogue and presented two monologues in separate parts. The colonialist nature of Zionism was among the main topics that the contributors discussed, and one of the prominent articles was Maxim Rodinson's *Israel, fait colonial*.[2]

Initially, many critics of Israel still discerned between 'smaller' Israel in its pre-war borders, and 'greater' Israel, the occupying power in the west Bank and the Gaza Strip. The first was legitimate, the second not. A smaller group of radicals adopted the Palestinian narrative, and argued that Israel was a colonialist state that had been founded on usurped Arab land. Rodinson in France and Eric Hobsbawm in the UK, among others, represented this radical position and were gradually joined by others, including some Israeli academics.[3]

The colonialist paradigm of Zionism

The Colonialist Paradigm is hardly original or innovative. Attempts to portray Zionism as a colonialist movement are as old as the Zionist movement and they have accompanied the Arab-Jewish conflict from its inception. The charge was already made by the first Palestinian Arab Congress that convened in Jerusalem in January 1919 if not earlier. Rashid Khalidi, for example, portrayed a local incident in 1913 as a symbol of the insurrection of Arab tenants against the Zionist/Jewish dispossessors, thus marking the beginning of Palestinian nationalism.[4] The late Prof. Baruch Kimmerling and Joel Migdal took its beginning even further back in time and linked it to the Syrian fellahin revolt against Ibrahim Pasha's occupying Egyptian army in 1834.[5]

What in earnest was the extent of Arab opposition to the Zionist enterprise at the beginning of immigration and settlement? Kimmerling found four examples – spread over 22 years – of press articles and petitions against the purchase of land by Jews. These, he claimed, proved Arab political and national resistance to land purchase by Jews in Palestine. This is poor evidence for the existence of genuine national opposition, especially since Kimmerling did not specify the scope of land transactions between Jews and Arabs in those 22 years.[6] At the same time, he ignored other – no less numerous – articles in the Arab press and petitions to the authorities in favour of the Jews and the blessing they bestow on the country. Some, at least, of these articles and petitions were indeed bought or subsidised by Jews, but this is true also for the contemporary Arab Anti-Zionist propaganda. It was encouraged and funded by private interests, and not always or necessarily out of national motivation.

Since the shaping of the new order in the Middle East and its division into mandates under the tutelage of the Western powers after the First World War, the Arabs of Palestine (they were not yet 'Palestinians') have portrayed themselves as a national liberation movement struggling against a foreign colonial power backed by the military might of British imperialism that tried to usurp their land. They raised anti-colonialist arguments in their appeals to the British government and to the League of Nations, as well as in their official and non-official deliberations with the various commissions that sought a solution to the Palestine problem in the 1930s and 1940s. However, colonialism was at that time legitimate and their arguments did not attract attention or inspire sympathy. World public opinion did not consider them stronger than the Jewish plight in Europe even before, and certainly after the Holocaust.

Since the late 1970s, however, anti-colonialist arguments fell on receptive ears, particularly in Western Europe that was haunted by post-colonial guilt feelings. Inspired by Edward Sa'id, the Palestinians endeavoured to demonstrate to the West the colonial nature of Zionism, particularly of 'Greater Israel' after the Six Day War.

Israeli post-Zionists of all creeds embraced to various degrees the Palestinians' arguments. Kimmerling, Pappé and others of their ilk were not the first Jews to argue that Zionism dispossessed the Arabs of Palestine and deprived them of their land and rights. They had been preceded by Jewish communists that as early as the 1920s objected to the Zionist enterprise because of its alleged colonialist nature and argued that one cannot remedy an injustice (to the Jews) by creating another one (to the Arabs). Their comrades in Palestine identified with Arab nationalism, accused Zionism of being an imperialist tool if not imperialism itself, and regarded Jewish settlement on the land as a capitalist exploitation of the Arab tenants.[7]

A large group of Jewish communists left Palestine and returned to the Soviet Union in the late 1920s and most of its members perished either in Siberia or in the Holocaust. Other Jewish communists repented and returned to Zionism on the eve of statehood or after the split of the party in the mid-1960s. More radical than the communists were *Matzpen*, an extremist anti-Zionist group that was active in Israel during the 1960s and 1970s and blamed Zionism for all the evils and wrongdoings of capitalism.[8]

In the late 1960s and the 1970s, several critical writers published books that criticised the Zionist past and the Israeli present. Prominent among them were Israel Ber, an ex-IDF senior officer and professor of military history in the University of Tel Aviv, who died in prison after being convicted of espionage for the Soviets; Uri Avneri, the editor of Israel's most popular weekly magazine in the 1950s, 60s and 70s, and a member of the *Knesset*; and Aharon Cohen (an autodidact scholar who founded and headed, together with Eliezer Bauer (Beeri), the Arab department of *Hashomer Hatza'ir* and Mapam (a Zionist left-wing party)).[9]

The centre of this school moved to the West in the late 1970s. Several books by former Israelis, as well as American and French Jewish activists of the New Left, presented an anti-Israeli/Zionist version of the history of Zionism and Israel. They stressed the injustice that was done to the Palestinians by the very foundation of Israel, regardless of its borders. Some of the authors were academics from various non-historical disciplines such as mathematics, chemistry, linguistics, literature and psychology. Others were well known journalists and writers.[10]

Since the late 1980s several new historians and critical sociologists have cultivated the stereotype of the colonialist Zionist immigrant by comparing the settling farmers in Rosh Pina or the pioneers in Deganya to the Dutch officials in the Netherland's Indies (now Indonesia) or the French 'Colones' in Algeria. Similarly, they have drawn similarities between the Jewish settlement in the land of Israel and the Boers (Afrikaners) in South Africa. They compared the United States' acquisition of Louisiana from France in 1803, and Alaska from Russia in 1867 with the purchase of Arabs' tracts of land by the Jewish National Fund. Similarly, they likened the attitude of the Jews to the Arab tenants that tilled these tracts with the Americans' handling of Hispanic settlers in Texas.[11]

"Political Zionism", Baruch Kimmerling asserted, "emerged and consolidated on the threshold of the colonial period in Europe, when the right of Europeans to settle in every non-European country was taken for granted".[12] It does not take an expert on colonial history to know that the colonial era in European history had begun much earlier, in the sixteenth century. Zionism emerged toward the end of that era and not on its threshold, and West European colonialism had been preceded by other colonialisms – Arab, Turkish and Russian – that no one dare mention in our politically correct academe.

Kimmerling's comparison of the transactions of Louisiana and Alaska to the land purchases of the JNF is peculiar. Many problems would have been saved or solved if the Zionist movement had the means to buy the Land of Israel in one fell swoop as the United States did in the nineteenth century, or had Britain and other powers really supported Zionism in the manner that he and other Post-Zionists claim. Precisely the slow pace of the Zionist enterprise's development, because of the need to purchase the land and the scarcity of resources, as well as the obstacles put in Zionism's way by Britain as a Mandatory Power, testify to the non-colonial character of the movement.

For Shlomo Sand, the comparison with the United States is redundant. In his view, Zionism is an occupying force in the manner of the Spanish *Conquistadores* in Latin America.[13] Ilan Pappé equates Zionism to Missionary activities in West Africa and to previous attempts by Christians to settle in Palestine and expel the Arabs from the country (i.e. the Crusades). He finds an "astonishing similarity" between the hidden wishes of Henri Gerren, the traveller and explorer of nineteenth century Palestine, and those of the Zionist leader Menachem Ussishkin, the chairman of the JNF: Gerren strove to revive the Crusaders' Kingdom of Jerusalem and Ussishkin aspired to resuscitate the kingdom of David and Solomon (so both of them were monarchists).

Referring to odd and unverifiable sources, Pappé further asserts that Zionist settlement in the Land of Israel strove from the beginning to dispossess the Arabs. He brings a dubious quotation of the Rabbi of Memel (Klaipeda, then a free German town in Lithuania), a "well known" Zionist leader by the name of Itzhak Rielf, who, according to Pappé, called in 1883 (14 years before the establishment of the Zionist organisation!) to expel the Arabs from the country. His second authority is Ussishkin's alleged ambition to purchase the bulk of the land of Palestine. The most "convincing" is his third authority: the Palestinian historian Nur Massalha, who collected quotations that in his view testify to a Zionist intention to dispossess and expel the Palestinian Arabs.[14]

The founders of the Israeli journal *Teoria Ubikoret* [*Theory and Criticism*], Yehuda Shenhav and Hanan Chever, opened an article on post-colonialism with a description of the battle in Tantura on 22 May 1948. They drew a direct line from that battle to the Israeli control of the territories and thence

to the American reaction to the events of 11 September 2001: "The atonement of thousands of innocent people in New York was replaced with the
atonement of thousands of helpless Afghans that were killed or became
homeless refugees". The common basis that Shenhav and Chever proposed
for the battle in 1948, Israel's rule of Judea and Samaria since 1967 and the
war in Afghanistan in 2002 is the concept of 'colonialism' – a mixture of the
past's sins and the present's injustices.[15]

Another, more serious endeavour to explain the formula that Zionism
equals colonialism was done by Amnon Raz-Krakotzkin in his unpublished
PhD dissertation. His study deals with Zionist historiography of the middle
ages and its contribution to Zionist colonialism through the negation of the
Diaspora. In fact, he blamed Israeli historians of complicity in a colonialist
cabal to eliminate the Arabs, and even conceal non-Zionist Jews from the
history of the Land of Israel.

Raz-Krakotzkin criticised two elements in the Zionist approach to the
nexus between the Jewish People and the Land of Israel: Benzion Dinur's
emphasis on the continuity of Jewish presence in the country; and the
romantic approach of part of the pioneers of the first and second waves of
immigration that regarded the Arabs as the descendants of the ancient
Hebrews of the first and second commonwealth period and a model for imi-
tation. Both approaches, he maintained, "did not leave room for the Arabs
and their consciousness. Their value was conditioned by the Zionist consciousness". In his view, this was the point of departure for the ignorance,
repression and total denial of the Arabs' claim for national rights in the
country.[16]

Raz-Krakotzkin argued that every historiographic project in the land of
Israel after the Balfour Declaration and World War One aimed to distance
the Arabs from the history of the land and portray it as a Jewish country. The
emphasis on the continuity of Jewish presence in the country and the Jews'
affiliation to the Land of Israel should have served the Jewish claim for rights
on and *in* the country. He asserted that an evident linkage existed between
Zionist historical writing and diplomatic activity. The historical claims, he
contended, were the foundation of the demand that Britain adopts an exceptional policy in Palestine that would disregard the national aspirations of the
native population and deny their right for a state or other political entity of
their own.

This statement, however, should have referred to evidence showing that the
British statesmen and officials read, or were supposed to read these Zionist
historical writings and were affected by them. The lack of such evidence is
one of Raz-Krakotzkin's principal flaws. It is highly doubtful whether any
British statesman and official ever read the writings to which Raz-Krakotzkin
referred. Apart from Sokolow's book on the history of Zionism from the
seventeenth century to the Balfour Declaration, and two volumes named
Palestine that were published by the ESCO foundation in the late 1940s, history books of Zionist writers were not written in English or translated into it.

Certainly, they were not on Lord Balfour's desk when he wrote to PM Lloyd George after the opening of the Peace Conference in Versailles in 1919:

> In the case of Palestine, we refuse, deliberately and justly, to accept the principle of self-determination... The justification of our policy is that we regard Palestine as absolutely exceptional. In our view the Jewish question outside Palestine has worldwide significance, and the Jews have a right to a home in their ancient country, provided this home will be granted to them without dispossessing or repressing the present inhabitants.[17]

British statesmen like Balfour and Lloyd George who accepted the Jews' affiliation to Palestine might have been influenced by Hebraist Christian scholarship but not by Zionist historiography.[18]

The Zionist political demands did stem from Jewish history, but not from Zionist historiography. Zionist diplomacy preceded Zionist historical writing by a generation at least, and influenced historians rather than was affected by them. Zionist historical writing did not aim "to convince the British" as Raz-Krakotzkin puts it. Dinur did not write English and was not translated into English, and when the fate of Palestine was decided in the Peace Conference in the wake of World War One he still lived in Russia, until his immigration in 1921.

In the eyes of Raz-Krakotzkin, the Hebrew University in Jerusalem symbolised Zionist Colonialism. Since its establishment, he argues, it was a colonialist university. It was not established for the indigenous population but for immigrants (this is true also for Harvard and all other IV League universities in the USA), and prevented the establishment of universities for the natives. Hence, he accused the University of being "a political weapon that denied education to the majority of the populace".[19]

Raz-Krakotzkin did not mean the graduates of Jewish high schools in the country that until the Second World War usually went abroad for higher education, but the local Arabs. However, the Palestinian Arab population was barely in the initial stages of elementary education. In 1925, the year of the Hebrew University's opening, Palestine had 49 Arab elementary and high schools in towns (29 for boys and 20 for girls) and 265 rural schools (all elementary, of which only 11 were for girls). They were attended by 16,146 boys and 3,591 girls, out of population of about 750,000. Most pupils attended school for four or five years only.

Twenty years later, in 1945, the total number of Arab pupils rose to 71,468, but only 232 studied in the 11th and 12th classes. Arab higher education had only 58 students.[20] In the mandate period, the Arab population that Raz-Krakotzkin complains about its academic discrimination did not need a university but elementary schools and teachers, and the British mandate developed the Arab education system considerably, as the figures show. The argument that the establishment of the Hebrew University prevented education from the Arabs is simply ridiculous if not stupid.

The Hebrew University also reminded UCLA professor David Myers of colonialism, but for a different reason. He compared the involvement of Weizmann and the Zionist organisation in the university's affairs with the relations between the patrons in the United States and the faculty and students of the American University of Beirut.[21] However, unlike the University of Beirut, the Hebrew University's mission was not bringing the light and inspiration of the West to the natives of the 'Old *Yishuv*' in Palestine, but to attract to Jerusalem Jewish scholars and students from the Diaspora and establish a world centre of Jewish scholarship.

Zionism is not colonialist

So far, I have presented the arguments for identifying Zionism with colonialism. What about the counter-arguments? Put simply, the implementation of Zionism required immigration and colonisation – just as the Spanish settled in South America, or the Pilgrims and others in North America, followed by a long line of Europeans who settled in North and South America, India and South-East Asia, Central Asia and Siberia, Australia, New Zealand and Africa. Like them Zionism, too, was assisted for a while by an imperialist power, Britain, though the reasons for British advocacy of Zionism were more complex and varied than pure imperialism. Here the similarity ends, and the comparison with colonialism fails to adequately explain the Zionist phenomenon. Zionism is indeed a colonizing enterprise, but it is not colonialist.

The founding father of Israeli sociology, Samuel Noach Eisenstadt, defined Zionism "a modern revolutionary settlers' society", resembling the Puritans in North America in the seventeenth century. Both movements, he argued, were ideological and revolutionary and later developed from agricultural to industrial societies having dynamic and modern economies. He explained this development as stemming from later waves of immigrants that differed from the idealist founders. In addition, he said, both societies succeeded in shaping democratic forms of government.[22]

Comparing two societies so different in scope and resources, over a time gap of 300 years, is a bold endeavour, but it blurs significant dissimilarities between the compared entities. Unlike emigration to America, ideological immigration to the Land of Israel did not end with the Second or third waves of *Aliyah*. Ideological and pioneering elements arrived in later waves of immigration and are still arriving. Zionist ideology emanated from a return to the past, while America promised to immigrants mainly a future. The Middle East was not a new world, but the cradle of the old one, burdened with all sorts of historical legacies and tensions: ethnic, religious, social, tribal and others. America offered pluralism, while Zionism strove to return the Jewish People to normality. The settlers in America annihilated the natives and brought their labourers/slaves from Africa. Excluding the first *Aliyah*, the Zionist pioneers competed in the labour market with the natives for manual jobs.

Derek Penslar has found several similarities as well as significant differences between the Zionist movement and national movements in India and South East Asia. David Myers also tried comparisons of this type. I doubt, however, if a comparison of national movements in Bengal or Thailand with Zionism is appropriate. In India and South East Asia two separate societies, the native and the Colonial-European, faced each other. By contrast, the European Jews were part of Europe even in the era of traditional society. They were one corporation among others in a corporative society. Although there may be some vague resemblance, unlike the national movements of the Third World Zionism did not emerge out of conflict with colonialism. The Jews' uniqueness as a non-territorial nation notwithstanding, their national development was part and parcel of the patriotic awakening that Europe underwent in the nineteenth century.[23]

Unlike the Spanish *conquistadores* and their successors, Jewish immigrants to the Land of Israel did not arrive in the country armed to their teeth, and did not strive to take it by force from the native population. The pioneer immigrants conceived the normalisation of Jewish life in terms of return to manual labour, not in exercising military power. Until the First World War, the idea of building a Jewish military force for achieving national and political aims interested a few visionaries and no more. Even at the end of that war volunteering into the Jewish battalions of the British army was controversial among young pioneers in Palestine.[24]

Taking a linguistic approach, until 1948 the Hebrew word *kibbush* (occupation, conquest) referred mainly to taming the wilderness and mastering manual labour and the arts of grazing; in its most militant form, it referred to guarding Jewish settlements. The term related mainly to competition for guard jobs against both Arabs and Jews.

Until the establishment of the *Haganah* Field Companies (the '*POSH*') in 1937, terms such as *gdud* (battalion) or *plugah* (company) referred to labour units, not to military ones. The armed Jewish force in the country emerged late, in response to attacks and threats on the part of the local Arabs and raids from the neighbouring countries. The key word in the process of building it up was 'defence'. As Anita Shapira wrote in *Land and Power*, the ethos of using force was defensive – at least until the Palestinian rebellion of 1936–1939.[25]

Since that rebellion, 'defence' was not perceived necessarily in tactical terms. Tactically, the *Yishuv*'s youth became aggressive, yet the use of the word 'defence' continued to symbolise a broader perception of the Zionist enterprise as constantly threatened by its Arab surroundings and, like in World War Two, also by other powers. The word implied that the *Yishuv* was the responding side and not the initiator of the threats; even if and when tactically it took the initiative, unleashed the first strike or shot the first bullet.

Unlike European settler societies in the former British dominions, to which the post-Zionists compare Zionism when they define it 'national colonialism' or 'colonialism that develops into territorial nationalism', Zionism voluntarily undertook restrictions compatible with democratic principles of self-determination. It strove to achieve a demographic majority in the Land of Israel before taking political control of the country. Furthermore, the Zionists regarded Jewish majority as a pre-condition for Jewish sovereignty. They believed that this condition was attainable through immigration, not by expulsion or annihilation in the manner of the Europeans' attitude to the Native Americans or the Aborigines.

In the 1930s, most Zionist leaders realised that attaining a majority in the whole of the country was questionable in view of Arab opposition and British fluctuation under Arab pressure. In view of the deteriorating condition of millions of Jews in Central and Eastern Europe, the Zionist Congress consented in the summer of 1937 to the partitioning of the country. Actually, partition was a Zionist idea, suggested by Weizmann primarily to preserve the Jewish majority idea and the Jewish character at least in part of the country. Maintaining the Jewish majority and character demanded, however, to combine partition with an exchange of populations or, so called, Transfer. Originally, this was not a Zionist idea, but the suggestion of the Royal Commission that recommended partition.

Economic theories of colonialism and sociological theories of migration movements are also inadequate when applied to the Zionist experience. Palestine differed from typical countries of colonialist emigration and settlement primarily because it was an underdeveloped and poor country. Usually, Europeans migrated to countries rich in natural resources and devoid of manpower to exploit their wealth. By contrast, Palestine of the nineteenth or early twentieth century was too poor to provide for its indigenous population. Before World War I, natives of Palestine – Jews and Arabs, Christians and Muslims, members of the Old *Yishuv* and second generation of the First Aliyah – emigrated to seek their future in America and Australia. Prominent examples are Edward Sa'id's father, or the Margolin family from the colony of Rechovot, whose son migrated to Australia and returned to Palestine in World War One as the commanding officer of a Jewish battalion of Royal Fusiliers.

Zionist ideology and zeal, as well as the import of Jewish private and public/national capital compensated for the lack of natural resources and accelerated the modernisation of the backward country. These two factors – ideology (except for a missionary one) and the import of capital – were totally absent in other colonial movements. Imperialist powers generally exploited colonies for the benefit of the mother country and did not invest beyond what was necessary for that exploitation. By contrast, the flow of Jewish capital to Palestine went one way. Neither Britain nor Jews abroad derived economic gains from the country. The purpose of the capital import was primarily to expand the country's absorptive capacity and increase the number of Jewish immigrants.

A central argument of those who claim that Zionism is colonialism concerns the taking over of Palestine's lands and the dispossession of the Arab tenants. The argument barely stands a critical test. Until 1948, the Zionists did not conquer but – unparalleled among colonial movements – bought land. Kimmerling shows how between 1910 and 1944 the prices of land multiplied by 52.5%. According to his data, in 1910 the price of agricultural land in Palestine was twice its average price in the United States, while in 1944 the proportion was 23:1. Between 1936 and 1944 land prices rose three times more than the cost of living.[26]

Under the circumstances, almost no Arab landowner could resist the temptation to sell land to the Jews. Palestinian and some post-Zionist Israeli scholars put the blame for the removal of the tenant farmers on foreign Arab landowners. They conceal the role of the resident land-owning elite families, those who led the Palestinian national movement. The list of sellers of land included members of all the Arab prominent clans in the country.[27]

Land trade has always been full of deceit and unfit transactions on all sides. However, they cannot alter the fact that one of the Palestinians' biggest failures was their failure to stop land sales, despite the violent steps they took and the numerous assassinations of land sellers, brokers and dealers throughout the twentieth century, before and after Jewish statehood. Upon statehood, the circumstances changed. State land was requisitioned and private lands were expropriated. But the state compensated private owners, either with money or alternative tracts, and individuals – local Arabs and land-owning refugees – continued to sell their holdings.

By contrast to other countries of colonialist emigration and settlement, the Jewish immigrants did not wish to integrate into the existing, mainly Arab economy, nor did they try to take it over. They laid the foundations for a new and separate economy, without the relations of mastery and dependence that usually characterised colonial societies.[28]

During the Mandate and in the early years of statehood, Jewish immigrants competed with native Arabs and Arab immigrants from the adjacent countries in the urban and rural, public and private manual labour markets – as agricultural labourers, in the building industry, as stonecutters, road builders, porters and stevedores.[29] *Kibbush Ha'avoda* [conquest of labour] had ideological, economic, social and political motivations, but such competition between white settlers and natives was inconceivable in colonial countries.

A cultural appraisal, too, excludes Zionism from the colonialist paradigm. Contrary to the colonialist stereotype, in most cases Jews who settled in the Land of Israel severed their ties with their countries of origin and their cultural past, at least in the first generation. Contrary to the East European national movements that cultivated popular vernaculars as a counter-weight to the imperial languages (German and Russian), Zionism abandoned the Jewish vernacular, the Yiddish, and favoured the return to the ancient, pre-exilic Hebrew. On the basis of Hebrew, it developed a culture that spread to all spheres of life, from the kindergarten to the academe, from technology to the arts and from slang to poetry. The revival of Hebrew began in Eastern Europe and preceded Zionism, but the Zionist movement and the *Yishuv* (the Jewish community in Palestine) adopted and developed it to its full extent. In the Land of Israel, Hebrew became the national language, spoken by all.[30]

Colonialist emigrants all over the world sought either a lucrative future or to escape a dreary present. Jewish immigrants to the Land of Israel also shared these motives, but their primary and unique aspiration, which distinguished them from all other colonialist movements, was to revive an ancient heritage.

The issue is complex, but its complexity by no means makes Zionism a colonialist movement or Israel a colonialist state, but rather the contrary. The false historical arguments have been raised primarily to influence the disputes of the present. From the beginning of the conflict, the Palestinian narrative has adopted the paradigm of a national liberation movement (Palestinian) struggling against a colonialist power (Zionism). Long after almost all other national-liberation movements have achieved their goals and thrown off colonialism, the Palestinians – who at least since 1967 have enjoyed far greater international support than any other anti-colonialist movement – are still more or less in the same place, if not worse.

This fact alone should have led the Palestinians and their sympathisers to re-examine their traditional paradigm. Instead, by cultivating the Zionist-colonialist allegation, they continue to avoid self-criticism and re-examination, and stick to the road that apparently leads nowhere.

Notes

1 Shlomo Sand, *The Invention of the Jewish People*, London: Verso, 2009
2 Maxim Rodinson, Israel, *fait colonial*, in Claude Lanzman (ed.), *Le Conflit Israel-Arabe, Les Temps Moderne*, June 1967.
3 Elia T. Zureik, *The Palestinians in Israel: A Study in Internal Colonialism*, London: Routledge, 1979; Uri Ram, The colonisation perspective in Israeli sociology, pp. 83–96, and Gershon Shafir, Zionism and colonialism: A comparative approach, pp. 55–80, both in Ilan Pappé (ed.), *The Israel/Palestine Question*, London/New York: Psychology Press, 1999,
4 Rashid Khalidi, *Palestinian Identity*, New York: Columbia University Press, 1997, pp. 96–111.
5 Baruch Kimmerling and Joel S. Migdal, *Palestinians: The Making of a People*. New York: Free Press, 1993.
6 Baruch Kimmerling, *Zionism and Territory: The Socioterritorial Dimensions of Zionist Politics*, Berkeley: University of California Press, 1983, pp. 14–15.
7 Matityahu Minz, Haumah Hayehudit – Hamtzaah Zionit? Beshuley Pulmos Hahistorionim [The Jewish nation – a Zionist invention? In the margins of the historians' controversy], in Pinchas Genossar and Avi Bareli (eds), *Zionut – Pulmos Ben Zmanenu* [Zionism – a contemporary controversy], Sde Boker, 1996, pp. 31–5.
8 Arie Bober (ed.), *The Other Israel: The Radical Case against Zionism*, New York: Doubleday Anchor, 1972.

9 Aharon Cohen, *Israel Veha'olam Ha'arvi* [Israel and the Arab World], Merchavia: Sifriyat Po'alim, 1964; Israel Ber, *Bitchon Israel: Etmol, Hayom Umachar [Israel's Security: Yesterday, Today and Tomorrow]*, Tel Aviv: Amikam, 1966; Uri Avneri, *Milchemet Hayom Hashvi'i* [The war of the seventh day], Tel Aviv: Daf Chadash, 1969.

10 Simha Flapan, *Zionism and the Palestinians*, London: Croom Helm, 1979; Idem, *The Birth of Israel: Myth and Realities*, London: 1987; Noam Chomski, *The Fateful Triangle: The United States, Israel and the Palestinians*, Boston: South End Press, 1983; Michael Palumbo, *The Palestinian Catastrophe: The 1948 Expulsion of a People from Their Homeland*, London: Quartet Books, 1987; Benjamin Beit-Hallahmi, *Original Sins: Reflections on the History of Zionism and Israel*, London: Pluto Press, 1992.

11 Baruch Kimmerling, *Zionism and Territory*; Yehuda Shenhav and Hanan Chever, Hamabat Hapostcoloniali [The Post-Colonial outlook], *Teoria Ubikoret* 20, Spring 2002, pp. 9–22; Ilan Pappé, Hazionut Kecolonialism – Mabat Hashvaati Al Colonialism Mahul BeAsia UbeAfrica [Zionism as colonialism: A comparative look on diluted colonialism in Asia and Africa], in Weitz (ed.), *Ben Hazon Lerevizia [Between Vision to Revision]*, pp. 345–65; Uri Ram, The Colonization Perspective, pp. 55–80; Gershon Shafir, Zionism and Colonialism, supra, pp. 83–96.

12 Baruch Kimmerling, Academic history caught in the crossfire: The case of Israeli-Jewish historiography, *History and Memory* 7/1, 1995, p. 41.

13 Shlomo Sand, Hapost-Zioni Kesochen Zikaron Lo Murshe [The Post-Zionist as an unlicensed agent of memory], *Alpayim* [2000], 24, 2000, p. 176.

14 Ilan Pappé, Hazionut KeColonialism, pp. 345–65.

15 Shenhav and Chever, Hamabat Hapostcoloniali, pp. 9–10.

16 Raz Krakotzkin, *Yitzuga HaLeumi Shel HaGalut: HaHistoriografia HaZionit VeYehudei Yemei HaBeinayim [The national representation of the Exile: Zionist Historiography and the Medieval Jews]*, unpublished PhD dissertation, Tel Aviv: 1996, p. 305.

17 Balfour to Lloyd George, 19 February 1919, FO 371/4179, British Archives (NA).

18 Raz-Krakotzkin, supra, pp. 322–3.

19 Ibid., pp. xii and 324–6.

20 The data is taken from A.L. Tibawi, *Arab Education in Mandatory Palestine*, London: Luzac & Company, 1956, pp. 45, 49.

21 David Myers, Between diaspora and Zion: History, memory and the Jerusalem scholars, in David Myers and David Ruderman (eds), *The Jewish Past Revisited*, New Haven: Yale University Press 1998, pp. 94–5.

22 Shmuel Noach Eisenstadt, Hamaavak 'Al Simley Hazehut Hacolectivit Ve'al Gvuloteiha Bachevra Haisraelit Habeter-Mahapchanit [The struggle for the symbols of collective identity in the post-revolutionary Israeli society], in Genossar and Bareli (eds), *Zionut: Pulmos*, pp. 1–5.

23 Derek Penslar, Zionism, Colonialism and Post-colonialism, *The Journal of Israeli History* 20, 2/3, Autumn 2001, pp. 84–120.

24 Yigal Elam, *Hagdudim Ha'ivriyim [The Jewish Battalions]*, Tel Aviv: Ma'arachot, 1973.

25 Anita Shapira, *Land and Power: The Zionist Resort to Force, 1881–1948*, Oxford: Oxford University Press, 1992.

26 Kimmerling, *Zionism and Territory*, p. 11.

27 An undated list (probably from 1944 or 1945) of more than 50 Palestinian notables who sold land to Jews, including the sellers' offices and the location of the sold lots, file S 25/3472, Central Zionist Archives (CZA),.

28 Anita Shapira, Hazionut Vehakoach – Ethos Umetziut [Zionism and force – ethos and reality], in Anita Shapira, *Hahalichah 'Al Kav Haofek* [Walking on the horizon], Tel Aviv: Am Oved, 1988, p. 37.

29 Anita Shapira, *Hama'avak Hanichzav – Avoda Ivrit, 1929–1939*, [*The unrequited struggle – Hebrew labour, 1929–1939*], Tel Aviv: 1977. For an opposing approach to the idea of "conquering" labour and its significance, cf. Baruch Kimmerling, *Zionism and Economy*, Cambridge, MA:, Schenkman,1983, pp. 47–56.
30 Ron Kuzar, *Hebrew and Zionism: A Discourse Analytic Cultural Study*, New York: Hawthorne, 2001.

14 Chaim Weizmann

From the Balfour Declaration to the establishment of the state of Israel.

Jehuda Reinharz and Motti Golani[1]

In Zionism's brief history, no figure did more than Chaim Weizmann for the establishment of the state of Israel.

If Jews, or at least Zionists and Israelis, remember Weizmann at all, it is as Israel's first president, a post he served in briefly, from 1949 to 1952. The better versed will recall his political haplessness in that capacity, imposed on him by Ben-Gurion, the country's first prime minister. They might also recall a second, earlier episode in Weizmann's life, his role in obtaining the Balfour Declaration – but nothing between that and his presidency. The well informed might also note that Weizmann was named president only after Albert Einstein turned down the job.

On October 31, 1917, the British government authorised Foreign Secretary Arthur James Balfour to send a letter to Lord Lionel Walter Rothschild, the most prominent name in British Zionism at the time. The letter stated that "His Majesty's government view with favor the establishment in Palestine of a national home for the Jewish people." Milner and Amery prepared the final draft of the Declaration and Balfour's office approved it. The foreign secretary signed it on 2 November. It was one more piece of paper, not of central importance, produced by the activist cabinet of Prime Minister David Lloyd George, which had as its major task ensuring that the outcome of the Great War, which was not going well at the time, would not be a total catastrophe for Britain. The letter aroused great enthusiasm among Zionists and Jews.

Was it already then, in November 1917, the famous declaration that some see as the basis for the establishment of the state of Israel just 30 years later, and which others see as the original sin that engendered the Jewish-Arab conflict? What actually happened was, as usual, more complicated. To paraphrase Simone de Beauvoir, the letter signed by Balfour was not born as the Balfour Declaration; it was made the Balfour Declaration. Why does Weizmann occupy such a small position in collective memory, despite the fact that, by the end of 1917, he had become the prime mover who transformed that piece of paper into a document of exceptional historical importance?

Famously, the Balfour Declaration is intimately connected to Weizmann's discovery of a biological process for producing acetone, a substance essential to the British war effort. According to legend, Weizmann turned the patent over to the British government, refusing any payment, a story enshrined in a brief dramatic fragment authored by the playwright George Bernard Shaw, *Arthur and the Acetone*. In the playlet, an astonished Arthur Balfour asks Weizmann, "Since you want none of the things that everybody wants, what the devil do you want?" "I want Jerusalem", Weizmann says. In his own not at all humble memoirs Weizmann would later respond to a similar claim in Lloyd George's war memoirs – "history does not deal in Aladdin's lamps".[2] It was an interesting response by a man who, when he wrote his autobiography in 1947, sought to take full credit for achieving the declaration.

Until 1917, Weizmann was an unknown scientific and political journeyman, learning his trade and perfecting his skills. Born in 1874 into a large family, Weizmann grew up in the Pale of Settlement of Czarist Russia. His supportive parents provided him with schooling that prepared him to set out, not yet nineteen years old, for the West. Weizmann was part of a huge wave of immigration from east to west at the end of the nineteenth century, a wave that included Jews, among them young people who sought 'globalisation'. That is, they sought secular, in particular scientific knowledge that would enable them to succeed in the world that stretched westward from Germany. Some of this modern disengagement from the conservative world of tradition and religion emerged from the encounter with the national idea. The young Weizmann devoted himself to Zionism and chemistry, in that order. Chemistry promised a good livelihood; in time it would also prove itself effective in enabling him to pursue his real passion, Zionist politics. Weizmann is perhaps the most notable exemplar of that small group of people who were prepared to sacrifice family, health, and academic career for the Zionist cause.

In Germany and then in Switzerland during the years 1893–1904, Weizmann emerged as a gifted chemical researcher and a lecturer with a winning personality. His great scientific opportunity came when, in 1904, he was named to the faculty of the University of Manchester. He was drawn in particular to the area that would later come to be called applied chemistry. His awareness of the need to make both economic and political capital out of his scientific work, which collective memory has much amplified, was his means of advancing his political agenda.

In any case, the juxtaposition of the University of Manchester and Weizmann's inclination to commercialise his discoveries (something hardly looked down on in today's academy), did not at the time work in his favour. In 1914–15 Weizmann parted ways, painfully, with the university. He was not dismissed, but he was not promoted to the rank of Professor as he believed he deserved. But there was also an attractive force that pressed him to end the academic phase of his life – Zionist politics, which by chance crossed his academic path just at that time his ability to promote the process he had discovered.

Weizmann's astuteness in politics and statecraft led him to promote the Zionist cause in the halls of government even as he pursued his scientific work. His hard, even Sisyphean labours in the political arena expanded as he came into contact with British leaders from the time he arrived in Britain in 1904, when he was a member of the second or even third rank of the Zionist leadership. He was a diligent student in all areas, in particular in politics. As a chemist, he was good, but there were better chemists than he. But he had few, if any, peers among contemporary Zionist activists when it came to his political talents, talents that have never been properly appreciated. For example, he learned from the Uganda controversy a central lesson that many of his generation did not grasp – one did not have to support the African initiative to realise that, for the first time ever, the most important European empire of the time, Britain, was treating the Zionist movement as a political interlocutor that represented the Jewish people as a whole.

Excited by this discovery, he determined to turn his life on the fringes of Zionist action from disadvantage to a surprising advantage. His political activity took place outside the university. He attended receptions and parties and talked with local and national leaders, journalists, businessmen, industrialists, intellectuals, and young activists. Soon he gained an invaluable patron in the person of the editor of the *Manchester Guardian*, C.P. Scott. In 1904, he met Balfour, then prime minister. And no less important, he gathered around him a group of young Jewish activists who knew the territory well. They understood, as he did, that business and British political connection were essential for the promotion of Zionism. Among these young friends were Simon Marks, Israel Sieff, Harry Sacher, and Julius Simon, all of who provided vital support in the two decades that followed. In short, Weizmann's presentation of the acetone process to the relevant officials in the Ministry of Munitions, Admiralty, and War Office, and the industrialisation of the process, were direct outgrowths of his contacts with high British officials.

Weizmann's instincts made him expert in the ins and outs of British politics and the important contours of the debates at the top levels of British government and, in particular, in the cabinet. His penchant for elitism and his ability to speak with his British interlocutors at eye level (in both senses of the word – Weizmann was six feet tall) made him an especially influential advocate. He did not entreat, did not ask to be pitied, did not use money as a lure. He internalised the mores of the society he lived in – less ideology, more political pragmatism, and a sharp awareness of the fine points of class distinction. For that reason, and because he was a Jew, not an Englishman, Scotsman, Welshman, or Irishman, he quickly became the consummate Briton.

Until late in 1917 Weizmann did not have a major achievement, neither scientific nor political, to his name. His academic career had, as noted, come to an end well before what should have been its high point. In the Zionist movement, Weizmann was situated far from the centre of Zionist activity, and he did not hold any significant Zionist post. True, in the summer of 1917 he was easily elected to head the English Zionist Federation, a position which provided him with a formal status he could use in his contacts with the government. He contributed to the British success, in June and July 1917, in preventing a separate peace agreement between the United States and the Turks and the latter's exit from the war. Weizmann was sent by the British government to meet with Henry Morgenthau Sr., a Jew who had been the American ambassador to Istanbul. Morgenthau was on his way to discuss the possibility of a separate American-Turkish armistice. Their meeting, and others with important figures, put an end to his mission before Morgenthau even reached his destination. The acetone process was an important contribution to the field of chemistry, but it would be difficult to argue that it was really critical in determining the manner in which Britain emerged from the war. The critical role it has been assigned in historical memory lacks proper historical proportion.

Weizmann played a role, certainly central from the Zionist point of view, in the genesis of the letter that later came to be called the Balfour Declaration. He volunteered for every mission to help the war effort, whether diplomatic or practical scientific. Weizmann understood two things – that it was important to think in terms of the British war effort, and that the neutralist policy of the World Zionist Organization was a dangerous one. With regard to the former, Weizmann studied the disagreement between those who advocated a separate armistice that would maintain the Ottoman Empire in exchange for peace on British terms and those who favoured conquering the territory of the Empire before the war ended. Weizmann used the little influence he had to push for the second option. A compact between Britain and Zionism, as well as between Britain and the Arabs of the Middle East, would certainly bolster the advocates of Britain becoming the imperial power in the region instead of the Turks. And Weizmann refused to accept the fact that the Zionist Executive had almost pathetically gone into self-imposed exile in Denmark so as not to take sides in a war in which Jews were killing other Jews in the mud on the European front. He maintained that the Zionists should come down on Britain's side.

Weizmann exploited Balfour's letter to the full. There is no other way of understanding his dazzling rise in the Zionist firmament and his ongoing promotion of the Zionist cause in Britain. But Balfour's letter had a dramatic influence on Weizmann's biography more because of what followed it than what led up to it. His utter identification with the Zionist project and his brilliant use of Balfour's letter, set him on the course toward historic success and also failure, from 1918 to 1948. It was no longer solely his own personal story.

To a large extent it was Weizmann who led the historical process that was so critical for Britain and even more so for Zionism, which principally involved the way in which Balfour's letter metamorphosed into a long-term binding political commitment. He understood that for the paper on which Balfour's letter was written to be worth something, action had to be taken. So he acted.

Weizmann was a convinced British imperialist for a good reason. He wanted to prove to the British that the Zionists were the most significant force on the eastern shore of the Mediterranean. Before he became part of the Zionist establishment, he persuaded Prime Minister Lloyd George to place him at the head of a Zionist Jewish delegation that would inform General Allenby's expeditionary force, which was then advancing northward to Damascus, about the Balfour Declaration, which was unknown to the supreme headquarters or those reporting to it.

Weizmann did three things. First, he repeatedly used the binding term 'declaration' when referring to the letter. Second, he claimed that the genesis of the Declaration lay in Britain's own interests. Third, he maintained that, as a British Jewish Zionist, he was the most qualified person to inculcate the Declaration into the minds of the British forces in Palestine. None of these were givens. Furthermore, within just a few months, between March and September 1918, Weizmann turned his delegation, which came to be known as the Zionist Commission, into the liaison between the British military government and the territory's Jewish population, and into a para-executive body that, in its various incarnations over the three (only three!) decades that followed, became the Zionist Political Department, the Zionist Executive in Palestine, the Jewish Agency Executive, the People's Administration, Provisional Government, and finally Israel's permanent government, in 1949.

By November 1918, the Balfour Declaration had become the operative British document regarding the conduct of British policy in the territory defined in 1922 as Palestine, after the separation of Transjordan into a separate entity. Weizmann astutely assented at the time to a British commitment to the Palestinian Arab cause, in exchange for the inclusion of the Balfour Declaration, verbatim, in the Mandate instrument ratified in July 1922 by the British Parliament and then by the League of Nations Council, which held formal sovereignty over Palestine.

Weizmann harnessed the momentum produced by the Declaration to tighten the British-Zionist connection and to fortify his own political standing within the Zionist movement. Despite coming from outside the international Zionist establishment, in July 1920 he was elected, ostensibly unexpectedly, as president of the World Zionist Organization. In 1921 he overcame the only real rival to his standing in the Zionist arena when he defeated Justice Louis Brandeis at that year's Zionist Organization of America convention in Cleveland.

There was a clear and present danger that a government in which the Declaration's sponsors, Prime Minister Lloyd George, Secretary of State for War Alfred Milner (who with Leo Amery had drafted the final draft of the Declaration), and Foreign Secretary Balfour himself would not consider itself bound by the statement issued in November 1917. Weizmann understood that it was not sufficient to have a British Zionist and a Jew, Sir Herbert Samuel, named to the post of high commissioner in Palestine. A high commissioner could not act on his own. The question was who would head the Colonial Office which, in 1921, assumed responsibility for Palestine from the Foreign Office. But even a sympathetic colonial secretary like Winston Churchill was insufficient. Weizmann had to ensure that the next prime minister would be committed to the Declaration, and no less importantly that the cabinet, parliament, and public opinion be favourable.

In 1922 it looked to many in Britain as if 'Chaim the Great' was pulling the strings of British policy in the Middle East and Palestine.[3] That was an exaggeration, of course. In June 1921 Weizmann returned from a long visit to the United States. It seemed to him that the British government was not doing all it could to live up to the Balfour Declaration's spirit. He asked Balfour, who was still foreign secretary, to invite the British political leadership to a private meeting. The colonial secretary and the prime minister attended, as did Lord Hankey, secretary to the Cabinet. Weizmann stood up and reprimanded them. None rose to put him in his place.[4] After the meeting, Weizmann nurtured Balfour. In the spring of 1925, he brought the elderly statesman to the cornerstone-laying ceremony for the Hebrew University in Jerusalem. The event quickly turned into an emotional festival in honour of Balfour himself, full of mutual admiration.

In October 1922, it seemed to Weizmann that his worst fears had come to pass. Lloyd George's government fell. The era of the national unity Lloyd George coalition was over. The Conservatives formed the next government and ruled Britain, with the exception of one brief interval, until 1929. But although they had opposed Zionism when in Opposition, they now decided, in 1923, to adhere to the Declaration, for the sake of preserving British interests.[5]

Weizmann spent much of his time in the 1920s trying to overcome Britain's parsimony towards Palestine. Churchill, Chancellor of the Exchequer (1924–29) held up for three years the government's guarantee for a Palestine Loan – notwithstanding the fact that it was needed as much by the British Treasury as by Palestine. As one scholar noted: "the overriding reason for guaranteeing the loan was to enable Palestine to repay its 'debts' to HMG and to satisfy the Imperial need for a deep-water harbour at Haifa".[6] In 1926 when Weizmann asked the government to guarantee a Zionist Loan to help the *Yishuv* overcome an economic depression, Churchill blocked the request. Not only that, but he overrode Colonial Office objections and insisted that Palestine's current budget surplus (£1.5 million in 1926) be used to subsidise TransJordan and from 1927, the Transjordanian (later Arab) Legion. Field-Marshal Plumer, the High Commissioner for Palestine, resigned in protest.[7]

Instead, Weizmann spoke of the Mandate, the charge that Britain had received from the League of Nations. In Britain, he warned that the award of the Mandate should not be taken for granted. At the League of Nations, he spoke enthusiastically about Britain's administration of the Mandate. He quickly gained an exceptional standing in the League's Permanent Mandate

Committee. Most of the parties involved favoured maintaining the status quo. Weizmann was the prime spokesman for this position. The relative calm in Palestine reinforced this.

Weizmann warned his colleagues against harbouring illusions about there being an alternative to the Anglo-Zionist alliance. He argued that Zionist activity in Palestine was possible only because of the Declaration. It thus would have been more accurate to call it, from the 1920s onward, the Balfour-Weizmann Declaration. It was this document that made it possible for the Jewish community in Palestine (the *Yishuv*) to grow and flourish to the point that it felt comfortable grumbling incessantly about its progenitors – Weizmann, the high commissioner, and the British in general.

But then a crisis overwhelmed Weizmann, the Zionist movement, and the *Yishuv*. Arab-Jewish tensions surrounding the Temple Mount (which the Muslims called *al-Aqsa*) heightened in 1928; in August 1929 a wave of Arab violence broke out. The underlying cause was the rapid growth of the *Yishuv* in the British incubator provided by the Mandate. The British were caught unprepared by the violence but eventually put down the riots. More than a hundred Jews were killed by Arabs; a similar number of Arabs died, most of them killed by the British. It was without a doubt a heavy blow to the *Yishuv*. Even worse was the about-face in British policy that grew out of it.

The hesitancy that Britain had displayed since 1922 now bore fruit. In June 1929 a new Labor-led minority government came to power. A commission of inquiry was sent to Palestine to investigate the causes of the riots; as a result of its report, in October 1930, the government published a new White Paper. The new policy re-interpreted the immigration policy of Churchill's 1922 White Paper: in future, the principle of 'economic absorptive capacity' would be applied to *all* of Palestine's population, not just the Jews, i.e. no Jewish immigration would be permitted so long as any Arabs remained unemployed. A further, cursory inquiry by a land specialist found that due to sales of Arab lands to Jews, nearly 30% of Arab rural families were landless, and almost the same number homeless. The Arab *fellahin* (peasant farmers), who had long been exploited by Arab landowners, were now being ejected from the land they had farmed as tenants by the Jews who had purchased their property, legally. The new White Paper stipulated that further land sales to Jews would be restricted to those blocs where they already held most of the lands.[8]

The conclusions reached by the British were largely baseless. The experts who studied the situation, correctly diagnosed the outcome but failed to properly define the problem. The Arabs resented the opportunities the British had given to the *Yishuv*, which the Jews had effectively exploited. The solution, Weizmann contended, was to promote the welfare of the *fellahin* on the personal and national levels, without retreating from the idea of a Jewish national home in the spirit of the Balfour Declaration.

Weizmann saw the either/or approach of Passfield and his cohort as catastrophic. You are mistaken, he angrily informed Prime Minister Ramsay

MacDonald. Passfield, he said, did not understand what he was talking about. You are harming the British interest and as a result the Zionist interest as well. You must immediately revoke this White Paper, he said, and immediately submitted his resignation from the presidency of the World Zionist Organization. He added that there would be implications during the prime minister's upcoming trip to the United States.[9] MacDonald appointed a new committee, headed by Foreign Secretary Arthur Henderson and including members from both the British government and the Jewish Agency, recently founded. An outside observer will find it difficult to understand the nature of this committee, in which negotiations were conducted between Weizmann's demands and the needs and constraints of the government. Henderson was sympathetic. Another central member of the commission, Malcolm MacDonald, the prime minister's son, had been swept away by Weizmann's charisma in 1929 and eagerly did his bidding.

The committee's work reached its climax in a scene that is hard to comprehend even today. On 13 February 1931, Prime Minister MacDonald took the podium in Parliament. He read into the Protocol his own personal reassurance to Weizmann that the latter had insisted on receiving in writing. Britain would not retreat from its obligations under the Mandate, and Passfield's policy was, for all intents and purposes, a dead letter.

The MacDonald Letter, as it came to be called, was a historic declaration hardly less important than the one named for Balfour. Never before or since has the British government openly announced that it was retracting a decision simply as a result of pressure from a citizen lacking any formal standing.

But this time around Weizmann did not manage to turn the MacDonald Letter into the MacDonald Declaration. The letter's timing and its context in Weizmann's life precluded that. The British Empire had suffered more blows and its government was weaker than Lloyd George's war cabinet had been. The British needed to treat the Arabs more carefully than it had done at the end of World War One. They sought to minimise the significance of MacDonald's Letter. Their attitude was that even if Britain had revoked the White Paper, it should never be forgiven. The confidence of Zionists on both sides of the Atlantic was on the rise thanks to Weizmann's successes, facing him with a more potent opposition within the movement than he had ever faced before.

In August 1929, Weizmann had established the broad Jewish Agency, composed of Zionists and non-Zionists. It was, without a doubt, one of the high points of his life. Quietly, without grand declarations, the Jewish Agency became the most effective instrument at the service of the Zionist enterprise during the 1930s and 1940s. The *Yishuv* labour movement was able to make good use of the Jewish Agency in the 1930s. It enabled Mapai to firmly establish its primacy in the *Yishuv*, and in the global Zionist movement as well. Weizmann had the wisdom to enable this historic encounter between Mapai and the Jewish Agency.

The MacDonald letter of 1931 enabled the Zionist enterprise to progress until 1937. It afforded the *Yishuv* another five years of free virtually unlimited immigration, during which it doubled its numbers, from 200,000 to 400,000. In the years 1932–39, the *Yishuv* expanded from 17 to 37 percent of Palestine's population. On the eve of World War Two, the *Yishuv* comprised a critical mass that could no longer be disregarded. In these years, a stable and full-fledged Jewish autonomous administration came into being, which served as the foundation for the establishment of the Jewish state a decade later.

Weizmann was the Great Enabler of the Zionist project. Without the framework provided by the British, even the *Yishuv*'s establishment of facts on the ground could not have been sustained. Few stood behind Weizmann in his balanced analysis of the objective and subjective failures (from the Zionist point of view) of the British government's Palestine policy, alongside the vital need to remain aligned with that country, because there was no alternative to the British Mandate. The Zionist arena settled accounts with Weizmann. No one cared that he had been at the head of those who argued the Zionist case to the British. It did not help him that he had been the most effective opponent of the new British policy. His achievement in securing the MacDonald Letter was of no help.

In July 1931, at the Seventeenth World Zionist Congress in Basel, Weizmann, after serving five terms as president of the World Zionist Organization, was not re-elected. An unholy coalition ousted him. Paradoxically, Weizmann collaborated with his opponents. It was now the era of mass politics, the time of the party, the time for agreements and compromises. A leader could no longer declare "you are either with me or against me". Weizmann understood democracy in a fairly primal way, without understanding its new political dimension.

Weizmann stumbled at the Congress when he declared that he no longer believed in the aim of achieving a Jewish majority in Palestine as a precondition for the establishment of a Jewish national home there. This struck at the keystone of contemporary Zionist thinking across the spectrum. Weizmann self-confidently refused to retract his statement even when his close associates demanded that he do so. When the Congress passed a resolution rejecting his statement, Weizmann took it as a vote of no confidence and resigned. Hurt and insulted, he left. Had he been less sensitive he could have held back and won re-election to the presidency, especially since his approach eventually won the day. Nahum Sokolow, close to Weizmann, was elected to replace him, and the new Zionist Executive was composed of his people and allies in the Labor movement.

When Weizmann voiced his opposition to seeking a Jewish majority in Palestine in the summer of 1931, it was not a slip of the tongue. Since the severe crisis with Britain in 1929–30, Weizmann reckoned that it was no longer possible to disregard the Palestinian Arabs, and that it would be both impossible and incorrect to rule over the Arabs. Of course, it was also unthinkable that the Arabs would rule over the Jews. The upshot of this principle of neither ruling nor being ruled was his objection to the impatience displayed by the Revisionists and their leader, Jabotinsky, who demanded shouting from the rooftops the 'ultimate goal' of Zionism: a Jewish state, here and now, in all of Palestine. It was just froth, Weizmann said, and a danger to the Zionist idea. Nevertheless, his failure was largely a tactical one. The fact that his approach was accepted by the Jewish Agency and Zionist Executives during Sokolow's tenure, from 1931 to 1935, and that this approach allowed Weizmann to formulate in the years that followed a plan based on an understanding that the Mandate, to which he remained committed, stood on a rickety foundation.

From there Weizmann naturally moved toward parity, an idea according to which, under any future political resolution, powers would be divided equally between the two peoples without regard to the proportion of Jews to Arabs in Palestine's population. He ended up endorsing partition into two independent states, one Jewish and one Arab.

Weizmann did not invent the idea of partition. But the minute he latched onto it, his standing in the Zionist movement and in Britain enabled him to take it from idea into practice. In his determination not to destroy entirely the British-Zionist fabric that the Zionists needed like air to breathe, and on the way to returning to the presidency (which would not be possible without his connection to Britain), Weizmann took much interest in the plan proposed by the senior Zionist diplomat Victor (Avigdor) Jacobson. The two agreed that the Zionist movement needed to go on a 'territorial diet' regarding its aspirations, and that it would be best off by pursuing a policy of 'national maximalism and territorial minimalism'. By that, they meant pursing the maximum national goal of an independent Jewish polity, while giving up the demand that the national home cover the entire area of Palestine. Jacobson thus proposed partitioning the country between the flesh and the bones – that is, giving the Jews the valleys and lowlands and the Arabs the central mountains, in the framework of a confederation of these two states with Lebanon, Syria, Transjordan, and Iraq, all under the protection of a British commissioner in Jerusalem.

Weizmann understood that only the British could make such a proposal. Were he to suggest it, it would be rejected not only by the Arabs, but also by the Jews. Out of office, his prestige actually grew when Hitler rose to power and Weizmann took responsibility for addressing the plight of the Jews of Germany, Austria, and Poland. His enhanced stature enabled him to further the partition idea.

The ever-active Weizmann discovered that the new crisis that began with the outbreak of the Arab rebellion in Palestine in April 1936 offered him an opportunity to promote partition. The British failed that same spring when they promoted the establishment of a Legislative Assembly, a cornerstone provision of the Mandate document, meant to pave the way for the establishment of an independent state in Palestine. Fifteen years too late, the Palestinian Arabs realised that such a body, in which they would enjoy a majority, would be to their benefit. The Zionists, who had in the past supported such a move, now refused to cooperate. In the end, Weizmann was able to induce Parliament to reject the plan on the grounds that it was inconsistent with the Mandate that Britain had received from the League of Nations. His success prompted the Palestinian Arabs to declare a general strike, which turned violent, to protest the Mandate administration's coalition with the Zionist movement.

In November 1936, the government established a Royal Commission of Inquiry into the causes of the Arab rebellion. Weizmann realised that this was the time to bring the partition idea to the front of his political efforts. Using the best of his backroom diplomatic skills, Weizmann persuaded the members of the commission, headed by Lord Peel, to issue a final report recommending the partition of Palestine. In July 1937 the British government endorsed the commission's recommendations, including the partition provision. According to the recommendations, the partitioned country would as a whole remain under British protection. The Arab state would be tied to Transjordan. Weizmann succeeded when it came to the principle of partition, but failed when it came to drawing the map. The Twentieth Zionist Congress, which convened in Zurich in the summer of 1937, accepted the idea of partition, but rejected the map proposed by the Peel Commission, under which the Negev and the western part of Jerusalem would not be included in the Jewish state. The Congress authorised Weizmann and the leaders of the Jewish Agency to continue negotiating the borders with the British government.

The Anglo-Zionist compact was not broken. True, Jabotinsky's Revisionist Party bolted the Zionist Organization when Weizmann returned to the presidency in 1935. But the rising leadership of the *Yishuv* labour movement, now the central political force in the Zionist movement, and the Jewish Agency Executive, stood by him. Weizmann could not have managed without the labour movement, and it needed him no less. Their agreement on the cardinal issues on the Zionist agenda, including the alliance with Britain, made this coalition into a force that it was difficult, if not impossible, to oppose.

The winds of war in Europe impelled the British to take rapid and brutal military action to suppress the Arab Revolt of 1936–39 that followed on the heels of the Peel Commission's partition proposal. The British were aided by the policy of restraint pursued by the *Yishuv* under Weizmann's leadership. The Arab Revolt tested British forces to the limit during the summer of 1938, but was finally put down during that winter. It is not possible to understand the outcome of the 1948 war without taking into account what happened to both sides during the years of the Arab Revolt.

But the winds of war in Europe doomed the partition plan promoted by Weizmann and Britain to failure. This time Weizmann was unable to persuade the British government not to reformulate its Palestine policy. London believed that it was vital to do so in order to guarantee the support of the Arab states during the coming war. Weizmann's admirer and student, Malcolm MacDonald, was now colonial secretary, and as such had the task of instituting a policy in the spirit of the idea that had failed in 1936 – a single state with an Arab majority and a Jewish autonomous regime that would serve as a national home. What the Zionists might have been able to stomach in the 1920s was unacceptable by this point. Furthermore, the new policy, codified in the MacDonald White Paper of May 1939, included provisions that were, for the Zionists, draconian. Especially painful was its stipulation that after five years, Arab consent would be required for the continuation of Jewish immigration beyond the scope of the quotas (75,000) established by the White Paper. The British needed the support of the Arab states and presumed, rightly, that the *Yishuv* had no alternative. Weizmann had no response to this snare, in which Britain turned against the spirit of the Balfour Declaration just as the *Yishuv*'s dependence on her – indeed, the dependence of the Jewish people as a whole – was greater than ever.[10]

Aware of Zionism's weak position, in 1939 Weizmann led an approach that was best summed up, after World War Two broke out, by his disciple, David Ben-Gurion, chairman of the Jewish Agency Executive: We will fight the White Paper as if there were no Hitler and we will fight Hitler as if there were no White Paper. As self-contradictory as it sounded, this formulation was the key to the success of Weizmann's policy during World War Two. The Zionist movement and the *Yishuv* continued to fight Britain's Palestine policy, primarily in the political theatre. But most of their efforts were directed at the little they could do to aid Britain, which until 1941 stood almost alone against Germany and its allies. In fact, the two halves of the statement were not equal. The fight against the White Paper necessarily took second place to support for Britain. Most of the effort was thus expended in that direction.

In London, Weizmann lobbied urgently but unsuccessfully for the establishment of a Jewish combat force to fight alongside the British. The constraints Britain faced in the Middle East, and the difficulty of enlisting American Jews in the war, prevented this from happening. At the same time, close to 30,000 Jewish men and women from Palestine responded to the pressing need of the time and to the call issued by the Jewish Agency and enlisted in the British army. Others engaged in secret missions on behalf of the British and in suppressing all those Jews in Palestine who sought to harm the British war effort.[11]

Weizmann, who in 1940 was inclined to believe in his personal ability to contribute to the British war effort, was welcomed by the British, who remembered the importance to Britain's victory in the previous war of his acetone production process. Along with Ernst David Bergmann, his right-hand man in the establishment of the Sieff Institute in Rehovot in 1934, Weizmann established a laboratory in London that worked on finding processes for the production of synthetic rubber, a vitally needed war material. He then tried to do the same in the United States. In both cases the processes he came up with were too expensive; furthermore, the oil companies opposed any attempt to replace oil.

Nothing could be more tragic than the ultimate sacrifice that Chaim and Vera Weizmann made to the British – and of course Jewish – war effort. Their son Michael, twenty-six years old, disappeared along with the rest of the crew of a Royal Air Force plane that set out in February 1942 on a mission to locate German submarines in the Bay of Biscay. Even when his differences with the British were at their height, the latter always recalled and respected the fact that the son of the president of the World Zionist Organization had fallen as an RAF pilot in the war against the Nazis.

As in World War One, in World War Two Weizmann's contributions to politics were far greater than his scientific ones. In 1942, Prime Minister Winston Churchill established, clearly as a tribute to Weizmann, a ministerial committee charged with re-examining the White Paper of 1939 and considering a return to a partition plan. However, in November 1944, Jewish terrorists of the *Lehi* organisation assassinated Lord Moyne (Walter Edward Guinness), the minister of state resident in the Middle East. The ministerial committee on Palestine policy, of which Moyne was an active member, ceased its deliberations. Churchill was deeply hurt. Moyne had been a personal friend and his murder had no precedent in the history of British-Zionist relationships. Effectively, Churchill abandoned Zionism.[12] He no longer received Weizmann, leaving the latter without a central tool in his political work, the personal conversation. Weizmann understood very well that a major blow had been dealt to the Zionist interest. He never forgave the dissident underground *Yishuv* militias for the harm they had done to the Zionist cause.

But far more important than this was the fact that Britain and its army saved the *Yishuv* from utter physical destruction, pure and simple. The magnitude of this achievement is so great that Weizmann, his colleagues in the Zionist leadership, and indeed collective memory have never found an adequate way of acknowledging it. Given the fate of Europe's Jews, the deadly danger that the Jews of Palestine faced from the German and Italian expeditionary force in North Africa cannot be overestimated. After and despite the White Paper of May 1939, Britain not only defended the *Yishuv* with the bodies of its soldiers, it also defeated the Axis forces and expelled them from North Africa, routed the forces loyal to Vichy France in Lebanon and Syria, put down the pro-Nazi rebellion in Iraq, and suppressed pro-Nazi sentiments in Egypt. At the end of the day, the British were central partners in the unconditional defeat of Nazi Germany, the liberation of the remnants of European Jewry who survived the death camps, and turned a blind eye to the migration of Jewish refugees and survivors from Eastern to Western Europe.

Weizmann wondered where the anti-British feelings that swept through the *Yishuv* and American Jewry after the war came from. It was difficult for him to grasp that the situation looked different to them than it did to him. He had not been to Palestine for five years, from 1939 to 1944, an especially critical period because he left Palestine in the midst of one wave of anti-British feeling, following the White Paper of May 1939, and next returned in the midst of another, following the assassination of Lord Moyne in November 1944. In between, Weizmann was cut off from the local mood. Faced with the catastrophe in Europe, many in the *Yishuv* were losing patience and developed expectations of what would happen after the victory of Britain and the Allies. Weizmann dismissed the feelings of American Jews as an expression of their pangs of conscience, not to mention annoying ignorance of Jewish and Arab affairs. Whatever the case, it was clear to him that he was losing his political hold, both in the *Yishuv* and in America, just as his base of support in Germany and most of Western Europe had been destroyed.

Weizmann still believed that the Zionist movement and the *Yishuv* should not cut their ties to Britain. He thought they should be grateful to Britain and himself and was convinced that, in its postwar weakness, Britain could, by action or inaction, determine whether the Zionist enterprise would succeed or fail. He was aware, especially after Labor's return to power in Britain in the summer of 1945, of the widening rift between Britain on the one hand and the Zionist movement and *Yishuv* on the other. He could not explain to a British government intent on unilaterally shedding Britain's empire why support for the *Yishuv* was consistent with British interests. He tried, but it seemed as if no one in London were listening to him.

All he had left were moral arguments. He made them to both sides. He argued to the British that they could not obviate their commitments under the Mandate and act against the helpless refugees for whom they had shed their blood. A Britain that did so would not be the Britain he knew and admired. Furthermore, Britain would hurt itself by doing so. As a loyal British subject, no less than as a Jew and Zionist, he was pained by his government's conduct toward the Jewish refugees and its refusal to reconsider partition. He had always had trouble being in the position of the victim, and perhaps for that reason he was not as effective as he could have been in this regard.

He made a clear demand of the *Yishuv* – anti-British terror was not only utter political, military and even physical suicide, but was also inconsistent with Jewish morality. It should be ceased immediately. Morality, he tried to explain, is not a burden but an asset; it is a source of power and guarantees the victory of justice even at a time when force needs to be used. Weizmann was by no means a pacifist.

As noted, following the assassination of Lord Moyne and Labor's subsequent rise to power, Weizmann's influence with the British government, the Zionist movement, and the *Yishuv* waned. But from a historical perspective, the decisive fact was that he placed the entire and not insignificant weight of his influence against the violence to which the Zionists veered in 1945–1946. Even when Ben-Gurion and his associates chose to be the Jewish Agency by day and the United Resistance Movement by night (October 1945–July 1946), there was no real clash between the British army and the *Yishuv*. Had such a clash occurred, in the context of Britain's sorry state after the war, it could have prevented the *Yishuv* from establishing a state not long thereafter. Nothing less. Weizmann stood, sometimes literally physically, between the extremist Zionists and the British.

Despite the turbulence in the Anglo-Zionist alliance, Weizmann did not ignore the United States. Weizmann had 'discovered America' in 1921, when it looked as if the British government were working in the Zionist interest. It arrived in tandem with the rise of American and the decline of Britain's power.

But Weizmann's alliance with the *Yishuv* was shaken in June 1942, when he and David Ben-Gurion, chairman of the Jewish Agency Executive since September 1935, clashed in New York. But too much weight has been placed on this admittedly painful and sensational confrontation. It was not a skirmish between equal forces, and it demonstrated the plight of both. Following the loss of his son Michael a few months before, he was emotionally weak and suffered a physical and emotional breakdown that summer. Under the circumstances, Weizmann had a hard time conceding authority and bringing others into his decision-making processes when that was clearly required.

Ben-Gurion, for his part, practically lost in the unfamiliar American landscape, and a long way from his home in Palestine, was on the verge of losing political control. It is hard to understand the clash between the two in any other way, given that they agreed on nearly all the cardinal questions and their differences were merely a matter of style. Neither did it help that Ben-Gurion, the junior figure of the two, admired Weizmann, while Weizmann treated Ben-Gurion with open contempt. The acrimony between them came in the wake of a major turning point in Zionist history. The previous month, a Zionist assembly in New York passed the so-called Biltmore Program, the first time the movement called explicitly for the establishment of a 'Jewish commonwealth' rather than a 'national home' in all of Mandated Palestine (a plan later ratified by Mapai). It was an expression of just how helpless the Jews and Zionists felt at the height of the war. Ben-Gurion quickly returned to Palestine, with Weizmann's assistance. The little that could be done in London and Washington was handled by Weizmann, his aides and, in the American case, local leaders.

Weizmann had been the person who established the political connection between the World Zionist Organization and the American government in Washington. He first met an American president, Calvin Coolidge, in November 1926, and had access to all subsequent presidents – Herbert Hoover, Franklin Roosevelt, and Harry Truman. In Washington, Weizmann acted on behalf of and under the sponsorship of the British government. The British embassy hosted him on his visits, held receptions in his honour, and its officials accompanied him to meetings with senior figures in Washington. Weizmann took advantage of this in multiple ways – to promise, support, criticise and threaten. He played a role in mitigating the differences between the two Western allies with regard to Palestine. Such differences, he believed, would be bad for the Zionist cause.

Despite this, Washington was hardly a bed of roses for him. He never gained in the State Department or White House the kind of cachet he enjoyed in Whitehall. He did not succeed in convincing the American government to provide financial support at the time of the economic crisis that threatened the *Yishuv* at the end of the 1920s. He also failed to obtain any significant American aid for Jewish refugees after the Nazis came to power.

But his work in the United States produced significant results after World War Two. He discerned the difficulties Britain faced and realised that its ally, the United States, was now calling the shots. Even though he was much weaker politically after the war, and even lost his formal position as president of the World Zionist Organization in December 1946, Weizmann was able to take advantage of his international stature, and his position in Britain and the United States, to further the Zionist cause. No other Zionist figure could simultaneously reprimand and understand Prime Minister Clement Atlee, while at the same time demanding of President Harry Truman that he support Jewish immigration to Palestine and further the partition idea, even though America's ally, Britain, believed that both were against its interests. He explained to his associates in the Zionist movement that they should boldly, even angrily argue, but without slipping into violence. This approach opened doors for him on both sides of the Atlantic.

It was Weizmann, more than any other Zionist figure inside or outside America, who had Truman's ear in the critical years of 1945–48. These were years in which the American president could dramatically affect the way in which the British Mandate would end. Weizmann was able to mould Truman's approach to partition, the refugee problem, the Anglo-American Committee of Inquiry on Palestine, the future map of the Jewish state, and American support, formal and informal, for its establishment. There can be no doubt that Zionist and, later, Israeli work in Washington was built on the foundation laid by Weizmann.

From 1917 to 1948, Weizmann's biography intersected with Jewish and Zionist history in a manner that could hardly be more relevant to the road that the Zionist movement took from vision to realisation. Perhaps inevitably, the two parted ways in 1948, when Israel was established.

Notes

1 Professor Reinharz is author of what has been called the 'definitive' biography of Weizmann; he published vol. 1 in 1985 and vol. 2 in 1987; vol. 3 (co-authored with Professor Golani): *Chaim Weizmann: Architect of the Jewish State*, was published in Hebrew in Tel Aviv, by Am Oved, in 2020; the English version is still to follow.
2 Bernard Shaw's satirical playlet was published in 1936. Two years later, Lloyd George published the first volume of his war memoirs, in which he claimed that *he* had held the said conversation with Weizmann; he related that when he asked Weizmann if there was some way that he could reward him for his contribution to the British war effort, the latter had replied: "Yes, I would like you to do something for my people". cf. David Lloyd George, *The Truth about the Peace Treaties*, London: Victor Gollancz Ltd., 1938, vol. 1, p. 349; also Chaim Weizmann, *Trial and Error*, New York: Schocken Books, 1949, p. 150.
3 See, for instance, Sahar Huneidi, Was the Balfour Policy Reversible? The Colonial Office and Palestine, 1921–23, *Journal of Palestine Studies* 27/2.

4 On the meeting, cf. *The Letters and Papers of Chaim Weizmann*, Jerusalem: Transaction Books/Rutgers Universities/Israel Universities Press, 1977, vol. 10, Bernard Wasserstein, editor, no. 298; also Michael J Cohen, *Churchill and the Jews*, London/Portland, OR: Frank Cass, 2nd revised edition, 2003, pp. 112–15.

5 Cf. Huneidi, supra, Michael J Cohen, *Britain's Hegemony in Palestine and in the Middle East, 1917–56*, London: Valentine Mitchell, 2017, Chapter 2; Bernard Wasserstein, *Herbert Samuel: A Political Life*, Oxford: Clarendon Press, 1992, pp. 241, 264.

6 Barbara Smith, *The Roots of Separatism in Palestine: British Economic Policy, 1920–1929*, Syracuse, NY: Syracuse University Press, 1993, p. 35.

7 Cohen, *Britain's Hegemony*, Chapter 3.

8 On the 1930 White Paper, cf. Weizmann, *Trial and*, Chapter 29 – indicatively, entitled: Attack and repulse; Cohen, *Britain's Moment in Palestine, Retrospect and Perspectives, 1917–48*, London: Routledge, 2014, pp. 220–8; on the land question, cf. Kenneth W. Stein, *The Land Problem in Palestine, 1917–1939*, Chapel Hill: University of North Carolina Press, 1984, and Yehoshua Porat, *The Palestinian Arab National Movement, From Riots to Rebellion, 1929–1939*, London: Frank Cass, 1977, especially Chapter 4.

9 Britain, still suffering from the shock waves of the 1929 Wall Street crash, was dependent financially on the United States.

10 On the 1939 White Paper, cf. Cohen, *Britain's Moment*, Chapter 13; Bernard Wasserstein, *Britain and the Jews of Europe, 1939–1945*, London: Institute of Jewish Affairs/Clarendon Press, 1979.

11 On Weizmann's proposal to mobilise a Jewish Division, cf. Michael J Cohen, *Palestine: Retreat from the Mandate: The Making of British Policy, 1936–45*, London/New York: Paul Elek, 1978, Chapter 6.

12 Cf. Michael J Cohen, The Moyne assassination, November 1944: A political analysis, *Middle Eastern Studies* 15/3, October 1979; Bernard Wasserstein, The assassination of Lord Moyne, *Transactions of the Jewish Historical Society of England* 27, 1982.

15 David Ben-Gurion's 'road map' to independence, May 1948

Tuvia Friling

Ben-Gurion spent the last days of World War Two in London. On 8 May 1945, when it was announced that Germany had surrendered, Ben-Gurion was in his hotel room watching the rejoicing Londoners from his window. Three years and six days later, on 14 May 1948, Ben-Gurion stood in the city of Tel Aviv and declared the establishment of the State of Israel. Shortly before leaving to attend the ceremony, he wrote in his diary: "At four o'clock independence was declared. In Israel, there was rejoicing and exhilaration. And again I stand mourning among the rejoicing". On his return from the ceremony, he started a new diary and in one brief sentence summarised the complexity of the moment: "We have declared the State. Its fate is in the hands of the army".[1]

For Ben-Gurion, the main lesson of the Holocaust and the fundamental solution to the anomaly of the Jewish People was the creation of a Jewish nation-state in Palestine. If someone had prophesied in 1939 that within less than a decade that state would come into being, he would have been viewed as an unrealistic dreamer. But what was for many no more than a distant hope served as Ben-Gurion's springboard and his platform for achieving that hope. Ben-Gurion had stood at the center of the *Yishuv*'s leadership for more than 45 years.[2] Not only did he help shape most strategic decisions and major policies, but he also participated in the implementation of most of them. He was a leader, not one who was led.

****

On 28 November 1945, the *Yishuv*'s Elected Assembly met in Jerusalem for a special session. The meeting took place against the background of the first acts of the 'Hebrew Rebellion', Britain's naval blockade and the intensive and violent searches conducted by the British army in the settlements of the Sharon area. The Labour government had announced that it had no intention of changing the White Paper policy, but favoured the repatriation of the masses of Jewish refugees in Europe back to their countries of origin.

With great emotion, Ben-Gurion shared with the audience what he had seen during his recent visit to the Displaced Persons camps in Germany and listed the lessons and imperatives to be learned. He warned that it would be hopeless for the British to try, whether by political or military means, to prevent the creation of their state.[3]

During the following, momentous three years until the declaration of Israel's independence, Ben-Gurion worked with his partners to implement the 'road map', which relied – first and foremost – on the establishment of a Jewish nation-state in Palestine. The entire infrastructure – political, economic, intellectual, social and military – was mobilised in this effort; from whatever could be achieved at the end of the war and the international arrangements that followed it; from what already appeared to be the decline of the British empire and the clumsiness and confusion the new British government. The Zionists' basic working assumptions on Britain's policy with regards the Jewish-Zionist question had all proven to be wrong. He determined to mobilise everything at the Zionists' disposal: the feelings of pain, frustration and anger of the survivors, and finally, from whatever the feelings of guilt – if there were any – among the leaders and citizens of the democracies with respect to the price paid by the Jewish People in the Holocaust.

The major strategies that shaped Ben-Gurion's 'road map' during the final years of the Mandate were:

- Political activity which primarily involved connecting between the spirit of the Biltmore Convention (see below), and the acceptance of 'a state now' policy, by all those who had opposed the idea, both inside and outside his camp. This included the 'sidelining' of Weizmann and embedding the change at the core of Zionist policy.
- Shaping the main pillars of the emerging State's defense policy: the definition of the 'main threat' and the buildup of power based on that policy.
- Detailed planning for the absorption of the millions of Jews that he planned to bring to Palestine.

Ben-Gurion was aware that his strategy would lead inevitably to a clash with Britain: in the Displaced Persons (DP) camps in Europe, on the routes to and in the various ports of Europe, on the shores of Palestine, on the streets of Jerusalem, Tel Aviv and Haifa, and in the political arena in Britain, the USA, and at the United Nations.

Between St. James and Biltmore and the expulsion of Weizmann from the Zionist Executive

Ben-Gurion's first effort was to transform the spirit of the Biltmore Conference that had taken place in May 1942[4] into a pragmatic platform. Biltmore had demanded the creation of a 'Jewish Commonwealth' after the war. Now, Ben-Gurion transformed it into the goal of 'a state now'. The decision to turn to the US was already made by Ben-Gurion in February 1939, during the St. James Conference.[5] Already at that point, he understood that Britain – for reasons of global policy and as part of the process of withdrawal in the face of Nazi-fascist pressure and the growing Islamic threat – had abandoned what been viewed by some of its statesmen as a commitment to realise the Balfour Declaration.

During the six years from the rise of Hitler to power until the Second World War, Ben-Gurion watched the rear-guard action[6] by the democratic world, whose price would be paid by the Jewish People and the Zionist movement. He pointed to the systematic steps Hitler was taking, the well-defined plan according to which he operated, Hitler's recognition of the nature of, on the one hand, his own people, and, on the other hand, that of the democratic nations. This is what Hitler viewed as the weakness of the democratic system and the complexity of its decision-making process and primarily the complexity of the decision to go to war.[7] Ben-Gurion pointed to the systematic violations of the various parts of the Versailles Treaty[8] – military, territorial and political – while the democracies acted as if they didn't notice. He also noted the political blindness which was expressed in, for example, the British reaction to the 'peace' speech given by Hitler in the Reichstag on 21 May 1935.[9]

During the 1930s, Ben-Gurion observed closely the series of international crisis in Europe. In his view, all of them were part of an historical process, one with its own internal, insane logic, that would lead in the end to a gargantuan war, in which the Jewish People would have to pay a heavy price. In February 1938, a month before Germany took over Austria, Ben-Gurion outlined with great precision what he expected: "Germany is swallowing up Austria – and tomorrow it will be Czechoslovakia's turn".[10]

In London, seven months later, in September 1938, Ben-Gurion witnessed the realisation of his predictions. He listened to Chamberlin's speech following the Munich Conference in which Germany's right to parts of Czechoslovakia was recognised. He wrote in his diary that after Czechoslovakia, it would be the turn of other small nations to be abandoned to their fate.[11]

From his point of view, the connection between events in Europe and in the Middle East was obvious. The surrender of Britain and France to the German *diktat* had undermined confidence in alliances and promises and had increased the prestige of Hitler and his totalitarian method. This would "leave deep footprints in the heart of the Arab world and make the work of Hitler's and Mussolini's agents in the Near East much easier". Now the relations between the Mufti Haj Amin el-Husayni and the Nazis would become even closer. Isolationist movements in the US would gain momentum, the peoples of Central Europe would run to make peace with the Nazis "and a new and horrible disaster would afflict European Jewry".[12]

Ben-Gurion had heard from Malcolm MacDonald, the Secretary of State for the Colonies: this time, "Germany has a case", as if Germany "deserved" the Sudetenland. "Woe to the world if they determine its fate!" He also described the weakness of the Jewish communities worldwide: the illusion that not every superpower would abandon them, their inability to act: what will they do? Protest?[13]

On 30 September 1938, the Western press published the details of the Munich agreement.[14] Ben-Gurion wrote in his diary. "Today is one of the blackest days in the history of Europe.[15] This is a period in which there is no respect for international commitments. A time of power politics and the Jews have no power".[16]

Ben-Gurion connected the democracies' capitulation in Europe and the situation in the Middle East. Already in 1936, there were rampant rumours of the destabilizing activity of Germany and Italy in the Middle East, who were not only fanning the flames of the Arab Revolt but also assisting the Arabs financially. Zionist Intelligence was accumulating evidence of the activities of Nazi and Italian agents in Palestine: their mobilising funds in Europe, shipments of weapons from Europe to Palestine, their espionage and dissemination of propaganda.[17] There was also information on the Mufti's personal involvement in this activity.[18] And all this was occurring under the watchful eyes of the Mandate authorities in Palestine. Ben-Gurion feared Britain was willing to placate the Palestinians with the same kind of appeasement shown to a different aggressor, namely Hitler.

Ben-Gurion understood that there was no point in trying to persuade Britain of the importance of the *Yishuv* to British interests in the region. For she had decided that as long as there was a risk of war in Europe, Britain would do nothing that might arouse the enmity of some one billion Moslems, spread out from India to Morocco. His assumptions were confirmed in May 1939, with the publication of the MacDonald White Paper, which severely restricted the purchase of land by the Jews and set a quota of 75,000 immigration permits during the coming five years.[19] The restrictions on immigration were not removed even after the destruction in Europe became officially known, in late November 1942. The permits were stretched out until the end of 1946.

After the St. James Conference, Ben-Gurion sought a different strategic partner for the Zionist enterprise – the United States. At the Biltmore conference in New York in May 1942, he and Weizmann put forward the demand for a Jewish Commonwealth in all of Western Palestine, to be created immediately after the war. Ben-Gurion acted alone on the plan's secret, intelligence component. He tried to convince William (Bill) Donovan, the head of the OSS (from 1945 the CIA), and Allen Dulles, his deputy, to view the *Yishuv* as a clandestine partner. He proposed that Donovan utilise the global dispersal of the Jews and the Zionists, and presented him with a number of possible channels for cooperation[20] Arthur Goldberg, a Jewish attorney who served later in the OSS[21] was working to establish relations with socialist organisations in Europe and to recruit from among them agents for espionage, propaganda, and sabotage. These organisations were a natural opposition to Nazi and Fascist groups. Ben-Gurion and his colleagues maintained their own connections with their European counterparts in the Socialist International and tried to exploit them for similar purposes.[22]

Thus, on arriving in the US, Ben-Gurion tried to also advance the clandestine side as part of the creation of a new political international orientation that he sought to adopt for the Zionist movement. He again made the same proposal to the Americans that he had already made in December 1942 to Donovan, then the head of the Coordinator of Information (COI). Donovan would be instructed by Roosevelt within a few months to establish the Office of Strategic Services (OSS).

In a meeting with Donovan, who was busy building his organisation and searching for agents, relationships and strategic partners, and in order to strengthen the prospects of his proposal, Ben-Gurion called on the support of members of the Emergency Committee of the Zionist movement in the US, including Robert Szold, Emanuel Neumann, Judge Harry M. Fischer, and established a broadly-based organisational infrastructure and a presence in strategic facilities such as ports, airports, factories, railways, etc. Later on, Goldberg was positioned in a station established in London and became one of Allen Dulles' senior associates in setting up the OSS station in Bern, Switzerland and was involved in the various activities organised from there.[23]

In a series of meetings, the proposal for collaboration was presented at length. A description was given of the Zionist movement's offices in Switzerland, Sweden, Turkey, and other neutral countries and their connections with related organisations in various locations in occupied Nazi territory. It was also stressed that Ben-Gurion was the one who could authorise such collaboration. It was recommended that they exploit his presence in the United States in order to reach an agreement.[24]

Allen Dulles advised his colleagues in Washington that Ben-Gurion's proposal be given serious consideration, as this was a connection that could serve as "a valuable source of information". He continued that he had been warned of the potential price of cooperation with the Zionists in the form of a reaction from the Arab world. Nonetheless, he recommended not panicking and advised it would be possible to exploit this partnership without being identified with the goals of the Jewish Agency.[25]

In May-June 1942, in other meetings held with senior officials at the Defense Department, Ben-Gurion tried to promote the idea that the *Yishuv* would provide a loyal stronghold of the US in the Middle East and that representatives of the Zionist movement would assist in the American war effort in other areas of the world.[26]

Thus, after the bitter disappointment with Chamberlain and the comprehension that neither Churchill nor his government would bring about a breakthrough, the two main pillars of Ben-Gurion's new strategy were the Biltmore Plan and the idea that the Zionists would work to establish a close, secret intelligence and operational partnership with the US.[27]

Whereas Ben-Gurion advanced the Biltmore strategy together with Weizmann, President of the World Zionist Organization at the time, his next move was to challenge Weizmann for the leadership of the Zionist movement. He succeeded in doing so at the 22nd Zionist Congress, held in Basel in late December 1946. This led to the marginalisation of the main opponent of Ben-Gurion's 'state now' plan, and to a new activist, political orientation of the Zionist movement.

During the dark days of the war, Britain's policies demonstrated for Ben-Gurion the limits of her support for Zionism: the continuation of the White Paper policy, her opposition to increasing the immigration quotas for Jews, even after late 1942 when everyone in Britain and the US knew that the Jews of Europe were being exterminated;[28] the disappointing result of the Bermuda Conference in the spring/summer of 1943.[29] Nor was there any reason to believe that there would be dramatic changes in its position towards the *Yishuv* and the Zionist movement even after the war. Ben-Gurion's slogan 'we will fight Hitler as if there were no White Paper – and fight Britain as if there were no war against Hitler'[30] had attempted to manoeuvre within the complex situation created by the war. But, in the end, it did not manage to overcome the irregularities of the situation. On the assumption that Britain would be unable to free herself of her political and economic interests in the Arab world, Ben-Gurion defined as baseless the rumours that the 'Big Three' had agreed in Cairo in early 1945 on the creation of a Jewish State.[31]

In May 1945, the Jewish Agency Executive wrote to Churchill, asking him to redeem his promise to Weizmann to set up a Jewish state in Palestine after the war. He replied that the Palestine question would have to wait until the peace conference.[32] This was described by Ben-Gurion as a major blow to the *Yishuv*. He defined Weizmann and the Jewish Agency officials in London and the US who were hesitant to recognise reality as "living in a paradise of fools".[33]

Churchill's defeat in the elections and the victory of the Labour Party did not bring about a positive change in British policy on the Palestine question. The first announcements of the new government regarding Palestine and the problem of the Jewish displaced persons in Europe (DPs) were ambiguous; from Ben-Gurion's perspective, they were another sign that there would be no positive change in British policy. Nor did he believe that the Labour government would behave like a party in opposition. His diary entries were characterised by a pessimistic outlook and his conclusion with respect to the attitude of Britain remained gloomy. The only thing that he felt had changed was the degree of urgency of the actions required: "Only a state now, massive *aliyah*, educational activity in the Diaspora, political pressure to free the Jews gathered in Eastern Europe ... can turn things around".[34] With respect to *aliyah* and a state, it was clear to him that they could be achieved only by armed struggle.

Ben-Gurion tried to persuade others of his viewpoint at the Zionist Convention held in London in August 1945. He claimed that there were strong anti-Zionist elements in the British establishment that were liable to prevent any positive turnaround in policy. Britain would try deception. Its government would not announce any new policy, it would simply continue the White Paper policy.[35] He analyzed the situation of the Jewish People after the Holocaust and presented in detail his political beliefs. He spoke of the need for a Jewish nation-state as the foundation stone of his philosophy, and practical implications. Although he was a part of the workers' movement and as such he saw the victory of Labour as highly significant, he declared that he would judge its actions solely from the Jewish-Zionist perspective.

Dr. Weizmann was right, said Ben-Gurion, when he emphasised that Zionism had no interest in one party or another. There were supporters and opponents of the Zionist idea within all the British parties. And there was no ignoring the fact that since the First World War the party had supported the Zionist enterprise and when Lord Passfield, the Colonial Secretary in Labour's minority government, published an anti-Zionist White Paper,[36] he was opposed by the entire party. Influential members of the movement, such as Ernest Bevin, had forced the government to turn the White Paper on its head.

Ben-Gurion went on to name all of the instances in which the Labour Party had adopted a decidedly pro-Zionist stance. The MacDonald Letter of February 1930 had opened the way for the large wave of immigration before the Arab Revolt in 1936–39. The party had also opposed the White Paper of 1939 and even proposed a vote of no-confidence in the government in reaction to the Land Law of 1940. He recalled that at its conference the previous year "the Labour Party had approved a far-reaching plan for Palestine, one of whose clauses went even further than the official Zionist program, in demanding not only a Jewish State but also the transfer of the Arabs".[37]

But despite the many expressions of Labour support Zionism, Ben-Gurion listed three reasons to dampen their enthusiasm:

a) Urgency: Even if the Labour government behaves as it promised when it was in opposition, there is a major gap in the degree of urgency: 'For us this is the primary and most urgent issue.... The suffering of the Jews in so-called liberated Europe does not give us rest.... However, for England, this is just one problem among many.

b) The ruling party cannot behave like a party in opposition, even it wishes to: It can no longer pass the responsibility for implementing its policy onto its rival.

c) England is a democracy at home, a dictatorship in its colonies..... Here [in Palestine] the principle of dictatorship prevails, and the colonial bureaucracy is largely anti-Zionist and has been so since the Balfour Declaration. It will remain in place and don't underestimate its power and influence even in the era of a workers' government.

Vigilance must be maintained and, if necessary,

it should be made clear to the English people, their representatives and their government what the White Paper is and how we will act against it. [...]

If the White Paper stands – after a reasonable time is given to political activity here in England and in America ... and no new policy appears ... there will be a rebellion against [its] brutal and illegal regime.

He continued:

I view it as my obligation to warn the Labour Party.... There are tens of thousands of Jews who ... want a place of respect for the Jewish People as well. And if this right is taken from them, they will stand up for what is theirs and will fight bitterly. They will not let this empire rule the Land of Israel after it has become a brutal dictatorship there, one that does not honor its obligations, does not stand behind what it says and does not recognize justice.... Either we are on the brink of the establishment of the Jewish State – since, without a state, the Jewish People cannot exist in this world ... or we are on the brink of a bitter struggle, one that Jews will take upon themselves – whatever price they will have to pay.[38]

British intelligence indeed monitored Ben-Gurion's statements and believed that he meant every word. It may also be assumed that they were aware of the clandestine preparations being made by the *Yishuv* and elsewhere for such an armed struggle.

On 4 October 1945, the *News Chronicle* published an interview with Reuven Shiloah, one of Ben-Gurion's closest aides. He warned the British government of the possible implications of continuing the White Paper policy – the invasion of Palestine by masses of Jews from Europe, of whom thousands would be "armed and desperate and would be willing to sacrifice their lives". He would not have made such a far-reaching declaration without Ben-Gurion's authorisation.[39] This was a clear signal to Bevin that the movement under his leadership would no longer tolerate the White Paper policy. No less so, it was also a signal to Weizmann that his time had passed, along with his pro-British policy.

The timing of the interview was also important. On 5 October, Bevin was due to meet Weizmann, and there was a need to inform them both of the rhetorical and practical boundaries for manoeuvrability from the viewpoint of activist elements within the *Yishuv*. As expected, Bevin did not conceal his views. He referred to Shiloah's interview as "a gun pointed at the head of Britain" and declared that the government of Britain could not deviate from the White Paper policy, which allocated 1,500 immigration permits per month, and could not grant 100,000 permits as a special allocation for the refugees in the displaced person camps – for fear that "the whole Arab world would rise up against Britain". Bevin continued that partition was not a solution, not even economically, and the establishment of a Jewish state was in any case, something that would take a long time. He concluded that he had already advised Attlee to avoid a decision on the question of Palestine and "to wait and see how things fall".[40]

In reaction, Ben-Gurion's announced that "the government of Britain has forced a war on the Jews" and that the continuation of the White Paper means a "war situation". He repeated his opposition to any further contact with British representatives until it was cancelled. Nonetheless, and despite Ben-Gurion's opposition, Weizmann and Bevin met again on 10 October. No advance was made. The meeting only deepened the rift between Ben-Gurion and Weizmann. Ben-Gurion demanded that the Zionist Executive be convened in Jerusalem. At the same time, he tried to recruit the leadership of the *Yishuv* to his side against Weizmann, on three main points:

1 Rejection of the immigration quota of 1,500 per month;
2 Severing contact with the British government and the Mandatory for as long as the White Paper policy was in place;
3 A declaration of the beginning of a Jewish rebellion, both in the Yishuv and worldwide, with the participation of the *Haganah, IZL*, and the *Lehi*.[41]

From Ben-Gurion's point of view, the die was cast, and within two days he wrote a letter of instructions to Moshe Sneh, signed with his nom de guerre – Avi Amos (the father of Amos). He commanded the *Haganah* to begin an uprising against England, determining the methods of the struggle, the means and the people it required.[42] He did not believe that an armed struggle could bring about the expulsion of the British from Palestine, but assumed that the Jewish struggle and the attempts to break the blockade in order to bring in thousands of Holocaust survivors would force Britain to carry on a deplorable and dirty war against refugees and survivors, which would resonate in global world opinion until Britain – an enlightened democracy, after all – would be forced to change its ways.[43]

Ben-Gurion spoke in similar terms at a press conference held in Paris on 16 October. To an audience of French journalists, news agencies, foreign reporters and representatives of the Jewish and Arab press, Ben-Gurion argued that the actions of the new government in England were a "continuation of the horrible policy of Hitler". He continued that the crisis in Palestine was not a conflict between Jews and Arabs, but between the Jews and the British government, and that since Palestine was not part of the British Empire, the problem was a matter for the United Nations. He warned that the Jews would never surrender to the immoral and illegal White Paper policy.[44]

This was the opening public shot of Ben-Gurion's confrontation not only with the British but also with those among his associates who opposed his policy. From here on in he was focused completely on the target of securing a Jewish state.

Simultaneously with the deterioration of relations with the British government, he was working to build a base of operations in France. On the political side, he sought to obtain the support of official French circles. On the practical-operational side, the infrastructure built by both the Yishuv representatives and the local Jews and Zionists was strengthened. British military operations against the *Yishuv* – Operation Agatha, the naval blockade, weapons searches and the arrests of the *Yishuv* leaders on 29 June 1946 (the 'Black Sabbath'[45]) showed that his fears were not unfounded.

Together with associates, he began locating individuals with military experience. He organised fundraising, set up offices and bases of operation, assembly points for weapons and vehicles. He met with the local Jewish leadership, leaders of the *Armée Juive*, members of the French underground, and with anyone willing to contribute their experience and contacts to the struggle. These were feverishly busy days during which Ben-Gurion met in Paris with emissaries of the *Haganah* and the *Mossad Le'Aliyah* Bet (illegal immigration organisation) who arrived from all corners of Europe. They provided him with detailed reports on preparations for the smuggling of immigrants, the purchase of ships and the activities of the Jewish Brigade.

According to the assessments of the British CID, they were dealing with a leader who was confident, consistent and locked on the target, an individual who embodied "passive and active opposition to the implementation of the White Paper or its continuation".[46] After he returned to Palestine in November 1945, after his first visit to the displaced person camps, British intelligence reported that Ben-Gurion "believes in the most extreme measures".[47] On 30 November, the Commander of Britain's military forces in the Middle East reported to the Ministry of War that since his return to Palestine, Ben-Gurion appears to have "absolutely been recognised as a leader".[48]

Ben-Gurion assumes the defense portfolio and defines the main threat

As the Chairman of the Jewish Agency Executive since 1935, and head of its Defense Department, a position he was appointed to at the 22nd Congress in December 1946, Ben-Gurion began to prepare the *Yishuv* for the approaching armed struggle. This involved a series of short- and long-term measures which gradually shaped Israel's defense conception, important parts of which are still in place until today.

On 26 March 1947, Ben-Gurion called a meeting with Ze'ev Shefer, the head of the National Headquarters of the Haganah. Shefer spent several hours explaining the structure of the organisation to him. Thus, Ben-Gurion who was already 60 years old and a civilian whose 'military experience' consisted of a short service as a corporal in the Jewish Legion during the First World War, began what quickly became known as Ben-Gurion's 'seminar', an intensive workshop in which he sought to transform his status from political leader to minister of defense in the approaching war.[49]

At that time, the *Haganah* had a name as a large and well-equipped underground organisation. In 1943, British intelligence believed that it had between 80–100,000 well-armed members. Even in Palestine, there were rumours of the organisation's great strength. The *Haganah*'s Intelligence service was reputed to know everything that happened in the corridors of power in Britain and in the Arab countries.[50]

But the truth was quite different. At the beginning of May 1947, the *Haganah* had about 45,000 members, of which only 2,200 *Palmach* (commandos) were fulltime. Most of the other members of the *Haganah* trained only intermittently, primarily in defence of the settlements, with light weapons, at no more than the company level. The weapons situation was not encouraging either. The organisation had no heavy machine guns, tanks, artillery pieces, planes or warships.

All of the weapons had been smuggled or self-produced and stored in secret stashes, which were in danger of being discovered and confiscated by the British, while the weapons' producers, smugglers, and concealers were in danger of being arrested.

Ben-Gurion found another weak spot in the operational doctrine of the *Haganah* command. The operational plans were based on the assumption that the most serious threat to the *Yishuv* was a local Arab uprising. The *Haganah*'s Plan B was updated several times during 1946, but it still centered on the threat of attack by local militias, which might be supported and backed by the British. This revealed that the *Haganah* had not studied or analysed a more serious scenario, namely an all-out attack by the regular armies of the Arab states.

In May 1947, Ben-Gurion commissioned reports on the strength of the regular Arab armies. What he learned from them caused him great concern. A coordinated attack constituted an existential threat to the *Yishuv*. Therefore, he set himself the goal of creating a regular army that would be capable of halting this eventuality. This led to the critical question of whether the *Haganah* was capable on its own of becoming a regular army. At the end of the first stage of his 'seminar', Ben-Gurion's answer was negative. In October 1947, he instructed the most senior officer that had served in the British army, to prepare a plan for the creation of an army:

> Assumption: The Arab world and the Arabs in the Land of Israel with the help of one or more Arab countries – and perhaps all of them – is liable to attack the *Yishuv*, with the goal of defeating it or even destroying it.[51]

During April-May 1946 Ben-Gurion decided to replace the core of the *Haganah*'s command with veterans of the Jewish Brigade, the unit that had operated as part of the British army late in the Second World War, whose commanders were familiar with the formations and structure of a regular army. He also made several structural changes in the National Headquarters and in the General Staff. Ben-Gurion's twin goals of creating a regular army and acquiring heavy weaponry prompted senior commanders of the *Haganah* to declare that the "old man has gone crazy". But he rejected the *Haganah*'s proposed budget and tripled it.[52]

From the autumn of 1947, his warnings of a genuine war appeared more plausible. After the UN Commission recommended the partition of Palestine, threats and declarations that heralded the coming war with Israel flooded out of Arab capitals. In October, the Syrians deployed thousands of infantry, armour and heavy weapons along Palestine's northern border in order to 'feel out' Britain's policy after the UN's recommendations. This was an ominous hint as to what could be expected once the British forces left.[53]

Ben-Gurion allocated funds to acquisitions and made changes in the structure of the relevant organisations. He sent Monya Mardor to Europe and the US to purchase planes and to recruit pilots and military experts and the head of the *Yishuv*'s military industries to order all of the raw material required. Some of the large sums required had been raised since July 1945, by means of the Sonnenborn Institute, the 'cooperative' of rich American Jews that Ben-Gurion had founded in the US.[54]

Ben-Gurion made a further strategic decision – if the *Yishuv* was attacked, the UN partition boundaries would be considered nullified and the *Yishuv* would try to expand them according to its needs and the possibilities available to it. This risked pitting the *Yishuv* against British forces and, needless to say, it required an army of a different type.[55]

The third component: planning for the absorption of the millions

The preparation for the absorption of the masses was the third component of Ben-Gurion's 'road map' on the way to a Jewish state. He commissioned studies of what physical infrastructure would be necessary for the absorption of millions of Jews who would arrive after the founding of the State.

He intended to prove to the free world that there was no basis for the limits imposed by Britain on immigration due to what it defined as the 'economic 'absorptive capacity' of the country. These preparations began prior to the Second World War.[56] He himself headed a steering committee, that acquired 12 subcommittees, composed of the top experts in the *Yishuv*. Ben-Gurion ordered them to assume that there was enough money to prepare a complete and fully detailed plan for the absorption of millions and to ignore political and economic constraints. Economists were asked to examine the possibilities for the development of industry and employment. Similarly, other experts – health, transportation and tourism – were asked to prepare detailed plans for the absorption two million Jews.[57]

Ben-Gurion endeavoured to convince his associates of the necessity of large-scale, accelerated immigration. Most of his experts believed that bringing in even a million Jews all at once was an unrealistic, even impossible task. Even those that supported large-scale immigration warned of what might be 'one of the larger catastrophes'. Most preferred a more gradual plan, to bring in one million in the first stage and another million when things had stabilised.[58]

Ben-Gurion's vision of one million immigrants was realised within a year – from the founding of the State and the opening of its gates to immigration. His determination was based also on his realisation that the agreement of the governments of Eastern and Central Europe to allow the emigration of their Jews was a window of opportunity that might shut at any moment.[59] It was an opportunity that government of a Jewish State created after the Holocaust could not afford to miss.

****

Ben-Gurion appreciated from an early stage that it was unwise for a people to base its future and its chances for survival on the goodwill of great statesmen and nations – even of the most enlightened democracies.

Ben-Gurion appreciated the great friends of the Zionist movement in Britain and admired the courage of the British soldiers and people. But he also saw the implications of British policy, which appeared already in the late 1930s, with appeasement. His deep admiration of the British people (especially of Churchill), its bravery, its democratic tradition and the way in which it stood up to the German attack during the blitz of London never diminished. But no less than what he saw and heard in Churchill's and England's greatest moments during the war, there were also what he saw at their lowest moments. In 1939, he concluded that Britain was essentially 'lost' as far as the Zionist movement was concerned. Her own imperial interests would always come first. During the 1940s and 1950s he came to distrust Britain to the point of detesting her.

Ben-Gurion behaved as someone for whom the reality that needed to be created was as real as the reality that needed to change. This was manifest when he defined the main threat to the *Yishuv* in defiance of the advice of most of the experts, in his decision to declare the State – in defiance of American warnings – and in his bold decision to bring in mass-scale immigration at an early stage.

Notes

1 Diary entry, 14 May 1948, Ben-Gurion archives (BGA).
2 In 1920, Ben-Gurion was elected to the Executive of the *Histadrut* (Workers' Union); in 1933 he was elected to the Executive of the Jewish Agency and in 1935 as its Chairman. In 1948, he was elected Israel's first Prime Minister and Defense Minister; he remained Prime Minister, with brief interruptions, until June 1963.
3 His speech was reprinted in *Ma'arachot*, vol. 5, Tel Aviv: Am Oved, 1957, pp. 9–32.
4 Ariel Feldestein, Meir Avizohar and Shifra Kolat (eds.), *Biltmore, Tokhnit Medinit* (Biltmore: A Political Program), Ben-Gurion Research Institute for the Study of Israel and Zionism, Sde Boker, (BG Research) 2012.
5 Tuvia Friling, *Ḥets ba-'Arafel: David Ben-Guron, Hanhagat ha-Yishuv ve-Nisyonot Hatsalah ba-Shoẋah [Arrow in the Dark: David Ben-Gurion, the Leadership of the Yishuv and Rescue Attempts during the Holocaust]*, Sde Boker, 1998, pp. 403–11.

6   Diary, 14 July 1936, 12 February 1938, 27 September 1938, 7 June 1940, and 8 September 1940, protocols of meetings, 7 June 1944, BGA.

7   Diary, 13 September 1938.

8   Conversation with Lord Melchett, 21 June 1935, London; 3 January 1939, New York, ibid.

9   Diary, 7 September; ibid., letters to Geula and Amos, 16, 22, 25 September 1935

10 Diary, 18 September 1938; ibid., Ben-Gurion to Geula, 15 March 1939, London; ibid., 24 March 1939, Paris; 28 April 1939, Tel Aviv, ibid.

11 Ibid., 14, 15, 18 September 1938; BGA, Correspondence Section, Ben-Gurion to Moshe Shertok, 18 September 1938.

12 Ben-Gurion to Shertok, 20, 21 September 1938, Ben-Gurion to Geula, 21 September 1938, BGA.

13 Ben Ben-Gurion to Shertok, 20 and 21 September 1938, ibid.

14 Diary, 30 September 1938.

15 Ibid, Ben-Gurion to Golomb, 30 September 1938,

16 Diary, 1, 2 October 1938; Ben-Gurion to Reiss and Kleinbaum, 3 October 1938; Ben-Gurion to Geula, Amos and Renana, 7 October 1938; Ben-Gurion to Dov Yosef, 18 October 1938, BGA.

17 Yoav Gelber, *Shorshe ha-Havatselet: ha-Modi'in ba-Yishuv 1918–1947* [*Growing a Fleur-de-Lis: The Intelligence Services of the Yishuv in Palestine, 1919–1947*], Tel Aviv: Ministry of Defense, 1992, vol. 1, p. 276, vol. 2, pp. 457–60, 650.

18 Ibid., pp. 278–9, 191–2, 273–7; Diary, 15 July 1936.

19 Friling, *Arrow in the Dark*, p. 155.

20 Diary, 1 December 1941, BGA.

21 Friling, *Arrow in the Dark*, pp. 381–530.

22 Tuvia Friling, '*Le-Halekh bi-Gedulot*' [*Ambitious Moves: Cooperation between the Revisionists Zionists and Anti-Nazi Germans in the Attempt to Defeat the Third Reich*], Study and Research Series, Jerusalem: Yad Vashem, 2015, pp. 18–21.

23 Correspondence between Emanuel Neumann, Goldberg, Dulles, May-June1942, RG 226, Entry 142, Box 5, US National Archives, (USNA)

24 Goldberg to A.W. Dulles, 5 June 1942, ibid.

25 A.W. Dulles to Robert Cresswell, 23 June 1942, ibid.

26 Friling, *Arrow in the Dark*, pp. 381–530.

27 Ibid., footnote 65.

28 Ibid., pp. 17–110.

29 On the Bermuda Conference, which opened on 19 April 1943, cf. ibid., pp. 130–2.

30 Meeting of Mapai Central committee, 12 September 1939, ibid., pp. 147–50.

31 Meeting of the Jewish Agency Executive, 15 March 1945, BGA.

32 On the memo and Churchill's response, see Michael J Cohen, *Churchill and the Jews*, revised paperback edition, London: Frank Cass, 2003, pp. 309–10.

33 Protocols of the meeting of the Political Committee in London, 8–14 June 1945, ibid. 'Avi-Amos' telegram, 7 October 1945; Yoav Gelber, *Toldot ha-Hitnadvut* [Hebrew: *The History of Volunteering*, vol. 3; *The Flagbearers*], Jerusalem: Yad Yitzhak Ben-Zvi, 1983, p. 376; on Ben-Gurion's and Weizmann's remarks about Churchill cf. Cohen, ibid.

34 Diary, 30 July 1945.

35 Ibid. 'Avi-Amos' telegram, 7 October 1945; summary of the Zionist Conference, August 1945, CZA, S-25-1212. Ben-Gurion speech, 'There is no future without a state,' BGA.

36 Cf. The Passfield White Paper, October 1930, Cmd. 3692, His Majesty's Stationery Office (HMSO), London: 1930.

37 Ben-Gurion, 'On the way to an army and the State of Israel – Situation of the Jews after the war', *Davar*, 30 April 1964, p. 2.

38 Ben-Gurion's speech reported in *Davar*, 3 August 1945, also Shabtai Teveth, *Ḳin'at Dayid: Haye Dayid Ben-Gurion* [*David's Envy: The Life of David Ben-Gurion*], Jerusalem/Tel Aviv: Shocken, 1977, p. 549.

39 39. Teveth, ibid., pp. 572–3.

40 Ibid., pp. 573–4.

41 Ibid., p. 575.

42 Michael Bar-Zohar, *Ben-Gurion*, vol. I, Tel Aviv: Zamora Bitan, 1987, pp. 525–6; Teveth, *Ḳin'at Dayid*, p. 577; Eli Shaltiel, *Moshe Sneh*, Tel Aviv: Am Oved [Hebrew], 2000, pp. 186–229.

43 Teveth, *Ḳin'at Dayid*, pp. 561–5.

44 Ibid., p. 579.

45 In this operation, the British arrested more than 2,700 individuals from the *Yishuv*, including members of the leadership. One of the operation's goals was to break the back of the *Haganah* command and to disable the civilian leadership of the *Yishuv*. In addition, the British searched numerous settlements looking for weapons, documents and operational plans.

46 Criminal Investigation Department (CID) – which reported to the Mandate government but also to other Intelligence agencies.

47 Friling, *Arrow in the Dark*, p. 385.

48 *Haganah* Archives, Tel Aviv, vol. 14, p. 380, Ben-Gurion file at the CID; W0275/120; weekly intelligence review no. 36, 23 November 1945, CO537/1742, A.J. Kellar (MI5) to John Martin (Colonial Office), 7 December, 1945; Supreme Commander to War Office, 30 November 1945, FO371/45387 E 9442, NA, Teveth, *David's Envy*, p. 627.

49 Teveth, ibid., pp. 653–60; Elhanan Oren and Gershon Rivlin (eds.), Introduction to *Yoman ha-Milḥamah: Milḥemet ha-'Atsma'ut*, [Hebrew: Introduction to the Diary of the War of Independence – 1948–1949], Tel Aviv: Ministry of Defense, 1982, pp. 708–9; Zahava Ostfeld, *Tsava Nolad: Shelavim 'Iḳariyim bi-Veniyat ha-Tsava be-Hanhagato shel David Ben-Gurion* [Hebrew: *An Army is Born: Main Stages in Buildup of the Army under Ben-Gurion's Leadership*], Tel Aviv: Ministry of Defense, 1994.

50 For this and following, cf. Teveth, *Ḳin'at Dayid*.

51 Ibid.

52 Ibid.

53 Ibid.

54 Diary, 18 June 1945, also. Tuvia Friling (ed.), *Biḳurim be-Gei ha-Haharegah* [Visits in the Valley of Death: Ben-Gurion's Journeys to Bulgaria, Sweden and the Displaced Person Camps in Germany], vol. I, (BG Research) 2014, pp. 1–11, 215–27.

55 Teveth, *Ḳin'at Dayid*.

56 Ibid., the chapter entitled 'From Biltmore to 5th of Iyar'.

57 Dvora Hacohen, *ha-Tokhnit le-Kliṭat Milyon 'Olim be-Reshit Shenot ha-'Arba'im* [The Plan for the Absorption of a Million Immigrants in the Early 1940s], booklet no. 18 October 1995, Institute for the Study of the *Keren Kayemet LeYisrael* (Jewish National Fund).

58 Ibid.

59 During his visit to Bulgaria in late 1944, Ben-Gurion coined the term the 'Red Paper', a play on the 'White Paper', referring to the danger that the East European countries under Communist rule would prohibit the emigration of their Jews. From 29 November 1947, there arose the additional danger of the oppression of Jews in Arab countries.

Part IV

Conclusion

16 Arab-Zionist negotiations during the Mandate

An unbridgeable divide

Laura Zittrain Eisenberg and Neil Caplan

Britain's almost 30-year administration of the Mandate was a period of escalating struggle between rival Jewish and Arab communities, each becoming over time more nationalistic and determined in advancing its mutually exclusive claims to the land. This clash did not preclude diplomatic efforts to arrive at a peaceful compromise of their conflicting aspirations. Between the end of World War One and the termination of the Mandate in 1948, Arab and Zionist leaders negotiated periodically in a variety of manners – directly, indirectly, under third party mediation, occasionally publicly and formally, usually secretly and informally. But all diplomatic efforts to bridge the chasm between them failed. Was this the fault of inept or dishonest negotiators, or was the gap between their competing national aspirations genuinely unbridgeable? An analysis of these futile Arab-Zionist negotiations adds to our understanding of why the decision on what entity would replace British rule after May 1948 would be made with the barrel of a gun and not by the tip of a pen.[1]

Explanations of the impasse

There are several possible explanations for the persistence of the Arab-Zionist dispute and the failure of the parties to reach an accord by the time the Mandate expired:

1 Some blame Zionist leaders for an initial indifference to the native Arab population in Palestine, and a failure to seriously reckon with its just concerns about its place in a Jewish homeland once Arab opposition could no longer be ignored or explained away.

2 Others single out the Arab community, whose rival political clans could not cooperate among themselves, let alone summon the leadership required to address Zionist interests with anything other than blanket rejection.

3 Generous observers take for granted the reasonableness and good intentions of both Zionists and Arabs and argue that the British, for their own selfish interests obstructed potential Arab-Zionist agreement by

deliberately sabotaging constructive contacts between the two peoples and inciting mutual suspicion.

4   Another explanation holds that a lack of sufficient contact among Arabs and Zionists prevented the majority of well-meaning Jews and Arabs from getting to know and understand one another. It was this mutual ignorance and the persistent misunderstanding of each other's intentions which led to distrust, dislike and hostility.

5   Leaders on both sides engaged in heavily 'tactical' negotiation activity that too often fell short of seeking a full-scale political accommodation, pursuing instead short-term gains and satisfying ulterior motives which created confusion and cynicism about their intentions.

6   Finally, there are those (some would call them 'realists') who believe that the basic minimum demands and aspirations of each side were, from the start, so far apart as to constitute a virtually irreconcilable conflict of interests.

There may be some truth in each of these explanations, but our analysis below suggests that the last two are the most accurate.

Negotiations as an extension of struggle

Perceptive Zionist and Arab leaders were quick to recognise the unlikelihood of a negotiated resolution but few were bold enough to speak about the impasse. As early as 1919, David Ben-Gurion observed:

> Everybody sees a difficulty in the question of relations between Arabs and Jews. But not everybody sees that there is no solution to this question.... There is a gulf, and nothing can fill that gulf. It is possible to resolve the conflict between Jewish and Arab interests [only] by sophistry. If we don't acknowledge this, and try to come up with 'remedies', then we risk demoralization.... We, as a nation, want this country to be *ours;* the Arabs, as a nation, want this country to be *theirs.*[2]

The Palestinian nationalist leader, Awni Abd al-Hadi, came to see the conflict similarly. "Some time ago", wrote Moshe Shertok in his note of a conversation between Awni and Haim Arlosoroff in early 1932,

> he [Awni] had come to the definite conclusion that there was no point whatever in negotiations or attempts to reach a mutual understanding. The goal of the Jews was to rule the country, and the aim of the Arabs was to fight against this rule. He understood the Zionists quite well and respected them, but their interests were fundamentally opposed to Arab interests, and he saw no possibility of an agreement.[3]

If the parties recognised that their goals were essentially contradictory, then why the dozens of negotiation episodes? To appreciate the reasons, we see how early on, Arabs and Zionists redefined the standard meaning of 'negotiation' to suit their own purposes. In the case of Arab-Zionist contacts during the Mandate period, however, the objective of negotiations was seldom about achieving a mutually acceptable accommodation in Palestine. Negotiations failed because a mutually satisfying solution was not their purpose in the first place. The tactical usage of the negotiating process for *other* ends, however, is perfectly consistent with the mutual recognition of the basic incompatibility of the parties' positions. In effect, Arab and Zionist representatives inversed the dictum of von Clausewitz: for them, diplomacy and negotiation were an extension of their basic 'war' by other (non-violent) means.

To better understand the failure of the parties to bridge the gap between 1920 and 1948, we offer an overview of their cumulative negotiating experience in terms of the high volume of Arab-Zionist contacts; the variety of purposes and motives for seeking negotiations; timing; the status of the negotiators; third-party considerations: and the proposed terms of agreement.

The wealth of negotiating experience 1920–48

This sheer quantity of Arab-Zionist encounters contradicts the argument that a lack of opportunities to interact is what allowed Arabs and Zionists to maintain uninformed and wrongly negative perceptions of the other's humanity and intentions. Apart from the often-congenial local relations forged between neighbouring Arab and Jewish villages and settlements, the Mandate period saw many thousands of contacts between representatives of the parties at all levels, up to and including secret discussions where political cooperation or an actual formula for peace was on the table. It is simply untrue that Arab and Zionist leaders were unfamiliar with one another's political programs; on the personal level, they often knew and even respected one another, all the while maintaining abjectly contradictory political objectives.

During the 1920s and 1930s, Zionist leader Dr. Chaim Weizmann met with dozens of Palestinian and non-Palestinian Arabs, seeking common ground which would accommodate the Zionist program in Palestine. British preparations for the Palestine Mandate included Weizmann's celebrated meetings and agreement (1918–19) with the Emir Faysal ibn Husayn, an optimistic relationship initially suggesting that friendly and fruitful negotiated arrangements between Arabs and Jews might indeed be possible. In late 1922, Weizmann held secret talks with Faysal's brother, the Emir Abdallah of Transjordan, inaugurating a 30-year clandestine relationship between the Emir and officials of the Political Department of the Jewish Agency in Jerusalem. Palestinian spokesmen, such as Awni Abd al-Hadi, Omar Salih al-Barguthi, George Antonius, and Musa Alami, periodically engaged in face-to-face dialogue with important *Yishuv* and Zionist figures. Throughout the duration of the Mandate, the head of the Jewish Agency, Ben-Gurion and Directors of its Political Department, such as M.D. Eder, F.H. Kisch, Chaim

Arlosoroff, Moshe Shertok and their designated representatives conducted exploratory and even serious negotiations with leading non-Palestinian and Palestinian Arabs.

At issue is not merely the quantity of contacts, which were many, but their quality as well. Most meetings were unofficial and secret; others were casual exchanges of views or information. The parties devoted much energy to sending out feelers, always trying to create the impression that the initiative came from the other side. These encounters, secret or open, took place in Jerusalem, or in Cairo, Damascus and Beirut, where Arab politicians, newspaper editors, religious leaders, entrepreneurs and cultural figures often received Zionist representatives hospitably, even while firmly rejecting the Zionist program. Some Palestinian Jews, operating independently, undertook personal missions towards establishing friendly contacts with Arab personalities, about which they periodically informed the Jewish Agency.

Obviously, few of these exchanges were of political significance; discussion of high policy was often in formalistic, rather than substantive terms, if it occurred at all. Yet, a fair number of Arab-Zionist meetings seriously attempted to define the terms of a possible agreement. Given the numerous Arab-Zionist encounters before 1948, it would be wrong to argue that a lack of direct communication or ignorance of the other party's true aims were at the heart of the impasse; there is no reason to think that an increase in contacts would have eliminated misunderstandings and led to peace. As Y. Harkabi once cautioned, "direct contacts between human groups do not always draw them together, but may make them realise how far apart they are and thus lead to further estrangement".

Purposes and motives

The political issues that dominated Palestinian-Zionist discussions during the Mandate period were the volume of Jewish immigration, continuing Jewish land purchase, communal representation in proposed self-governing bodies, electoral politics in mixed Arab-Jewish municipalities, and economic and security hardships caused by the Arab general strike and rebellion of 1936–39.[4] Each one of these was fraught with complications and a threat to the parties' overarching and mutually exclusive aspirations; together they constituted a virtually impossible nut to crack. However, on both sides there were an interesting variety of motives for initiating and conducting negotiations.

Sometimes both Arabs and Zionists found themselves simultaneously interested in negotiations for the purpose of derailing some unwelcome action on the part of the British. Thus, as early as 1921, the Emir Abdallah and the Zionists discussed their shared interest in the re-unification of Palestine west of the Jordan river with Transjordan, to the east, although their conflicting visions of who would govern that reunited Palestine made common action impossible. Likewise, Zionist and Arab opponents of the British partition plan of 1937 were potential partners for negotiations – but, again, with drastically different visions of what should replace Peel's plan to divide Palestine. More often than not, however, the two sides had their own reasons for engaging in talks.

Zionist motives

Occasionally, despite their scepticism regarding the outcome of talks, Zionist leaders recognised the tactical advantages of appearing reasonable and conciliatory to important third parties, such as British authorities or world public opinion. Thus, when trying to rectify serious political setbacks after the Passfield White Paper (1930) and prevent the issue of the MacDonald White Paper (1939), Weizmann launched a diplomatic offensive designed to prove to the British that their contemplated concessions to Arab demands need not be so far-reaching, since Zionists were demonstrably capable of negotiating seriously with reasonable Arab leaders. As Arab opposition became increasingly severe, Zionist decision-makers also needed to prove to their internal critics that they were doing everything possible to explore the chances of an agreement, following up on more leads than were perhaps warranted according to the appraisals of their own 'Arab experts'.

Under threat of Arab violence, Zionists sometimes thought it prudent to engage in talks in order to defuse some imminent danger. Thus a Zionist agent in Damascus during the tense spring of 1920 believed that his cordial conversations with Arab politicians, even if they led to nothing politically, were at least contributing to improving the security situation.[5] Perhaps the classic example of this type of negotiation was Golda Meir's unsuccessful efforts to persuade Abdallah to abstain from the planned Arab assault on Israel in May 1948. Abdallah's agreement would not have resolved the political problem in Palestine, but would have greatly improved the security situation for the Jews by keeping Jordan's Arab Legion, the most powerful army in the Arab coalition, from entering the fray. On the local level, peace pacts between Jewish settlements and neighbouring Arab villages or Bedouin tribes served a similar purpose, of providing security and peaceful day-to-day relations, without attempting to resolve larger political questions.

Deadlock with the recognised, uncompromising Husayni leadership in Palestine led Zionists periodically to initiate advances to the latter's rivals, primarily the Nashashibis, who became known, by default, as 'moderates' or 'the Opposition'. Ideally, Zionist assistance to so-called moderates would have led to their replacing so-called extremists in positions of power, from which they might one day have undertaken to welcome Zionist activity in Palestine for the benefit of all its inhabitants. But given the dynamics of Palestinian political organisations and the widespread consensus against losing the country to the Zionists, it was wildly unrealistic to imagine negotiations between the Jewish Agency and members of the Opposition leading to such an outcome.

We must not conclude, however, that there were no Zionist overtures for talks with Arabs motivated by the sincere desire to conclude a far-reaching agreement. The important caveat is that such optimistic initiatives seldom came from official leaders of the Jewish Agency, but rather from concerned individuals usually acting independently. Thus, Haim Margaliut Kalvaryski presented full-blown peace plans to Arab leaders in 1919–20 and in 1930; likewise, Dr. Judah L. Magnes discussed plans for a binational solution with the Arabs, in 1929 and 1937–38. On the other hand, Ben-Gurion's talks with Arab leaders (1934–38) dealt in broad terms with ultimate solutions to the emerging Arab-Zionist impasse. They were of an exploratory nature only.

Arab motives

Arab motives for entering into talks with Jews were also mixed, with even fewer (if any) actually envisaging an overall accord such as those suggested by Kalvaryski and Magnes. From their position of perceived strength as the country's majority during the Mandate period, there was little incentive or compulsion for them to accommodate themselves to Zionist claims. But Arab leaders in Palestine occasionally saw the tactical advantages of using the Zionists in their political manoeuvring *vis-a-vis* the British. For example, in their attempts to revive discussion of self-government for Palestine after rejecting three consecutive British proposals during 1922–23. Talks with Zionists were used then as a pretext, whether to create the impression within the Arab community that the initiative for a Legislative Council was coming from the British and/or the Jews, or to give the appearance to the British that the Jews were not as solidly opposed to a council as the Zionist leadership professed to be.

A mercenary instinct often brought Arabs to make overtures in search of Zionist resources, while Zionists often invited or entertained such contacts out of a desire to win hearts and minds among the Arabs. The need for financial backing for the publication of a newspaper was one recurring motive, which dovetailed nicely with the Zionists' desire for a better image in the Arabic press. Other Arabs sought backing for the establishment of a political club or party which might, they hinted, be less hostile to Zionism. A person with ambition for a government post might also seek surreptitious Zionist support, again with the inference that, if successful, the Zionists could count on a friend in high places. In this way some Arab leaders sought to use Jewish money to further their struggles against their rivals. Individuals seeking to sell land to Jews also sought audiences with Zionist representatives. Unsurprisingly, most of these interactions were kept secret, at the Arabs' insistence.

Heated local contests for power, such as the Jerusalem municipal elections, occasionally provided catalysts for Arab overtures to Jews. Thus in 1927, the 'extremist' Husaynis were not averse to attempting to strike a deal with the Jerusalem Jewish community by which the latter would abstain from voting, so that their rivals, the Nashashibis, might be more easily defeated at the polls. The Jews demurred and supported the more accommodating Nashashibis.[6] As the Mandate wore on, such Arab-Jewish political coordination became increasingly rare and counter-productive because of the de-legit-imisation suffered by any Arab party accused of collaboration with the Zionists.[7]

Timing of negotiations

Considerations of timing produced circumstances that prevented actors from entering negotiations, propelled them to the negotiating table, and encouraged or prevented flexibility once there. Often, Arabs and Zionists came to the table not so much when conditions seemed ripe for peace as much as when "the status quo seemed more painful or dangerous than a potential negotiated compromise".[8] Like protagonists everywhere, Arabs and Zionists were reluctant to negotiate from positions of perceived weakness or under the threat of violence; unfortunately, they similarly lacked the incentive to make concessions from positions of perceived strength, illustrating the vicious circle captured in the Middle Eastern adage: 'When I am weak, how can I compromise? When I am strong, why should I compromise?'[9] In the aftermath of the Arab riots of 1920, 1921 and 1929, for example, a strong case was made in Zionist circles that the psychological moment was not right for talks with Arab leaders, who might infer that violence was an effective way to force Jewish concessions.

A peace overture was often a temporary ploy, used to overcome a real or anticipated setback. Overtures were also timed to capitalise on a recent advantage (real or imagined) vis-a-vis the other side. Observing the intersection of timing with the influence of the British 'third party', Musa Alami wrote about the Zionist leaders in the months between the issue of the Shaw Report (limiting Zionist activity) in March 1930 and the MacDonald Letter (nullifying those limits) in February of 1931:

> even the most violent among them became very friendly towards the Arabs during this period. For the first time, the Jews wished to come to some understanding with the Arabs. Several meetings took place and all sorts of promises and programmes for cooperation were drawn up. But curiously enough, the Jews stopped those negotiations immediately upon the publishing of the MacDonald Letter. The Arabs therefore felt that so long as the British are backing the Jews, the latter will always disregard the Arabs.[10]

From his research into diplomatic manoeuvres during 1936–39, one scholar found similar calculations affecting the Arab side:

> The feelers put out by Zionist and Arab leaders ... were in the main political subterfuge, designed either to gain political advantage or to avert political disadvantage.... During the winter of 1937–38, it was to the

Arab advantage to prove the Peel Commission on 'conflicting national-isms' wrong, and avert the partition of Palestine.[11]

World War Two largely militated against serious negotiations between Pales-tinian Arabs and Zionists, especially during the period of Nazi successes, which had their echoes in Palestine, especially on Arab and Jewish percep-tions of their own relative strength. Expecting the imminent downfall of European Jewry and awaiting Hitler's victory, Arabs anticipated a rapid decrease in Jewish bargaining power and hardened their stance accordingly. The same assessments produced a life-or-death desperation that made Zionist leaders that much more unlikely to scale back their demands for a sovereign Jewish home in Palestine and even less inclined to negotiate with anyone offering anything less.

After the War, the Zionists launched an ambitious diplomatic offensive on the [non-Palestinian] Arab front, attempting to arrange for Egyptian Prime Minister Isma'il Sidqi and King Abdallah in Transjordan to join the Zionists in advocating for partition and the creation of a Jewish state in some part of Palestine. In return, Sidqi expected the Jewish Agency to press the British to rapidly conclude negotiations for their evacuation of Egypt; Abdallah was looking for financial largesse and for the Zionists to lobby the British in favour of Abdallah's 'Greater Syria' aspirations, including the annexation of the Arab parts of a partitioned Palestine. These efforts failed, largely because the Zionists were unable to influence His Majesty's Government to provide Sidqi or Abdallah with what they needed from London.[12]

By the end of the Mandate, bitterness and mistrust had increased between Zionists and Arabs in Palestine, whose infrequent meetings were progressively "farther removed from the reality of an imminent 'solution by force'".[13] HMG referred the Palestine problem to the UN in February of 1947. Shortly after the adoption of the UN Partition Plan in November of 1947, Colonial Secretary Arthur Creech Jones announced that Britain would terminate the Mandate on May 14, 1948; preparations for the departure of all British troops and functionaries began immediately. This stiffened the belief on both sides that the likelihood of a negotiated solution was almost nil and that their attention and energies would be much better spent preparing militarily to realise their national goals.

Status of the negotiators

When weighing the prospect of talks with the other side, Arab and Zionist representatives had to consider the status of the proposed interlocutor. Suc-cessful negotiation required negotiators who were authorised by or had the backing of those in power who could persuade their community to go along with whatever agreements reached through the bargaining process. Arab-Zio-nist peace efforts suffered from a Catch-22 dilemma: "Anyone willing to negotiate with me can't be worth negotiating with". Arabs and Zionists often refused to meet with one another's 'hawks', whom they believed to be impervious to reason, but were also not enthusiastic about creating contact with the 'doves' on the grounds that they were not truly representative or capable of 'delivering the goods'. Ideally, Zionist leaders would have liked to deal with a single, strong, recognised leader who would not subsequently be repudiated by an opposing sector of Arab opinion. The closest Palestinian to fit the bill, however, was their most committed opponent, the Mufti, Hajj Amin al-Husayni, whose popularity and legitimacy derived largely from his maximalist positions and refusal to negotiate or compromise with Zionists. Leading notables of the Nashashibi family were not averse to talks with the Zionists, but they commanded considerably less support and exerted less influence within the Palestinian Arab community.

Many times, one or both of the parties at the table had neither the authority nor the power to negotiate and deliver on concessions and promises. Meddlers were the bane of the official spokespeople on both sides, who often found themselves engaging in damage control necessitated by unofficial representatives from their own camps making overtures to leading personalities on the other side. The desire of these freelancers for personal gain or to 'do good' usually led them to propose compromises that the recognised leadership subsequently repudiated, thereby increasing the level of confusion and mutual suspicion between the two communities. Arab negotiators had to realise that although Magnes or Kalvaryski might offer them appealing terms, only the recognised Zionist authorities, such as Shertok and Ben-Gurion, had a chance of making good on their end of a bargain, even if their terms were less attractive. Many of their Arab interlocutors were well-informed and well-intentioned, but not charged by the Palestinian leadership to speak in its name. Speaking about Musa Alami after several conversations with him in the summer of 1936, Shertok observed that Alami might be "the equivalent among the Arabs of Dr. Magnes among the Jews – a very charming person eager to see Arab-Jewish differences settled, but representing no one".[14]

Finding little sympathy or success among the Palestinian Arabs, a truism of Zionist diplomacy evolved by which it was sufficient to develop positive economic and social relations with the Palestinian Arabs, while reserving political relations for a leader of the wider Arab movement *outside* Palestine. Zionists hoped to find someone prepared to concede Palestine to the Jews in exchange for certain services – Jewish capital, technical skills, cutting edge agricultural and scientific techniques, international political support – applied to the Arab world as a whole. The hope and presumption were that a major Arab leader would be able to influence Palestinian Arabs to go along with such an arrangement. Initially Weizmann's circle thought Emir Faysal, ostensible heir to a proposed Greater Arab Kingdom (excluding Palestine) might be their man; his brother Abdallah in Transjordan was another candidate, who was willing to go quite far in negotiating with the Zionists, but not far enough.[15] Throughout the Mandate period Zionists focused their diplomatic efforts on building bridges with a number of prominent Iraqi, Egyptian, Syrian, and Lebanese personalities, but the latter's demand for secrecy and their lack of influence with the Arabs of Palestine rendered them ineffectual. In the course of his meetings with Arab leaders during the mid-1930s, Ben-Gurion offered Zionist support for and membership in a regional Arab federation in exchange for Jewish sovereignty in part of Palestine. In the late 1930s and early 1940s, H. St. John Philby, a British Arabist and sometimes advisor to King Abd al-Aziz Ibn Sa'ud, proposed the Saudi King as the potential rallying-point of pan-Arab unity who might concede Palestine to the Jews in return for financial assistance and Zionist political influence on his behalf in Washington and London. Weizmann and his London associate, Prof. Lewis B. Namier, found this gambit particularly appealing, but the King was never as interested as Philby had suggested and the scheme never got off the ground.[16]

It is not entirely facetious to say that Zionists were perhaps among the most ardent pan-Arabists, hoping that Palestinian Arabs would replace their local attachments with a wider nationalism. Most Palestinians, however, were not so devoted to the ideal of pan-Arabism or to an individual non-Palestinian pan-Arab leader as to be willing to forgo the option of an independent Arab Palestinian state. Rumours that members of Faysal's court were negotiating with Zionists in this spirit in June 1920 provoked the following rebuke from a Palestinian member of the Syrian Congress:

> Up until now we have been silent, but in the future we will be unable to be silent and will not agree to Palestine's being sacrificed on the altar of [Syrian] independence.... The Government must ... deliver specific instructions to its emissaries to reject all the rumors connected with the Zionist question.... The Palestinians have been silent until now because of the honor of the Syrian state; but wretched Palestine has been devastated.[17]

Likewise, allegations of secret negotiations between Zionists and a committee of Syrians in Cairo in 1922 evoked a stern warning from the Haifa Arabic newspaper, *al-Karmil*: "Anyone who thinks that the sacrifice [of Palestine] is likely to help save another [Arab] spot is suffering from a repugnant brain disease and should stay out of the world of Arab politics until he gets well".[18]

Third-party considerations

Those who believe that a solution could have come about if only Arabs and Jews had been left to settle their differences, can point to the hard fact that Arab and Zionist leaders were never independent agents, free to consider any and all options in direct talks with one another. Their leaders always had to take into consideration the wishes and interests of powerful outside forces, such as the Turks, prior to 1914, and the British (and French) during the Mandate.

Our reading of the evidence is not that peace-loving Jews and Arabs were the victims of the machinations of imperial powers, but rather that, in the pursuit of their national goals, both sides could expect more by turning to outside powers than to each other. The unity and independence sought by pan-Arabists after 1918 depended on what the British and French governments were prepared to allow; Faysal's agreement with Weizmann did not reflect spontaneous affection or anticipation of the advantages which might accrue to his cause from world Jewry, but rather the belief that Arab independence, which depended on Great-Power decisions, might be more easily won if he cooperated with his British patrons, who were advising him to be 'nice' to the Zionists.

Likewise, Dr. Weizmann's personal diplomacy with Arab leaders after World War I was not based solely on the Zionists' independent judgment but also on their assumption that such a policy would please the British. After all, it was the British, not the Arabs, who had the power to press for international recognition of the Balfour Declaration and to implement its policies in Palestine. This pattern repeated itself throughout the Mandate period; Zionists and Arabs looked to the British for what they wanted most, and turned to each other when it appeared that such a move would be useful in furthering their respective positions *vis-a-vis* the all-powerful British.

Vacillations in British policy – made in London but applied in Jerusalem, with frequent discrepancies in the spirit of the two – also had their impact on Arab-Zionist negotiation attempts. Arab and Zionist perceptions of the drift of British attitudes and policies strongly influenced decisions whether to negotiate or to abstain from contact with each other. Under the terms of the Mandate, British officials found themselves in the thankless situation of administering the country under the 'dual obligation' of promoting the Jewish national home while at the same time protecting the "civil and religious rights of all the inhabitants of Palestine, irrespective of race and religion' and preparing the country for 'self-governing institutions".[19] Vigilantly watching how HMG's representatives implemented these obligations left each side feeling, at one time or another, that the British were unduly favouring the other. This perceived favouritism had the effect of rendering the preferred party arrogant and unyielding and the aggrieved party resentful, thus undermining hopes for a reasonable settlement. This comes out clearly in Musa Alami's rebuke of Moshe Shertok in 1936:

> the Jews were not in fact interested in reaching an agreement with the Arabs, since they depended on the English, and as soon as their situation improved somewhat they completely forgot about the existence of the Arabs.[20]

Conversely, the Zionists frequently complained that the Arab belief that *al-dawla ma'na* [the [British] government is with us] contributed to a spirit of defiance more likely to lead to rioting than to a willingness to negotiate with the Jews.

Often behind Zionist and Arab complaints about British policy lay an implicit desire for an imposed solution to the conflict, rather than one freely negotiated between their leaders. The Zionists consistently hoped that the British would apply the Balfour Declaration policy so sympathetically and so firmly that the Arabs would be forced to accept the fact of a permanent and flourishing Jewish national home. The Arabs, through their protests, non-cooperation and violence, aimed to convince the British to abandon the Balfour Declaration, and impose majority Arab government on a capped Jewish minority. To the extent that HMG allowed Arabs or Jews to believe it might impose their maximum demands upon the other, neither side felt compelled to make the hard choices and difficult concessions – needed for a negotiated settlement. Despite the lip service to the notion of reaching an Arab-Zionist understanding directly, each party behaved in a way which undercut the negotiating process and invited an imposed solution.

At times, Britain appeared to be pursuing its Palestine policy in consultation with Arab and Zionist representatives, and British officials went through the motions of 'mediating' between them and attempting to hammer out an arrangement acceptable to all. Thus, the Churchill White Paper of 1922 followed an exchange of correspondence between the Colonial Office with the Zionist Organization and a Palestine Arab Delegation, and several bilateral meetings with each. Likewise, the MacDonald White Paper of 1939 followed the St. James Round Table Conference at which Jewish and Arab representatives were invited to discuss various proposals for a mutually acceptable policy. But the truth was that the ostensible mediator had preferences of his own and a preponderance of power compared to the relative weakness of the parties in conflict. The Churchill White Paper, Britain's Palestine policy from 1922 to 1939, was really an imposed solution (rejected by the Palestine Arab Delegation), as were the drastic changes set forth by an exasperated Chamberlain government in the 1939 White Paper (which both Zionists and Arabs rejected, albeit for different reasons).

A third party of considerably lesser import was the non-Palestinian Arabs, the Zionists' preference for whom as negotiating partners was previously addressed. To the extent that Zionist leaders saw a better chance for reaching an agreement with them and focused their energies accordingly, talks with Palestinian Arabs received significantly less serious attention.

The proposed terms of agreement

For realists, the crux of the problem for arriving at a negotiated settlement was always the unbridgeable gap between even the minimalist positions of the contesting parties. But did those positions remain frozen and static, or was there some scaling-down of the original, maximalist demands, over the course of the Mandate?

The conventional wisdom of negotiation and diplomacy would lead us to expect that, like participants in other bargaining situations, Arabs and

Zionists had two positions: a) an initial, *tactical* position; and b) an ultimate, *essential* position. The difference between these two positions is known as the 'room for manoeuvre', i.e., the disposable items which can be given up during negotiation so as to arrive at a settlement with one's essential position largely intact.

An examination of the terms of the proposed ZionistArab agreements during the Mandate period suggests that on the whole, official spokesmen did not leave themselves much leeway. With few exceptions, there was very little scaling-down of the original, official demands of each side. The Arab position was that Palestine was an Arab land and should remain so. The addition of a new Jewish population to the demographic and political picture was perceived as illegitimate, and insufficient reason for modifying the claim to an independent Arab Palestine. The logic of the argument and the overwhelming (albeit lightly declining) Arab majority suggested that capitulation to Zionist demands was unjust, absurd and unnecessary. In the future Arab state of Palestine, Arabs argued, Jews would enjoy minority rights, but the majority had the right to protect its status either by halting or restricting further Jewish immigration, to ensure that the Jewish population remained a minority. The maximum size of this minority, as a percentage of total population, was one of the subjects debated during negotiations.

Even in the larger, pan-Arab context, Arab terms did not go much beyond this. The Emir Faysal appeared (briefly) to consider a separate 'Jewish Palestine' but he soon changed his position to accepting Palestine as a Jewish province within his promised Arab kingdom. Twenty-five years later, the Lebanese Maronite Church negotiated a treaty with the Jewish Agency which recognised an independent Jewish Palestine in exchange for its support for an independent Christian Lebanon. But the Church had minimal political influence in Lebanon and none in Palestine.[21] The Emir Abdallah and other non-Palestinians who contemplated an exchange of services with Zionists were willing to countenance a special status for Jews within Palestine, but never allowed for an independent, predominantly Jewish state in Palestine.

The willingness to reduce official demands was slightly greater on the Zionist side, but not enough to entice the Arab side into a negotiated agreement. The classical 'dream' was that Palestine (ideally on both sides of the Jordan) should ultimately become an independent Jewish state; this state would be prepared to participate in a confederation of Middle Eastern states if its neighbours recognised it and agreed to live in peace with it. When the historic opportunity for a small Jewish state within a partitioned Palestine presented itself in 1937, the official response of the 20th Zionist Congress, after much anguished soul-searching, was favourable in principle.[22] Ten years later, the United Nations Partition Resolution offered a (larger) independent Jewish state in a part of Palestine and Ben-Gurion accepted this final scaling down of Zionist demands. However, this apparent 'concession' was not enough to form the basis of an Arab-Zionist agreement, but led instead to a slide to war resulting in Israeli independence.

At the unofficial level, Arab and Jewish personalities explored a wide gamut of logical possibilities for an accord. Many of these efforts were known to the recognised leadership of each side, but failed to earn official sanction. On the Zionist side, several prominent personalities, acting in their individual capacities, believed that the maximalist Zionist goal of a Jewish state in all of Mandatory Palestine was unachievable, given the steadfastness of Arab hostility and the disinclination of the British to adopt and enforce a position wholly favorable to the Zionists. These mavericks began, as early as the mid-1920s, to formulate alternative terms which they hoped would win Arab acceptance. Itamar BenAvi was among the first to propose a federal Palestine with Arab and Jewish cantons. The *Brit Shalom* group and its successors tried in vain to convince both Arabs and Jews that the only solution lay in a unified, bi-national Palestine, where each national community would enjoy equal rights and exercise equal powers, regardless of their actual numbers in the population.

In the early days of the 1936 Arab General Strike, Judge Mustafa al-Khalidi approached a fellow jurist, Gad Frumkin, and suggested a joint search for an end to the strike and perhaps even an Arab-Zionist accord. Frumkin brought in Judah Magnes and three other prominent Palestinian Jews, who became a 'Group of Five' in negotiations with Khalidi: Musa Alami and other Palestinian Arabs who served in the Mandatory government, including some with contacts close to the Mufti. In those unofficial talks, 'the Five' were willing to forego the goal of a Jewish majority, and entertained Arab proposals which envisaged a fixed population balance (e.g., 60:40) which would have maintained a permanent Arab majority.[23]

These and later variations of peace proposals failed to win the confidence of the vast majority of Zionists, or even an echo from the Arab camp. A few Arabs were willing to consider the additional protection of Jewish rights that could have come about through some form of communal autonomy or Jewish cantons, but always within a sovereign Arab Palestine. The range of logical possibilities seems to have been fully probed and exhausted in Arab-Zionist negotiations prior to 1948; the disposition of Palestine by force, when the Mandate expired, was inevitable.

Conclusion

The generalisation that for every conflict there is a negotiated resolution is highly questionable. The divide between Zionists and Palestinian Arabs was indeed unbridgeable during the Mandate period. Both sides' increasingly nationalistic insistence on what became irreconcilable red lines, combined with their tactical manipulation of diplomacy, made the Arab-Zionist conflict in Mandatory Palestine one that had no peaceful, rational solution, no possible basis for agreement through voluntary compromises. Each party was so motivated by the righteousness of its cause, that it felt it *had to,* and that it could *afford* to, hold out for something very close to its full demands.

Consequently, each side waited for circumstances to force the opponent to modify his terms. Those circumstances arrived on 14 May 1948, when the last remnants of the hitherto all-powerful British administration departed, leaving Zionists and Arabs to unsheathe not their pens but their swords to determine whose claim to Palestine would prevail.

Notes

1 This chapter updates and significantly elaborates upon Neil Caplan, Negotiation and the Arab Israeli Conflict, *The Jerusalem Quarterly* 6, (1978), pp. 3–19.
2 David Ben-Gurion speech to the *Va'ad Z'mani*, 10 June 1919, J1/8777, Central Zionist Archives (CZA).
3 Awni Abd al-Hadi quoted in Moshe Shertok report, 12 February 1932, S25/3051, CZA.
4 Neil Caplan, *Futile Diplomacy,* Vol. II: *Arab-Zionist Negotiations and the End of the Mandate* London: Frank Cass, 1986; Routledge, 2015, pp. 29–40, 73–7, 118–29.
5 S. Felman, Damascus report, 28 January 1920, Z4/25082, CZA.
6 Neil Caplan, Arab-Jewish contacts in Palestine after the First World War, *Journal of Contemporary History* 12, 1977, pp. 659–61.
7 Hillel Cohen, *Army of Shadows: Palestinian Collaboration with Zionism, 1917–1948*, Berkeley/Los Angeles: University of California Press, 2008.
8 Kenneth W. Stein and Samuel W. Lewis, *Making Peace among Arabs and Israelis: Lessons from Fifty Years of Negotiating Experience*, Washington, D.C.: United States Institute of Peace, 1991, pp. 14–15, Harold H. Saunders, *The Other Walls: The Arab-Israeli Peace Process in a Global Perspective,* rev. ed., Princeton: Princeton University Press, 1991, pp. 24–5, 121.
9 Quoted in Thomas L. Friedman, *From Beirut to Jerusalem,* New York: Farrar, Straus, Giroux, 1989, p. 194.
10 Musa Alami, 'Present state of mind and feelings of the Arabs of Palestine', September 1933, p. 9, memo enclosed in Wauchope to Cunliffe Lister, 23 December 1933, 37356/I, CO733/257/11, British National Archives (NA).
11 Michael J Cohen, Secret Diplomacy and Rebellion in Palestine, 1936–1939, *International Journal of Middle East Studies* 7/3, July 1977, p. 404; Caplan, *Futile Diplomacy II*, pp. 70–7; Monty Noam Penkower, *Palestine in Turmoil: The Struggle for Sovereignty, 1933–1939.* Vol. II: *Retreat from the Mandate, 1937–1939,* New York: Touro College Press, 2014, pp. 416–18.
12 Caplan, *Futile Diplomacy II*, pp. 142–7; Neil Caplan and Avraham Sela, Zionist-Egyptian Negotiations and the Partition of Palestine, 1946, *Jerusalem Quarterly* 41, Winter 1987, pp. 19–30.
13 Caplan, *Futile Diplomacy II,* p.140.
14 Shertok quoted in Cohen, Secret diplomacy, p. 389.
15 Laura Zittrain Eisenberg and Neil Caplan, *Negotiating Arab-Israeli Peace: Patterns, Problems, Possibilities,* 2nd edn, Bloomington: Indiana University Press, 2010, pp. 74–5.
16 Caplan, *Futile Diplomacy II,* pp. 133–8; Yehoshua Porath, *In Search of Arab Unity,* London: Frank Cass, 1986, pp. 81–97.
17 Izzat Darwazah, quoted in Yehoshua Porath, *The Emergence of the Palestine-Arab National Movement,* London: Frank Cass, 1974, p. 89.
18 Quoted in Porath, ibid., p.114.
19 Mandate for Palestine (24 July 1922), articles 2, 6, accessed online 13 February 2019 at https://naip-documents.blogspot.com/2009/09/document-6.html. For discussion,

see Neil Caplan, *The Israel-Palestine Conflict: Contested Histories*, Oxford: Wiley-Blackwell, 2010, pp. 59–65.

20 Quoted in David Ben-Gurion, *My Talks with Arab Leaders*. Transl. from Hebrew by Misha Louvish and Aryeh Rubinstein, ed. M. Louvish, Jerusalem: Keter/New York: Third Press, 1972, p. 85.

21 Laura Zittrain Eisenberg, *My Enemy's Enemy: Lebanon in the Early Zionist Imagination, 1900–1948*, Detroit: Wayne State University Press, 1994, pp. 136–144.

22 Text of the resolutions are quoted in *Palestine: A Study of Jewish, Arab, and British Policies*, New Haven: Esco Foundation for Palestine, Inc 1947, vol. 2, pp. 854–5; also accessed online 11 February 2019 at https://en.wikisource.org/wiki/Zionist_Peel_Commission_resolution; cf. Michael . Cohen, *Palestine: Retreat from the Mandate: The Making of British Policy, 1936–45* London/New York: Holmes & Meier, 1978, pp. 35–8; Itzhak Galnoor, *The Partition of Palestine: Decision Crossroads in the Zionist Movement*, Albany, NY: State University of New York Press, 1995, Chapters 9–10.

23 Caplan, *Futile Diplomacy II*, pp. 35–40, Shmuel Dothan, 'Attempts at an Arab-Jewish Agreement in Palestine during the Thirties', *Studies in Zionism* 1/2, 1980, pp. 220–4; Cohen, Secret diplomacy, pp. 385–7.

Select bibliography of English sources

James Barr, *A Line in the Sand: Britain, France and the Struggle that Shaped the Middle East*, London: Simon and Schuster, 2011.

Nicholas Bethell, *The Palestine Triangle: The Struggle for the Holy Land, 1935–1948*, New York: Putnam, 1979.

Neil Caplan, *Futile Diplomacy*: vol. I: *Early Arab-Zionist Negotiation Attempts, 1913– 1931*, vol. II: *Arab-Zionist Negotiations and the End of the Mandate*, London: Frank Cass, 1983/1986 (both re-issued by Routledge in 2015).

Hillel Cohen, *Army of Shadows*, Berkeley: University of California Press, 2008.

Hillel Cohen, *Year Zero of the Arab-Israeli conflict 1929*, Waltham MA: Brandeis University Press, 2015.

Michael J Cohen, *The Origins and Evolution of the Arab-Zionist Conflict*, Berkeley: University of California Press, 1987.

Michael J Cohen, *Churchill and the Jews*, revised paperback edition, London: Frank Cass, 2003.

Michael J Cohen, *Britain's Moment in Palestine: Retrospect and Perspectives, 1917–48*, London/New York: Routledge, 2014.

Michael J Cohen, *Britain's Hegemony in Palestine and in the Middle East: Changing Strategic Imperatives*, London/Portland OR: Valentine Mitchell, 2017.

Kais M. Firro, *A History of the Druze*, Leiden: Brill, 1992.

Martin Gilbert, *Churchill and the Jews*, London: Simon and Schuster, 2007.

Yosef Gorni, *Zionism and the Arabs, 1882–1948: A Study of Ideology*, Oxford: Clarendon Press, 1987.

Aviva Halamish, *The Exodus Affair: Holocaust Survivors and the Struggle for Palestine*, Syracuse: Syracuse University Press, 1998.

Sahar Huneidi, *A Broken Trust, Herbert Samuel, Zionism and the Palestinians*, London/New York: I.B. Tauris & Co. Ltd, 2001.

Mustafa Kabha, *The Palestinian People seeking Sovereignty and State*, Boulder, CO/ London: Lynne Rienner Publishers, 2013.

Elie Kedourie, *England and the Middle East, The Destruction of the Ottoman Empire, 1914–1921*, London: Bowes & Bowes, 1956.

Issa Khalaf, *Politics in Palestine: Arab Factionalism and Social Disintegration, 1939–1948*, Albany: SUNY Press, 1991.

Rashid Khalidi, *Palestinian Identity: The Construction of Modern National Consciousness*, New York: Columbia University Press, 2009.

Baruch Kimmerling, *The Palestinian people: A History*, Cambridge: Harvard University Press, 2009.

Gudrun Krämer, *A History of Palestine: From the Ottoman Conquest to the Founding of the State of Israel*. Princeton: Princeton University Press, 2008.

Jacob Metzer, *The Divided Economy of Mandatory Palestine*, Cambridge: Cambridge University Press, 1998.

Rory Miller, *Divided Against Zion: Opposition in Britain to a Jewish State in Palestine, 1945–1948*, London/New York: Routledge, 2000.

Yehoshua Porat, *The Emergence of the Palestinian-Arab National Movement, 1918–1929*, London: Frank Cass, 1974.

Yehoshua Porat, *The Palestinian Arab National Movement: From Riots to Rebellion, 1929–1939*, London: Frank Cass, 1977.

Itamar Radai, *Palestinians in Jerusalem and Jaffa, 1948: A Tale of Two Cities*, London/ New York: Routledge, 2016.

Jehuda Reinharz, *Chaim Weizmann*, vol. II: *The Making of a Statesman*, New York: Oxford University Press, 1993 (vol. III, in press).

Jonathan Schneer, *The Balfour Declaration: The Origins of the Arab-Israeli Conflict*, New York: Bloomsbury, 2010.

Tom Segev, *One Palestine, Complete: Jews and Arabs under the British Mandate*, New York: Little, Brown, 2001.

Tom Segev, *A State at Any Cost: The Life of David Ben-Gurion*, New York: Farrar, Straus and Giroux, 2019.

Anita Shapira, *Land and Power: The Zionist Resort to Force, 1881–1948*, New York: Oxford University Press, 1992.

Colin Shindler, *The Triumph of Military Zionism: Nationalism and the Origins of the Israeli Right*, London: I.B. Tauris, 2006.

Kenneth W. Stein, *The Land Question in Palestine, 1917–1939*, Chapel Hill: University of North Carolina Press, 1984.

Bernard Wasserstein, *The British in Palestine: The Mandatory Government and the Arab-Jewish Conflict, 1917–1929*, London: Royal Historical Society, 1978.

Bernard Wasserstein, *Britain and the Jews of Europe, 1939–1945*, London/Oxford: Institute of Jewish Affairs/ Clarendon Press, 1979.

Chaim Weizmann, *Trial and Error*, New York: Schocken Books, 1949.

Index

Note: Page numbers in **bold** type refer to **tables**
Page numbers followed by 'n' refer to notes

'Aali al-Kilani revolution 80
Abd al-Aziz, King Ibn Sa'ud *see*
    Faysal, Emir
'Abdallah, Emir of Transjordan 139, 142,
    144, 145, 151, 272, 273, 276, 277;
    meeting with Weizmann 271;
    negotiating terms 281
Abrahamic Declaration (Storr's label for
    Zionist claims to Palestine) 31
Abu-Rukon family 129
activism, Christian versus Druze
    passivism 121–5
Activist-Revisionist Front manifesto 216
Adler, Chief Rabbi Herman 2070
adventurism 215–16
agrarian population, Palestinian 87, 89
agreement, Zionist–Arab proposed terms
    of 280–2
Agricultural Party 85
Ahimeir, Abba 210–11, 213–14; teacher
    and organiser 214–16
'Akka 73–4; earthquake (1927) 72–3;
    high school 72–3; Zu'ayter's relocation
    to 73–4
Al Jama'a al-Islamiyya 127–8
al-Istiqlal newspaper 79
al-Istiqlal Party 69, 70, 143
Al-Karmil 66
al-Qassam, Sheik 'Izz al-Din 125
al-Alami, Musa 150, 166–7, 183, 275,
    277, 279; and Group of Five 282;
    rebuke of Shertok 279
Ali, Muhammad 138
aliyah: second (1904–) 66, 288; third
    (1920s) 210, 288; fourth (1920s) 211
Allon, Yigal 130

Altman, Aryeh 218
Altneuland (Herzl) 158
Alza'ama Alhqqa (The True Leaders) 80
American Congressional Committee on
    Foreign Affairs, hearing regarding
    Balfour Declaration (1922) and report
    163–4
American Jews 247, 248, 263
American opinion on Palestine 36
American University of Beirut 71–2;
    Zu'ayter at 71–2
Amery, Leo 37, 235
Amlanim 210
anarchistic militarisation, of Great Arab
    Revolt uprising 128
Anglo-American Committee of Inquiry
    (AAC) 43n52, 47; memorandum from
    Jewish Agency 167
Anglo-American Mission to Poland
    (1919) 32
Anglo-American relations, and Bevin 46
Anglo-Iraqi Treaty (1930) 148
Anglo–Zionist Alliance, post-World War
    Two 248–9
al-Ansari, Sami 111–12
anti-government actions, by Arab Revolt
    rebels 112–13
anti-Jewish prejudice, of British elite 3
anti-Semitic stereotypes 14–15, 18–19, 49
anti-Semitism 25, 48–9; and Bevin 46,
    47, 48; Churchill's opposition to 45;
    mistreatment of Jews in Second Polish
    Republic 32; modern 221; protest risk
    in England (1938) 52; riots in Britain
    (1947) 47
anti-Zionism, Christian 108–9

anti-Zionist obstructionism, Baggallay's 35
Antonius, George 109
appointed commissions, in Arab
    municipalities 90
appropriation, collective Arab patronage
    of the Palestinian cause 149–51
Arab Army 18
Arab Club (*al-Nadi al-Arabi*) 16
Arab consciousness 66
Arab economy 181, 183
Arab Executive Committee (AEC) 138
Arab expansion to the North 20
Arab government, majority 28
Arab Higher Committee (HAC) 125,
    197, 204n32; members 86; Second 87
Arab identity, modern 66
Arab independence 21, 173, 183, 184;
    British guarantees of 17
Arab Independence Party 78, 79
Arab Kingdom 20, 21; Faysal's view of
    Palestine's inclusion 23
Arab land brokers 196–7, 200
Arab League 40, 48, 136; collective
    patronage over Palestine 151; Military
    Committee 151; and Palestine
    Question 149–51
Arab League Pact 149–50
Arab monarchs 144–5
Arab Nation Fund (*Sunduq al-Umma*) 200
Arab National Congress (Bludan, 1937)
    145–6
Arab national consciousness 66
Arab National Party 85
Arab nationalism 71, 80, 224; Zu'ayter
    as creator 81
Arab Nationalist Bloc 85
Arab nationalist movement 1; opposition
    to Zionism 111; supra-state 140
Arab nationalist party, primary core of 71
Arab nationalists: perception of Zionism
    139; and restoring Syria to the
    Turks 24
Arab organisations, dedicated to
    Palestinian Arab cause 29
Arab Palestinian General Congress 68
Arab Reform Party 86
Arab Revolt (1936–9) 33, 86, 90, 123,
    125–32, 140, 146, 165; first phase 179;
    leaders 67; marginalisation of minority
    groups 5; middle class shelters from
    113–14, 115; suppression 245; village
    versus town 111–14
Arab Revolt against Turkey (1916–18) 18
Arab rule 20

Arab states: defying 145–7; domestic
    stability 152; and Palestine Question
    139–41; Palestinian-Arab leadership
    143–9; Palestinian-Arab national
    movement 136–54; perception of
    Zionism 139
Arab unity 71
Arab volunteer force 144
Arab-Christians, as minority group 5
Arab-Islamic consciousness,
    domestic-regional nexus 137–42
Arab-Palestinian leadership, at national
    level 83–7
Arabic, Zionist newspaper in 164
Arabs: Christian 108–11; civil and
    religious rights 2, 5, 192, 279; of
    Palestine 223; rights of 39, 127, 148,
    160, 165, 192, 224, 226, 281, 282,
    see also Palestinian Arabs
Arab–British–Jewish relations, and
    Jewish immigration 6
Arab–German alliance 148
Arab–Israeli War (1948) 5, 115, 120, 202
Arab–Zionist dispute, explanations
    269–70
Arab–Zionist negotiations during
    Mandate 269–84
Arlosoroff, Awni and Haim 270
Armenians 108, 114
army: Arab 18; British 37; Jewish 207,
    218, 262–3; Palestine defence 76;
    Zu'ayter's call to youth 76
Army of Deliverance 151
Arthur and the Acetone (Shaw)
    236, 250n2
Ashkenazi Jews 33, 39
Al 'Assa 127–8
assimilation, of Jewish immigrants 16
al-Atrash, Sultan 130
al-Atrashi, Abd al-Ghaffar 129
Attatürk, Kemal 50
Attlee, Clement 54, 58, 250
Auschwitz 55, 56, 60n60, 61n66
Austria 254
Austrian Jews 180
autonomy, local, for Palestine 16
Avneri, Uri 224
Ayan social class 121

Baggallay, H. Lacy 34, 35, 36
Balfour, Arthur 15, 26, 50, 121; letter to
    Lloyd George 227; letter to Lord
    Rothschild 235, 238–9; and
    Weizmann 240

Balfour Declaration (1917) 2, 14, 15, 17, 24, 49–51, 108, 173, 174, 280; Arabs' demand to abolish 162; Article IV 21; Article VII 21; British intentions of 179–80, 279; call for abolition 162, 280; Christian opposition to 122; drafting 235; international recognition 279; opposition to 32, 67, 122; securing 8; and Weizmann 212, 235–6, 238–40

Baron, Salo Wittmayer 30

Begin, Menahem 205, 216–17, 218; and Jabotinsky 6

Ben Ze'ev, Menahem (Begin pseudonym) 218

Ben-Avi, Itamar 282

Ben-Gurion, David 7–8, 37, 56, 57, 164, 169, 270–1; acceptance of UN Partition Plan (1947) 281; on benefits of Jewish immigration 183; defence portfolio and threat definition 261–3; on land sale possibilities 198; letter to HC MacMichael 199; and MacDonald White Paper (1939) 246; negotiations 271–2, 274, 277–8; rejection of proposal 165–8; road map to independence 252–66; 'seminar' 261–2; visit to United States (1942) and cooperation plan 255–6; and Weizmann 249, 259–60; *Yishuv* leadership 252

Ben-Zvi, Yitzhak 130, 165

benefit theory *see* blessing thesis, Zionism to the Arabs

Ber, Israel 224

Bergmann, Ernst David 246

Berlin, Isaiah 1

Bermuda conference (1943) 218

Bet Sefer le-madrikhim Betar 214

Betar 208, 212–13, 214, 215, 218; conference (1938) 217; Jabotinsky's role for 215–16

Bevin, Ernest 4–5, 45–8, 58, 58n8, 59n12, 258, 259–60; and anti-Semitism 46, 47, 48; in Commons debate on Palestine (1949) 47–8; shortcomings 48

bi-national Palestine (*Brit Shalom*) 282

Bible 31

Bibring, Adelbert 212

Biltmore Conference/Convention (1942) 37–8, 249, 253, 255

binational solution (Magnes) 274

blessing thesis, Zionism to the Arabs 223; benefit theory 159, 164–5, 168–9; concept 157; first phases 157–60;

official Arab response 161–4; as political-national gain 166; rejection 167; Zionist critics 160–1

Bols, Major-General Sir Louis 15

Bolsheviks 214

Bolshevism 49, 210

book publishing, Palestine/Palestinian references 67–8

Boulangisme 205

bourgeoisie, Palestinian-Arab 5, 115, 126; government officials in 103; lifestyle 111, 112–13; neighbourhoods 104–5, 108; resentment of 112; values 114

Bowman, Humphrey 72–3, 74

boycotting, of Jewish economy 150

Brit Ha-Biryonim 214–15

Brit Shalom 282

Britain: Arab-Muslim resistance to 148; Department of Education 72–3; elite's anti-Jewish prejudice 3; favouritism to both sides 279; and Hejaz 19; immigration policy 177–81, 184–5; Labour Party 258–9; military administration (1918–20) 87; muddled policy making 14–15;

Palestine policy 245–6; and Palestine Question 257, 264; partition of Palestine policy retreat 146; perspectives on conflict of interest between Palestinian Arabs and Zionists 3–5; policy on the Balfour Declaration 279; policy fluctuations on immigration 177–81; policy fluctuations under 'dual obligation' 279; support for Zionist project 168; and *Yishuv* 247–8; Zionist policy of cooperation with 173

British Army, Jewish division refusal 37

British Commonwealth 56

British elite, anti-Jewish prejudice of 3

British Empire, and Moslem World 36

British politics, Weizmann's understanding of 237

British Zionist Federation 8

Buber, Martin 168–9

al-Buraq protests (1929) 74

Butler, R.A. 36

cadetism 207

Camp, Major J.N. 22

Canaan, Tawfiq 167

Canada, Jewish Legion base 217

capital, Jewish 181–2, 187n52, 230

Caplan, Neil 13

Census, Palestine (1931) 194
Central European Jews 36
Chamberlain, Neville 8
Chazars 32, 35, 39
Chever, Hanan 225–6
Christian Arabs: marginal players in national movement 108–11; population 109–10
Christian middle class 102–3, 122; disproportionate 119–20; response to Palestinian-Arab Revolt (1936–9) 111–14, 114–15
Christian middle class–Palestinian Arab values gap 109–10
Christians: anti-Zionism 108–9; Arab-speaking 66; and Druze differences 131; educated middle class 102–3; Greek Orthodox 122; Hebrew-Israelite blood 34; intellectuals 121; low response to GAR 132; Mandate benefits 120; minimal participation in Great Arab Revolt 127; population (1931) 119–20; in public sphere 121–5; refugees from Arab–Israeli War (1948) 120; revolt against in Great Arab Revolt 126; rights of 120; urban bourgeois status 127
Christian–Muslim divide, over domination of Christians in government organisations 108
Churchill, Winston 4–5, 15, 45–61, 162–3, 177; anti-Semitic skeletons of 48–9; and the Balfour Declaration 49–51; in Cabinet meeting (1921) on Zionist policy 50–1; in Commons debate on Palestine (1947) 57; in Commons debate on Palestine (1949) 47–8; defeat in 1945 election 257; support for Jewish State in Palestine 53–5; support for Jews and Zionists 45; and Weizmann 247; Zionist disillusion with 55–7
Churchill's White Paper on Palestine (1922) 22, 28n51, 175, 191–2, 280
Cilicia, withdrawal of British forces from (1919) 23
city growth: in late Ottoman period 102; upper-middle class development 103
civil rights, of Arabs 2, 5, 192, 279
civil versus political society (Vashitz) 110–11
civilian unrest, Arab-Jewish 198
clan-politics, Arab 91
clans, *Hamulas* 121, 131n12
Clausewitz, Carl von 271

Clayton, Brigadier General Gilbert 14, 19, 20
Cleveland, Ray L. 34–5
co-existence, Jewish–Arab 159–60
Cohen, Aharon Chaim 129, 224
Cohen, Hillel 131
Cohen, Michael J. 37
collectivism, Islamic 124
colonial 'intrigue' 13
colonialism: is Zionism? 221–34; Shenhav and Chever on the concept 225–6; Western 6, 137, 139, 159, 225
colonialist Zionist immigrant, stereotype 224
commissions of inquiry 192, 241, *see also* Peel Commission (1936–7)
communal violence 191, 192
communism 122
communist movement, Christians in 126–7
communists, Jewish 224
consciousness: Arab-Islamic 137–42; Palestinian Arab 66
consumer products, possession of 106
Coolidge, Calvin 249
Cornwallis, Kinahan 23
Crossley, Anthony 33, 36
Crossman, Richard 61n68
Czechoslovakia 254

Damascus 19; Arab government established in 67
Darwaza, Muhammad 'Izzat 25, 70, 197
Davies, Clement 54
Decembrists 213
defence, by armed Jewish force 229
defence army, for Palestine 76
democracy, parliamentary 214
demographic race, Arabs–Jews 183, 184–5
development, brought by Jews 183
Diaspora 226, 228
Dinur, Benzion 226, 227
diplomacy: conventional wisdom of 280–1; Zionist 277
diplomatic manoeuvres (1936–9) 275–6
Diston, Marshall 49
disturbances: (1920s) 111, 173, *see also* riots
Dizengoff, Meir 164
Doar Hayom 214
domestic Arab politics 140
domestic instability, in Arab states (late 1930s) 140

Donovan, William (Bill) 255, 256
Druze 121; British policy towards 124;
and Christians differences 131; from
Lebanon 129; from Syria 129; identity
formation 124–5; and Jews connection
130; low participation in Great Arab
Revolt 132; as minority group 5;
peasant population 121; peasants 130;
peasants' murder 129; as persecuted
group 130; political activity during
GAR 128; politics of 124, 125; public
sphere 121–5; refusal to recognise a
separate religious community 124;
revolt against in GAR 126; village
attacks by Palestinian rebels and
aftermath 128–9; Zionist movement
plan to move villages to Hauran
Mountains 130; Zionist policy
on 130–1
Druze in the Jewish State, The (Firro)
129–30
Druze-Lebanese volunteers 129
duality, British support for Jews and
Arabs 192
Dulles, Allen 255, 256

East Prussia 37
Eastern Europe 221; great Jewish
centres 30
Eastern European Jews 22, 31, 35, 36;
origins 36, 42n35
economic absorptive capacity (of Jewish
immigration) 175–7, 179, 183, 191–2,
241; assessing 181–2; definition 175;
deviation from 184; post-World War
Two 263
economic boom, in Palestine
(1933–5) 184
economic crises, Jewish community
(1923 & 1925–9) 178, 180
economic projects, joint Jewish–Arab 164
economy: Arab 183; Arab and Jewish
181; Jewish 182
Eden, Anthony 36, 37
educated elite, Palestinian 123
educated middle class, mainly
Christian 102–3
education: for males and females 105;
multi-lingual 105; needs for Palestinian Arabs 227; Palestinian nationalist
65; state systems 139
effendis: land purchases by 194–5;
Muslim 131; of Palestinian Arabs 165,
166; Zionist opposition of 165

Egypt 143–4, 145, 150; Islamic
associations 138; Islamic groups 140;
and Palestine Question 141; pan-Arab
aspirations 147; regional leadership
146–7; royal court 147
Eisenstadt, Samuel Noach 228
Elders of Zion 17; protocol 162
elections: irregular local 91; Jerusalem
municipal (1927) 274; Legislative
Council of Palestinian Arab Congress
boycott (1923) 84, *see also* local
municipal elections
electricity, banning from 'Jewish'
company 112
eligible voters, local elections 88, 90, 91
elites: British 3; new Arab entities rule
142; Palestinian educated 123;
Palestinian family 68, 87, 91;
Palestinian resident land-owning 231
Emek Hepher 193
English Zionist Federation 207, 237
Epstein, Yitzhak 159–60
ethnological reasons, Crossley's argument
about Jews returning to Palestine 33
Europe, international crisis (1930s) 254
European Jews 34, 229; origins 41;
permission to return to Europe 40
eviction, of Arab tenants 196
exclusive Jewish work 181–2
Executive Arab Committee 68
extermination of Jews 218, *see also*
Holocaust

factionalism, of Palestinian family-based
traditional elite 68
Faisal Ibn al-Husayn 67
Faisal, King *see* Faysal, Emir
Falastin 114, 120
family elite, Palestinian 68, 87, 91
family rivalries, Arab 84–5
Faraj, Raja 128
farmers, Arab 21
al-Farouki, Sheikh Suleiman 127–8
Farouq, King of Egypt 141
fascism 211, 213
fatwa, against selling land to Zionists 196
favouritism, by Britain to both sides 279
Faysal, Emir 13, 17, 18, 19, 20, 22, 23,
24, 82, 142, 277, 278; meetings with
Weizmann 271; negotiating terms 281
Faysal–Weizmann Agreement (1919) 4,
13–28, 18, 25, 143, 279
federal Palestine proposition
(BenAvi) 282

Feldschuh, Reuven 212
fellahin (Arab peasant farmers), exploitation and ejection from land 241
Fertile Crescent: domestic Arab politics 140, 141; ruling elites of 142
Filastin 66, 67, 127–8
financial backing, needs for newspapers 274
Firro, Kais 124, 129–30
food products, European/American 107
Foot, H.M. 195
Forming A Nucleus for the Jewish State 1882–1947 201
France: Ben-Gurion's base of operations in 261; *Boulangisme* 205; Mandate for Syria and Lebanon 174; and Syria 4, 14, 20, 23, 24, 25
Franz von Sickingen (Lassalle) 209
Freedman, Benjamin 39, 40
Frumkin, Gad 282
Fu'ad, King of Egypt 138

Gaselee, Sir Stephen 35, 36
Gaza 88
Gaza Strip 202
General Islamic Congress (1931) 138–9
general strike, Palestinian-Arab (1936) 143–5
German Jews 180
Germany: Jabotinsky's predictions about 206; Nazi 53, 149, 217, 247; pro-German policy 148–9, *see also* Nazism
Gerren, Henri 225
Gilbert, Martin 45, 60n48
'glacier of Jewry' (Namier on Eastern European communities) 30
God, belief in 31
Goldberg, Arthur 255, 256
Golden Square 148
Gorni, Yosef 13
governance, local in British Mandatory Palestine 87–90
government officials, in Palestinian bourgeoisie 103
Grand Mufti of Palestine 148
Great Revolt *see* Arab Revolt (1936–9)
Greater Israel 223
Greater Syria (*bilad al-sham*) 16, 67, 85, 121, 142, 276
Greek Orthodox Christians 122
Greeks 108, 114
Green Hand band 111
Greenberg, Uri Zvi 211
Group of Five 282

Ha-Am, Ahad 167
Ha-Madrikh 218
Ha-Poel Ha-Tza'ir 160
Ha'aretz 214
Haber, Leo 40; *The Khazar Poet* 40
al-Hadi, Awni Abd 13, 24, 165, 166, 270
Haganah 260–3, 266n45
Haiduc-Dale, Noah 123, 131
Haifa 73, 103; socioeconomic dynamic 122
Halperin, Yirmiyahu 217
Hamulas (clans) 121, 131n12, 133n12
Hankin, Yehoshua 195
Hapoel Hatzair 210
al-Haram al-Sharif (Temple Mount, Jerusalem), Zionist threat to 137
Hardy, Oliver 36
Harkabi, Y. 272
Harlo, Ahmad Abdullah 70
Hasan, Manar 115
Hashemites 16, 17–25, 149; from Hijaz 142; glorified by Lawrence 18; rulers 142, 143
al-Hashemiyya school (Nablus) 72
al-Haya al-Maqdisiya 77
Haycraft Commission (1921) 173
Hayutman, Isaac 164
Hazan, Yaakov 165
Hebrew Labour 164–5
Hebrew language 231–2
Hebrew Rebellion 252
Hebrew University (Jerusalem), as symbol of Zionist colonialism 227, 228
Hejaz, and Great Britain 19
Heller, Daniel 213
Herut 6, 218
Herzl, Theodor 158–9, 159, 190
Hidden Question, A essay (Epstein) 160
High Commissioner 89, 90, 91
Higher Arab Committee (HAC) 112, 143–7, 150
Higher Arab Institute (HAI) 151
Hijaz 17
Histadrut 7, 166; Congress (1934) 165; Congress (1937) 166; submission to UNSCOP 167
History of Palestine (al-Barghuti and Tawtah) 67–8
Hitler, Adolf 34, 51, 148, 180, 246, 254, 255, 257, 260, 276
Hoare, Sir Samuel 52
Holocaust 7, 46, 205, 217–18, 252, 253, 258; survivors 38, 260

Hope-Simpson, Sir John 38, 178, 182, 187n52
Hourani, Cecil 40
House of Commons debates 47
Husayni clan 16
al-Husayni (Husseini), Haj Amin 1, 17, 68, 84, 85, 86, 87, 89, 110, 113, 123, 127, 131; forced exile 146; head of HAC 143; and Nazis 154; opposition to 165; return from exile to Egypt 151; and as strong negotiator 277; support for mobilisation against Zionist aspirations 137–9
Husayni (Husseini), Musa Kazim 17, 23–4, 75, 84, 85, 162
Husayni party 114
Hushi, Abba 129, 130
Husseini, Ibn 'Ali 142
Husseini, Jamal 39, 40, 147
Husseinis 16, 85, 86, 89, 91, 127, 139, 143, 274; deadlock outcomes 273
Husseini–Nashashibis divide 84, 85, 86, 88, 90, 91, 139, 144, 146
Hyamson, Albert 182
hybridity, intercultural 107, 108

Ibn Sa'ud 139, 144, 145
identity: Arab modern 66; Druze 124–5; Eastern sense of 67; formation and affiliation 80–1; Jewish 221–2; modern Palestinian Arab 66, 67; Palestinian Arab national 65, 67–8; pan-Eastern 67; pan-regional Arab 66
illegal immigration, of Jews 185
Illustrated Sunday Herald 49
immigrants: annihilation of Jewish 16; Khazar Jews to Eastern Europe 30
immigration, Jewish to Palestine *see* Jewish immigration to Palestine
immigration to United States: closed-door policy 180; laws 179
imperialism, British 2
impoverishment, rural Arabs 194
independence: achieving Palestinian 75; Arab 17, 21, 173, 183, 184
Independence Party of Palestine 86
injustice, by foundation of Israel 224
integration, Arab–Christian 127
intellectuals: Arab 65, 67, 69, 222; Christian 121
intelligentsia, Jewish labour movement's 210
inter-Arab divisions, over Palestine 151

inter-Arab politics, and Palestine Question 142
inter-Arab tensions 142
intercultural hybridity 107, 108
'iqal (headdress) 112
al-Iqdam 74
Iraq 141, 144, 145; anti-Hashemite coup (1941) 151; Hashemites in 142; *Mufti* in (1939–41) 147–9; pan-Arab nationalists and army leadership 148; politics 148; propaganda bureaus 150
Irgun B'Yisrael 217
Irgun (Zwai Leumi) (IZL) 6, 59n9, 205, 213, 216–17, 218; side to take in World War Two 217
Iron Wall, The (Jabotinsky) 161–2
al-'Isa, 'Isa 114
Islam 123; as control 132; holy sites 137; and Judaism 6
Islamic collectivism 124
Islamic identification 66
Islamic movements, supra-state 140
Islamisation 5, 132; among Great Arab Attack fighters 128; of Great Arab revolt 125, 126; of nationalism 140; of Palestinian national struggle against Zionism 123
Islington, Lord 84
Israel: independence 281; Land of 208, 221; as nation state of Jews 222, *see also* Jerusalem
Israel (State of) 129, 252; pillars 6
Italy, fascism 211

Jabotinsky, Vladimir 243–4, 245; and Begin 6; Begin's criticism and challenge to his authority 216–17; cultivating youth 211–13, 215–16; *Homo Homini Lupus* 207; idea of parliament 214; ideological influences on 205–6; influence of poetry on 208; move to the right and antisocialism (1917–) 209–11; poetry influence on 208; sense of fatalism 207; views on parliament 214; views on World War One 206–7; visit to Poland 211–12
Jabotinsky, Ze'ev 161–2
Jacobson, Victor 244
Jaffa 103; Jewish Immigrants' hostel 173; population after Arab–Israeli War (1948) 120; socioeconomic dynamic 122
al-Jama'a al-Islamiyya 127–8
Jawhariyya, Wasif 106

Jerusalem 25, 102, 103; Christian population after Arab-Israeli War (1948) 120; 'garden suburb' 104; Hebrew University 227, 228; as Islamic holy site 127; mayors 91; municipal elections (1927) 274; municipality 91
'Jew-baiting' by Churchill 49
Jewish Agency 186n20, 191, 201, 218, 256, 276; agreement with Lebanese Maronite Church 281; British sanction of 190; constitution 167; Executive 257, 261; negotiations 271–2; special memorandum to Anglo-American Committee of Inquiry (AAC) 167
Jewish Arab settlement 13
Jewish Army 207, 218; Ben-Gurion's goal for 262–3
Jewish Brigade 55, 57
Jewish capital 181–2, 187n52, 230
Jewish Chronicle, The 49, 52
Jewish combat force, to aid World War Two Britain 246
Jewish Commonwealth 37, 249, 253, 255
Jewish communists, return to Soviet Union 224
Jewish economy, boycotting of 150
Jewish Fellowship 38–9
Jewish geographic development 190
Jewish immigration to Palestine 6, 8, 22, 172–88; absorption of the masses 263–4; after MacDonald letter 242–3; Arab fear of 173; Arab reaction to 184; Arab veto 52, 53; and Arab–British–Jewish relations 6; assimilation 16; ban 173; benefits 167, 168; between the world wars 175–7; Britain's policy 184–5; Britain's policy fluctuations 177–81; British Administration categories for 176, 191–2; ceiling on 173; cessation call 173; change from economic to political issue 33; Churchill's restriction plans (1938) 52–3; as control 167; ebb and flow (1920–48) 191; economic impact 173, 183; from Eastern European 22; ideological to Land of Israel 228, 229; illegal 185; impact on Palestinian Arabs 182–3; of Jewish Holocaust survivors 7, 8; and labour 184; limited rate 142; political high level principle 179; preferential status 180; quotas 52, 53, 145, 174, 246, 257, 260; regulation 178; restriction 51, 192, 199, 255, 281; statistics 243; stopping of 192–3; suspension (1921) 191; threat of 66,

see also economic absorptive capacity (of Jewish immigration); land sales by Arabs to Jews
Jewish independence, road map 252–66
Jewish labour movement 164, 165, 242, 245
Jewish Legion 207, 212, 215; based in Canada 217; origins of 208
Jewish majority 33, 87, 142, 172, 177, 230; Weizmann's opposition to 243–4
Jewish military force 206, 208, 229
Jewish minority, capped 280
Jewish nation-state in Palestine 252–3, 258; Ben-Gurion's road map 253–66
Jewish National Committee (*ha-Vadd ha-Leumi*) 164, 167; Committee for Our Relations with the Arabs 164; proclamation to the Palestinian Arabs (1947) 167–8
Jewish National Fund (JNF) 197–8, 200; documentation 195; land purchases 193, 201, 224, 225
Jewish National Home 2, 6, 22, 23, 57, 166, 174–5; British support 142, 192, 235; demographic growth of 184; physical growth 190
Jewish nationality, denial of 222
Jewish Outlook, The 39
Jewish Palestine 20
Jewish refugees 38, 52, 173, 180, 218, 247–8, 250, 252, 259
Jewish settlers, ties severing with land of origin 231
Jewish State 6, 17, 22, 197, 244, 276; Arab public resistance to 145; Churchill's support for 53–5; infrastructure 8, 9; land area 201–2; physical requirements 189; prevention 38; sovereign 172, 173
Jewish Telegraph Agency 57
Jews: American 247, 248, 263; Ashkenazi 33, 39; Austrian 180; Central European 36; and Druze connection 130; Eastern European 22, 31, 35, 36, 42n35; economy 181, 182; European 34, 41; European and return to Europe 40; German 180; identity 221–2; land purchase restrictions 33; nation building 192–7; nationalism 221; power and influence myth 26; rights of 2, 22, 31, 37, 38, 39, 123, 127, 181–2, 226–7, 281, 282; Russian 39; wealth and influence 18–19
jihad (struggle for freedom) 75, 77, 79, 80

jobs: in public and municipal works 182;
 types in Palestine labour market 181–2
Jones, Arthur Creech 276
Jordan, Arab League 273
journalism, in late Ottoman period 120
Journey to the Land of Israel 2040, A
 (Lewinsky) 157–8
Joyce, Colonel 19–20
Judaism: conversion to 32, 33, 38, 39, 41;
 and Islam 6; Khazar conversion to 35;
 and Zionism differences 123
Judeo-Bolshevik bogey 15
Junblatt, al-Sitt Nazirah 129

Kabha, Mustafa 126
Kalvaryski, Haim Margaliut 131,
 274, 277
al-Karmel 120, 278
Karmi, Ghada 113
Karmi, Hasan 113
Karmi, Mahmud 113
Katznelson, Yosef 214
Kedourie, Elie 17, 35
al-Khalidi, Judge Mustapha 282
Khalidi, Rashid 125–6, 223
al-Khalidi, Yousef Ziaa al-Din 158–9
Khanifas, Sheikh Hassan,
 assassination 128
Khazar theory 30, 32, 34, 36, 38, 39, 40
Khazars 4, 30–44; conversion to Judaism
 35; origins of 30, 39
Kheyr (Khir) family 124, 125
al-Khouri al-Baytjali, Iskander 112
kibbush ha'avoda (conquest of land) 231
kibbush (occupation/conquest) 229, 231
Kimmerling, Baruch 223, 224, 225, 231
Kincaid, Charles A. 34
kinship: Ottoman structure 87; and
 Palestinian social structure 83
Kishinev pogrom (1903) 208
Kitchener, Lord Herbert 17
Koestler, Arthur 40
Kook, Avraham Isaac Hacohen 168
Kristallnacht 32, 51, 60n37
kufiyya (headdress), enforcement 112

labour: certificates 176, 178;
 immigration 184
labour market, Arab 182
labour movement, Jewish 164, 165;
 Yishuv 242, 245
Labour Party, British 257–9;
 Ben-Gurion's response to support of
 Zionism 258–9

Labriola, Antonio 206
land: Arab sources 192–7; linking people
 to 189–91; *musha'* system of tenure
 194; state-owned 231; Zu'ayter's call
 to protect 76
land brokers, Arab 196–7, 200
Land of Israel 208, 221, 222; ideological
 immigration to 228, 229
Land and Power (Shapira) 229
land prices 198; increase 200–1, 231
land sales by Arabs to Jews 6, 8, 19, 189–90,
 191–2, 196, 223, 231; consequences 193;
 failure to stop 231; mid-1930s to end of
 Mandate 197–201; motivations for
 192–7; official plan 201; percentages
 201–2; restrictions 33, 241; small owner
 protection 196; transfer regulations
 circumventing 199–201
Land Transfer Regulations (1940)
 193, 199
Landless Arab inquiry (1933) 195
landlords, Arab 165
lands of origin 47
Law of Execution (Amendment)
 Ordinance (1931) 196
Lawrence, Thomas Edward 4, 13, 14, 18
League of Minorities 129
League of National Liberation 127;
 members 122–3
League of Nations 24, 138, 145; Council
 186n20, 239; Mandate for Palestine 2,
 174, 185n7; and Weizmann 240–1
League for Peace with Justice in
 Palestine 39
Lebanese Maronite Church 281
Lebanon 22, 146, 150; Druze from 129;
 French Mandate for 174
Legislative Assembly, plan failure 244–5
Legislative Council of Palestinian Arab
 Congress, boycott of 1923 elections 84
Lehi 217, 247
leisure habits, middle class 106
Lenin, Vladimir 211
Les Temps Modernes 222
Levant 139
Levi, Sylvain 22
Levin, Dr Shmaryahu 24
Levontine, Zalman 160–1
Lewinsky, Elhanan 157–8
lifestyle, bourgeois: of Palestinian Arabs
 104–8
Ligue antisémitique de France
 (Dumont's) 205
Likud 218

Lilienthal, Alfred 39
al-Liwa' 111
Lloyd George, David 15, 18, 49, 50; coalition's Palestine policy 50; dismissal of Military Occupation regime 3; government of 4, 20, 235, 239, 240; letter from Lord Balfour 227; memoirs 250n2
loans, to Arabs 20
local governance in Palestine 87–90
local municipal elections 5, 83, 91; (1927) 88–9, **92–3**; (1934) 89–90, **94–5**; (1946) 90, **96–7**; regulations 88

MacDonald, Malcolm 32, 53, 241, 245–6, 254
MacDonald, Ramsay 33, 241–2; letter to Weizmann (1931) 137, 242–3
MacDonald's White Paper on Palestine (1939) 2, 8, 33, 51–3, 147, 174–5, 179, 180–1, 185, 198–9, 246, 255, 258–60, 280
McMahon–Husayn agreement (1915) 39
MacMichael, High Commissioner 199
Magnes, Dr Judah L. 166, 274, 277, 282
Majlisiyeen 84
Mandate for Syria and Lebanon 174
Mandated Palestine: description 1; population 172
Mandatory government 146
Mapai 7, 218, 242, 249
Mardor, Monya 263
Margolin family 230
Margulies, Heinrich 194
Mark, Merav 122
Martin, J.M. 40
Marxism 122, 123, 205
Massalha, Nur 225
Matzpen 224
maximalists (of Jabotinsky movement) 216; rise of 213–14
Mayors 87, 88; appointment 90; from opposition 90
meddlers in negotiations 277
media 29; Khazar theory promotion in 39
mediation, by British 280
Meinertzhagen, Colonel Richard 50
Meir, Golda 273
mercenary instincts, in negotiations 274
merchants, peasant indebtedness to 194–5
Mesopotamia 24, 50, 139
Michels, Roberto 211

Mickiewicz, Adam 208
middle class: intellectual 65; Muslim and Christian and the national movement 108–11; Palestinian Arab 5, 102–18; and Palestinian Arab national movement 115; rise of 102–8, *see also* Christian middle class
Middle East: Churchill's policy for (1945) 54–5; colonial 'intrigue' in 13–28; pre-World War Two destabilising by Germany and Italy 255
Migdal, Joel 223
militant Zionism 6; origins 205–20; and romantic nationalism 208–9; youth 211–13
militarism 216
military force, Jewish 206, 208
Military Occupation regime (1918–20), dismissal by Lloyd George 3
Military Zionism 6
Milner, Alfred 235
minorities, national 209
minority groups 5
Mir'at al-Sharq (Mirror of the East) 67, 74–6; Zu'ayter's writing for 76
Mitri, Michel 134n47
mobilisation: of religion 132; of resistance to Zionist aspirations in Palestine 137
moderate Zionism 21
moderates, Nashashibi 273
modernisation, and growing interest in Palestine Question 139–40
modernity, Palestinian Arab 106
monarchs, Arab 144–5
money lenders, Palestinian Arab 195
Money, Major General 14–15, 20
Monroe, Elizabeth, on the Balfour Declaration 2
Moody, Sydney, conversation with Shuckburgh 3–4
Morgan, J.P. 58
Morgenthau, Henry 238
Moroccan revolution 72
Mossad Le'Aliyah Bet 261
Mosul 20
Moyne, Lord 36–7, 53, 57; assassination 247
Muadi family 124
al-Mu'arada 84, 123
Mufti 114, 196; Grand, of Druze 124; in Iraq (1939–41) 147–9
Mukhtars 87, 88, 91, 107
multi-lingual education 105

Munich Agreement (1938) 255
Municipal Corporations Ordinance
    (1934) 89, 90, 91
Municipal Councils 88
municipal elections *see* local municipal
    elections
Municipal Franchise Ordinance
    (1926) 88
municipalities 87–8, 89, 90, 91;
    Palestine 87
Municipalities Ordinance (1877) 87, 88
musha' system of land tenure 194
Muslim Brotherhood of Palestine 87
Muslim Brothers (MS) 137
Muslim Higher Council 68
Muslim majority, Sakakini's fear of 109
Muslim Youth Organisation 85
Muslim-Christian Association (MCA)
    16, 67, 68, 83–4, 108, 131; seats in 121
Muslim-National Associations 131
Muslims 122; in bourgeois neighbourhoods
    108; grievance over overdominance of
    Christians in government organisations
    108; holy places 137
Muslim–Christian societies: demands of
    121–2; post-Ottoman period 121
Mussolini, Benito 211, 213, 214
My Talks with Arab Leaders
    (Ben-Gurion) 166
Myers, David 228, 229

Nablus 69, 72–3, 74; Zu'ayter's teaching
    in *Al-Najah* National School 70, 78–9
Naffa, Zaid 129
Nakba (disaster) 115, 202
Namier, Lewis 30–1, 278
Nashashibi, Raghib 84, 85, 86
Nashashibis 89, 123, 127, 131, 144, 274,
    277; as 'moderates' 273
Nashashibis–Husseini divide 84, 85, 86,
    88, 90, 91, 139, 144, 146
nation building 192–7
nation-state, modern 221
national army for Palestine 76
National Bloc Party 86
National Defence Party 85
National Islamic Council 127
National Liberation League 87, 122–3
national liberation movement, Arabs of
    Palestine 223
national minorities 209
National Party 123
nationalisation, of fledgling Arab
    states 140

nationalism 72; Arab 71, 80, 81, 224;
    Islamisation of 140; Jewish 221; local
    and pan-Arab 65–82; Palestinian 5,
    83; Pan-Arab 81; romantic 208–9;
    Ukrainian 209
Nationalist-Islamic Associations 127
Nazi Germany 53, 149, 217, 247;
    appeasement by Chamberlain's
    government 53; pogroms 208, 209,
    218, *see also* Holocaust
Nazism 33, 35, 46, 51, 205, 217, 218;
    defeat of 46
Near East, restoration of 24
Nebi Musa see riots
negotiating experience, Arab–Zionist
    (1920–48) 271–2
negotiations, Arab–Zionist 13; Arab
    motives 274–5; conventional wisdom
    of 280–1; different meanings 271; as
    extension of struggle 270–5; from
    positions of perceived weakness/
    strength 275; proposed terms of
    agreement 280–2; purposes and
    motives 272–7; resolution 270; status
    of negotiators 276–8; third-party
    considerations 278–80; timing of
    275–6; Zionist motives 273–4
neighbourhoods: Arab middle class 103;
    bourgeois 104–5, 108
New York Herald Tribune 39
New Zionist Organisation 213
News Chronicle 259
newspapers 66, 67; Arab and reporting of
    debilitating land sales from Arabs to
    Jews 196–7; financial backing needs
    274; late Ottoman period 120; Zionist
    in Arabic 164
Newton, Frances 31
non-Palestinian Arabs 280; talks with
    Zionist representative (1908/1913–14) 16
Nordau, Max 207
al-Nqqash, Zaki 70

obstructionism, anti-Zionist
    (Baggallay's) 35
Occupied Enemy Territory
    Administration (OETA) South 13
Odesskie Novosti 205–6
Ormsby-Gore, William 3, 179
Orthodox Christians 122; attacks by
    rebels 131
Orthodox Church, Palestinianisation of 123
OSS (US, Office of Strategic Services)
    255–6

298   *Index*

Ottoman Empire 66, 69; administration
    87; Jewish immigrants as citizens 16;
    leading families 84–5; millet system
    83, 120; newspapers 120; reforms and
    economic/social change 102
Ottoman Land Law (1858) 193
Ottoman Land Registration Law
    (1864) 193
Ottoman Municipalities Ordinance
    (1877) 89
Ottoman Rule 20
Ottoman Syria 13
Ottoman Vilayet Law (1864) 87

Palestine: population 172; population in
    1930s 70, 103; population in (1931) 103,
    194; power struggles (Arabs) 178;
    urbanisation 122; urban–rural
    population fissure 102; *Yishuv*
    population 2
Palestine Arab Cause, The (Canaan) 167
Palestine Communist Party 87; members
    122; split in ranks 122
Palestine Loan 240
Palestine Mandate: Article VI 190–1;
    termination 276
Palestine population: (1931) 103; after
    World War One 70; Jewish
    (1882–1948) 189
Palestine Question 136–54; and Arab
    League 149–51; and Arab states
    139–41; and Britain 257; and Egypt
    141; and inter-Arab politics 142;
    regionalisation of 143–5; solution
    within Iraq/Transjordan/Palestine 147
Palestine State, with Arab–Jewish shared
    government 174–5
Palestine triangle 172–88
Palestine Youth Congress 86
Palestinian Arab Congress 84; decision
    to boycott 1923 elections 84; executive
    committee 85; (1919) 6, 223; (1928) 84
Palestinian Arab leadership 91; and Arab
    states 143–9; leaders' land sales to Jews
    196, 197; mistrust of the military 125;
    policy 109; policy and bourgeoisie 115
Palestinian Arab National Movement 68,
    102; Arab states 136–54; and middle
    class 108–11
Palestinian Arab Party 85, 87
Palestinian Arabs 16–17; agricultural
    class 194; anti-government actions by
    Revolt rebels 112–13; boycott of 1923
    elections 84; civil and religious rights

2, 5, 120, 192; civil society collapse
    114; civil versus political society 110;
    clan-politics 91; consumption patterns
    107; Council of Ten 21, 22; *effendis*
    131, 165, 166, 194; elite 4–5, 68, 123,
    127; food consumption 107; general
    strike (1936) 143–4; identity 67–8;
    leadership 83–7, 91, 125, 143–9; local
    councils 5; as majority in Palestine 51;
    middle class 5, 102–18, 119–20, 122;
    national identity 65, 68; national
    versus personal/regional/sectarian
    values gap 110–11; nationalism and
    Zu'ayter 65–82; new social class 122;
    notables 195; origin of 34; perspective
    on Zionist aspirations in Palestine 5,
    137–9; pluralism 119; political clubs
    16; political parties 5; political parties
    and local self-governance 83–101;
    possession of consumer products 106;
    public and municipal works jobs 182;
    public resistance to Jewish State
    establishment 145; religion as control
    132; religious and civil rights 2, 5, 192,
    279; religious authority only political
    leadership in Palestine 83; rights of 15,
    19, 21, 31; stigmatisation by Lawrence
    18; Zu'ayter's criticism of leadership
    75–6, *see also* local municipal elections
Palestinian Christians, non-elite
    classes 123
Palestinian Free Party 85
Palestinian National Congress (1919)
    10n11
Palestinian National Movement 5, 132
Palestinian nationalist movement: Christian
    role in 121; sectarianism in 127
Palestinian People's Party 85
Palin Report into *Nebi Musa* riots
    (1920) 3
Palmach 114
pan-Arab nationalism 65; Zu'ayter
    creator of 81
pan-Arab nationalists, Iraqi 148
pan-Arab unity 142, 278
pan-Arabism 66, 67, 85, 86
pan-Arabists 278
pan-Eastern identity 67
pan-Islamism 85
pan-regional Arab identity 66
Pappé, Ilan 1–2, 225
Paris Peace Conference (1919) 190
Parliamentary Conference of the Arab
    and Islamic States (Cairo, 1938) 141

Parsons, Laila 128
partition of Palestine 52, 173, 174, 198,
    230, 259; British retreat from policy
    146; Churchill's plans 53–4, 55–6,
    56–7; Peel Commission plan 197, 245;
    with a small Jewish state 281; UN
    plan 151, 167, 202, 263, 276, 281
Pasha, Ibrahim 65–6, 223
Pasha, Nahhas 141
Passfield's White Paper (1930) 7, 8, 138,
    178–9, 241–2, 258
passivism, Druze versus Christian
    activism 121–5
patriotism, Begin on 216
patronage, of Arab League 149–51
peace: Catch-22 dilemma for efforts 276–7;
    Kalvaryski's plans 274; local pacts 273;
    overture ploy 275; proposals 282
peasants 5; Arab 21, 165; Arab
    indebtedness to notables and merchants
    194–5; Arab land registration
    requirements 193–4; inducing hostility to
    Jews in 20; and land sales to Jews 195–6;
    rights of Arab 21, 193–4
Peel Commission (1936–7) 90, 141, 145,
    172–3, 174, 179, 183, 184–5, 245, 276;
    report 197, 245
Penslar, Derek 229
Perry, Glenn A. 41
Philby, H. St. John 278
Piłsudski, Józef 209, 212
pluralism, Palestinian society 119
pogroms 208, 209, 218
Poland 208–9; Anglo-American Mission
    to (1919) 32; arrivals from 211
Polish Jewry 32, 218
Polish Legion 209
Polish military, training of *Irgun* mem-
    bers 217
Polish State 32
political coordination, Arab–Jewish
    274–5
political elite, British 4–5
political high-level principle 179
political institutions, Palestinian 5, 83
political Zionism 191; Kimmerling
    on 225
politicisation, of fledgling Arab
    states 140
politics: domestic Arab 141; Druze 124,
    125; Iraqi 148
Porath, Yehoshua 111, 131, 278
post-war consensus, after Nazism
    defeat 46

press: Arab 16; monitoring of Palestinian
    by British 76–8
Price-Gordon, Assistant District
    Commissioner of Ramallah 113
propaganda: bureaus (Iraqi) 150; Faysal's
    fear of enemy 20; pro-Turkish 21; by
    Zionists 6, 38
Propes, Aharon 217
protests: about Arab secession of 'south
    province' 22; al-Buraq (1929) 74; risk
    of anti-Semitic in London 52
public sphere, Christians in 121–5

Qalqilya, elections in 88–9
al-Qassam, Sheik 'Izz al-Din 69, 79–80,
    86; funeral of 80
Qatamon, conquest 114
al-Qawuqji, Fawzi 144; and Army of
    Deliverance 151
Question that Outweighs All Others, A
    (Epstein) 159–60
quotas: Jewish immigration 145, 174,
    246, 257, 260; refugees 180

race, literature on Jewish origins 35
Rahman, Sir Abdur 39, 43n62
Raz-Krakotzkin, Amnon 226–7
Raziel, David 217
Red Army 50
Réflexions sur la violence (Sorel) 205
refugees: German 180; Jewish 38, 52,
    173, 180, 218, 247–8, 250, 252, 259;
    quota 180
regionalisation, of Palestine Question
    143–5
Religious Communities Ordinance
    (1926) 83
religious rights, of Arabs 2, 5, 192, 279
religious sectarianism, of Ottoman
    structures 87
Remez, David 161
reunification, of Palestine west of the
    Jordan with Transjordan 272
Revisionism 216, 217, 218
Revisionist conference (Krakow,
    1935) 216
Revisionist Zionism 6, 212, 213, 214;
    maximalist wing 211
revolutionary syndicalism, of
    Sorel *et al.* 205
revolutionary Zionism 211
Reynolds, David 45, 56
richesse, Jews' fabled 4
Rielf, Itzhak 225

right-wing Zionism *see* militant Zionism
rights: Arab civil and religious 2, 5, 192,
    279; of Arab peasant and tenant
    farmers 21, 193–4; of Arabs 39, 148,
    160, 165, 192, 224, 226; of Christians
    120; of Jews 2, 22, 31, 37, 38, 39, 123,
    181–2, 226–7; of Jews and Arabs 127,
    281, 282; of Palestine to be indepen-
    dent 149; of Palestinian Arabs 15, 19,
    21, 31; of prayer at Wailing Wall 137,
    138, 142
riots: anti-Semitic (1947) 47, 59n17; Arab
    against British in Palestine (1921) 50,
    275; Arabs against Jews (1929) 84, 85,
    89, 127, 138, 142, 241, 275; Arabs
    against Jews *Nebi Musa* (1920) 3, 13,
    15, 275
Roach, Commissioner Keith 76–8
Rodinson, Maxime 6
romantic nationalism, and militant
    Zionism 208–9
Roosevelt, Franklin D. 180
Rose, Norman 47
Ross, Sir Dennison 36
Rothschild, James de 33–4
Rothschild, Lionel Walter 207; letter
    from Lord Balfour 235, 238–9
Round Table Conference in London
    (1939) 146
Royden-Shaw, Dr Maud 31
ruling elites, of new Arab entities 14
Ruppin, Dr Arthur 16
rural sector 195–6; Arabs engaged in 194
rural violence, on Arab peasant farmers 194
Russia 209–11; Jews 39
Russification 209

Sabella, Bernard 120
Sacher, Harry 207
Sa'id, Edward 223
al-Sa'id, Nuri 144, 147–8
al-Sakakini, Dumya 105
al-Sakakini, Hala 104, 105
al-Sakakini, Khalil 73, 103–4, 106–7,
    109–10, 111–12, 116n8, 126; letter to
    son Sari 104, 109–10
al-Salahiyya school (Nablus) 72
Samson (Jabotinsky) 212
Samuel, Sir Herbert 2, 3, 177–8, 239
Samuel, Sir Stuart 32
Sand, Shlomo 222, 225
sansculottes ideology 215
Sa'ud of Najd, House of 142, *see also*
    Faysal, Emir

Saudi Arabia 144, 145
Sa'ud–Hashemite rivalry 142
Savinkov, Boris 210
Scott, C.P. 237
sectarianism, within Palestinian
    nationalist movement 127
self-governance, Palestinian local 83–101
self-government, Arab national 174, 274
September 11th attacks (2001) 226
settlements, Zionist, benefits to Arabs
    159–60
Shapira, Anita 229
Sharia court system 124
Shatara, Fuad 163
Shatta village lands 193
Shaw, C.V. 40
Shaw Commission (1930) 178
Shaw, George Bernard 150n2, 236
Shefer, Ze'ev 261
Shehada, Bulus 74–5
Shenhav, Yehuda 225–6
Shertok, Moshe 165–6, 270, 277; lecture
    (1940) 169; rebuke by al-Alami 279
Shiite community 124
Shiloah, Reuven 259
Shlush, Yosef Eliahu 164
Shua'ib, Prophet 124, 125
Shuckburgh, Sir J., conversation with
    Moody 3–4
al-Shuqayri, Ahmad 73–4
al-Shuqayri, Sheikh Asaad 127
al-Shura 72
Sidqi, Isma'il 276
Six Day War (1967) 222
Smilansky, Moshe 160
Sneh, Moshe 260
social change and modernisation, Arab,
    and public interest in Palestine
    Question 139–40
Socialist Zionists, explaining Arab resis-
    tance despite the blessing 165
socio-religious groups, Jews as 35
Sokolov, Nahum 207, 243
solution, Zionist and Arab 'wish' for
    imposed 280
Sonnenborn Institute 263
Sorel, Georges 205
Southern Syria, name for Palestine? 21
Soviet Union, return of Jewish
    communists to 224
Spears, Sir Edward 31, 38
Spinney's department stores 107
sports 105–6
state education systems, Arab 139

State of Israel *see* Israel
'state now' policy (Ben-Gurion) 253, 257
state-owned land, Arab 231
stereotypes: anti-Semitic 14–15, 18–19, 49; of Churchill and Bevin 4–5
Stern, Avraham 216, 217
Stern Gang 217
Stewart, Rt. Rev. W.H. 31
Storrs, Sir Ronald 29, 31, 40
sulha agreement, after Druze village attacks 129
Sunni Muslims 124
supra-state Arab nationalist and Islamic movements 140
Supreme Islamic Council 127
Supreme Muslim Council 86, 108, 124, 137
Sursock lands 193
Surya al-Janubiyya (southern Syria) 67
Sykes, Sir Mark 4, 14, 18, 19
Sykes-Picot Agreement (1916) 21
Syria 18, 19, 145, 263; Druze from 129; and France 4, 14, 20, 23, 24, 25; French Mandate for 174; land purchases by Sursocks 193; National Block 143; Ottoman 13; and Palestine 24; revolution 72; Southern 21; and Turkey 24; United 22; withdrawal of British forces from (1919) 14, 23

tarbush (fez) 107, 112
Tarif family 124
Tarif, Sheikh Amin Tarif 124–5
Tarif, Sheikh Tarif Muhammad 124–5
Tartars 32
Taylor, A.J.P. 57–8
Tel Aviv 25
tenant farmers, Arab 21, 193–4
Teoria Ubikoret 225
Tibawi, Abdul Latif 13, 195
Totah, Khalil 112–13, 113
Totah, Selim 163
al-Toubbeh, 'Isa 107
al-Toubbeh, Jamil 107–8
Touqan, Ibrahim 109
Toye, Richard 49
Transjordan 51, 239, 240, 245; reunification of Palestine west of the Jordan with 272
Treaty of Versailles (1919) 254
Trevelyan, Humphrey 26
Truman, Harry 250
Turkey 17, 50; Arab Revolt against (1916–18) 18; entry into First World War 207; and Syria 24

'Turkifisation' 66
Turkish national movement 132

Ukrainian nationalism 209
al-'Umar, Dahir 66
unemployment, Arab 182
United Nations Educational, Scientific and Cultural Organisation (UNESCO) 34
United Nations Special Committee on Palestine (UNSCOP) 39; *Histadrut* submission to 167
United Nations (UN) 55, 57, 75; Partition Plan (1947) 151, 167, 202, 263, 276, 281
United Resistance Movement 248
United States of America (USA) 55; Ben-Gurion's visit (1942) 255–6; closed-door policy 180; Congress 169; immigration laws 179; OSS (Office of Strategic Services) 255–6; Puritans 228; Senators' visit (1936) 197; Weizmann in 248–50
United Syria 22
unity: Arab 71, 149; Pan-Arab 142
universities, for Palestinian Arabs 105
urban bourgeoisie, Arab 113
urban notables, Arab peasant indebtedness to 194–5
urban society, Palestinian Arab 115
Ussishkin, Menachem 23–4, 161, 225
usury, Palestinian Arab 195

values, Christian–Palestinian Arab gap 109–10
Versailles Treaty (1919) 254
village versus town, in Palestinian-Arab Revolt (1936–9) 111–14
villagers: action during Mandate/Revolt 114–15; middle class attitude to 113
violence: Arab communal 191, 192; Arab rural 194, *see also* Arab Revolt (1936–9)
volunteer force, Arab 144
volunteers, Druze Lebanese and Syrian 129
voting rights, of Palestinian resident males 89

al-Wahhab, 'Abd 108
Wailing Wall 19; Jewish right to prayer dispute (1929) 137–8, 142
Warsaw Ghetto Uprising (1943) 218
Wasserstein, Bernard 36
Wauchope, Sir Arthur 84

weapons, *Haganah*'s 262
Weitz, Josef 197–8, 201
Weizmann, Chaim 7, 8, 13, 54, 56, 57, 58n8, 235–51; agreement with Faysal 4, 13–28, 143, 279; in Arab–Zionist negotiations 273, 278; astuteness in politics and statehood 236–7; and Balfour Declaration (1917) 212, 235–6, 238–40; becomes President of the World Zionist Organisation 239; and Ben-Gurion 249, 257; Churchill's partition promise to 55–6, 56–7; discovery of biological process to produce acetone 235–6; family background and early career in chemistry 236; letter to Chamberlain 189; letter to Zionist Bureau about the British 25; meetings with the Palestinians (1918–19) 16–17, 271; opposition to Jewish major-ity 243–4; partition plans 244–5; personal World War Two loss 246–7, 249; post-World War Two 248–9; success at Paris Peace Conference (1919) 190; understanding of British politics of 237; and United States 248–50; work on finding processes for synthetic rubber production 246; as Zionist autocrat 15–16; in Zionist movement 237–51
West Bank 202
Western colonialism 6, 137, 139, 159, 225
Western Wall, march to (1924) 214
White Papers on Palestine: Churchill's (1922) 22, 28n51, 175, 191–2, 280; MacDonalds's (1939) 2, 8, 33, 51–3, 147, 174–5, 179, 180–1, 185, 198–9, 246, 255, 258–60, 280; Passfield's (1930) 7, 8, 138, 178–9, 241–2, 258
Williams, Rushbrook 36
Woolley, Sir Leonard 36, 37
working classes: Arab 67; Jewish 210
World War, First (1914–18), Jabotinsky's views on 206–7
World War, Second (1939–45) 217, 257; assessments of outcome 276
World Zionism 8
World Zionist Congress (Basel, 1931) 243
World Zionist Organisation (WZO) 190, 238, 242, 257; Weizmann as President 239
Wright, Captain Peter 32

al-Yarmouk 73, 74, 81
Yeivin, Yehoshua Hirsh 211
Yishuv 25, 83, 90, 121, 128, 132; Ben-Gurion's leadership 252; and Britain

247–50; Britain's military operations and attacks against 261, 263; labour movement 242, 245; militias 247; population 2; rapid growth 241; saving from World War Two destruction 247; self-defence 172–3; youth 229
YMCA 105–6
Young Turks 66
youth 79; cultivation by Jabotinsky 211–13, 215–16; militant Zionism 211–13; Poland 211–13; Polish Jewish 212–13; recruitment by Zuʿayter for defence army 76; *Yishuv* 229; Zuʿayter's criticism of 77

Zionism 6; apathy to 50; Arab opposition to 14–15, 20, 162; Arab resistance despite 'blessing' 165; Arab states' perception of 139; British military's opposition to 14–15; British support for 31; case against 38–9; Christian opposition to 31, 108; Churchill in Cabinet meeting (1921) on policy 50–1; Churchill's support for 45; as colonialism counter-arguments 228–32; and colonialism differences 6; colonialist paradigm of 223–8; definition (Eisenstadt) 228; Druze policy 130; goals 25, 167; ideology 230; is it colonialism? 221–34; Islamisation of Palestinian national struggle against 123; Jewish challenge to 191; and Judaism differences 123; limits of Britain's support during World War Two 257; militant 205–20; moderate 21; national movement's opposition to 111; Palestinian Arabs opposition to 16; perspectives 6–9; policy (1921–2) 50–1; political 191, 225; propaganda 38; reaction to Bevan's speech (1945) 47; Revisionist 6, 210–11, 212, 213, 214; revolutionary 211; self-image 168; slowing down 198–9, *see also* blessing thesis, Zionism to the Arabs
Zionist Bureau 25
Zionist Commission 165, 239; Weizmann's report to (1918) 20
Zionist Congress: Basel (1946) 257; Vienna (1913) 16; Zurich (1937) 161, 173, 230, 245, 281
Zionist Convention, London (1945) 257–8
Zionist enterprise, Arab opposition to 223–4

Zionist Executive 176
Zionist Loan 240
Zionist Movement 15, 108, 129, 191; collaboration with post-war neutral countries 256; plan to transfer Druze villages to Hauran Mountains 130; self-image 168
Zionist newspaper, in Arabic 164
Zionist Organisation 173, 176, 177–8, 186n20; acceptance of economic absorptive capacity 176–7
Zionist Political Committee meeting (1945) 56
Zionist resources, Arab quest for 274
Zionist settlements, advantages for the Arabs 159–60
Zionists: disillusion with Churchill 55–7; goal between wars 172–3; land sales to 196; land to develop 19; secret understanding with King 'Abdallah 151
Zionist–Palestinian conflict (1930s) 69

al-Zirakli, Khayr al-Den 77
Zreq, Qustanten 71
Zu'ayter, Akram 5, 65–82; at American University of Beirut 71–2; demonstrative writings (1929–39) 74; father's death influence 70–2; from teaching to journalism 74–6; important life stages 69–70; incarceration 76, 80; *Ink on Paper* article in *al-Haya al-Maqdisiya* 77; as leader of the revolution and organiser of the 1936 protest 79–80; Leader of the Youth name 80–1; pressure from British officers over his press articles 76–8; relocation to 'Akka 73–4; return to Nablus 72–3; *Tea and Blood* article in *al-Haya al-Maqdisiya* 77–8; teaching at Nablus *al-Najah* National School 70, 78–9; teaching in Iraq 79; *Youth* article in *al-Haya al-Maqdisiya* 77
al-Zuhor 73

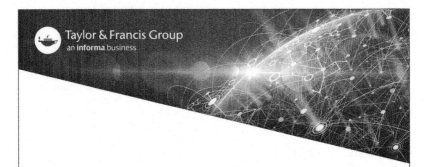

Printed in Great Britain
by Amazon

43483136R00178